Ralph, 1st Duke of Montagu (1638-1709) Power and Patronage in Late Stuart England

By

Steven Hicks

Acknowledgements

My greatest thanks must go to His Grace the Duke of Buccleuch, for kind permission to use the archive of his ancestor Ralph Montagu at Boughton House and many of the photographs with which this book is illustrated. Gareth Fitzpatrick, Director of the Living Landscape Trust at Boughton, has been unfailingly kind, helpful and supportive over the many years of this work's gestation and I owe him a great debt. Crispin Powell, latterly appointed Archivist there, has also offered considerable assistance. I also wish to thank Dr. Jeffrey West and John Crompton who kindly read over my manuscript and made many helpful suggestions, and the staff at Lambeth Palace Library. Finally many thanks to Dr. Robin Eagles of the History of Parliament Trust who generously allowed me to mine the references he had used for his unpublished article on Ralph for *The History of Parliament: the House of Lords, 1660-1832*.

Forward by

The Duke of Buccleuch, KBE

At Boughton House one is constantly reminded of my ancestor Ralph, Duke of Montagu; from the exterior by his remodelling of the mediaeval house and in the interior as a result of his lavish patronage of the arts.

Much of Duke Ralph's legacy at Boughton is due to his support of the plight of the Huguenots through his patronage of craftsmen and professionals. This saw these religiously persecuted Protestant immigrants from France integrated and contributing to many areas of national life.

I therefore warmly welcome Steven Hicks's biography of him, with its extensive research within my Family's Archives, which has resulted in this being the first book on Ralph Montagu to be published in this country.

It affords us all the opportunity to read and learn much more about this complex and fascinating man.

Preface

Ralph Montagu first came to my attention more than a decade ago when I read the story of how he wooed his second wife in the guise of the Emperor of China in Christopher Simon Sykes' "Private Palaces". I was amused and impressed by his chutzpah, and so tried to find out more about him. This was before the internet had come 'of age' and it was not an easy task. I visited Boughton, the house which owes so much to Ralph, and this fuelled my interest. I read the printed volumes of the letters which he had written as ambassador to the court of Louis XIV and was able for the first time to hear the voice of the man himself. I discovered that the original letters from which the printed version derived were housed at the Northampton County Record Office and, in deciphering Ralph's appalling handwriting I felt not only closer to him, but also found that the Victorian transcribers had left out anything which they considered incidental. Whilst the omissions added little to the story of Charles II's relations with Louis, they often shone a little more light on small facets of Ralph's character and life and so I began to create a true record of them. The NCRO also holds other papers relating to Ralph, and I was kindly allowed to examine the rest of the archive at Boughton House which is now in the care of his descendant the Duke of Buccleuch & Queensbury. Despite this wealth of original documentation no biography of Ralph had ever been written other than one produced by Edward Metzger in 1987 which, printed and sold in the USA, was unobtainable in this country.

A constant problem for historians writing about this period is that 1 January 1678 "Old Style" in England was also 1 January 1679 "New Style" and the former was not the first day of a new year. In the Old Style the year started on Lady Day, 25 March whereas the New Style year began on 1 January. New Style has been used as consistently as possible in this study. The calendars of Spain, Portugal, France and most of Italy had adopted the Gregorian calendar in 1582 and so moved nine days ahead of England, but the fact that this was at Papal instigation discouraged most Protestant nations from following suit. Britain changed in 1752 (and Greece not until 1923). This is doubtless why it is possible for Ralph to be writing to his sister from Paris on 5 July 1678 and yet arrive in London three days earlier.

Another difficulty is money – it is extremely hard to convert sums quoted by Ralph's contemporaries into modern day values. Whilst multiplying by 100 is a simple way to catch a sense of a value without searching the internet for inflation tables, even using the latter is not much more scientific since inflation has affected different commodities in different ways (tea, coffee, sugar and chocolate were extremely expensive in Ralph's day). An unskilled labourer in London might earn two shillings a day, whilst Samuel Pepys, a senior civil servant, received just under £1 (£350 a year).

Introduction

Historical biographies can shine unique lights on the period in which their subjects lived. So much of what is written about English history has a narrative flow full of dates, notable events and great people but such overviews perforce lack the personal. The historical biography reminds us that these events were moulded by people - like us in some ways but very different in others – and that those events often had a material effect on those who lived through them. My intention is not only to enable the reader to learn about a life from the past but also to understand Ralph's place in the history of his age. Ralph Montagu's life spanned a period which is rarely considered as a historical whole – from the Restoration of 1660, through the Glorious Revolution and well into Queen Anne's reign. He was not only acquainted with monarchs, offering advice to Charles II, talking in private with Louis XIV, helping William III to a crown, but also with the greatest men of that period – politicians (such as Danby and Sunderland), generals (Marlborough and Schomberg), philosophers, scientists et al. It was the great scientist Robert Hooke who designed his London house which would later hold the British Museum, and the philosopher John Locke, one of the most famous of Enlightenment thinkers, who acted as his physician for some time. Pepys wrote about him and Congreve dedicated "Way of the World" to him. Ralph also had close personal relationships with important and independently minded women, including Charles II's sister Madame, the beautiful Duchess of Mazarin, and his first wife Elizabeth Wriothesley, Countess of Northumberland. His second wife may have been insane, but she was the richest woman in England. Ralph seems to have found working through the wives and mistresses of influential men to be one of the best ways to achieve his ends. Indeed this was remarked on by his contemporaries – women seemed to appreciate his talents more than men did.

Ralph's life is usually only considered to be of note by historians of the later seventeenth-century for his role in bringing down Charles II's chief minister Danby. Charles consequently dissolved the Cavalier Parliament which had sat for more than seventeen years (the longest Parliament in English history) to save Danby from impeachment. But his political life encompassed far more. Twenty-one years old at the time of the Restoration, and closely related to the earls of Sandwich and Manchester who had been influential in the king's return, he was well placed to benefit from this family connection. The unexpected, violent death of his older brother five years later made him the heir to the estates and title of his father Lord Montagu. As ambassador to France from 1669 – 1672 and 1676 – 1678 he had the difficult task of maintaining Charles's constantly changing relationship with his cousin Louis XIV, and it is from this period that the bulk of his letters come. Having been poorly rewarded by his monarch and suddenly finding himself in disgrace, his career ruined in part through the accusation of the king's former mistress that he had seduced her teenage daughter, he used the protection gained from being elected as an MP to reveal the king's acceptance of bribes from France for his neutrality at the same time as Danby had been asking Parliament to vote him money for war against France. In the period of Ralph's life politics changed irrevocably. The two political traditions named 'Tory' and 'Whig' came into being and Ralph was most definitely in the latter camp. Many of the divisions that had led to the Civil War resurfaced as the fear of Catholicism grew and Ralph was in the vanguard of the movement to exclude James, duke of York, from the throne and promote the duke of Monmouth in his stead. The king, however, had learnt from his father's experience and proved adept at embracing the ambiguities needed to cope with the changed political culture that he had found at his restoration. He had to both remember and forgive the revolution and the regicides, to be a king and yet be familiar to his people as the 'Merry Monarch'. His obduracy won out – few of his subjects wanted another civil war. Some of Ralph's friends and relations were executed for plotting against Charles. He was extremely lucky not to be amongst them but considered it politic to take his family to France for two years.

When James came to the throne Ralph didn't allow the fact that he had done all he could to prevent such an occurrence stop him testing the water to see whether he would be welcome at court. However the rumours that he was about to achieve office came to nothing perhaps because, ambitious as he was, he balked at converting to Catholicism (a sure way to James's favour). Ralph then played a leading role in advancing William III's cause at the time of the Glorious Revolution – indeed he informed the king that his persuasion of a few uncertain peers to add their votes to his had tipped things in William's favour. Following this he became a Whig grandee, influential in brokering ministerial appointments and acting as political tutor to his near relation Charles Montagu (later earl of Halifax). I believe that the story of Ralph Montagu is unusual in this period in providing insights to England's political development, at both the highest level and in the county, together with its cultural development. His cultural tastes, springing from his own character together with his long experience of Louis's court and a period in self-imposed exile in that country, seem to have been influential. He created Montagu House as his London residence, of grandeur appropriate to the place he considered he and his family held in society, painted and furnished by the finest craftsmen. Despite being acknowledged at the time as one of the greatest houses the city has ever had, the watercolours and floor-plans that still survive have received little academic interest.

Both political and cultural spheres are well illustrated through extant archives and letters. The foundation of this book is built from original documents, primarily the Montagu archive which holds a wealth of material that gives evidence of Ralph's life - letters, notes, annual accounts, lists of servants, bundles of creditors' bills - and deserves to be better known. Further primary material can be found in the manuscripts collections in the British Library and Bodleian, and in the printed volumes of the Historic Manuscripts Commission. The letters are extensively quoted, not only so that readers can hear contemporary voices but also so that they can come to their own view of characters and motives. (Letters could be full of gossip and written with self-interest in mind, such that it is not easy to discern an objective truth, if such a thing can be said to exist). This may also serve to help others writing about this period, by providing a hoard of information garnered from many places which they can use, just as I have done from the sources cited in the bibliography. My text is therefore an historical narrative largely based on primary sources of which sufficient exist to render secondary sources irrelevant beyond general context.

I hope that the reader will, by the time they have reached the end of this book, agree with me that Ralph Montagu is a character worth knowing, and one who deserves his place in the mosaic of history.

Ralph Montagu's arms as a single man (the earl's coronet was added later).

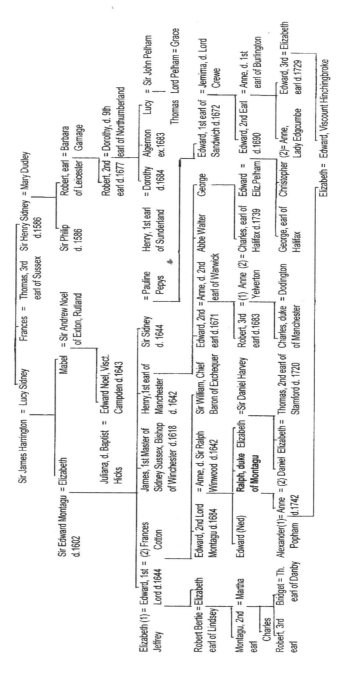

Montagu Family Connections

Ralph Montagu: Marital connections

Henry Cavendish, 2nd = Frances   Grace = Gilbert Holles
duke of Newcastle   Pierrepont   3rd earl of   Clare
d.1691

Margaret =   John, duke   Grace (2)=
d. 1716   of Newcastle   Th. Lord
                            Pelham

Thomas Pelham Holles
duke of Newcastle
d.1768

Catherine = Thomas, 6th earl of
d.1712   Thanet d.1729

Rachel (1) =Thomas Wriothesley   = (2) Elizabeth, d. Francis
de Ruvigny 4th earl of Southampton   earl of Chichester, d.1646
d.1640   d.1667

= (3) Frances, d. 2nd duke
      of Somerset d.1680

(1)=(2) Ralph (2) = (2) Elizabeth (1) Christopher, 2nd
       duke of Montagu   (1654-1734) duke of Albemarle
       (1638 - 1709)

Ralph   Winwood   Anne = (1) Alexander Popham
(1679-89)   (1682-1702)   d. 1742 (2) Daniel Harvey

John Churchill, duke = Sarah
of Marlborough d.1722   d.1744

Anne (2)   = Charles, 3rd earl =   (1) Arabella
(1684-1716) of Sunderland d.1722   d. 1698

Elizabeth = Rachel =   (1) Francis, Lord Vaughan d.1667   Josceline, earl of (1) = Elizabeth
         d.1723   (2) William, Lord Russell ex.1683   Northumberland d1670 (1646 - 90)

Edward =
Noel, Visct.
Camden

Wriothesley = Elizabeth, d. & h.
2nd duke of   Josiah Child
Bedford

Wriothesley, 2nd earl
Gainsborough

Henry, Lord Ogle d.1680 (1) = Elizabeth
s. of 2nd duke of Newcastle   d.1722
Thomas Thynne k. 1682 (2)
Charles, 6th duke of   (3)
Somerset d.1748

Rachel (2) = Scroop, 1 st duke of = (1) Elizabeth
Bridgwater   d. 1744   (1687-1714)

Frances, 2nd   =   Henrietta, duchess
earl of Godolphin   of Marlborough d.1722

John, 2nd duke of = Mary
Montagu (1690 - 1749) (1689-1751)

Chapter 1
Family and Advancement

Over the course of the twentieth century the use of class as a way of pinning a person to their place in society, slowly gave way to a simpler determiner of wealth (muddied in recent decades by celebrity). When Ralph Montagu was born in 1638 (as for centuries before and afterwards) the family he was born into – its ancestry, whose child he was and to whom he was related – was extremely important, as will frequently be shown in this work. His family were fortunate that in about 1450 a prosperous yeoman called Richard Ladde decided to adopt his wife's family name of Montagu. Her great-great-grandfather was Sir Simon, a grandson of the first earl of Salisbury and of the 2nd Lord Monthermer (who was himself grandson of King Edward I and Queen Eleanor of Castile). It is believed that Sir Simon inherited Hanging Houghton in Northamptonshire from his wife (land which passed by descent to Ralph) and so became the first Montagu to live in the county.

The career of Richard Ladde's grandson began the family's rise to prominence. Edward Montagu went into the law, a particularly successful way of rapidly attaining wealth and position under the Tudors. Legal adviser to the Abbey of Peterborough, he was knighted in 1537 and rose to become Chief Justice of the King's Bench the following year and of the Common Pleas in 1545. This meant that he was well placed to benefit from the dissolution of the monasteries in the 1540s, when he was able to add lands in Northamptonshire which had belonged to St Edmundsbury Abbey to those at Boughton, Weekley, Warkton, Geddington and Barnwell purchased earlier. (Boughton was bought in 1528). Many other families who would dominate Northamptonshire life arrived at this period: the Spencers at Althorp, Cecils at Burghley, Comptons at Castle Ashby and Brudenells at Deene. Less fortunate for Chief Justice Montagu was his involvement in drafting Edward VI's will, naming the Protestant Lady Jane Grey as his successor rather than Mary: the latter had him imprisoned in the Tower of London, despite the fact that he had objected to the insertion of Lady Jane's name but had been overruled. He seems not to have learned from this experience – in Mary's reign he was to swear that her father's will had been tampered with to exclude the Stuarts from the succession.[1] He died in February 1557, some eighteen months before the death of Mary and ascent of Elizabeth. By his third wife Sir Edward had eleven children. The eldest, another Edward, seems to have lived a long life away from the Court. He made a good marriage with Elizabeth, daughter of Sir James Harrington of Exton in Rutland and Lucy Sidney.

---

[1] Robert Persons Certamen Ecclesiae Anglicanae, ed J. Simons (Assen, 1965) p.171

(She was niece to Frances Sidney, countess of Sussex, the foundress of Sidney Sussex College, Cambridge, and cousin to the poet Sir Philip Sidney and his brother Robert, viscount de L'Isle). Elizabeth bore him four sons and a daughter. The eldest, Edward, seems to have made some additions to the house at Boughton, taken care of his estates and added to the family's wealth to the extent that in 1621 he was able to purchase a barony from James I and so become Lord Montagu. It was said that he paid £10,000 for it. (Many others did the same, such that the number of peers grew from fifty at Elizabeth's death to 130 twenty-five years later). He played his part in county politics - Montagu influence was usually supreme in the eastern part of Northamptonshire and so managed the election of one knight of the shire to Parliament, whilst the Spencers controlled the western part and so the other seat – and he was a moderate puritan, sponsoring 'godly ministers'. In 1606 he initiated the parliamentary bill for a public thanksgiving every 5 November for the failure of the Gunpowder Plot. Despite his religious views he was nonetheless loyal to Charles I and was consequently imprisoned by the Parliamentarians in 1642, early in the Civil War. He was released under house arrest to his London home where he died two years later in his eighty-second year.

Lord Montagu's younger brothers did not inherit the family estate and so had to make their own way in the world. Henry entered the law, became Chief Justice of the King's Bench in 1616, Lord Treasurer in 1620 and Lord Privy Seal in 1628. He was rewarded with the earldom of Manchester. James entered the Church and was the first Master of Sidney Sussex College before becoming bishop of Bath & Wells[2] and then bishop of Winchester. In the early 1600s he was dean of the Chapel Royal, and so close to King James. He supervised one of the teams of theologians who created the Authorised Version of the bible which was printed in 1611. The youngest brother Sidney was an M.P. for over forty years (he represented Wells in 1614, perhaps due to his brother James's influence as bishop there). He married Pauline Pepys and their son, yet another Edward Montagu, became earl of Sandwich at the Restoration in 1660. Lord Montagu's own son Edward, the 2nd Lord, married Anne, daughter of Sir Ralph Winwood (another Northamptonshire man). Sir Ralph had been ambassador to France 1601-1603, and then to the Netherlands. At a time when King James's ministers were divided into those for or against Spain he was in the latter camp, and as a Secretary of State from 1614 he encouraged Walter Raleigh to attack the Spanish fleet and South American settlements..Consequently his death in 1617 was fortuitous – he may well otherwise have shared Raleigh's ruin the next year when King James

---

[2] The great doors he gave to Bath Abbey after restoring it, prominently displaying the Montagu coat of arms, are still there.

decided to improve relations with Spain. Edward's wife Anne had three children who survived infancy: Edward (generally known as Ned), Elizabeth (Betty) and Ralph, (the subject of this biography) who was born in the London house of his grandmother, Lady Winwood, and baptised with his grandfather's name at the church of St. Bartholomew the Less, Smithfield on Christmas Eve 1638. Anne died in September 1642 and her mother seems to have taken on the care of the grandchildren.

The period of Ralph's youth was one of the most turbulent the kingdom had ever seen: less than a year after his birth Scots parliamentarians were raising an army to oppose King Charles I and the Civil Wars would soon begin. Although the 1st Lord Montagu favoured the royalist cause many other family members were for Parliament and against the King's political and religious agenda. Lord Montagu's cousin, the 2nd earl of Manchester, was one of the five MPs who the King had wanted to arrest when he entered the House of Commons with soldiers in 1641 and he became a general of Parliament's forces, commanding at the 2nd Battle of Newbury with Cromwell as his lieutenant. The two men had been at Sidney Sussex College together. In 1644 another cousin (the future earl of Sandwich) was one of the colonels who supported Cromwell's denunciation of Manchester for indecisiveness, and stated that Manchester had opposed the war from the beginning. It shows that even those Montagus in opposition to the King didn't necessarily support each other, and this Edward's father was a Royalist. He had raised a regiment of infantry at the age of eighteen in 1642 and became Parliament's General at Sea in 1656. His brother-in-law, the Northamptonshire landowner Sir Gilbert Pickering, was Cromwell's Chamberlain (and cousin to Dryden). Ralph's father was sufficiently trusted by Parliament to be one of three peers appointed to receive the captured King from the Scots in January 1647at Holdenby House, Northants and stayed with him until June when Cornet Joyce appeared with troops to claim the King's person as the Army's guarantee against a deal being done behind their backs between Parliament and the Scots. Later that year Lord Edward hosted Thomas Fuller at Boughton, where he wrote "*Cause and Cure of a Wounded Conscience*" reflecting on the losses both he and the country had suffered through civil war. As a fellow countryman (born at Aldwinkle, Northamptonshire) and having taught at Sidney Sussex, Fuller would have been greatly welcomed.[3] In December 1648 the future earl of Sandwich and his father-in-law were amongst the 148 MPs purged (i.e. removed) from Parliament by Colonel Pride on behalf of the army, as being insufficiently radical. On 4 January, when the Lords were asked to discuss a proposal to try the King for treason, Manchester argued that this would be in contradiction to the fundamentals

---

[3] Fuller is most famous for "The History of the Worthies of England", published after his death.

of English law. (He had been desperately trying to negotiate with Charles I to achieve a settlement). Two days later the House of Lords was abolished, and the King was beheaded at the end of the month.

Ralph was then ten years old and letters from that year survive, sent by Lady Winwood to her son-in-law from her country house at Thames Ditton, that show she was kept well informed about her two grandsons studying at Westminster School.

'Your sons are both very well on Monday last. I am very glad you will have them to Boughton in August, for if you should leave them alone at school, as in your lordship's last letter to me you were pleased to write you would, it would quite have disheartened them, I think, from learning; for in truth they must have a little recreation sometimes, and take a little air for their health's sake, so it will do very well that their sister and they meet together at Boughton... I know my son will not fail to bring your daughter from Quainton to you about that time' (July 5).

'I thank God we are all well here, and so I hear your sons are at Westminster, Ned was ill one day only, but was very well the next again, and I hear Ralph looks very pale. I fear they buy fruit and eat too much of it' (July 25).

'You will see by Mr Busby's letter that poor Ralph has got the small-pox. As soon as it was suspected, Mr. Busby moved him into a house in the stable yard, and sent for Dr. Wright, who, being ill, sent the apothecary instead, and would have sent a nurse, but Mr. Busby did not wish either of them to see him. As he has now been ill five days and is said to be doing well, I think we had better leave him in the hands of his master...who, as you will see, expresses much love and care towards him. Edward is quite well so far, but I advise that he should be sent to Lady Montagew's, and then if he falls sick he can be nursed there. Meanwhile he can go to school, and he and his man can still dine at Mr. Busby's. I am of Mr Busby's opinion that the boys have been riding too much in the heat, drinking beer when they were very hot, and eating too much also: and I believe Betty will do the like as long as she is abroad'[4] (Undated). Dr Busby was a renowned classicist and educator, and managed to hold his post for nearly fifty-seven years, through the Civil War, Restoration and Glorious Revolution. Dryden, Locke, Wren, Prior and Ralph's cousin Charles, the future earl of Halifax, were all his pupils. It is interesting that Ralph did not go on to Sidney Sussex, the 'family college', as his brother, father and uncles had, or enter the law, which had been a proven route to success for various members of the family.[5] Three letters which his brother Ned wrote

---

[4] Small beer was drunk in preference to water, which was more easily contaminated.
[5] Early in 1666 Lord Montagu intervened in an election to the college via his cousin the earl of Manchester, who was Chancellor of the University, showing the continued family interest in the college's affairs. Cal SP Dom March 12th 1666

in about 1650 to his father indicate that he was a troublesome teenager: one in Latin states his determination to work harder in future, another expresses his sorrow for past misdemeanours and implores his father to restore him to '*the sunshine of his favour*' and the last has a postscript asking for some money, as he has none. There are no similar letters from Ralph, just a poem in Latin of eight lines by him (a eulogy marking the death of Henry Hastings) published by the school in 1649 as part of *Lachrymae Musarum*. It suffers by comparison with another poem in the work, by Dryden.

The Montagu family had already distanced themselves from the army radicals and once order began to break down in 1659, following Cromwell's death, they were willing to be convinced that restoring Charles II to the throne was the best way of avoiding anarchy. Sandwich was with the fleet off Denmark and Ralph's brother Ned was with him. The Royalists hoped that Sandwich would bring the fleet over to their cause and chose a most unusual agent in Cromwell's nephew Tom Whetstone, a naval captain who had been discharged for professional incompetence and disobedience. At Copenhagen in the autumn he contacted Ned, who had shipped with him and was known to be a royalist agent, and gave him letters and instructions to encourage Sandwich to change sides. [6] The time was not yet ripe. The next year Sandwich's diary records that on April 10 '*The Hon. Edward Montague came on board the Naseby about noon and went off again in the evening. [In margin: To the King in Flanders]*' and on the 18th '*In the morning the Hon Edward Montague came on board the Naseby [In margin: returned from Flanders with letters to me from the King & the Duke]*'. Samuel Pepys, a cousin and agent of Sandwich, records his curiosity about what was going on: '*This morning very early Mr Edward Montagu on board, but what was the business of his coming again or before without any servant and making no stay at all I cannot guess*'. On the 4th Charles had issued the Declaration of Breda which promised a general pardon, religious tolerance and arrears of pay for the army. General Monck, in charge of the army, had secretly pledged his allegiance to Charles and had a hand in the contents of the Declaration which was not made public until May 1, by which time Sandwich had been persuaded to support the restoration. Manchester, for his part, had been elected Speaker by the ten peers who returned to the Lords when the Convention Parliament met on 25 April.

On May 2 1660 the newly elected Parliament begged the King to return from exile and Sandwich commanded the fleet that brought him back. Charles acknowledged his debt by refusing to go ashore at Dover in the

---

[6] R. Ollard *Edward Montagu, 1st Earl of Sandwich, "Cromwell's Earl"*, (London 1994) p.68

brigantine that had been fitted out for the purpose, preferring Sandwich's own barge. An earldom, the Garter and the post of Master of the Wardrobe were a more permanent reward. Ralph was twenty-one years old. He must have shared in the joy and celebrations that met Charles's return and hoped that he and his brother would find advancement at the restored Court. Given his extended family connections, he was well placed to do so. Pepys's diary gives occasional insights into that connection – on 24 June he and Sandwich dined with Lord Montagu at the latter's house in Little Queen Street (now the northern end of Holborn Kingsway) and three years latter he records that on 15 May Lord Montagu and his brother dined at Sandwich's[7]. Manchester had been appointed Lord Chamberlain at the Restoration and seems to have been on good terms with his cousins, having forgiven Sandwich's attack on him in 1644.[8] We know from Pepys that the Earl used his influence to get Ned elected as MP for the port of Sandwich in Kent during the Spring of 1661 (he had already tried unsuccessfully to persuade the voters in Weymouth and in Hastings to do so). This influence came from running the Navy (hence Pepys' employment as Clerk to the Naval Board). In August Ned was entrusted with the very large sum of £5,000 to help prepare the fleet for its voyage to Lisbon to bring Catherine of Braganza back to England for her marriage to King Charles. (Pepys and Lady Sandwich feared '*that he will not do it to my Lord's honour, and less to his profit*'). Nonetheless it is clear from surviving letters amongst Sandwich's papers that Ned was one of his prime agents: '*I was sent for by my Lord Chancellor. As for your business here*' he has negotiated a payment of £4,000 for the Earl's costs in going to Lisbon as Charles's representative.[9] '*I received this day one of the 22 of July from Alicante with an inclosed to my Lord Chancellor which I immediately delivered. It gave great joy to the King and my Lord Chancellor for they were in no little trouble for the uncertainty of your health. I hope by the date of yours and your intending the next day for Algiers it will fall out right for our meeting in Portugal*'.[10] Both Ned and his father acknowledged the help they received from their relative who was riding so high in royal favour. '*Before I give you any account of your last commands I must discount the last expressions of your letter as more than are dew to me since I never yet had so good an opportunity as I desire to express how much I am your servant...I spoke to the Lord Chancellor*

---

[7] In September 1663 Pepys went to visit Sandwich at Hinchingbroke, his country home, only to find that the earl had gone to Boughton and in July 1665 Sandwich's daughter seems to have been at Boughton shortly before her wedding.

[8] At the end of August 1665 Manchester advised Sandwich that it would be to his advantage to put to sea soon since, if the Dutch returned to port unopposed, that would give ammunition to his enemies at Court. (Carte Ms. 223, fol. 309)

[9] Bodleian Ms. Carte 223, f. 232. 22 August 1661

[10] Ibid f. 234. 26 August 1661

about the town of Huntingdon in order to do what you recommended on their behalf and he answered me he would favour them and do their business whenever they applied themselves to him...Lord Oxford, Mr Hide, my brother and many more of your humble servants present themselves to you' (Ned to Sandwich).[11] (The earl of Oxford clearly wanted Sandwich's favour – in December he wrote directly to him, having missed Ned when *'I went to Mr Montague's lodging today'*).[12] *'I must return humble thanks for the favours I have received from you at my late being at Hinchinbrook... If your Lordship sees an opportunity at court I desire you to make known how sensible I am of his Majesty's goodness to me, though I have been unkindly dealt with by my fellow peers, and the express words of the Act are that the commissioners may abate any that complain after the tax is set if it be not returned to the Exchequer...I hope at Christmas to have the happiness to wait upon your Lordship here and at Hinchingbrooke'* (Lord Montagu to Sandwich from Boughton).[13]

The extended family's ties were strengthened by the mutual obligation of services performed by one member of the family for another– for example Lord Montagu's brother William, a lawyer, helped Sandwich in his legal and financial affairs.[14] There is evidence that Ralph was doing well at Court and had already forged his own connections in a letter he wrote to his father on June 21 1661 from London saying that he was going out of town for a month with the duke & duchess (probably a reference to the Yorks) to drink the waters at Tunbridge and *'Today the Portugal Embassador dines publicly with the King at Whitehall...If I am not obliged to go to the Progress, at my return from the waters I will come and pay my duty to your Lordship in the county'*. Ralph may well have lived with Ned. (Pepys records a visit to Ned's chamber in July, where he heard a Frenchman play the guitar *'most extreme well, though at best methinks it is but a bawble'*). The next month Ralph received the perquisite of being appointed Keeper of Hartleton Lodge in Richmond Park jointly with his brother-in-law Sir Daniel Harvey, which brought him £25 p.a. Any source of income was to be welcomed. Ned at least certainly seems to have lived beyond his means - two years before the Restoration and his coming to court the King's Bench had recorded a very large debt of £1,800 and Ralph stood bail. There is an implication in Pepys's writing that Ned wanted to be taken seriously as a man of business but because he left servants and *'many other things of consequence'* in a state of confusion when he rushed off to Lisbon at the start 1662 the King and Court joked about him. Pepys was told that he had disappeared leaving Sandwich to pay bills of £1,000

---

[11] Ibid f. 246. 1 July 1661
[12] Ibid f. 244. 5 December 1661
[13] Ibid f. 260. 5 October 1663
[14] Bodleian Ms. Carte 73, f. 345. 16 January 1661

and couldn't properly account for £2,000 of the £5,000 entrusted to him. The same source told *'many more scurvy stories of him and his brother Ralph'*. It would have been a salutary lesson to Ralph on the financial hazards of court life. The 6th earl of Westmorland condemned his father for expecting rewards that never came: *'a warning to all not to spend their estates to serve at court in expectation of being afterwards repaid or rewarded. Tis an action all courtiers smile at.'*[15]

On March 1 1662 Sandwich brought the fleet that was to accompany the Queen back to England to anchor by the Belem monastery in Lisbon and recorded that Ned came on board to give him his commission and instructions. (He had apparently been there since January 16 when Sir Arnold Braems reported that his ship had arrived and he had 'this evening gone on shore').[16] It was six weeks before she was ready to leave, on April 14, and then as soon as they were at sea the Queen and all her ladies were sick. On the 26th Sandwich *'waited upon the Queen in the morning to know her pleasure concerning making the best of our way and sending Mr Montague before for England in the Princess with letters from the Queen'*. Thus in early May Ned brought the King news that the Queen would by that time be at the Scilly Isles. He then returned to the coast and on Tuesday May 13 at noon boarded Sandwich's flagship which was by Dunnose Point, off the Isle of Wight. The next day the Queen disembarked at Portsmouth. The King arrived on the 20th and they were married the following day.

All this activity seems to have gained both Ralph and Ned posts at Court: they were appointed Master of the Horse, Ralph to Anne, duchess of York (the King's sister-in-law) and Ned to the new Queen. Ned's uncle William Montagu also benefitted from the creation of a household for Catherine – he became her Attorney General. The posts allowed direct access to members of the royal family and so offered the potential of further advancement (and perhaps solvency for Ned). It is clear that despite Pepys' views the brothers were still in favour with Sandwich – they are recorded as dining with him in *'great company'* on July 16.[17] Ralph was to be further favoured by the King who had decided on an alliance with Louis XIV of France. Aware of how unpopular this alliance with a Catholic power would be with his subjects, he wanted to explore ways that this might be done without raising suspicion, and decided the best intermediary would be his sister, Henrietta Anne, (known as Madame), Louis' sister-in-law. Ralph was sent to France as messenger. It is clear from the texts of the letters Ralph carried that he was *'so well instructed as he will informe of all that passes here'* so that there would be

---

[15] BL Add Ms 34223, f.4
[16] Ibid f. 531. 16 January 1662
[17] Pepys, vol 2, p.265

no written evidence of what Charles was trying to achieve. Ralph must have been impressed by the magnificence of Louis's Court and certainly liked Madame, for Charles wrote to her in February 1663 just after he had returned to London that he was surprised her husband had allowed Ralph to stay with her so long *'for he is undoubtedly in love with you'*. [18]

However Ralph was soon to see how fickle royal favour could be. Ned had been getting into trouble, as Pepys happily noted in his diary. The "affronts" he had offered Hugh Cholmely, another of the Queen's servants, led to a duel in August 1662 which Ned lost, having in the fight been driven back into a ditch. He followed this up by borrowing £400 from his patron Lord Sandwich and at the end of the year fell out with Lord Chesterfield, the Queen's Chamberlain, (the imputation was that Ned was trying to control access to the Queen) and so was *'quite broke at Court with his repute and purse'*. Worse still, in February 1663 he abused Sandwich. Ned had sent his servant Eschar to ask Sandwich to sign off the accounts for the Lisbon voyage but was asked to attend on the Earl in person. Pepys records that Ned charged Sandwich with ingratitude, *'that he had received his earldom, garter, £4,000 per annum, and whatever he is in the world, from him'* and further abused him before the Earl calmed him (not wanting the world to see an argument in the family) and Ned broke down in tears. It would seem that this tension arose from Ned's financial straits - it is likely that his post gave him honour rather than remuneration – courtiers' stipends were usually much in arrears but they were expected to maintain a high standard of living as a consequence of their role. There was clearly enmity between Pepys and Ned, the former being open with his criticisms of the latter, such that Ned had told Sandwich that *'there was a fellow in the town, naming me, that had done ill offices, and that if he knew it to be so, he would have him cudgelld'*. Pepys opined that Ned owed everything to Sandwich and may have freely expressed that opinion, wounding Ned's pride. Perhaps there was an element of jealousy too. Additionally Ned apparently informed the Lord Chancellor that he had been behind Sandwich's action in bringing the fleet over to Charles before the Restoration which, though containing some truth, clearly showed ingratitude towards his kinsman and patron. Pepys also records that Ned's only remaining friend was Sir Henry Bennet, who had been made a Secretary of State the previous October, and he believed that friendship arose only from their similarity *'in the same matters of lust and baseness'*. Bennet had apparently promised Ned an annual pension of £2,000 and an earldom. News of Ned's conduct (and probably of his debts) reached his father and caused a rift, which was apparently sufficiently severe that the King stepped in to help (his letter also makes reference to Ralph): *'I am glad to hear that my recommendation of your son to your*

---

[18] C.H. Hartman *Charles II & Madame* (London 1934) p.68

kindness hath so good effect, for he hath asked my leave to go and see you...I shall be glad to hear that you have given like encouragement to his brother, of whom I have a very good opinion, though he hath not had the like occasions of serving me so considerably: for whose sake, and for your own good affection to my service, you shall always find me ready to entertain any opportunity of doing you a good turn, or to any of you relations, as...Your affectionate friend Charles R'. November 28 1663.

Although things seemed to have been smoothed over, six months later Ned was in disgrace again and he was now dismissed from his post. *'His fault, I perceive, was his pride, and most of all his affecting to be great with the Queen and it seems indeed had more of her ear than anybody else, and would be with her talking alone two or three hours together; insomuch that the Lords about the King, when he would be jesting with them about their wives, would tell the King that he must have a care of his own wife too, for she hath now the gallant: and they say the King himself did once ask Montagu "how his mistress (meaning the Queen) did"'* (Pepys). Bishop Burnet, in his "History" notes that the Queen, never having had an admirer before (nor after), asked the King what people meant by squeezing one's hand. The King told her "love" to which she responded *'Then Mr Montagu loves me mightily'*. Perhaps Charles was not prepared to be on the receiving end of jokes about marital fidelity (though he often made such jokes), or it may have been an irritation too far from a courtier. The Queen's response to her husband's action was not to replace Ned until after his death, and the person then chosen was his brother Ralph. Ned was understandably reticent in telling anyone, especially his father, what had happened, and so said at Court that he had been given leave to make a parental visit. Lord Montagu must have been angry at all that had transpired, and concerned for the future of the family and its estates when his eldest son came to inherit. One must assume that Ralph was occupied with his place in the York's household. Sir Ralph Esher records a brief conversation from this period, stating that he had been introduced to Sir Philip Herne *'by my namesake Ralph Montagu (afterwards so great a man, and ambassador)'*. *'Sir Philip'* said he *'here is a gentleman desirous of the honour of your acquaintance upon a ground very remarkable, considering he is one of the court. He has fallen in love with you regard for the truth.'* [19] There is also a mention of his presence in the household: *'The Duchess, who took after her father, swallowed her objection [to the Duke's walking round the room all evening, at the heels of some lady] by the help of a great appetite for beef and lobster, to say nothing of ale. She cared no more for her shape than the Chancellor. Montagu reckoned one evening that she sent her gentleman to the sideboard five times before supper.'* [20]

---

[19] *Sir Ralph Esher: or adventures of a gentleman of the Court*, vol.1, p.237
[20] Ibid. vol. 3, p.13

There seems to be no record of Ned's activities for more than a year, but it is likely that he found reason to absent himself from London by sailing with Sandwich in the fleet sent out in July 1664 to fight the Dutch. He is recorded by Sandwich as being with him in mid April 1665 and so he probably fought at the Battle of Lowestoft on June 3. Ralph was certainly there as a volunteer on the duke of York's flagship the Royal Charles (York was Lord High Admiral) and would later recount his memory of the events to Dr Burnet.[21] Sir Ralph Esher was with him, and recorded his own experiences of the great battle between two hundred ships: *'the novelty, the noise and the mystification, fairly took away my sense for the moment. I believe Montagu said something to me, which I did not very well understand.'* [22] They seem to have been the quarter deck, as aides to the Duke, and were lucky not to share the fate of Mr Boyle and Lords Falmouth and Muskerry, decapitated by chain-shot. The ship that had engaged them was the Eendracht, commanded by van Obdam, admiral of the Dutch fleet. After several hours of conflict that ship blew up, killing the admiral and almost all his crew. *'A little after the explosion, and when the mind had become, as it were duly sensible of its extreme terribleness, I shook from head to foot like a frightened horse.'* Sandwich suffered the taking of his ship, but it was recovered by Prince Rupert. The two brothers had experienced a terrifying and exhilarating battle which ended in a resounding victory for the English. Esher's postscript: *"'A truce, gentlemen, to melancholy stories'* said Montagu, as we rode up the Thames in the Duke's shallop, *'they make his Highness think of Lord Falmouth.'* So we changed the conversation and returned to those of the gay survivors."[23]

Whilst Sandwich then went to see his wife, Ned and Ralph may have gone to Boughton. In July the Court left the capital for the healthier air of Salisbury. The duke and duchess of York went too, and as a member of their household Ralph may have followed. The Great Plague that had started in April, and would over the course of a year kill some 100,000 people (perhaps 20% of London's population), was increasing its grip on the city. The Montagu clan escaped its effects but disaster was to follow. On Sunday 16 July Sandwich records that *'Captain Talbot came in to us with the Garland from Southwold Bay and brought Mr Edward Montague on board the Swiftsure as a volunteer this voyage'*. The fleet decided to take advantage of an agreement with the Danes to share the booty they would remove from the large number of Dutch merchantmen in the harbour at Bergen. Unfortunately the Danish governor insisted he had no instructions from Copenhagen to allow this, despite Ned's attempts at

[21] Burnet's *History of my own time* ed O.Airy, vol.1, p.391
[22] *Sir Ralph Esher* ibid. p.275
[23] Ibid. pp.275, 279.

persuasion (he having been chosen to negotiate). On August 2 (after some indecision, which allowed the Dutch to prepare), Sandwich's deputy Rear Admiral Tyddiman attacked with fourteen ships. Ned was sailing with the eighteen year old earl of Rochester and George Windham. Before the battle they had a conversation that Rochester, and (more fully) Burnet, recorded. Ned was sure he would die and Windham thought he might. Rochester tried to persuade them, on oath, that if they were killed they would later appear to him and tell him of the after-life. Only Windham would agree. The battle started at five in the morning and lasted for over three hours, the English blinded by smoke on the wind coming from the harbour. Despite his presentiment Ned *'generously staid all the while in the place of greatest danger'* as did Windham but towards the end of the action *'he fell on a sudden into such a trembling that he could scarce stand: and Mr. Montagu going to him to hold him up, as they were in each others Arms, a Cannon Ball killed him outright, and carried away Mr. Montagu's Belly, so that he died within an hour after'*. It was rumoured that he wrote a letter in his own blood to the Queen before he expired. 400 other men were killed. It is interesting that Lord Chancellor Clarendon wrote to Sandwich *'Were poore Ned Montagu to be lost, I am glad the circumstances of it were much to his advantage, and do not warrant his dying a Romanist if that be true'*.[24] When Sandwich visited Lisbon three years later, in 1668, he paid several calls on a daughter of the duke of Medina-Sidonia, Donna Maria, a nun at the Alcantara. On learning of his close relationship to Ned, she told him of the young man's secret conversion when in Rome aged eighteen or nineteen. The Pope had apparently so interested himself in the matter as to give him his personal leave to conceal & deny his change of religion. Donna Maria claimed to have heard of it from Ned when he had spent three months in Lisbon in 1662. Did Sandwich keep this confidential? It is curious that Sandwich received a letter from a Sister Maria de la Cruz in Lisbon in July 1666, thanking him for his letter and offering her condolences on the death of Ned.[25] He responded that he hoped to pay her a visit when the public business of his embassy to Lisbon was over. It would have been a great shock and further blow if he had told Lord Montagu of it.[26] Was it Ned's faith that made him refuse Rochester's request to swear an oath that he would return as a ghost?

Ralph had lost his only brother, who may have been his confidante, friend and ally – it is possible the brothers lodged together at the Court in Whitehall rather than with their father in Little Queen Street, encouraging and supporting each other in their ambitions. Something of this may be

---

[24] Bodleian Ms.Carte 223, f. 287. 28 August 1665
[25] Bodleian Ms.Carte 73, ff. 460, 462. 22 July 1666
[26] R. Ollard "Cromwell's Earl" p.203

read into the letter from Ralph (in York) to Sandwich on August 20 1665. *'My Lord I understand by Sr Thomas Clifford that your Lordship has already taken some care about my Brothers body, but I fear he is not embalmed well enough to keep. Therefore pray give order to Mr Pierce the chirogion to have a care that he may be embalmed over again and made to keep as long as possible. I believe he had noe english servants with him when he was killed, therefore pray let some of yours attend the body till my father sends for it away and in the meane time be layde in – church. I beg your pardon for givin you this trouble and am...'* [27] [28] Ralph also undertook to clear his brother's debts. Ned left a letter for his father before he went to sea. *'If this letter comes to your hand it is after my death. I hope that and my repentance and the many hearty submissions I have made to you will have wiped away all your displeasure'.* He asked that those persons who have lent him money shouldn't suffer loss. *'I have nothing to add but to assure Your Lordship that my repentance is real and that it [comes] in my heart'.* The *'particular of my debts'* includes Mr Cuthbert of Oundle, the draper, cousin Sidney Montagu, *'upon bond when I went into France'* and his servants for 3 years wages, Thomas Kipps, Peter Eschar and Thomas Cave. Ralph has annotated it: *'All these debts and others very considerable not mentioned in this paper I paid before my marriage... out of kindness and respect to my brother's memory and for the honour of the family, out of the advantages I had raised by my own industry without troubling my father or bringing any encumbrance upon the lands or estate that was to descend to me'.*

Ned's death benefitted Ralph of course, because he became heir to the Montagu title and estates, and his position in society rose in consequence. One clear benefit was his promotion into Ned's place as Master of the Queen's Horse, with its welcome salary of £365 p.a.,[29] although this had not been automatic. When any place was available there were always plenty of well-connected candidates. Sir George Carteret told Sandwich in September that a nephew of the Lord Treasurer was to have it.[30] A chance remark in a letter from someone at court shows that it was York who secured the place for Ralph. *'The business of Master of the horse to the Queen has become one of the notablest intrigues you have known a great while, you shall have all the particulars when we meet. In the mean time, I will only tell you that at the Duke's most violent prosecution, Mr Montagu was received into the post on Wednesday last.'* [31] Having witnessed Ned's

---

[27] Bodleian Ms. Carte 223, f. 151

[28] Sir Thomas Clifford (later Lord Clifford of Chudleigh) has joined Ned in the negotiations with the Danes.

[29] Cal. SP Dom May 10th 1667: Warrant to Board of Greencloth to allow 20s a day in lieu of a diet of 3 dishes of meat to Ralph Montagu, master of horse to the Queen

[30] Bodleian Ms. Carte 75, f. 352. 11 September 1665

[31] Egerton Ms. 2538 fol. 260 from Merton College 7ber 30 1665

death in battle York seems to have decided that it was right for his brother to succeed him. Despite Ralph's higher profile the only surviving record of his activities over the next two years seems to be a letter from Arlington dated 3 July 1666 which implies that Ralph was again in France, less than three years after his first visit.[32] He may thus have been away from the capital at the time of the Great Fire of London at the start of September.

Those who went to court did not do so merely for the honour of serving the King and his family. For those who chose not to go into the law or the church it could lead to even greater social and financial reward though, as we have seen, the risks were also greater since one was dependent on royal favour and had to fight to keep it in the maelstrom of gossip and intrigue. Ralph was clearly ambitious for greater things than his dead brother's post. He had enjoyed the experience of his mission to France (the King wrote to his sister that he *'has even had a very pleasant visit thanks to the good treatment he received from those in authority'*) and seems to have started to explore how the King might be persuaded to send him back to the most splendid Court in Europe as ambassador. Patrons were needed to support him. The Venetian Ambassador explained to the Doge that there were two power-groups at court, the Lord Chancellor supporting the Queen, while the earls of Bristol and Arlington, and others high in the King's favour, supported his mistress Barbara Villiers. It had become clear when Charles insisted on making the latter one of his new wife's Ladies of the Bedchamber, and permitting her to give birth to their second child at Hampton Court (where Charles had brought Queen Catherine for their honeymoon), that her power had not been decreased by the King's marriage. It was thought that the Montagu family interest, headed by the earl of Manchester as Lord Chamberlain, also inclined to her. One of the ways for Ralph to access her favour was through his sister Betty. The loss of Ned must have made the siblings even closer, a closeness that clearly lasted all their lives, not least because they seem to have had similar characters. The letters he wrote to her from France were addressed to his *'Dearest Sister'* from *'Your most affectionate brother'*. Betty had married Sir Daniel Harvey (brother to William Harvey, who described the circulation of the blood). We know that she was a close friend of Barbara because in the summer of 1667, after one of her many arguments with the King, Barbara took refuge with Lady Harvey at her house in Covent Garden. On previous occasions she had visited her uncle in the country, but now she needed to stay on the scene - Lord Chancellor Clarendon, her enemy, was about to fall. On June 10 a Dutch fleet captured the fort of

---

[32] Bodleian Ms. Carte 46, f. 329. Lord St. Alban's letter to the King speaks, uncertainly, of M. de Beaufort's being at Rochelle; Mr Montagu affirms it positively, in a letter to the writer; asserting that he is to accompany the new Queen to Portugal, before he comes hither

Sheerness on the Medway, burned thirteen ships and towed away Charles' flagship, which Sandwich had commanded when he brought the King back from exile (it became a Dutch tourist attraction). For the rest of the month there were fears of invasion. The Second Dutch War had been opposed by Clarendon, who thought that France was the greater danger (not knowing of his royal master's overtures to Louis XIV), but Parliament was baying for blood and so eventually the King bowed to pressure and unjustly exiled him.

Barbara was related to one of England's greatest and most influential peers, the duke of Buckingham, and it was through him that Ralph lobbied for the post he wanted. He wrote to Henry Bennet, Lord Arlington at Bath on July 20 1668: '*Since your Lordship went out of town, my Lord of Buckingham spoke twice to the King about declaring me his Embassadour for France. The first time the King asked him whether he did not think I was too young; the second time he asked him what he thought of my Lord Sunderland's going: whereupon my lord Duke says he gave him some reasons in favour of me, which made him insist not upon my Lord Sunderland, but yet did not at that time resolve anything. Now, my Lord, since the King has himself taken away his own objection by naming a younger man than myself to the same employment he thought me too young for, I hope your Lordship will be so kind to me in your next letter to the Treasurer to say something that may move the King to determine in my favour'.* Arlington was the person named by Pepys as being Ned's only remaining influential friend three years before. As Secretary of State for the South he was responsible for southern England and diplomatic relations with the Catholic nations and therefore key to Ralph's ambition to be Ambassador to France.

By August 16 the King had given in to all this persuasion: '*Ralph Montagu's character being approved, he goes ambassador to France*'.[33] Ralph started to prepare himself: '*Mr Montagu and Lord Trevor attend my lord (Arlington) constantly at Goring House*'.[34] He wrote to Arlington on October 10 that '*After I had waited on the Queen at Audly-End, I returned hither to attend the Commissionaires of the Treasury for the allowance your Lordship told me were settled upon Ambassadors*'. The State Treasury Books show his frequent attendance on them, such as the entry for October 20: '*Mr Montague called in: moves for money for his embassy*'.[35] Since Ralph had already years of experience of holding an office paid for by the State he can surely have had no delusions about becoming rich as a direct result. Charles spent lavishly and so was always in need of funds, which Parliament was loath to award him. As a

[33] Calendar State Papers Domestic
[34] Cal SP Dom
[35] State Treasury Book for the year, p.463

consequence office holders were constantly petitioning the secretaries of state, Lord Treasurer and others for money due. The Treasury told Ralph that he could have £1500 to purchase what he would need, but that this would be recouped from the £100 weekly allowance. Ralph pointed out that Lord Keeper Coventry's brother had recently gone as ambassador to Holland and was given an advance of £3000 which wasn't recouped from his weekly allowance. Intelligence money and extras were to be allowed.[36] The State Treasury Books provide several examples of Ralph's extraordinaries, such as this from a decade later. (Expresses refer to post personally carried by a messenger, and were thus likely to arrive much quicker at their destination and not be read by agents of the French postal service).

August 17 1678	£	s	d
To ten expresses at 30l each	300	0	0
To two expresses at 30l each, one at 40l	100	0	0
Given to an express sent from England	15	0	0
For new year's gifts to the King & Queen of France, Princes of the blood & ministers' officers	150	0	0
For postage of letters	140	0	0
For intelligence	80	0	0
For lodging & stables at St. Germain	70	0	0
For the same at Versailles	80	0	0
For extraordinary charges of journeys thither & sending servants within the year	160	0	0
Laid out more than I drew bills for upon account of the troops	90	0	0
[Interest or discount paid] for advance of money I took up for the troops	36	0	0
Upon my allowance of 100l per week for [ordinary] entertainment	173	0	0
Exchequer fees for the sum of 1,622l 2s 6d for extraordinaries	57	7	6
[Interest or discount] given for the advance of 2,600l viz 20 guineas	21	13	4
	1473	2	10

To understand the background to Ralph's embassy requires some knowledge of English foreign policy at this time. Put as simply as such matters allow, Charles II was pro-French. He was, of course, half French himself (and one quarter Italian through his Medici grandmother), and

[36] Cal SP Dom December 1668

Louis XIV's cousin. His sister had married the King's only brother the duc d'Orleans, known as Monsieur (and so she was Madame). Charles's mother still lived in France and he had spent two years of his exile there. He must have been envious of Louis's power, unhindered by a parliament. This bond was reinforced by his dislike of the Dutch, England's fiercest commercial, maritime and colonial rivals. Additionally, the pro republican Dutch faction tried to keep power in their own, patrician, hands and allow Charles's nephew, Prince William of Orange as little influence as possible. The Venetian ambassador reported in 1672 that Charles was convinced that the hatred of the Dutch for England was hereditary, that it increased because of trade rivalry and became implacable owing to the pretensions of the United Provinces.[37] The King thought that Dutch defeat would increase English trade and so sufficiently swell royal revenues through the tax thereon that some independence from Parliament could be had. He did not see France as a rival in the same way, but many Englishmen were anti-French not only due to historic enmity but more particularly to France's Catholicism. The duke of Buckingham was the leader of the pro-French faction, less out of conviction than in the hope of ruining Arlington, his rival for the King's ear, who was pro-Spanish. Charles recognised that the French had demands on Spain (and on all the countries with which it had land boundaries) which would lead to war and then England would have to choose sides. Louis had been annoyed by the outbreak of the Second Dutch War – at that time Holland and England were on good terms with him and he was encouraging Portuguese opposition to Spain, so expecting that when his father-in-law Philip IV of Spain died and his feeble brother-in-law succeeded the way would be clear for him to take advantage of the situation. As a consequence in 1666 he came into the war against England on the Dutch side. He had no intention of fighting, but knew the declaration would put the Dutch under obligation, dishearten England and warn Spain away from strengthening ties with England, as Arlington's ambassador, Sandwich, had been trying to do. Sandwich did succeed in this the following year because the Spanish realised Louis's promise of non-aggression wasn't to be trusted: he had taken his army into the Spanish Netherlands, which he claimed were the property of his wife. Arlington was surprised at '*how willingly men, of all qualities, run into the Spanish service, and openly protest against the French*'.[38]

In mid-December 1667 Arlington and Buckingham met with the French ambassador, the marquis de Ruvigny, and stated that any Anglo-French treaty had to be anti-Dutch. Holland was not to divide the Spanish

---

[37] Cal SP Venetian xxxvii, p.244

[38] T. Bebington ed., Lettres du Comte d'Arlington au Chevalier Temple (aux Comtes de Sandwich, & de Sunderland; & aux Chevaliers Fanshaw, Godolphin, & Southwel), (Utrecht 1701) vol. I, p.165

Netherlands with France, Ostend and Nieuport were to be given to England so that Parliament could see the benefit of a French alliance, and a commercial treaty was to be concluded. Louis would only agree to the latter. Normally this statement of positions would be followed by lengthy diplomacy to find common ground but Arlington was concerned that, if the French and Spanish made peace, English neutrality would be worthless, so he wanted a prompt agreement. Just as Louis's second offer arrived, annoying Charles by being little better than his first, Holland and Sweden agreed to enter a Triple Alliance with England to preserve the Netherlands against all enemies (including France). To complete Arlington's joy his rival Buckingham was disgraced for killing his mistress' husband, the earl of Shrewsbury, in a duel (watched by the countess, who supposedly cared for her lover's horse whilst he was thus occupied). Consequently the Privy Council's committee for foreign affairs was reorganised, and became known as the Cabal (coincidentally the initials of its members' titles). Arlington's secretary, Joseph Williamson, became its secretary, and he was able to get his nominee, Sir John Trevor, appointed as his fellow Secretary of State, for the North. The two Secretaries, with the Lord Treasurer (then the earl of Southampton), were Charles's chief ministers

The King saw the Triple Alliance as a way of demonstrating to Louis that his response to English overtures was unsatisfactory and that, much as Charles leaned towards France, he needed to properly treated. Louis saw things differently – he made an agreement with the Emperor that when the enfeebled King Carlos of Spain died his realm would be divided. The Hapsburgs would take Spain, Milan and the West Indies, whilst France would have the Spanish Netherlands, the Franche-Comte and the Two Sicilies. In April 1668 France and Spain made peace, as Arlington had feared, and Louis took part of Flanders as a 'down payment'. Arlington responded by negotiating to bring more countries into the Triple Alliance, insisting that if there was to be rapprochement with France the first step should be the promised commercial treaty. The City of London had long felt that the current balance of trade was unfair, an attitude hardened by Colbert's imposition of 100% duties on imported manufactured goods in 1667. (Colbert had been appointed Finance Minister by Louis in 1665). Louis instructed his new ambassador to England, de Croissy (Colbert's brother), to stall for time and to try to bribe Arlington with £25,000 plus £2,500 a year. Charles was still determined to secure a French alliance: in December he told his sister that he was sending her a cipher, so that they could correspond in secret for the first time and he announced that he would prorogue Parliament to October 1669, since he was not in need of money. Now he needed to get Arlington on-side. He seems to have done this by revealing that he intended to convert to Catholicism, thus playing to Arlington's sense of loyalty to his monarch and making him realise that he had to go along with the intention to ally with France if he wanted to remain in office. Arlington may well have thought that if all went well the proposed alliance could be scuppered by excessive demands likely to be made by the French or, if it was written into the treaty that the first step should be the public announcement of Charles's conversion, further steps might never take place. (There was no immediate prospect of the country being willing to accept a Catholic king).

This was the state of English foreign policy when Ralph stepped onto the stage as ambassador to France at the age of thirty-one, armed with his instructions issued to him by Arlington.[39] On March 10 1669 he *'with a small retinue, has arrived at Calais, and intends furnishing himself with Frenchmen'*. (Twenty-five horses had been sent ahead of him at the start of February).[40] He reached Paris on the 25th. Two days later Ralph sent Arlington the first of the many letters he would despatch during his stay in Paris, stating that he had arrived, had called upon the Queen before her dinner, and later upon Madame, followed by her husband, Monsieur. There were practical matters to be sorted out. *'I am forced at present to lie in an ill lodging not fit to be seen in, for as soon as I came to town I found the house Mr de Moulin took for me not fit for a dog to lie in, & yet with the time I have paid for already, and am to pay, it will cost me a year's rent. I have found...one of the best houses in Paris...I hope to have it and go into it before Easter, by which time I hope to be ready for my Public Audience'.* (The ill lodging was in the Rue de Richlieu. It wasn't until October that he was able to move into *'one of the best houses in Paris'* in the Faubourg St. Germain, near Queen Henrietta Maria's home). He was clearly very cross about the accommodation, writing to Lord Trevor in relation to de Moulin, one of the embassy staff, that he *'has put mee to a great many inconveniencies. I will not trouble the Secretary of State with the particulars, but my sister will let you know them all. I came yesterday to this Towne & today wayted upon the Queen, who hath been indisposed when I mett Madam. I went afterwards in the evening to the Palace Royall to wayt on her & after that shee told me I was to goe to Monsieur, wch. I did accordingly, who recd mee mighty kindly as I could expect'.*[41] Before the public audience *'On Monday I am to have a private audience with the King. I could not well have it sooner because he has been this week every day out of town at St Germaines & Versailles, at both which places he is a-building'.* The Public Audience was a diplomatic minefield. The "Princes of the Blood" (members of the extended royal family) always insisted that their carriages should go before the ambassador's in the procession marking his official arrival in Paris, and in that to the palace next day, but

---

[39] Thirteen articles, issued 22 Feb. 1668/9. BL Add Mss.32094 fo. 216.
[40] Cal SP Dom
[41] BL Add Mss.23894 fol.3

he represented the King of England and so this could be seen as a slight to his royal master. Ralph was told by Monsieur and Madame that no other ambassador, not the King of Spain's, the Emperor's, or even the Pope's, insisted on precedence. The last English ambassador had been forced to make his audience without the Princes as a result. The expedient finally arrived at was to have Queen Catherine's coat-of-arms on his coach (since Ralph was her Master of Horse), and so it could go after the King of France's and before the Queen's: *this rank I take is judged by everybody as the most honourable*. It is worth giving a full description of the event which must have been one of the most memorable days in Ralph's life (and also gives a flavour of splendid ceremonial long since passed).[42]

On Thursday April ye 25th in the afternoon, His Excy attended by divers English nobility and gentry in a magnificent Train and Equipage at L'Hostel de Rambouillet, a house appointed for that purpose about a mile from Port St. Antoine was met and complimented by ye Mareschall de Belfonds & Monsr. Bonueil, Master of Ceremonies; besides other gentlemen who, in the name of the Most Xtian King, Queen, Monsieur, Madam & all the Princes of the Blood congratulated his Excies.' Arrival here with their Bienvenues, accompanying him with their several coaches to conduct him into Paris, which were ranked in this manner

Four gentlemen and six Pages on horseback rode first before the King's coach wherein was his Excy the Duke de Belfonds & Monsr de Bonueil, next unto which went his Excies two coaches, the first of State and the other part of the train, & then followed the Queen's coach and those of Monsieur, Madame & all the Princes of the Blood, in the foremost of which all the Ambassadors retinues were placed, his Excies twelve footmen attending him by the coach side. Thus the Ambassador proceeded to his house in the Rue de Richlieu. Being come to his house was there complimented more ceremoniously & by persons of great quality from all the forementioned, which his Excy returned with much civility, meeting them on the stairs at their entrance & accompanying them to their coaches. The Most Xtian King having appointed the morrow for his Excies Publique Audience, Monsr de Lorrain (a favourite of Monsieur) & Mr De Bonnueil came in the King's coach to conduct the Ambassador thereunto. His Excies coaches kept the same rank as at the Entrée...& entered the Louvre with a very splendid train & was brought to the presence below stairs, where having expected about half an hour, his Excy was conducted up into the Hall where the Most Xtian King was in his Chaise of State...with Monsieur by him & after three reverences the Ambassador had made the three ascending steps, the King at the same time bareheaded

---

[42] Xtian is an abbreviation for Christian.

standing, they both covered, when his Excy made his Harangue in English, which was after read in French by Monsr du Moulin.

In the afternoon in the same form the Ambassador had a public audience of the M Xtian Queen who was attended by many great Ladys, & then the Dauphin was complimented by my Ld Ambr, as well as his younger brother the Duk d'Anjou & his sister, which put a conclusion to the ceremonies of the day. The next day he had public audience of Monsieur.

Abel Boyer's obituary of Ralph gives a wealth of other details: there were 74 pages and footmen in rich liveries, 12 led horses, 18 English noblemen and gentry, 4 rich coaches with 8 horses each, and 2 chariots with 6 horses '*made as fine and costly as Art and Workmen could contrive*'. Ralph rode in the King's state coach, '*passing through multitudes of spectators, who were astonish'd at the grandeur and applause of the English nobility*'. Two days after his entrance Ralph had his first public audience with the King, '*which for a distinguishing Mark of Honour he had in his Most Christian Majesty's Bed-Chamber, and even within the Rails round the Bed, where the King stood to receive him. His Excellency having made his Speech in French, and delivered his credentials, the King answered him in very obliging Terms, both in relation to his Master and himself; and then his Excellency presented to the king the English Noblemen and Gentlemen of his Retinue: which being over, he had an Audience of the Dauphine and the rest of the Royal Family*'.[43] Monsieur then entertained him at a public dinner '*at his Noble Seat of St. Cloud, where he had the Honour to see those most exquisite Gardens beyond Comparison, the finest in all France; and he did him the Honour to Walk to the end of his whole garden with him, a Favour that Prince was not used to bestow on any, even of the Princes of the Blood. After this, he was entertain'd in particular at Versailles for a considerable while, where he had all the Gardens at his Command, and the most extraordinary Fountains and Water-works were ordered to be Play'd always at his entrance*'.[44] Whilst he was at Versailles he was invited to dine with Monsieur de Livry, Master of the King's Household, and afterward had a long conversation with Louis '*the Fountains playing all the while*'. Ralph began the negotiations for a treaty "*with the French King in the Apartment of Monsieur de Louvoy, the King of France's Chief Minister, where the Ambassador often dined*'.

Although this first hurdle had been overcome there were plenty of others to be tackled in an era when precedent and precedence were so

---

[43] *The Court in Mourning. Being the Life and Worthy Actions of Ralph, Duke of Montagu* (London 1709)

[44] A. Boyer *The History of the reign of Queen Anne digested into Annals* (London 1710) Remarkables of the year 1709, p.365.

important. Ralph wrote to Trevor: *'There will now be another dispute about visiting the Princes of ye Blood, whether I am to do it first or no, as other Ambassadors doe. I desire the King's pleasure in that'*.[45] Whether you visited them before they visited you, met a visitor at his coach when he arrived, at the foot of the stairs to the main rooms, at the top of the stairs, at the door to the reception room, in the reception room but you rose from your chair, or if you remained seated, all indicated your view of the worth of your visitor and consequently whether he would feel insulted or not. Ralph reported that he could not visit the Prince de Conde, as King Charles wished, because the Prince would only permit it if he met Ralph at the top of the stairs of his residence, whilst on the return visit Ralph would be expected to meet the Prince at his coach. The Savoy ambassador wanted to know whether, if he visited, he would be treated as representing a kingdom rather than a principality. Who was the first to doff his hat and incline a bow similarly indicated who outranked the other – one of Ralph's complaints about de Moulin was that on occasion the latter had not removed his hat when Ralph entered, the latter asking whether he thought he was there as a companion rather than a servant. (April 17). This was not simply a diplomatic issue, or Ralph being overly sensitive – when the Commons came into the House of Lords they were to stand hatless whilst the peers were seated and 'covered', and when in 1689 the constitutional ramifications of the revolution were being taken in the privileges committee spent a lot of time discussing the circumstances under which peers could wear their hats in the monarch's presence. One sometimes imagines a courtly dance taking place: *'Two days since my Ld Ambassadour met the Prince of Tuscany in Monsr Tamboneau's garden, where they made many compliments and turns'* (An entry of August 31 1669 by William Perwich, Ralph's secretary, some of whose letters also survive). When a Turkish envoy had an audience with the French Foreign minister in November 1669, the latter lay on a couch. Perwich records: *'The Turk was introduced by a gentleman and made most profound reverences according to his manner, which were returned by a tip of the hat and a nod that he should sit down, at which time the Turk was presented with a dish of coffee'*. Ralph or Perwich would write frequently to England to enquire what Arlington thought was appropriate and what previous ambassadors had experienced.

Intelligence was to be gathered from talking to French ministers, the ambassadors of other nations, and English ambassadors travelling through Paris. One such was Lord Winchelsea, who arrived on his way home from Turkey in June, after eight years in Istanbul. It had taken him fifteen days to travel from Rome. (His replacement was Ralph's brother-in-law Sir Daniel Harvey, appointed Ambassador to Constantinople in 1668, where

---

[45] BL Add Ms 23894 f.8.

he died four years later). Ralph had written early in his embassy that *'it will be very hard in this country to learn anything of consequence, they being all here much readier to ask questions of what concerns other people than answer anything that concerns themselves'*. (April 10). Learning things of consequence was central to an ambassador's role – Perwich noted on June 28 1670 that *'there are some English marchants in company at Marseilles, called Hills, who have offred my Ld Ambr punctuall information of all that passeth & particularly ye persons directed for any adresse to Sr Thomas Allin. I have in my Ld's name incouraged them'*. Charles also employed spies, hence the £80 spent on intelligence shown in the list of costs dated April 1678. Shortly after Ralph arrived he had to defend one of these, Rene Petit, Charles's agent in Picardy, Normandy and Brittany. Colbert complained that he had been libelled by Petit, but Perwich says that he was simply *'too bold in his expressions...What greater proof can wee have of them opening our lettrs'*. (He complained about how often the French were doing this. A packet from Spain had been kept by them for eight days and they had removed letters to Arlington and Trevor). The French ambassador in London gave Arlington a note of complaint about the man but Ralph was unable to elicit from Louis's ministers what offence he had committed and responded to Arlington that if Charles *'would oblige the French Ambassador to breake off all commerce of all the English spies that come to his house he would not fill his letters nor give fresh intelligence of all the scandalous and false reports both of the King and the government as he does'* (December 7). English visitors of note who passed through Paris would call at the Embassy and useful information gained could be about England as well as France: *'Mr Bridgman, my Lord Keeper's son, who has no great brains or a strong head, one night with Father Patricke and I drinking a glass of wine, I put him on talking about his father'* (May 8 1669). Information might be gathered even when shopping. *'I went to Martiall's* [a famous Parisian drapers] *and I saw a present which I am sure must cost a thousand pounds packing up. I found since it was for my Lady Castlemaine...I asked him whom it was for, but he could not, or would not, tell me. I asked him who paid him; he told me the king of France'* (May 3). At Yale there is a manuscript which purports to be Ralph's diary from November 1669 to June 1671 but seems (as far as translation of the French written in an appalling hand allows one to say) to be intelligence collected. It includes notes on the French forces in Holland (numbers in each regiment, officers names), discussions on taxation etc.[46]

Ralph settled into his embassy and decided he needed to change some of his staff. He had been unhappy with de Moulin ever since the debacle over

---

[46] "Diary of Ralph Montagu" Beinecke Osborn fb. 191

his accommodation: '*Mr. de Moulin I find apprehends that I am jealous lest his parts should eclipse mine. I confess my Lord, I am extreme jealous of him but it is of his folly & indiscretion*' (April 6 1669). A month later: '*As for Mr du Moulin I assure you that it is as much for your sake as my own that I would be rid of him for he is an absolute spy of Lord Trevor's, who I must needs advise you every day more and more to have a care of*' (May 18). Ralph eventually accused him of taking a cut when exchanging money and sent him packing. He suggested to Arlington that he be replaced with Mr. Vernon '*who was a schoolfellow of mine, and, without being partial to him, as witty and modest and understanding a man as ever I knew of his breeding and education. He has been all the world over, and speaks French and Spanish and Italian better than ordinary Englishmen do*' (May 22). Ralph felt that he ought to have been helped in his work by his relative, the Abbe Walter Montagu (son of the 1st earl of Manchester). The Abbe had met Queen Henrietta Maria during the negotiations for her marriage to Charles I and had become close to her after his conversion to Catholicism in 1635 at the age of 30.[47] Banished from England by Parliament in 1649 he had become part of the Regency Council in France and Henrietta Maria's spiritual adviser as well as Madame's almoner. He was thus well placed to secure French help for Charles II's restoration in 1660.[48] The Abbe was also on good terms with Sandwich, as the letters he sent to the latter concerning the education on Sandwich's son in France over a period of two years attest.[49] He may have been influential in Ned's conversion. It is likely the two men met when Ned was a royalist agent during the Commonwealth. Though his elderly relative was clearly in a position to be well informed, Ralph complained in May 1669 ' *de Moulin... keeps a constant correspondency with Abbe Montagu, I believe unknown to your Lordship, and he presently tells Mr de Tellier all he knows. Abbe Mountagu is in France as my Lord Chamberlain is in England, and extreme useless to me, for he is grown very ignorant and out of fashion*'. (The Lord Chamberlain was the Abbe's brother, the 2nd earl of Manchester).

In fact it was Abbe Montagu who, due to his closeness to the two royal families, and his faith, was being employed to translate documents concerning the secret part of the treaty between England and France of which Ralph was in ignorance. The Catholic Lord Arundell had arrived in France shortly after Ralph, ostensibly to see the Queen Mother, and met with him occasionally. The true reason for his visit was to do the

---

[47] Walter had written "The Shepherd's Paradise", an eight hour masque, for her in 1633 (with sets by Inigo Jones). He is the only Montagu to appear in a famous novel - Dumas's "The Three Musketeers" (Chap. 43 "The Red Dovecote Tavern").
[48] Bodleian Ms. Carte 223, ff. 600, 602.
[49] Ibid. ff. 59,61,63,65,67,69

diplomatic rounds offering an offensive and defensive league towards all and against all, helped by the Abbe. The league was not to conflict with the Triple Alliance, and the French navy had to stop ship-building. Charles's conversion to Catholicism would be supported by Louis with money and troops if necessary, after he had put loyal Catholics into key offices and persuaded Parliament to allow liberty of conscience. (It is difficult to know how much of this fantastic scenario was Arundell's and how much Charles's). Since Vienna had rejected a French proposal regarding the Spanish Netherlands, and with the Dutch expressing opposition to Louis's expansionism just before Arundell arrived, Louis was at this point all the keener for an English alliance. Ralph apparently had no sense that diplomatic negotiations were going on behind his back - as early as May 3 1668, when '*Madame did as good as own to me that she is sure that in a short time England and France will join. I am sure she cannot know any such thing, but Sir Ellis Layton, who is employed by Ruvigny to gain my Lord Buckingam, makes it be believed, to get a little more money; and I dare confidently say he is a spy, that tells all he does know, and a great deal that he does not know*', he was discounting indicators that others knew more than he did. On Louis arrival at St. Germain from Chambord on October 20 Ralph greeted him publicly with a list of complaints in the name of the Triple Alliance against the King's many violations of the Treaty of Aix-la-Chapelle. Did he not notice Arundell, who had returned from a brief trip to England with further instructions?

In June 1669 Charles was concerned that Louis wanted to bring the French ambassador into the secret and opined that it wasn't time to inform either him or Ralph.[50] Ralph's continued concern was to make Arlington a persona grata to the French court, which still considered him to be pro Spanish and therefore anti French. Madame was close to both Kings, and shared that view of Arlington. '*I have watched an opportunity of speaking privately with Madame, which was not easy, she keeping her bed...but this day Monsieur being gone to St. Germaine's ... appointed me between one and two o'clock. I desired, before any other discourse, to know her reason for being dissatisfied with your Lordship. She told me that she had no kind of anger in the world to you, but she believed that you slighted her and her friendship...She asked me if I would answer for you. I told her I would. I was the willinger to put you upon good terms with her, because I find the King's letters – some of which she showed me, because she is proud of them, but yet in great confidence – that he writes to her of very private matters, and speaks his mind of all things very freely to her. I think, my Lord, if you approve it, it would not be amiss if your Lordship writ a civil letter to her, and send it to me for her, wherein you may take notice of how*

---

50 C.H. Hartman ibid p.256

I answered to her for you, and how ready you are to make it good. I find here that the French Ambassador does you all the ill offices that can be here, and says, if it were not for you, France and England would join'. Ralph knew that something more tangible than words would help Arlington's case (and, of course, increase Ralph's reputation in the eyes of both parties). He wrote to his sister on July 19: '*There is a business which I would have you propose to my Lord Arlington. I believe he may do it the easiest that can be, and it is a thing that may hereafter be of great consequence to him and all his friends. You may propose it to him, and afterwards he is a better judge than either you or I what is better to be done. You know I have writ formerly to you that if ever there could be any money spared, it were very fit for the King to make Madame a present. In the first place, the King really owes it her, and when the Parliament gave her, at her coming into England* [at the Restoration], *ten thousand pound, the King desired to make use of it, and never gave her a penny of it'.* Ralph then suggests that, since it looked as if some of Catherine of Braganza's dowry would actually be paid by the Portuguese, £5,000 of it should go to Madame. He thought it best to keep the payment quiet since Henrietta Maria's allowance had been stopped by Charles and she might raise a complaint as a consequence. The King agreed to the plan and on August 26 Ralph was able to write to his sister that when Madame heard the news '*She says my Lord Arlington is such a kind man that it is impossible not to be his friend...You never saw anybody perkt up as she is since this money, and it makes her so sure to my Lord Arlington that he had better have given it out of his own pocket than not a-got it her...there are certain jewels in pawn which she would fain have out against the winter before her husband knows that they are there'.* He mentions that Madame had showed him some letters from her brother which mentioned Lady Harvey. '*I dare tell you he is kinder to you, and you have more credit with him than you think you have; for all he says of you is as of one that he has a good opinion of, and believes loves him better than anybody'.* It is clear that he has considered how he might be rewarded, perhaps helped by his sister's 'credit', for he continues '*I know you have a mind to be a Lady upon your own account as well upon Sir Daniel's, and therefore I intend...to engage Madame to write to the King about my father's business; but pray first ask my Lord Arlington's opinion'* of the idea that Lord Montagu be given an earldom one must assume. Madame was indeed in great need of money. Ralph later wrote to his sister: '*Abbe Clermont, a man of great quality and one of the greatest gamesters in France...partly won of Madame, and partly paid to other people what she had lost, as much as made her four thousand louis d'ors in his debt. This man, about a month ago, left off being an Abbe, and has bought a place of Gentleman of the Robes to the King, for which he is to pay fifty thousand pistols and...he could not make* up this sum unless Madame paid him...She sent for me and told me of the business, being very unwilling Monsieur or the King should know of it'. Ralph had to advance her 5,500 louis until such time as the promised money came from England. He finishes his letter by saying 'If I get well of(f) of this, I promise you, I will never meddle with such businesses again' (December 12).

Ralph passed on his views of Louis's chief ministers: 'Mr Tellier and Mr de Lionne, by what I can guess, are two as cunning and able men as can be; for Colbert here, by that little that I saw of him, he is very vain and very pedantical; he affects being mighty eloquent, and run(s) himself into speaking nonsense presently' (May 24 1669). He even gave an opinion of Louis himself: 'The King here is the least beloved and esteemed by all his servants, even in the nearest about him, that ever king in the world was, because of his ill-natured and proud usage of them upon all occasions. They have no way of complaining of it, as a very witty man told me the other day, but by extolling the King of England's using of people, which they say angers and vexes the French King more than anything they can say. He is the same to the women, except to one, as he is to the men, and a little while ago some ladies were a-commending the king of England before him. He appeared a little nettled at it, and said "Women always love adventurers, but I do not credit myself for being any less of a gentleman for not having been chased out of my kingdom"' (July 26). He continued to supply Arlington with information on all he heard in Paris, whether gossip or not: 'There is a great noise here of the Duke of Buckingham and you being fallen out...My Lord Buckhurst is extreme sensible of your kindness to him...your Lordship can make use of and trust my Lord...The Duke of Richmond bids me tell you he will stand by you' (September 6). A few days later Ralph wrote to Charles to tell him that his mother had died. As he told Arlington on the 11th 'She went to bed pretty well, and about two a clock in the morning, as her servants went to give her something, they found her a-dying'. He went on to explain that although the earl of St. Alban's, her Chamberlain, sent an express to England with the news, he did not tell Ralph, who happened to find out about it only an hour later 'by chance'. Since this would have been at three in the morning it is likely he had an informant in the household. He then sent privately to her nephew King Louis to have the house sealed up, as was customary when royalty died. Not knowing of his agency, St. Alban's railed at Ralph for such an indignity. 'I am sure without this my Lord St Alban's would not have left a silver spoon in the house...I would not have any but his Majesty know I did this, because it makes one have enemies to no purpose...I shall be at very great expense for mourning. I have all my coaches and some fifty servants and three rooms of my house to be in mourning...P.S. I find by some discourse with my Lord of Richmond, that if *the King sends an Ambassador into Poland, you would oblige him in getting him named'.* A little later he estimated the cost of mourning (three coaches, two for the town and a travelling coach, three rooms to be hung with black cloth, fifty servants etc) to be £1,000. The cost was actually £1,203 9s 3d.[51] *'I am like to spend the winter as I have spent the summer, upon the high way. For between St Germain, St Cloud and Colombe I have hardly sat still a day since I have been in France'.* (These were the country residences of the King, Monsieur and Madame, and Queen Henrietta Maria. Shortly after his arrival he had taken a small house at St Germain to save the commute between there and Paris. He had written on May 4 1669 that if he stayed in Paris *'a man shall be as much a stranger to all that passes as if he were in England and seeing sometimes teaches one more than hearing'.* Perhaps remembering Paris's anti-royal sentiments during the Fronde rebellion of his youth, Louis never spent a great deal of time in the city). On the 25th he had a ceremonial audience to offer the King condolences on the death of his aunt and after the public audience was over *'the King appointed me to come to him into his closet where I spoke to him according as...the King my master commanded me'.* He made himself useful by making an inventory of the late Queen's valuables, giving money to the right charities, and offering suggestions: *'Pray tell the King that there is a very pretty service of gilt plate...will serve his Majesty for his new lodgings'* (October 27). *'There is some pieces of crimson and gold brocard, a very fine stuff, and will make his Majesty a very fine bed...There will be enough almost, I believe, to hang the alcove of the chamber too. If the King pleases, I will have it made up for him here much handsomer and cheaper than it can be in England'* (November 9). It is clear that Ralph would miss his regular contact with the Queen Mother's household, which was mainly English: *'I am shortly like to be much alone. My Lady Duchesse of Richmond...and all the good company of the queene mothers family being preparing for England'* (December 7). [52]

Madame was still in mourning for her mother when on November 26 Ralph told Arlington that more grief had been heaped upon her. The bishop of Valence had been forced to give up his position as Almoner to Monsieur after advising him *'not to live in so scandalous a way as he did both to God and man with the Chevalier de Lorraine'.* Lorraine had become Monsieur's lover at the age of fifteen in 1658 (Monsieur was three years older), two years before Madame wed. The bishop had also produced love letters from Lorraine to one of Madame's ladies which were very unflattering to Monsieur. The bishop had been exiled to the country but, taken *'very ill of the stone'*, he had secretly returned to Paris to consult a

---

[51] State Treasury Books Nov 15 1699 p.297
[52] Cal SP Dom Account of expenses of his mourning death of the Queen Mother totalling £1,328

doctor and looked likely to die. His steward wrote to the governess of Madame's children (Madame de Chaumont) who had been friends with the bishop and the latter replied that, though it had been foolish of him to come to Paris, she would have been willing to visit him in his hour of need if she had not been sick herself. In fact, feeling that her position had been bolstered by the success of the treaty between her brother-in-law and her brother, Madame had asked him to bring to Paris letters which she hoped would discredit Lorraine (who had moved into her house). Tipped off by the doctor, royal agents raided the bishop's lodging. Although he managed to get rid of the documents in the privy, they found Madame de Chaumont's letter which resulted in the King telling Monsieur that she should be *'turned out of her place'*. Madame asked Ralph to intercede for her servant and confidante with Louis. He did so, but *'after arguing the thing a great while, I could have no other reason for his doing the thing than that he resolved it. All France, as well as Madame, look upon this as a very harsh thing, and the rather because that Madame de Montespan, who hates Madame and Madame de St. Shoumon particularly, is at the bottom of this business...The King told Monsieur, who can hold nothing and so told Madame again, that he believed Madame would complain to her brother, the King of England, and perhaps he would take it so ill that he would not be his friend. "Well," says he, "let her be whose sister she will, she will obey me." I tell you these particulars because by such circumstances you may sometimes judge of men's humours, and so take your measures for matters of greater consequences. The king's chief pleasure here is to domineer and insult over those that are in his power, and I will conclude with thanking God, both for you and myself, that we serve so good a master'* (November 26).

Encouraged by Madame, Ralph wrote to both Arlington and the King: *'I would humbly propose to your Majesty what Madame has already discoursed to me of, which is, that your Majesty would tell the French Ambassador in England, that you know the Chevalier de Lorraine is the occasion of all the ill that your sister suffers, and that she is one that you are so tender of that you cannot think the French King your friend, whilst he suffers such a man about his brother, by whose counsels he doth every day so many things to Madame's dissatisfaction...In case your Majesty does not approve of this way, nothing could be more for Madame's comfort, as well as credit, than that your Majesty should desire to have her make a journey to you into England in the spring...If you shall think this improper too, Madame would then desire that you would let fall to the French Ambassador that you are informed how unkindly she is used here, but that she had desired you to take no notice of it, but only, if you please, not to live so freely, nor do the French Ambassador so much honour, as you used to do. You Majesty may perhaps think me impertinent for writing* of this, but I assure you, Sir, not only all the French, but the Dutch, the Swedish, and Spanish Ministers are in expectation of what your Majesty will do in this business, for they all know Madame is the thing in the world that is dearest to you; and they whose interest it is to have your Majesty and the King here be upon ill terms, are very glad he has done a thing which they think will anger you' (December 12).

Ralph wrote to Arlington on the same day: 'I am not afraid that the King's using Mr. Colbert coldly should return upon me, for the King here lives at so much distance and strangeness with me...sometimes I go two days together to St. Germain's without being able to get to speak with any of the Ministers, and all they answer at the door is, when I ask for any of them, "Il travaille pour le Roy"...I will say nothing to you of Mr usage of Madame, but if she had married a country gentleman in England of five thousand pound a year, she would have lived a better life than she doth here; for Mr, though he be a very wise Prince, doth, as Sir Daniel used to, take a pleasure to cross his wife in everything'. (The Sir Daniel referred to is doubtless Ralph's brother-in-law). It might be wondered why, given the treatment she received from the French king and his brother, she continued in her endeavours to bring Louis and Charles closer together.

King Charles resolved on seeing his sister, but more for reasons of state than as a loving brother. Louis announced in January 1670 that 'on Easter Monday he will set forth towards Flanders, to visit all the new conquered places and fortifications. He will go first to Callice [Calais], and so to all the towns he has on the sea coasts. He intends to be two months in his journey. The Queen and all the Court go with him'.[53] The Dutch and Spanish were worried that the stated purpose of the visit hid the opportunity it would give Louis to lead his troops against another of their towns but in truth it would also allow quicker communication between the two monarchs so that the counterpart copies of the treaty could be signed. Madame was delighted at the prospect of seeing her brother again, as Ralph reported in a letter to Arlington of January 20, which he ends with 'I find my father so delighted with the King, that I believe he would be glad to put himself to service too. I wish the King would make him a Lord again, as my sister desired Sir Daniel should be a Knight again'. It was five months since he had alluded to an earldom when writing to his sister. A fortnight after this letter Monsieur behaved so appallingly that even Louis could not ignore it. 'The Bishop of Langres...was possessed of some four thousand pistols a year, in two abbeys, which upon his death were in Monsieur's disposal...The Bishop fell sick some six days ago, and upon Thursday the news came to St. Germain's that he was dead. I happened to be in Madame's chamber when Mr heard it, who, before a great deal of company, told the Chevalier de Lorraine that he would give him those two

---

[53] RM to Arlington January 11

benefices, though it seems the King had already told Mr that he would never consent that the Chevalier de Lorraine should have them, not thinking him a man of a life fit for Church benefices. Mr...went to see the King, who was a-going to Versailles. Mr came from the King so discontented with some discourse that passed between them, that he presently sent for his coach and declared he would leave the Court, since the King used him so; and my Lord Abbot Montagu being there...so far prevailed with Mr, as though his coach and guards were at the door, to stay till the King came back. At the King's return Mr had another conversation with the King, in which both were both so dissatisfied that Mr came presently away to Paris, and the Chevalier de Lorraine was taken prisoner.[54] Despite the fact that this must have been the very thing that Madame wished for most, she knew that Monsieur would blame her for his lover's removal, blameless though she was, and that she would still have no peace (he had said *'qu'on ne me rend le Chevalier'*). So she interceded with Louis before leaving with her husband for their country residence, which gained her credit, though the King would not of course submit his royal will to his brother's.

In his letter to Charles of February 5 Ralph praised Madame's behaviour towards his royal master and related that, having agreed things in advance with her, he had asked for a private audience with Louis and told him that Charles was grateful for all he had done for Madame and, now that she had lost her mother, he commended her to Louis's care as the person in the world he loved and cared for most. Louis naturally made all the right noises. Ralph then took *'the boldness to say a word or two to you in my own concerns. Madame was please in her last letter to recommend me to your Majesty for a Commissionaire's place in the Treasury, which I hear this post you have bestowed on Mr Grey. Sir William Coventry's is yet indisposed of. If your Majesty thinks me capable or worthy of such employment, your Majesty may bestow that upon me without any increase in expense to yourself, for five Commissionaires, which were the number at first, will cost you no more than four; and your Majesty will enable me the better to support the expense I am forced to be at here, which, by reason of the Court's never being in a place, is treble what any Ambassador has been at this twenty year. I humbly beg your pardon, Sir, for this presumption, but I confess it would be the greatest satisfaction in the world to me to owe my good fortune to your Majesty's choice and favour, rather than to the importunity of any of my friends'.*

Ralph bolstered his claim with a letter to Arlington a few days later, on the 8th, when having said *'I do not doubt but that you will stand my friend in this business"* he follows with *"This thing will be an absolute settling of my fortune, which, you know, with my brother's debts, my father's*

---

[54] RM to Arlington February 1

37

liberality, and what I am forced to spend here, is on no good condition....I have spent already, and I have been here but ten months, above nine thousand pistols, not reckoning my equipage, towards which the King gave me fifteen hundred pound, and afterwards out of the Prizes a thousand, which did not near serve'. It seems that this may not have gone down well with Arlington, for on the 24th Ralph says that he has heard as much, apologises, but stresses that Madame is pleased to think that she has been served well by him and has often pressed him to name something she could ask of her brother for him.

Madame's problems and petitions for financial assistance were by no means Ralph's only concerns as ambassador. Letters went to Arlington every couple of days full of news and rumour: *'There is nothing more hot in this Court nor more taken for granted, than the Prince of Condes being King of Poland'* (April 30 1669). *'I came hither to see a review of all the troops that was made today...As the King was riding along about three o'clock he spied Mr de Berrie, Mr de Lionn's son, coming to him; so he ride up to meet him...After he had talked with him apart, he came up to the company, and with a great deal of trouble told us that they had chosen and crowned a King in Poland, one Michael Bisnobesky, a young man of four and twenty year old, that nobody has ever named before'.* (July 4 – the news had taken two weeks to arrive). Often others wrote for him: *'I have made Mr Vernon one of my secretaries write a letter of all the foreign news. If your Lordship likes it and thinks it better than when I write with my own hand I will continue sometimes to make use of him, sometimes of Mr Perwich'* (June 16). Since Ralph's handwriting was appalling, with erratic spelling and almost no punctuation, it would have been interesting to see Arlington's response, especially since the latter had been told by the King in April that Ralph had the better hand. *'His Majesty now can be able to contradict those that told him I could not write'* (April 11). *'Versailles that has cost so many millions is to be pulled down and they talk of building the most magnificent thing that ever was seen'* (June 19). Often there was personal advice to Arlington: *'There is great expectations of the Parliament. Colbert writes word that you are a lost man whenever it meets, but if you will be for the French they offer to save you.... I swear the Ministers here, with all their great abilities and understanding, know no more of England than they do of Persia; and I do not wonder at it, considering the dexterity of their Ambassador, that gives them such good intelligence; and lest you think me like him, I will say no more'* (July 26).

There was also news of Candia in Crete (Heraklion). The Turks had taken the rest of the island from the Venetians and in 1648 laid siege to the capital. The siege lasted for twenty-one years. In 1669 a French expedition not only failed to lift it but one of its biggest warships sank, and the force returned home. Two months later the city surrendered. There is not as much correspondence surviving as might be expected on the subject of Spain, the Netherlands, and the Triple Alliance but, of course, the real work was going on elsewhere. Monsieur, in his pique, was opposed to his wife meeting her brother, perhaps hoping that Louis would give in to blackmail and allow his lover to return from exile in Italy. What Louis did do was give Monsieur an increase in his annual income; he then settled half of it on the Chevalier. In return he grudgingly agreed to permit his wife to sail to Dover and stay for three days *'but Mr will by no means hear of her coming to London'* (April 16). Ralph was pleased that King Louis had decided not to take all his ministers on his journey into Flanders, so not obliging him to *'go in a great equipage'*. By the time of his letter to Arlington of April 29 the details were almost settled. Whilst he had thought he might get out of making the trip *'she has commanded me to attend her at Lisle, the 21st of May...About the 22nd of May Madame desires my Lord St. Alban's may be at Dunkerque with the yachts...and by the 26th Madame hopes to be at Dover, where she desires that if the King will give himself the trouble to come, that nobody of the women should be there, to spare that trouble to the Queen and Duchess, because she hopes, upon the King's letter to the King and Mr, that they will consent she may go along with the King and Duke to London'*. Madame would have had no memories of London, having fled at the age of three, but they never did consent. Ralph duly arrived at Lille, on19 May. Ralph suggested that the opportunity be taken to press the French diplomatically - Louis wanted Charles to release him from his promise not to use his army for a year. *'We shall do well to make use of this conjuncture and gain what points we can of them, especially something in this Treaty of Commerce'*. William Perwich: *'Last night my Ld Ambassador arrived here...desires to be excused from answering till next post being so weary after so long a journey, and having little to acquaint your Lordship with. The King is expected here on Friday next and all magnificent preparations are making for rendering his reception more glorious of fireworks, bonfires and fountains to run with wine. Here are about 5000 foot and horse in garrison, and near the same at Arras, where at the Ambassador's approach my Ld Douglas as the head of his regiment made him a compliment of volleys and great guns from the ramparts'*. (£500 had been promised to Ralph to pay for his journey, so whilst he promised *'good husbandry'* he was able to enjoy his break from Paris). Three days later Ralph visited Tournai, where he was shown round the newly completed citadel and given a sumptuous feast by the governor.

We hear nothing from Ralph between 23 May and 7 June, and then *'It is some days since I writ to your Lordship, there having been nothing of consequence worth troubling you with. In the last letters Mr Perwich mistook and killed the Duke of Lorraine instead of the Duke of Florence'* followed by *'I find all the foreign Ministers here extremely alarmed at this interview of the King and Madame, and extremely impatient to know the result of the negociatio*n (June 21). They would have been even more alarmed if they had known the details of the secret Treaty of Dover:

'The King of England will make a public profession of the Catholic faith, and will receive the sum of two millions of crowns to aid him in this project, from the Most Christian King, in the course of the next six months. The date of this declaration is left absolutely to his own pleasure. The King of France will faithfully observe the Treaty of Aix la Chapelle, as regards Spain, and the King of England will maintain the Treaty of the Triple Alliance in a similar manner. If new rights to the Spanish monarchy revert to the King of France, the King of England will aid him in maintaining these rights. The two Kings will declare war against the United Provinces. The King of France will attack them by land, and will receive the help of 6000 men from England. The King of England will send 50 men-at-war to sea, and the King of France 30'. Charles was promised Vlissingen and land which would allow control of the Scheldt (and therefore of much Dutch trade) and there were to be separate articles to provide for the Prince of Orange.

Good news came out of the meeting at Dover for Ralph. After congratulating Arlington on the announcement of the betrothal of his only child to the King's illegitimate son Henry (later duke of Grafton), Ralph reported that Madame had told him that the King intended to make Lord Montagu an earl, and that this would be *'more acceptable to him now, I believe, than it would have been formerly, because, since his late appearing at Court, he cannot but be satisfied that it is wholly upon his own account, and out of the personal esteem and kindness the King has for him, and not at all upon my consideration'* (June 21 1670). It had been an eventful few weeks, but the following days were to be even more so. On Saturday June 28 Ralph visited Madame and, after she had complained that Monsieur was still treating here appallingly, she told him of the alliance that had just been concluded between her brother and Louis, and of their intention to attack the Netherlands. Next day she was dead. She had just celebrated her twenty-sixth birthday when at *'4 in the afternoon finding herself hot within, she drank 2 or 3 glasses of juice of chicory, immediately whereupon finding a marvellous alteration all over, she cried out she was poisoned'*. [55] Ralph had been on his way to see her when she fell ill and he asked her several times whether she did believe she had been poisoned. She shrugged and told him not to repeat anything of the sort to her brother, who she loved above all things in the world; her only regret in dying was

---

[55] *The despatches of William Perwich : English agent in Paris, 1669-1677, preserved in the foreign state papers of the Public record office, London* Royal Historical Society (London, 1903)

leaving him. She made Ralph promise her that he would pass this message on to the King.[56]

'*The strained relations which existed in the last months of her life between her Highness and her husband and the instantaneous manner of her death after she had taken the water as mentioned has caused the people, who always take the worst view, to conceive the suspicion of poison...It was accordingly decided...that the body should be opened in the presence of ten of the most celebrated physicians of this city*'.[57] This was carried out in the evening of the next day. Ralph, Abbe Montagu, Lord Salisbury, and two English doctors (one an expert in female diseases) were also there. Perwich: '*No sooner was ye upper skin enter'd but all the house was filled with the most horrible stench that anybody ever smelt. She was all rotten within, her liver wasted, & this ye generall opinion of ye Doctors, that they wonder'd not why she dyed then, but that she lived soe long. She was stuff'd up with bile*'. The diagnosis was cholera but it is now thought that it was acute peritonitis caused by the perforation of a duodenal ulcer. Despite the post-mortem '*the king strongly resents the mischievous change in the sentiments of the English Ambassador here. In the first few days after Madame's death he agreed with the others in declaring it natural. A few days later he changed his mind, withdrew this truth and by harmful offices is inspiring mistrust and ill feeling between these governments*'.[58] There is an intimation in a letter he wrote to Arlington on July 19 that he may truly have changed his mind. The Dutch ambassador in London spread the same rumour, doubtless hoping that a consequential chill in relations between England and France would benefit his own country. On Tuesday 2 July the King, Queen and Dauphin came to Paris to offer condolences to Monsieur, and sent the Governor of Paris to Ralph '*to assure him that Madam's losse was as sensible to him as if it had been the Queen his wife, and will give him Audce* [audience] *in a day or two*'.[59] The five year old Princess Anne, who had been under the care of Madame, her aunt, returned sadly to London at the end of the month, when Abbe Montagu took the opportunity of a letter of condolence to King Charles to remind him of the request his late sister had made to give Lord Montagu an earldom. Ralph had lost his most influential patron.

Life and diplomacy went on. The wrangling between France, Sweden, Holland and Spain over who was to decide upon what in accordance with the peace of Aix-la-Chapelle was interminable. Ralph tried to protect England's trade with France, particularly that of Jersey and Guernsey:

---

[56] C H Hartmann
[57] Venetian Ambassador to the Doge, Cal SP Venetian p.217
[58] Ibid p.225
[59] Perwich despatches

'there must be great care in our new Treaty of Commerce, or else all the trade of these islands will be utterly destroyed, which is a thing they drive at here' (July 30). *'My Lord Ambassador is gone this morning to St Germains to deliver in a Memll [memorial] upon our London Merchants' complaint'* (Perwich, September 6); *'the great minister [Colbert] refused to give my Ld Ambr an answer in writing to the Memll I sent you a copy of about our woollen manufacture. Indeed the whole designe is to ruine all our trade to France & promote their wine manufactures'* (ibid, October 1). *'My Marseilles correspondent tells me that upon my Ld Ambr's complaint at Court, the seamen they debauched from on board our merchants' ships were released, & from Rouen they complain of ye extravagant great dutys laid upon our English importations, as 125 livres on 100 barrils of sea coales'*. (ibid, October 15). In August 1670 the duke of Buckingham was sent by Charles to make a treaty with Louis which would be the official version of the secret Treaty of Dover (omitting the clause concerning Charles's conversion of course). He was surprised at the speed with which it was agreed. *'My Lord Duke of Buckingham is here ever since Monday, and is just now in his tailor's hands, fitting himself this night to go to St. Germains...There is a lodging furnished for him in the King's own house at St. Germains; one of the King's coaches and eight footmen ordered always to wait on him, and a table to be kept for him'* (August 13). Buckingham was also charged with reminding Louis of the English merchants' grievances. His Grace having laid the ground, Ralph submitted a statement of those complaints a few days later. *'Mr Colbert is the occasion I believe of all the ill-usage our English merchants receive in France, to weary them out of trade, and to encourage his own manufactures. My Lord Duke has discoursed the matter here thoroughly with the King, and I think has partly convinced him how impossible it is for him to have what he desires from England till he has first satisfied the nation of his good intentions towards them, by not pressing so hard upon us in point of trade'* (September 15). On the same day that Ralph wrote this letter to Arlington he wrote another, having discovered that the latter had told Abbe Montagu that he wasn't yet *'thoroughly satisfied'* with Ralph. He believed that the French Ambassador was partly to blame, not least because Ralph had taken him to task over his behaviour towards Arlington. *'As for my Lord of Buckingham, I have done all that man can do to send him away well satisfied with me; if I have succeeded I shall think I have done no small matter. Upon all discourses I have had with him concerning your Lordship, I find he pretends to be very fair, but I cannot but let you know that he has a great opinion of my Lord Ashley, Orery, and Sir Thomas Osburne. Your best way with him, if I may advise you, is to let him see you do not want him much; for I am confident you are the much stronger of the two, and whilst he knows that, there is no danger of*

him...Mr. Porter, that delivers this, will give you by word of mouth a perfect account...I thought this a better way than writing a long tedious letter, and there are many circumstances that cannot be writ...(P.S.) Pray burn this letter'.

It might be thought that this information about Buckingham was given as a reminder to Arlington that it was always good to have friends and supporters. Ralph certainly felt free to give advice to his superior: on October 20, having again expressed his acknowledgement of the gratitude he owed *'in being so just to me as not to let all the ill offices which I perceive people have endeavoured to do me make any impression in you to my disadvantage"* he follows up with *"Since I left England I hear that Secretary Trevor has not been the man he ought to be towards your Lordship, considering that he owes all his fortune and preferment wholly to you. You know, my Lord, I was always so much concerned for you, that I was one of the first that gave you warning of him, and one of the first that suspected what I see since has followed, and I am sure no man spared him less than I did'.* In December the treaty was signed by the Cabal Ministry in London. Ralph reported that he had been informed of one of Buckingham's servants, Douty, being in Paris. He had taken *'a private scurvy lodging by the Rue St. Honore. I knew of his being in town by chance, and had him watched. He went at once to Mr de Lionn's, and another time to Mr. Colbert's'.* The Duke had left behind a musician, Smith, *'to perfect himself'* who had become friendly with Mr. Vernon, Ralph's secretary. Vernon saw Smith in the street and asked if he would like to go with him to visit Douty at his lodging. At their meeting Vernon suggested that they might be more comfortable drinking at the ambassador's house. *'So at night he came; and drinking with my servants he had forgot that in the morning the occasion of his journey was to see his brother at St. Omer...and the reason now was to buy clothes for my Lord Duke and my Lady Shrosbery...and twenty other frivolous excuses'.* Next day Douty told Smith he would cut his throat for having betrayed him to the ambassador's people. The letter has a post script: *'I forgot to tell you that, to disguise himself, Douty, though he has a great head of hair, puts on a periwig'* (December 14). Buckingham was angry that his secret had been uncovered: *'I have been advertised from intimate friends of his how much he is privately my enemy, and the resolution he has of being as he calls it revenged on me for advertising of you concerning the courier he sent into France'* (January 28 1671). Ralph says that it was his duty to report to Arlington and, though doesn't fear the Duke, asks his master to report the facts to the King.

In December there had been suggestions that Louis would move against the Netherlands early in the new year. He had stated his intention to visit newly built fortifications in Flanders, beginning with Dunkirk, accompanied by 40,000 soldiers and 10,000 horse. The new Dutch ambassador told Ralph that he understood Charles was having his fleet prepared for the spring, and some great men at the French court had told him it was to be used against his country. Ralph disingenuously *'told him if he took to heart and believed all discourses that are made in a country where people are so apt to talk as they are here, he would have a very uneasy time of it'* (December 3). Inadvertently illustrating the truth of this, Ralph wrote on the 11th: *'You cannot imagine how blanc this Court were at the news that came out of England of the Parliament's readiness to supply our master with the money he desired; I could hardly make them believe it. I suppose they do imagine that if the King be put into so good a condition, by the affections of his subjects at home, he will have less need, and not have so great dependencies on his neighbours abroad; or they imagine that, being upon equal terms with the King here, it will cost them more before they can get him of their side. There is nothing so certain, my Lord, that notwithstanding all the greatness and strength of France that you both know and hear talked of, it will be impossible for them to go on with any of their great designs if they cannot have the English on their side. I am sure your Lordship is wise enough, whatever part we take, to make the most advantageousest terms that can be, both for the King and the nation...As for the affairs of this Court, Madame de Montespan and her friends are in the greatest power'.* Less than a week later he heard that Parliament hadn't granted Charles the supply he wanted.

Ralph also gave news of another marriage, *'which you will wonder at'*, of la Grande Madamoiselle, the forty-three year old only daughter of Louis's uncle the Prince of Conde by his first wife Marie de Bourbon, duchess of Monpensier (whose title she had inherited). In the wars of the Fronde, when her father tried to wrest the crown from his brother, she had (at the age of twenty-four) led the army that took the city of Orleans. A few months later she was in command of the Bastille and sheltered the Prince of Conde and his defeated troops. Her great wealth would have made her an ideal bride for Louis, but she was eleven years older and her conduct hadn't endeared her to him. Perhaps for this reason, and concern that her vast estates would pass outside the royal family if she had an heir, Louis was prevailed on (supposedly by de Montespan) to rescind his consent for her marriage to the duc de Lauzan two days before the wedding. According to Ralph the King sent for her to come to his closet, she supposed to sign the contract, but he told her that he had realised that the marriage would be dishonourable to her, since it would be thought that the only reason for marriage with one below her in rank was because the groom was a favourite of his. Louis then told Lauzan that though he had kept him from so large a fortune, he gave his word that he would take care of him. Next year the prospective bridegroom was whisked off to the

Bastille, and then to Pignerol, to join Louis's former finance minister, Fouquet, and Dauger "the Man in the Iron mask". Lauzan was imprisoned for ten years (an improvement on Fouquet's nineteen years and Dauger's thirty-four) until la Grande Madamoiselle agreed to settle extensive properties on Louis and Montespan's oldest child. Even then she was not permitted to marry, so when she died, at the age of sixty-five, the Palais de Luxembourg and all her other properties passed to Monsieur, as Louis had intended.

The new year saw Ralph making suggestions concerning the subsidy that Louis was to pay Charles under the terms of the treaty for equipping the English fleet (as Louis would have viewed it) or to help Charles not to have to rely on Parliament. He tells Arlington that he has seen the treaty which Buckingham had facilitated, and that the Dutch suspect nothing, indeed almost everyone in Paris thought that England and France would fall out. But he is concerned that unless the money was sent over in strictest secret suspicions would be aroused *'for there are here and in England many people that do not wish the union between the two Kings; and if I may venture to advise, it were much safer and would be much more secret if the money that is to be paid in February were put into Spanish pistols* [currency], *which should be...put in some ballot of merchandise, and conveyed from hence all the way by water into England. It may be done at the same time that the person that the king sends over to fetch my Lord Abbot Montagu's statues and pictures, and he nor nobody living know of it'*. The French foreign minister's suggestion of bills of exchange was foolish since *'it will be impossible that so great a sum can be returned and the Dutch not find it out, who have spies and intelligence amongst all the banquiers of the world'* (January 17). If the transfer of the money waited until the pictures and statues were packed up, it didn't go until late March, when Ralph mentions on the 21st that it was almost done and also tries to interest the King in Abbe Montagu's orange trees (he apparently had one of the finest orangeries in France). Ralph also had pressing personal concerns. He had requested that, when King Louis went to Flanders in late April 1671, he should return to England, not least to save the expense of having to travel with him. His *'troublesome or clamorous debts'* would need to be paid first and *'I am in the greatest necessity and want of money that can be, having not had one penny from the King these last ten months; my credit is quite at an end'* (January 28). Yet even then he felt able to send a coach to Arlington next month as a present. *'I am over-stocked with coaches, and therefore I do as when a country is over-peopled, transplant...I hope, if I come to England, your Lordship will prevail upon his Majesty that I may not, for the time that I am to stay, give much attendance at Court, but that I may have leave to spend most time with my father'* (February 24).

On April 8 he writes that he intends to leave Paris around the 20th, a few days before Louis set out, fearing that it might be difficult to procure horses for the journey if he left it later. He was *'just now a-going to Versailles, to deliver his Majesty's letters to the King'* and then he falls silent for five months until he returns to Paris.

Edward Montagu, eldest son of Edward 2nd Lord Montagu

Elizabeth Wriothesley, Countess of Northumberland

Closterman - Ralph, 1ˢᵗ Duke of Montagu

Michael Dahl - Ralph, 1st Duke of Montagu

Copyright of the subject

Genari - Ralph when 1st Earl of Montagu (painted 1679)

Chapter 2
Of Marriage, Mansion and Mistresses 1671-1676

On March 23 1671 King Charles had written to Ralph instructing him to return to England for discussions whilst Louis was away. There seems to be no record of Ralph's other activities during the five month break from his embassy. Presumably he spent time with his father, as he had intended, in London or at Boughton, and with his sister. He may also have attended the funeral of his relative the earl of Manchester, the Lord Chamberlain, who died on May 5 just a few days after he reached London. The one thing that we can be sure of is that he purchased the post of Master of the Great Wardrobe from his relative the earl of Sandwich on August 12 for £14,000. Modern financial equivalents can only be an estimate, but this might be some £27.5m (based on average earnings) in 2014. Sandwich had never been a very rich man and lived lavishly, embellishing his fine house at Hinchingbrook, so was probably in need of the money. It might be that he still had not paid the £5,000 agreed for his daughter's dowry on her marriage in 1670 to Sir Richard Edgcumbe – being blessed with many sons and daughters created a large financial liability. One wonders where Ralph, even with possible help from his father, obtained such a sum. He may well have borrowed, at least in part, against the promised £2,000 p.a. income from the post.[60] (In addition his deputy received £200 p.a. for doing the work). The price paid – seven times the annual income of the post – was the usual amount expected for what was, in effect, an annuity.

Ralph returned to France in late August 1671. He had started to prepare for this at the end of July but the royal yachts were with the King in the West. He arrived at Dover on the 20th and was reported to be waiting for fair weather. Setting sail at eight next evening on the "Henrietta", *'they had a stormy night, as the seamen judge'*. Apparently the yacht had to turn back and at five in the afternoon of the 23rd Ralph went on board a second time.[61] Even then his ship had to wait two days at sea before it could enter Calais harbour because of the continuing squall. On 3 September he travelled to Dunkirk to meet the marquis d'Estrades, (the French ambassador to the Netherlands) and give him letters from the King and Arlington. The Marquis professed his devotion to Charles's service and said that the King could have got more for Dunkirk if he had asked. He then complained that Buckingham had undermined his reputation with Louis. *'From this he fell to talk of the present alliance that is like to be between France and England, but by his discourse I perceive he knows nothing but by guess, and by some discourses held to him by the Prince of*

---

[60] Calendar State Treasury Books 1669-72
[61] Cal SP Dom 1671

Conde, who is certainly trusted with the secret'. It took four days for Ralph to reach Paris, and he waited until the day after he had seen Louis at Versailles on the 11th to report again, with the news that de Pomponne had replaced the recently deceased de Lionne as Foreign Minister, a great surprise since he had been closely associated with the disgraced minister Fouquet. In London Ralph had apparently discussed with Charles a plan to suggest to Louis that, rather than provide him with between 4,000 and 6,000 troops, the French king should be allowed to raise up to 10,000 English troops at his own cost. Ralph had been discouraged by Marshal Turenne and some others who knew of the treaty, being told *'that it would put scruples and jealousies into the King's head here, as if your Majesty were wavering in your resolutions of going on with the war'* and Buckingham had made matters more difficult by having boasted of the excellent troops that he would bring to France. Ralph persisted and tackled Louis's chief minister de Louvois himself (having first prepared the ground by discussing the idea with some of the minister's trusted colleagues) who in turn talked to Louis and secured agreement. Ralph subsequently wrote to Charles on the 23rd to tell him of this coup. It is worth quoting the letter at some length in order to see how Ralph took the opportunity to further undermine Buckingham's reputation.

At the same time I proposed this I assured the King that your Majesty would permit him to make levies of English in your country, in case he desired it...to the number of ten thousand. To which Mr de Louvoy has also now replied, that his master has such a value of the English, and thinks it may be a terror to his enemies to have English in his army, that he doth intend to raise some, but will not yet resolve of the number till he can tell upon what terms he may raise them, and upon what pay...and withal recommended to me to desire your Majesty, that as he is willing to spare your purse, that you will also be so kind to him as, in the raising of men, order it so that he may have them on reasonable terms; which if that can be, he believes he shall constantly entertain a body of English, which should always be ready for your service if ever you have occasion for them.

Therefore, if I may be so bold as to advise your Majesty, you cannot do anything more advantageous to yourself than to facilitate the French King's levies, because, if once they are on foot and upon reasonable terms, you may be confidant, as long as this war lasts, of being eased of the burthen of paying any forces yourself, which will be an expense of very near four score thousand pound a year saved, and a very popular thing to your people and Parliament.

I must give your Majesty an account of one great motive that has induced them here to release your Majesty...But first I must beg of you, Sir, not to believe that (it) is out of malice to the Duke of Buckingham, who is not my friend, for I only tell you what Mr. de Louvoy told me. He says they conceive your Majesty to be under an engage(me)nt to give him command of those forces you were obliged to send over, and they have conceived so ill an opinion of him, for his last behaviour toward you in the Parliament, that they do not look upon him as a man well-affected to Monarchy, and consequently likely to play a thousand tricks when once he has such authority in his hands; and that they know for certain that he and his friends desired to keep well with the Presbyterian and fanatic party, who never were well-affected to a French alliance and could never be persuaded that they would join unanimously for the destruction of Holland, which is a Commonwealth, and such they believe wish in England, if they had the power to compass it.

He told me at the same time that they were so alarmed at a news of the French Ambassador's, of my Lord Ashley's being to be surintendant des finances, creature de Mr. de Boukingamm, because they are afraid your affairs would be in people's hands they cannot think at bottom well-affected either to Monarchy, or the great design you are now upon.

I told (him) upon this discourse, that I believed it was natural for your Majesty, if the Duke of Buckingham did not command the forces that were to come to France, to desire it might be the Duke of Monmouth, who would be followed by all the young nobility of England.

With this letter to the King went another for Arlington in which Ralph, after saying that he had been at Versailles for a few days talking to de Louvois and others about this business, reveals that it wasn't his verbal skills alone that had achieved a beneficial outcome for his master. He had employed the persuasive power of bribery. Ralph had had '*a private commerce*' with a sister of Madame de Fresnoy, de Louvois' mistress, who '*governs him*'. She had passed through Calais in the spring as he was about to return to England. Seeing his yacht in port, she had gone on board to look at it, joking with the captain that if Ralph had been there at the time she would have gone with him to visit England. He had used this opening as an opportunity to visit her and she responded that if he brought her something back from England it would give her the opportunity to mention his kindness to de Louvois. '*So accordingly I sent her some slight things to the value of ten or twelve pounds*'. He renewed his acquaintance with her on his return and suggested that, if her sister was able to sweet-talk the Secretary for War into persuading Louis to accept Ralph's suggestion, he would make the sisters '*a considerable present*'. He had promised a jewel worth 6,000 crowns for Madame de Fresnoy and another of 2,000 crowns for her sister, or the money if they preferred. He expressed the hope that Charles wouldn't think it money wasted because these presents of £2,000 would save him £500,000. The other talk in the autumn of 1671 was of marriage: Marshal Turenne (one of France's greatest ever military commanders) was offering his niece in marriage to the duke of York, though Ralph knew that Louis was going to propose his cousin, Madame de Guise (the duchess of York had died less than six months before). He also discovered that Buckingham had been so annoyed at losing the prospective command of the English forces in France that he wrote directly to Louis saying it was a '*malicious project*' of Ralph's.

On December 9 the earl of Sunderland arrived in Paris to replace Ralph as ambassador so that he could go to London and talk directly with the King. On the 11th he had a last audience at St. Germain and the next day a servant reported to Arlington that he was concentrating on '*preparations for his speedy departure, which will be on Tuesday next'*. On the eve of that departure a letter arrived from Arlington which threw his plans into confusion. Charles had commanded Ralph to see whether he could extract four million pounds from Louis to pay for an extra thirty ships for the war, since the Dutch fleet was so strong. Ralph responded in his missive to Arlington of December 15: '*Your Lordship's of Dec. the 1st came to me last night at about 11 o'clock. I have ever since been thinking and contriving which way to bring to pass what his Majesty commands me to attempt, which would be the greatest joy in all the world to me, if I could succeed in it; but I confess I see on all hands very great difficulties, and the chief is, I am afraid the King here has not so much money as the world does imagine'*. Nonetheless, he seems to have realised that attempting this would reinforce his position as the main interlocutor between the two kings, and help protect him against Buckingham, so drafted a letter for Charles to send Louis with the proposal : '*if there is anything in the style not after the manner that Kings write to one another, it is easily mended. But I have framed it directly to the King's humour here…I will not communicate the thing here to any of the Ministers, but go directly to him with the letter; and to speak, as one ought to do always, respectfully of Kings, he often takes a pride and vanity to do things of his own head'*. On Christmas Eve Ralph gave the letter to Louis at St. Germain, advanced all the arguments in favour of the proposal with which he had been armed, added one of his own (that the Dutch would employ any seamen not in English service), and was turned down for lack of finance. '*I found his Christian Majesty extremely perplexed and startled at the proposition, like as if he had some suspicion that our master may waver in his resolutions about this war'*. After an hour's conversation Ralph was sent on his way, with the usual compliments. The delay in Ralph's London trip had allowed him in the third week of December to head the English gentry then in Paris at an audience with Monsieur to congratulate him on his marriage (less than eighteen months after his first wife's death). His new wife Elizabeth

Charlotte was the daughter of the Elector Palatine, and so a grand-daughter of King James I.[62]

Ralph finally arrived in London just after Christmas. *'On Saturday night Montagu arrived here from France. He pretends he came upon his own occasions, to settle things about his office in the Wardrobe, but tis certainly believed he comes upon some public account, for an ambassador must not leave his employment (without order) upon any pretence of private affairs. The King and Duke were private with him 2 hours that night'*.[63] Few could have believed Ralph's story that he was making a private visit - in January 1672 the Venetian ambassador in London noted that Ralph has *'arrived from Paris and will soon return. It is not true that the confidential relations between these two crowns are broken'*.[64] His Northamptonshire neighbour Christopher, viscount Hatton wrote to a friend on the 13th that Ralph had been in England for three weeks and had been made a Privy Councillor on the 2nd. *'And I assure you, a great man he is'*.[65] He returned to France a month later, his letter of February 12 written from Calais saying that he had *'arrived here last night beyond my expectation, the wind proving fair to bring me from Dover'* and had met with Buckingham's steward, returning from Paris, presumably still lobbying for military command. On his way Ralph had an accident, which William Perwich underplays in his letter of the 17th: *'My lord Ambassador arrived here on Monday night, and by the way his little Charriot breaking into pieces down a hill, his Exce. through God's mercy had no other harme than a bruise on his Arme'*, but Ralph offers this as an excuse for not writing on the 21st, since *'I was really so ill of a bruise in my arm that I could not do it'*. He had, however, been well enough to see Louis that day and recommend gaining Sweden as an ally in the forthcoming war for which *'The preparations here go on very vigorously both by sea and land'*.

---

[62] Despite stating that her husband needed rosaries and holy medals draped in the appropriate places before he could perform his spousal duties, she gave him a daughter (mother of the future Emperor Francis I) and a son and heir whose line would provide future Kings of France. Fortunately, unlike his first wife, Elizabeth Charlotte was a robust woman, plain of face and plain speaking, and so a little better equipped at surviving her difficult marriage. In 1682 she had to endure the exiling of Louis's illegitimate son, the fourteen year old comte de Vermandois, who had been living with the Orleans and of whom she had grown fond. He had been seduced by the Chevalier and the twenty-one year old Prince of Conti, and died the following year. Although closer to her husband in his last years, she was probably at her most content after Monsieur died in 1701. After burning all his lovers' letters – she the perfume from which she declared made her nauseous – she enjoyed more than twenty years of widowhood.

[63] Verney Ms mic. 636/19 Sir Ralph to Edmund Verney, 28 Dec. 1671
[64] Cal SP Venetian January 8, 1672
[65] Hatton Correspondence vol. 1 p 54

He had also pressed on Louis the need to follow through on the commercial treaty.

Being a Privy Councillor brought little financial reward. He wrote to Arlington: '*I have not these eight months past been able to get from...the Treasury one penny of my daily entertainment; nor, since I have been Ambassador in France, have I been able to procure any money upon the King's assignations, which were so bad that I was forced to give my own bond...so that in effect I have served abroad these three years upon my own account*'. Worse still his credit was being affected by news from England such that '*I am torn a-pieces by all that I owe money to*'. This news was of Charles's Stop of the Exchequer – the gold-merchants had refused to lend the King more money, so he had suspended interest payments from the Exchequer, which would bankrupt many of them. Added to this difficulty, the imminent death of Louis's eldest daughter would cause Ralph more expense for mourning, and during Lent the few Parisian butchers allowed to sell meat demanded ready money. At least he was able to portray the Stop as a royal means of putting off the necessity of holding a Parliament in order to raise finance (which would give that body an opportunity to object to the war). Ralph used this ploy in March because the French were discussing whether the English alliance was favourable to them, and what England would do if they chose the Spanish Netherlands as a target rather than the Dutch. In addition '*I found at my return here, that they had been very uneasy upon the last proposition of turning the ships into money, and many here, the wisest of them, particularly Mr. de Turenne and Mr. Colbert, looked on it as a trick of ours*' (March 7). He was having to make a lot of effort to keep the French to the various terms that had been agreed, and repeated to Arlington all that he heard (not least from Louis) that indicated their intention to do otherwise. His letters are full of news about the preparations for war, the departure of the French ambassador, and the uniform that the duke of Monmouth's troops were to wear (he had to send a sample to London, so that the yellow cloth chosen could be made up as Louis wished). There were occasional alarms when Ralph heard that Charles had cavalierly made a statement that would cost England dearly. He had said, for example, that if the French liked Monmouth's regiment then in the following year they could have more English soldiers free of charge. At the end of March Charles issued the Royal Declaration of Indulgence, giving religious liberty to Protestant non-conformists by suspending the penal laws that punished recusants. Parliament suspected, rightly, that this would be followed by similar liberty for Catholics and so would force its withdrawal the following year in return for funding the war.

Ralph's debts were still much on his mind, not least because his embassy would come to an end once Louis went on campaign. '*I took the liberty to trouble your Lordship in one of my former letters concerning an order for mine from the Treasury for my entertainment from Midsummer last to Michaelmas, which is stopped... My servant that has solicited Mr. Treasurer...gives me little hopes, unless your Lordship does me the favour of moving the King in it. If, for example's sake, he shall not think fit publicly to change it, any other way that he will please furnish me with the like sum will be as good to me; but I can no ways in the world make shift without it. I had spent money here long before his Majesty stopped my assignments. I must be taking my leave here in a month, about which time the King will be going into the field, and I shall make but an ill figure, both for my master and myself, to be left in pawn; for though I may make a shift to come away without paying all my debts here, yet there are some that will be so clamorous and dishonourable that it will be impossible for me to stir till they are satisfied'* (March 26). *'I have, since my employment here, lived at much a greater rate than formerly the English Ambassadors used to do. At my coming hither I was guided by Madame, who for the King her brother's credit ordered me to do so, and I have been forced ever since to continue the same expense; and I flatter myself that by the access and introduction it has given me with all the people here, that the King my master has been much better served by it; yet your Lordship can bear me witness that I have never troubled his Majesty for anything, nor in my three years' time had any extraordinary paid to me, only for the mourning of the Queen Mother, and something for my journey into Flanders. I know how precious a thing ready money now is in England, and therefore in this conjuncture I would be as little as pressing upon his Majesty as possible can be. All I desire is that he would be pleased to order my ordinary allowance to be paid to me'* (April 2).

He had been allowed to sell materials from the "Sapphire", a ship which ran aground in the Scillies in 1670, but this is unlikely to have yielded much.[66] Similarly he had been granted £1,000 from the sale of captured ships in May 1669 but it was noted in November 1674 that this had been paid to him as part of his embassy equipage, so he never truly received the grant. He wasn't even able to obtain non-monetary recognition – a separate letter to Arlington the same day, (which the latter endorsed as private), after complaining that Buckingham had been trying to undermine his embassy by accusing him of being *'a Spaniard'* (i.e. anti French) alludes to an offer which Louis had made to commend his services to Charles. It is apparent from another written a few days later that Ralph

---

[66] Cal SP Dom Nov 16 1670 King to Lord Admiral. *The Sapphire ran aground on the coasts of Sicily some months ago, and part of her guns, tackle etc was saved, but in places so remote that it would be a great charge to bring them to the stores. You are therefore to give order empowering Ralph Montagu, Ambassador to France, to sell the same for his own use, as a reward for services*

had suggested the Garter might be an appropriate reward, since he says that out of all the reasons that Charles gave for refusing it the only one that he considered genuine was that Arlington hadn't received the honour. It is clear that Ralph was worried that the minister *'might take it ill of me to pretend to a thing which you have not, and which you deserve so much better...You know me to be so true a servant of yours, and so steady in all your interests, that I flatter myself to believe you are so kind to me that you will rather be glad than sorry at any advantage that happens to me, especially when it may be to put me in a condition of making some return of all the obligations I owe you; at least in keeping my corner against your enemies and mine'*. A month later Arlington was to be given a greater honour than the Garter – the marriage of his only child and heiress to Charles's son by Barbara Villiers. Ralph received nothing. Learning that Buckingham had been made a Commissionaire of the Prizes, after having been told that none were to be made when requesting the post for himself earlier in the year, couldn't have improved his outlook. As for his Mastership of the Great Wardrobe, *'you know with what difficulty I purchased it, to save my credit at home and abroad; and yet, as the matter is ordered, it is so far from being a credit or advantage to me, that it has prejudiced both'* (April 13). He was clearly disillusioned about his choice of career, which wasn't bringing him the rewards he had hoped for. In a sentence written to Arlington which would hold good as encapsulating his view for years to come: *'In all things concerning my person or my fortune the King has shown me little favour or good will and yet I know not why, for I never displeased him...for upon my account I can never expect his Majesty will think I deserve anything'* (April 12). Ralph had to rely on the recommendations of others.

Ralph was put to additional expense in having to house the duke of Monmouth and Mr Godolphin for a fortnight, but at least that gave him the opportunity to prevail on the latter to write to Arlington, suggesting that it was the right time to remind Charles of the reward he had for so long promised Lord Montagu for his services. The visit must also have allowed Ralph to build on his acquaintance with Monmouth (whose claim to the throne he would later support in preference to the duke of York's), and remind him that he had put his name forward to be the general of the English forces in France, rather than Buckingham's. After his farewell audience with Louis at St. Germain on April 22 he had to make plans to leave with just a few servants, asking for a protecting convoy to be at Calais for him by the 25th since *'The Dutch may perhaps expect a greater booty of me than they will find'*. In fact he didn't leave until the start of May, with a farewell gift of a miniature of Louis surrounded by diamonds. He had apparently stayed for some time at Versailles *'to enjoy all the*

Diversions of the Season'.[67] His baggage was certainly back by the end of May – a State Treasury Books entry for May 22: *The Treasury Lords to the Customs Commissioners to open at the lodgings of Ambassador Montagu at the Mews 49 cases & 4 trunks of wearing apparel belonging to him arrived from France & now stored in Southwark.*[68]

Ralph therefore had no diplomatic role during the Third Dutch War. It was perhaps as well – after all the plotting and preparation it did not go well. The English navy proved unable to overcome the Dutch, and at the Battle of Sole Bay in June the earl of Sandwich was killed on his flagship. On sighting the Dutch fleet the French had sailed in the opposite direction. When the Dutch offered Louis all their southern fortresses, which would have made continued Spanish occupation of the southern Netherlands untenable, and a considerable amount of cash, Louis only asked for the least important Dutch port that Charles desired, and then made further demands on his own account which he knew would be refused. He was intent on capturing Amsterdam and crushing the Dutch. Even though he knew that William of Orange, who had been appointed Captain-General of the Dutch forces, had ordered the water defences to be flooded, he thought that by waiting until winter he would be able to advance over the ice up to city's walls. Charles tried to exploit the situation by coming to a separate agreement with William but the terms Arlington and Buckingham offered the Prince were considered unacceptable. Because the Dutch fleet controlled the sea Baltic grain supplies could get through, so the population could not be starved into submission and the winter was not sufficiently cold to freeze the water defences. In 1673 the navy was again unable to overcome the Dutch and Louis found the vulnerability of the Spanish Netherlands too great a temptation to resist – he besieged and took Maastricht which led to the Emperor and the Spanish allying with the Dutch. Louis had to withdraw his armies. The public mood in England changed. Parliament passed the Test Act, requiring that all holding public office should take communion from a Church of England priest and the country was flooded with Dutch printed pamphlets accusing Charles and Louis of wanting to make England Catholic again. Reacting to public opinion Charles's ministers began to support the Dutch and the King told Louis that, for his own survival, he needed to make peace. A treaty was signed but the French continued the war until 1678, ending it with few gains for the money spent except the Franche-Comte.

There is little information of how Ralph spent seven months in England. We have only six inconsequential letters written to Arlington (such as one from October asking for his embassy chaplain to be

---

[67] *The Court in Mourning. Being the Life and Worthy Actions of Ralph, Duke of Montagu* (London 1709)
[68] Cal State Treasury Books p.1242

considered for a Canterbury cathedral post). He apparently sailed back to France from Dover, with Count Schomberg, in the "Henrietta" on November 16 [69] and wrote to Arlington from Paris on December 20: *'present my humble duty to his Majesty, and let him know, according to the leave he was pleased to give me, I go tomorrow towards Italy, where I will ramble for two or three months'.* He had reached Marseilles by the time he wrote next, on January 16 1673, asking for help in pressing the Treasury for payment of his dues and saying that he did not intend to visit Rome *'lest people should think I go about business'* (i.e. become a Catholic). What he did, and where he went, for the next six months is unrecorded (though he was back in Paris by mid April), but it is clear that during 1673 he wooed his future wife. This doubtless made him consider what he could offer her by way of status – she was from a higher level of the aristocracy than he was – such that he wrote to Arlington once more. *'I hope that it may be now a favourable conjuncture for your Lordship to finish a thing for me which you have often told me you would use your utmost endeavours to see done. It is the making my father an Earl. You know [how] long his Majesty has promised it me, and yet since he has done the same thing for many others, and left me out. It was also one of the last things he promised Madame, and methinks if it were but that alone, it might prevail against all the ill offices of my enemies, and the little merit I have...I have not been unlucky in serving his Majesty in things that have been very advantageous and profitable to his public affairs, and in others that have concerned very nearly the honour of his own private person; and if I have ever offended him, it was only in an ambition of having a particular mark of his favour towards me, which is a fault very pardonable in any one who serves a Prince...All my enemies give out I am disgraced; all my friends believe it, and with some good reason, when they see his Majesty is not kind enough to me to make good a promise'* (April 15).

Among the visitors to Paris during Ralph's embassy had been the earl and countess of Northumberland. Perwich notes on January 18 1670 that they had taken Queen Henrietta Maria's town house for a year, intending to spend time there after they returned from Rome. Josceline Percy, the 11th Earl, was twenty-five years old and had perhaps decided on a foreign trip after the death of his baby son in 1669. However, less than six months after their arrival, Perwich records *'the sad news of my Ld of Northumberland's being dead at Turin, in his returne from Rome, of a violent burning fever. His corps is on its way, as well as his afflicted widow. The losse of this nobleman is the greater because ye family is extinct for want of issue male'* and on June 18 *'My Lady Northumberland is here on her way to England'.* Ralph's letters however do not mention this attractive young, rich widow he would marry three years later. That

[69] Cal SP Dom

she was, unsurprisingly, much wooed by others is shown by an incident related by Attorney-General Sir Heneage Finch to his son the next year, in September 1671. She had apparently been staying with her half-sister Rachel at Woburn Abbey before moving with the company there to Lord Sunderland's seat at Althorp. One of the company was Henry Savile '*who hath long been countenanced by my Lady Northumberland, whether as her dead Lord's friend or as envoye and ambasciatore d'amore from a great person* [the duke of York] *nobody knows, but he presumed so farr upon it that at Althorp, having got from my Lord Sunderland a master key on pretence of going into the billiard, he made use of it at one o'clock at night to enter my Lady Northumberland's chamber in his shirt and nightgown, and there kneeling down by the bedside told her, Madam, I am come with great confusion of face to tell you that now which I durst not trust the light with, the passion with which I serve and adore you. She with amazement rung the bell, but not daring to trust to that leaps out of her bed and at another door which H. Savil was not aware of, opens a way into the gallerye, through which she ran barefoot and knockt at the chamber door where Lord Ashby's lady was lodged and made shift to get into bedd...leaving H. Savil to meditate how to come off this adventure. He presently retires to his lodging and writes a letter to my Lady Northumberland in which he would turn all this to ridicule as if the house had been haunted*'.[70] Savile left early next morning, later pursued by the Countess's brother-in-law and others. They couldn't find him in London and were told he had fled to France.[71]

There is a rare description of the Countess in Paris from April 1673 by Madame Sevigne (made on the 15th, the same day Ralph wrote to Arlington complaining of his lack of royal favour). Sevigne records that the former paid her a visit and that the Countess was '*strikingly beautiful, but I cannot find a single trait in her face that is so alone, nor where the slightest hint of youth remains. I was surprised. She is, with all that, badly dressed, no grace, I was shocked.*' The next month Sevigne received a letter telling her that '*Montagu has gone. It seems his hopes were reversed. I believe that something has gone wrong.*'[72] The courtship clearly did not

---

[70] HMC Finch Mss vol.2, p.3

[71] Savile was one of Lord Rochester's greatest friends. The younger brother of George, later marquis of Halifax, he had probably been the duchess of York's lover, had frequent duels and insulted her husband the Duke so often that at one point he was dismissed from court. Like Rochester, his personality enabled him to be forgiven a good deal. He replaced Ralph as ambassador at Paris in 1679, the same year that Rochester sent his friend (for a second time) a young Frenchman he had enjoyed. (Both friends would die of venereal disease, and corresponded about their symptoms and treatments).

[72] "Madame de N me vint voir hier. J'avais ete la chercher avec Mme de Coulanges. Elle me parut une femme qui ete fort belle, mais qui n'a plus un seul trait de visage qui se soutienne; ni ou il soit reste le moindre air de jeunesse. J'en fus surprise. Elle est, avec cela, mal habillee, point de grace; enfin je n'en fus point de tout eblouie." "Montaigu s'en va; on

run smoothly. One of the few sources of information we have about that courtship is in Abel Boyer's "The History of the Reign of Queen Anne: Remarkables of the Year 1709". In Ralph's obituary he mentions that '*It was said that Mr Montague had a secret Commission sent him, to win over to him* [Charles] *a certain English Lady then in France, and who passed for the greatest Beauty of that Age, and had an immense Fortune...the Vertuous Lady, to shun the unlawful Embraces of the King, retired to France, where Mr Montague, instead of being an addresser for the King, becoming an humble Suitor for himself. The Lady had no difficulty to determine, whether she should Sacrifice her Honour to obtain the contemptible Name of Mistress or worse to her Sovereign or joyn honourably with a Man of Rising Fortune, and who, by his Management of the Post he was then in, shew'd he was not unlikely, or unqualified, to be in time one of the greatest men in the Nation. Therefore it was reported that when the King asked her afterwards, What she could see in Montague to make her choose him for a Husband? She answered with a great deal of readiness of Wit, The same that his Majesty saw in him to choose him for an Ambassador; intimating, that it was the Ornaments of his Mind, and the shining Qualities she saw in him that recommended him to her choice, rather than his Person. In short, Mr Montague, having obtained the consent of the Lady, they came privately over from France, and were Married at Titchfield in Hampshire...Mr Montague has a very large Fortune with his Lady, for besides the Estate in old Southampton Building in Holbourn, an Estate in Warwickshire of about 2500l. per Annum, was left to her by the Lord Dunsmore; so that one way or other, her Fortune was computed at about 6000l. per Annum*'. In the event of her death without heirs this estate was to be enjoyed by Ralph during his lifetime. Letters to Sir Joseph Williamson give the gossip: '*The Towne now is full of the marriage which they say is concluded between Mr. Montagu and the Countess of Northumberland...& that his Majesty has given consent, & to honour it will make him as high in dignity as her husband...& people say shee, having mist her ayme of Dutchess of Yorke, will no longer continue a widdow*'. Interestingly the rumour that she might marry the widowed duke of York, and so become part of the royal family, was still prevalent only two months before she married Ralph: '*The Countess of Northumberland...the people say his Royal Highness is to marry her, and that shee, seeing the other fayle, came home on purpose to receive the motion, and its much liked by all the people and his Royal Highness's*

---

did que ses esperances sont renversees. Je crois qu'il y a qulequechose des travers dans l'espirit de la nymphe" May 19 1673 E. B.de Fonblanque *Annals of the House of Percy, from the Conquest to the opening of the nineteenth century*, vol 2, pt.2 p.489

servants'.[73] To what does *'seeing the other fayle'* refer? Had the marriage to Ralph hit a hitch, since there is an implication that she had been abroad? What turn might history have taken if she had become duchess of York. The Duke clearly preferred a Catholic bride and, a little over two months after Ralph's own wedding, married Mary, duchess of Modena of whom *'The common people here, and even those of quallyty in the country, beleeve she is the Pope's eldest daughter'.*[74] However it came about, *'Yesterday morning Mr. Montagu went down to Titchfield, my Lady Eliz. Nowells, whither the Countess of Northumberland went before, & there to-morrow they are to be marryed; & they say he shall be made Earl of Chichester, a title entayled upon her father by her grandfather the old Lord Dunsmore, who was so created'.*[75] The marriage took place on August 23 1673 at Titchfield, the Wriothesley family seat. To mark the occasion Lord Montagu *'settled most of my lands upon my Sonne who to my great comfort and content hath marryed a noble and virtuous Lady'.*[76]

Far more negative contemporary opinions of Ralph's character were recorded than positive ones, and historians have consequently held an almost entirely negative view of it, yet this marriage indicates that Elizabeth saw something in him to persuade her not only to give up a certain amount of personal liberty, but her title and her only child too. Her family was greater than Ralph's: not only had her husband been an earl of very ancient lineage, but her father Thomas Wriothesley was 4th earl of Southampton, and Lord High Treasurer of England from the Restoration until his death in 1667. Her grandfather may well have been Shakespeare's lover and the dedicatee of the Sonnets. Her mother was daughter and heiress of the earl of Chichester (one of his other titles was Lord Dunsmore). Her late husband's estate was worth some £42,000. All this Ralph would have had in mind when he tried again to get his father made an earl in April: on her marriage Elizabeth became plain Mrs. Montagu (although she was known as the countess of Northumberland for the rest of her life). Under the terms of her late husband's will, she lost custody of her six year old daughter Betty to her mother in-law, a member of the Howard family, with whom she was on bad terms. James Vernon to Williamson: *'My brother has gone to Boughton with Mr. Montagu and his lady; they will be in town the next week. The day after they were married the Countess Dowager sent a gentleman with a letter to Titchfield to claim the little Lady Betty'.* The Williamson letters also show that public opinion thought this act was *'of extreme hard digestion, and no stone will be left*

[73] W.D. Christie ed. *Letters addressed from London to Sir Joseph Williamson while Plenipotentiary at the Congress of Cologne in the years 1673 and 1674* (Camden Society 1874) Letter of June 13 1673 p.38
[74] Ibid Letter to T. Derham 5 November, 1673 p.63
[75] Ibid pp. 176 & 179
[76] Lord Montagu's Will of October 1673, PRO Prb.II.379

unturned, if either King or Parliament can be prevailed with to keep up the mother's right'. The newlyweds refused to give the girl up, such that 'the Towne has already disposed of her to my Lord George and made the mother a Dutchesse'.[77] Ralph's new wife wrote to Dr. Mapletoft, Lord Northumberland's old tutor, to whom Betty had been sent: 'I am very glad the dear child is soe well, and since you think it necessary to remove her out of that aire I do intend to send my coach to Farnham...to bring her hither on Thursday. I leave her wholly to your care to remove her when you think fitt...and pray take care to defend her from her grandmother, who has not soe much civillity left as to come and speake to me her selfe; but by a letter has lett me know that she does expect to have her delivered up; if not, she must use force. Poor childe pray God send her health, and protect her from all the designes that are upon her at this time'.[78]

After the marriage in Hampshire, the newlyweds went to Northamptonshire for Lord Montagu's blessing and more celebrations. On August 27 Elizabeth told him 'My Lord I am extremely obliged to your Ldshp for the kind invitation you are pleased to make me... I am sure there is nothing that I doe with so much impatience long for as the waiting upon your Ldshp... Mr Mountague have promised me to bring me to your Ldshp that soe I may have the opertunity of professing to you with what reality I am My Lord, your Ldshps most obedient daughter and humble servant'. One of those invited to Boughton was Sir Justinian Isham of Lamport, a neighbouring landowner. He had written to Lady Long on the 16th :'You may heare by this that my Country man Mr Montagu hath concluded all for his marriage wt ye Lady Northumberland, ye Writings being days since sealed by ye father ye Lord Montagu here. For some time there was very small probabilitie of it how soever it hath bin lately wrought about. This might be newes for ye Mercurie Gallant' (an ephemeral periodical). He went with his wife and daughter and in another letter recorded that the bells of the parish churches in Northamptonshire were re-roped to ring the happy couple into the county.[79]

Only a few months after the festivities Elizabeth was visiting her husband in the Tower of London. 'Mr. Montagu was standing in the circle in the withdrawing room, the King present, when the Duke [Buckingham] comes in hastily to go to the King and pulls Mr. Montagu by the shoulder to make way, who, holding back, somewhat angrily asked who is there, the Duke replying, It is I, and will come by; You shall not, said Mr. Montagu, upon which some fierce words more of I will and you shall not passed

[77] Williamson Letters, from Sir Robert Southwell, August 31, 1673 p.198
[78] E.B. de Fonblanque, Annals of the House of Percy, from the Conquest to the opening of the nineteenth century (London 1887) p. 490, drawing on Alnwick Mss DNA: F/2
[79] N. Marlow, The diary of Thomas Isham of Lamport (1658-81), kept by him in Latin from 1671 to 1673 at his father's command (Farnborough, 1971)

between them, when Mr. Montagu bid the Duke follow him. Being both come out of the Queen's rooms, Mr. Montagu challenged the Duke to go immediately and fight, and so make only a rencounter of it, and not a sett duel, the Duke would not, but told him he should heer of him at such a place the next morning, upon which they parted. Mr. Montagu was no sooner got home but the King, who had been informed...sent to secure him, the Duke keeping out of the way till the Tuesday following, when he went to the King; and the next day the whole business was heard at the Councell'.[80] A different version of events was also circulating:

'Mr Montagu offering to pass by the Duke of Buckingham in the drawing room, his Grace resisted him, but Mr Montagu said he must go that way, and rushing by offended the duke so much as to make him lift up his foot at him, which made Mr Montagu desire him to go to some other place with him, but no notice was taken of it'.[81] Ralph was sent to the Tower on December 3. Before he went he wrote to Arlington for help: *'Just now the Serjeant-at-Arms was with me with an order to go to the Tower. I am very willing to obey the King's demands, but the words of the order are drawn up, I suppose, with an intention of further inconvenience to me, for it is expressed,* "for challenging the duke of Buckingham in the King's presence"; *which interpretation to the words(s)* "Follow me" *was made by the Duke of Buck friends, whereas I meant nothing but the avoiding a noise in the King's presence. Therefore I desire, if it be possible, that the King may be moved to have the order altered, for you know the Duke of Buck chicon enough, that if it be taken for granted I challenged in the king's presence, he may pursue it farther, and I do absolutely protest against any such thing'.* He was released after three days *'through the earnest solicitation of his friends'* and put under house arrest for a while. This seems to have been considered sufficient punishment, for nothing more is recorded of the matter. The clear enmity between the two men had long been evident and the previous year Ralph, as Master of the Wardrobe, petitioned the lords of the Treasury to set a date to hear his complaint *'that during his absence in France the Duke of Buckingham invaded the rights thereof... his Majesty declares he will be present'.*[82]   Duels between the nobility were common – a few months earlier Ralph's relatives, the young earls of Manchester and Sandwich, had not let their shared Montagu blood prevent them from duelling *'about the keeping of the swans'* for example (presumably over being Keeper of the King's Swans, Manchester have been granted that office the previous year).[83] By the summer of 1674 any disgrace that may have fallen on

[80] Williamson letters, from Robert Yard, December 8 p.89
[81] Cal SP Dom December 5 1673 and Thomas Derham to Williamson.
[82] Cal SP Dom August 21 1672
[83] Williamson letters June 13 1673 p.38

Ralph had clearly lifted since his name was added to those of Sunderland and the Lords Keeper and Treasurer as committee members discussing the Treaty of Commerce with France.[84]

Ralph's new marriage apparently had problems other than how the Countess was to keep the custody of her daughter, though the thought that the loss could happen at any moment must have been a strain. Even at the time of her wedding the Countess's friends had apparently not been happy about the match (it had been *'much to their dissatisfaction'*).[85] *'My Lady of Northumberland and her new husband Mr. Montagu, have already begun to differ upon the report risen from him, as she sayes, that he bought her of her mayde for 500 l pa; and the Towne now talks of parting them'.* [86] Perhaps Ralph had been unwise enough to make a joke to that effect, not thinking of the power of gossip. Less than a month later: *'Mr. Montagu and his lady begin already to live like man and wife, neither caring a rush for the other, which makes her marryng of him more and more to be wondered at, and that for him shee should refuse not only Mr. Savill but Mr. Gray too; the reason that some give is this, that Mr. Grey was so unfortunate as to have an uncle that had no – ergo – but that Mr. Montagu has a sister that has one'.*[87] A fortnight after that Sir Gilbert Talbot writes to Williamson *'Your friend Ralph Montagu hath managed his matter soe that he and his Countess lye in two beds, the reason sayd to be strong jealousy of the old mistress'*.[88] Metzger suggests this was a reference to the duchess de Brissac with whom Ralph had been friends. The Countess's year ended miserably: *'My Lady Northumberland has miscaryed and is very ill this week, which is increased by her husband's being not yet free from his restraint'.*[89]

There seems to be no record of Ralph's activities, other than his marriage and arrest, from early 1673 until the end of July 1674 when we first hear of his intention to build a London house for himself and his new wife (and the family they would have hoped to have) in Robert Hooke's diary: *'To Flamstead at Tower and Coffee house in Mark Lane. He spoke about R. Montacues house and new quadrant'*.[90] Hooke's life neatly encapsulates this age of the polymath, when one of Britain's greatest mathematicians (Newton) spent much of his time as Master of the Mint writing religious works and a great astronomer (Wren) was to achieve

---

[84] Cal SP Dom July 24
[85] Williamson letters August 25 p.183
[86] Ibid October 10, 1673 p.99
[87] Ibid November 5 1673 p.63
[88] Ibid November 13 p.71
[89] Ibid December 17 p.99
[90] H. W. Robinson & W. Adams ed., *The diary of Robert Hooke F.R.S., 1672-1680 : transcribed from the original in the possession of the Corporation of the City of London* (London 1935)

fame as an architect. Hooke was a couple of years older than Ralph and had, like him, been at Westminster School. He had worked for Robert Boyle, the natural philosopher, at Oxford University, and became Curator of Experiments for the Royal Society shortly after it was founded in 1660. Between that time and his work for Ralph on Montagu House he had discovered "Hooke's Law of Elasticity", which led to his development of the hairspring, enabling pocket watches to keep reasonable time, and he had printed "Micrographia" giving microscopic, telescopic and biological observations (famed for its large scale drawings of a flea and a louse, and for coining the word "cell" to describe biological organisms). He also argued for an attracting principle of gravitation and would go on to discuss this with Newton who he would later accuse of not acknowledging the contribution his ideas made to the latter's famous "Principia". In the year that he produced the designs for Ralph's house he published "An Attempt to Prove the Motion of the Earth from Observations". This suggested that *'all bodies whatsoever that are put into a direct and simple motion, will so continue to move forward in a straight line, till they are by some other effectual powers deflected and bent';* and that *'these attractive powers are so much the more powerful in operating, by how much the nearer the body wrought upon is to their own Centres'* i.e. the gravitational pull larger planets exert over smaller ones. Like his mentor Wren, Hooke had also acted as an architect, designing the Bedlam Hospital for lunatics and the Monument to the Great Fire of London. (This is the largest freestanding stone column in the world and was also intended to serve as a scientific instrument – a hinged lid in the flaming urn at the top opened, and the whole column acted as a zenith telescope). He assisted Wren with the Royal Observatory at Greenwich in 1675, where Flamsteed took up his post as the first Astronomer Royal.

Ralph's marriage had not only helped to provide the funds for such an expensive undertaking as the erection of a house which would manifest his position in society, it also helped provide the site: in 1675 he paid £2,600 for seven acres of Southampton Fields (where the British Museum now stands) to one of his wife's half-sisters, Rachel, wife of William, Lord Russell.[91] The 4th earl of Southampton had started to develop this part of Bloomsbury shortly after the Restoration and Rachel brought the Bloomsbury and Covent Garden estates to the Russell family, together with Southampton House which faced Bloomsbury Square, to the east of the new Montagu House. The gardens of the two houses adjoined each other and both fronted Great Russell Street which Strype described as *'a very handsome, large and well-built Street, graced with the best Buildings in all Bloomsbury, and the best inhabited by the Nobility and Gentry, especially the North Side, as having gardens behind the Houses; and the*

[91] L.G. Schwoerer, *Lady Rachel Russell : "one of the best of women"* (London 1988)

Prospect of the pleasant Fields up to Hampstead and Highgate. Insomuch that this place by Physicians is esteemed the most healthful of any in London'. It must have had great attractions for rich merchants who wanted to move out of the densely-packed, noisy City. Strype goes on to say that *'for the stateliness of Building and curious Gardens, Montagu House hath the Preminence, as indeed of all Houses within the Cities of London and Westminster'*. It certainly outdid Southampton House, built some twenty years earlier as a long low building with a single roofline, in external appearance alone. There is no record of Hooke's plan, nor detailed record of its appearance, but the sketch of it in a map by Ogilby & Morgan of 1682 shows a clear division of the sections and high roofs, so it probably looked much like Hooke's Ragley Hall in Warwickshire, which survives. An arched entrance in a high brick wall fronting the street, surmounted by an octagonal turret topped with a wooden cupola, gave access to the courtyard in front of the house. Behind the wall ran an Ionic colonnade and the wings of the house to left and right containing the stables and offices had doorways flanked by Ionic pilasters. The house itself was entered by steps from the courtyard and was 168' long and 57' high (51m x 17m).

On 10 October 1683 John Evelyn: *'Visited the Duchess of Grafton, not yet brought to bed, & dining with my Lord Chamberlain (*her father Arlington*), went with them to see Montagu House, a palace lately built by Lord Montagu, who had married ye most beautiful Countess of Northumberland. It is a stately & ample palace. Signor Verrio's fresca paintings, especially the funeral pyre of Dido, on the stayrecase, the labours of Hercules, fight with the Centaurs, effeminacy with Dejanira, & Apotheosis, or reception among the gods, on ye walls & roofe of the greate roome above, I think exceedes anything he has yet don, both for designe, colouring, & exuberance of invention, or what they so celebrate at Rome. In the rest of the chamber are some excellent paintings of Holbein & other masters. The garden is large, and in good aire, but the fronts of the house not answerable to the inside. The court at entrie, and wings for offices, seeme too neere the streete, and that so very narrow and meanely built that the corridore is not in proportion to ye rest, to hide the court from being overlook'd by neighbours, all which might have been prevented had they plac'd the house further into ye ground, of which there was enough to spare. But on the whole it is a fine palace, built after the French pavilion way, by Mr. Hooke, the Curator of the Royal Society. There were with us my Lady Scroope, the great witt, and Monsr. Chardine, the celebrated traveller'*. Verrio's work here and at Windsor was later destroyed, but one can gain some idea of what the rooms would have looked like from his later work at Chatsworth and Burghley. He may well be the *'Italian* *painter at Mountacues'* mentioned by Hooke and brought back by Ralph in 1672 from Paris to make designs for the Mortlake tapestry factory.[92]

Through Hooke's diary one can chart the progress of the work over six years, and see something of Ralph's daily activities too. Hooke finished the final design on February 16 1675, but Ralph was in the country and not back until the 22nd when he approved it and Hooke then whisked it off to show the Portuguese ambassador. The estimates were approved by Ralph on Friday, March 5, just before he went off to Newmarket (probably to join the King and court at the races). The master bricklayer was to be Thomas Fitch, who had made a fortune after the Great Fire rebuilding many of the City's churches. The names of the master joiner, carpenter, mason, painter, smith are also recorded – the whole gamut of craftsmen needed for such a house. The turret clock was provided by Thomas Tompion, the greatest maker of the age (Ralph paid him ten guineas for a watch too, in December 1677). We know from Hooke that Ralph played tennis (sometimes with the King), visited Wren and Garraway's Coffee House (in Change Alley, Cornhill, where tea was first sold in England) either in his carriage or sedan chair, and spent time with his sister (April 22 1676: *'With Mr Mountacue at Lady Harvys, discoursd about chimney pieces, ceelings, wings etc*).

1675 saw the arrival in London of a woman who would become one of Ralph's closest female friends. Hortense Mancini had come to visit her cousin's daughter Mary of Modena, duchess of York. Hortense was one of five beautiful sisters who had been brought to Paris at an early age by their widowed mother, to seek the protection of their uncle, Cardinal Mazarin, chief minister of France. Her sister Marie was supposedly the first mistress of Louis XIV, and one of her brothers tasked with seducing Monsieur. All the sisters married well. Laure became the mother of the duc de Vendome, a famous general, and Olympe gave birth to Prince Eugene of Savoy who would later lead an army against his French cousin Vendome. Hortense's hand (and dowry) had been requested by the exiled King Charles - his adviser, Abbe Montagu, wrote to Mazarin on December 20 1659 requesting that he *'will not promise your niece Hortense in marriage to anybody until I have had the honour of speaking to you'*.[93] But Mazarin considered that Charles's prospects were too uncertain. After the Restoration six months later Mazarin changed his mind and offered a twenty million livre dowry. Clarendon thought a French match inadvisable and so foundered a marriage that might have made both parties happy and produced heirs. Instead she was married in 1661, at the age of fifteen, to the duc de La Meilleraye, almost twice her age. Though one of the richest

---

[92] Christopher Brown in "Art & Patronage in the Caroline Courts: Essays in honour of Sir Oliver Miller" ed. D Howarth (Cambridge 1993)
[93] Correspondance Politique: Angleterre, Paris CA 71, f.188

men in Europe he was mentally unstable. Many stories were told of him: that he wanted to have the front teeth of his daughters removed so that they could not be as flighty as their mother for example, and he certainly had chipped off or painted over the genitalia of the fine art collection which Hortense had inherited, together with great wealth, from her uncle. Despite this he fathered four children by her in as many years (four of his granddaughter's children would become mistresses to Louis XV). She was rescued from the convent in which her husband later incarcerated her by her brother Philippe and went to stay with her sister Marie, in Rome. Here they entertained the exiled Chevalier de Lorraine and his brother. When Marie left her husband Hortense sought refuge with the duke of Savoy, who housed her at Chambery and had an affair with her. After his death in June 1675 she was turned out by his widow and her own husband deprived her of all sources of income. Ralph seems to have come to her rescue. He may well have hoped that she would supplant Louise de Kerouaille, who had in her turn supplanted Barbara Palmer, duchess of Cleveland as King Charles's mistress. Indeed, this is what was claimed by St Evremond, who was close to Hortense during her many years in London and also knew Ralph well. (He said that the latter had met her at Chambery). One reason Ralph and Arlington may have had for promoting her was that she was not interested in playing politics, simply in enjoying herself. She set out for England with her eight servants, including her Moorish page Mustapha, dressed as a man. A rough crossing from Brill in December 1675 forced her to land at Sole Bay near Southwold in Suffolk, from whence she rode on horseback to London.

Mistresses had a central place in Court politics because of their unique intimacy with Charles. This allowed them (and through them those they favoured) to ask things of the King when in his company, at a time when he was most likely to be relaxed and in good humour. How much influence they truly had is extremely hard to distinguish, but it is certainly the case that the illusion (if such it was) of power over the King afforded them power over others. The patronage system meant that, having achieved power, obliging others with favours reinforced the alliances necessary to maintain it, whilst at the same time demonstrating it. Barbara had been Charles's mistress in exile and her ability to maintain this position after the Restoration and exploit it to gain power, rank and wealth greatly encouraged others. Buckingham, Arlington and the Montagus recognised that they couldn't rely on her to advance their interests. The Venetian ambassador may have once described them as all being with her in the party that opposed Clarendon, but only a few months after the latter's fall she had become friendly with his daughter, the duchess of York, and her husband, and so supported Clarendon's son against the attempts of Buckingham and Arlington to remove him from his post of Lord

Chamberlain to the Queen. Her success in this seems to have moved them to try to discredit her with the King. Ralph's sister, Lady Betty Harvey, was enlisted to help them. In late December 1668 the court was gossiping about the dinner which Buckingham had arranged to reconcile Arlington with George Porter, a minor courtier. Lady Betty proposed a toast to Arlington and all his friends, and to the confusion of Porter's former friends. This was taken to mean Barbara and the Yorks. She also used her famed wit against Barbara's conduct in front of the King and Queen. Barbara retaliated, eventually calling Lady Betty a hermaphrodite who had turned against her because she had spurned her sexual advances. Lady Betty responded that she was amazed that she could say such a thing, since Barbara was famed for never spurning anyone's sexual advances.[94] Early in the New Year the campaign continued. Barbara arranged for an actress playing the part of Sempronia in the staging of "Cataline's Conspiracy" (to overthrow the Roman Republic) to caricature Lady Betty, to loud applause. Although Sempronia was recorded as having been beautiful, intelligent and lucky in life and marriage, she also lacked morals and was a conspirator, acting independently of her husband. Lady Betty got her kinsman the Lord Chamberlain to imprison the actress, but as Pepys records, Barbara *'made the King to release her, and to order her to act it again, worse than ever, the other day, where the King himself was'*. By the third performance Lady Betty had primed people in the audience to hiss and fling oranges at the actress. Buckingham tried to get Charles to command the actress to make amends to Lady Betty but was told that this would cause too many other people to come forward demanding similar satisfaction for the insults they had received. Realising that the campaign had failed, Buckingham presented himself at Barbara's house for reconciliation (even if its sincerity was doubted) and Lady Betty retired to hers and only received close friends.[95] 1669 was an eventful year for her - there was a scandal when she killed one of her pages, *'a young knight of 14 or 15 years, & with his own sword'*. She claimed that he had attacked her but it was rumoured he had *'boasted of receiving some favour from her'*.[96]

Many at Court had an interest therefore in undermining Barbara's power by providing Charles with a more amenable mistress and thought that they had found a suitable candidate in Louise de Kerouaille. A Breton, she had been one of Madame's attendants and accompanied her to Dover in 1670 where King Charles is likely to have seen her and shown interest. Bishop Burnet later asserted that Buckingham encouraged Charles.

[94] PRO 31/3/120-121 de Croissy to Lionne, 24 December, 1668 & 31 January, 1669
[95] PRO 31/3/120-121 de Croissy to Lionne, 24 Dec 1668, 14 & 31 Jan 1669
[96] W. Westergaard ed., *The First Triple Alliance: The Letters of Christopher Lindenov, Danish Envoy to London 1668-72* (Yale 1947) p.111

Certainly William Perwich reported to Arlington on September 17 1670 that Buckingham had left the previous day, returning from his diplomatic trip to arrange the Treaty, together with the Count de Grammont and '*the beautiful young Lady Madame Keroel, quandon maid of honour to Madam, who I hear is to have the same rank with her Majesty in England*'.[97] But he squandered any goodwill he had garnered by sending her off to Dieppe and then, apparently forgetting she was there, going to England himself via Calais. (Ralph wrote to Arlington on the 24th that he had previously informed Godolphin she was waiting for the yacht to be sent to her that Buckingham had promised). She was still in Dieppe when Ralph wrote again on October 15. Arlington and the French ambassador Colbert de Croissy both promoted Louise and a conversation between them recorded a year after her arrival gives an indication of what was hoped for.[98] Arlington wanted the King to have a mistress who well born (unlike Nell Gwynn) and good natured (unlike Barbara Palmer), and so would be amenable to mutually beneficial arrangements with those who courted her favour. Louise's apartments were in Whitehall and so everyone could have access to Charles there, if welcome, whereas the '*little creatures*' and actresses who Buckingham encouraged Charles to bed tended to monopolise that access. Arlington told Louise to take care of the King's favour, ensure that he always found pleasure in her company, and not tax him with business or speak ill of those who served the King. Lady Arlington had a woman to woman chat and told her to be submissive to Charles unless she preferred to return to France and enter a convent. De Croissy agreed to help, giving Louise a sign of French royal approval and informing her of her obligations to Arlington. He rightly anticipated privileged access for himself and future French ambassadors to Charles through her – so much so that in October 1682 the Dutch ambassador complained about this special treatment. He was forced to back down because royal visits to mistresses were unofficial and so couldn't be challenged.[99]

Arlington and many others were disappointed that Louise hadn't lived up to their expectations of her and hence placed theirs hope in Hortense as her replacement in the King's affections. Hortense's arrival in December 1675 caused a sensation in London, sufficient for the Calender of State Papers (Domestic) to record a purported conversation:

Some days before the poor coffee-houses fell under persecution two French gentlemen went to Garraway's near the Exchange, when some company invited them to their table, and the conversation began

[97] PRO letter 116
[98] AAE, CPA, 101, de Croissy to Louvois, 8 October, 1671
[99] PRO 31/3/153 Barillon to Louis XIV 28 October, 1682

1st Coffist *have you not heard of the courier arrived three days since with a retinue that marked him for a man of great quality?*

2nd Coffist *I saw him and his attendants alight from their post horses, terribly weather-beaten, having rid in the late storms.*

1st Frenchman *I now understand, was in not in Bedford Street, Covent Garden?*

1st Coffist *Yes*

1st Frenchman *Then I will tell you that the person you saw was indeed an extraordinary courier and one of great quality.*

2nd Frenchman *In truth it was not a courier, but a very illustrious courreuse*

1st Frenchman *The courier you saw alight, booted and spurred, covered with mud was the fair Duchess of Mazarin herself.*

2nd Frenchman *It was in very truth that new Queen of the Amazons who is come to conceive a martial race by your Alexander*

4th Coffist *She could not have taken a better way of recommending herself, for both vigour and soundness, than by riding astride, booted and spurred, 500 miles on a post horse in the depth of winter....I think it much more honourable for Great Britain to have its monarch subdued by a famous Roman dame, than by an obscure damsel of Little Britain or by a frisking comedian...*

3rd Coffist *A great wit and profound statesman...protests that the French king, finding Carwel too weak both as to extraction and interest, to wed thoroughly the concerns of France, has sent the King over a new mistress that shall do it to the purpose...I shall tell you then another more reasonable and not so far fetched. It is said for certain that the ingenious gentleman, Mr Ralph Montagu, so lucky in remote contrivances, having made great acquaintance with this Duchess when she resided at Chambery, has by concert with Arlington prevailed with her to come over, they hoping that the King taking to love her, she may be a means of ruining the Lord Treasurer, who is thought to be much strengthened by the Duchess of Portsmouth*

1st Frenchman *These gentlemen are not too well informed, who persuade themselves that a niece and heiress of Cardinal Mazarin, having claims to money at Court, can be engaged to take part against the Minister who is in favour and holds the purse...*

2nd Frenchman *I shall content myself with telling you, that the Duchess of Mazarin is in reality so charming that, if your King kisses her but once, I hold her of Portsmouth as done for.*[100]

A clear indication of Ralph's involvement in Hortense's arrival is the statement that she came to Bedford Street, where his sister Lady Betty

---

[100] Cal SP Dom 1675/6 p.474

lived. She arranged for Charles to meet Hortense there.[101]. The French ambassador sent the same news back to Paris in January 1676 [102] and seven months later reported '*I am told by Madam Harvey, sister of Monsieur de Montagu, the most intriguing and the cleverest woman in England, that Madame Mazarin is extremely satisfied with the conversation she has had with the King of England, and that she is counting strongly on the protection and good office of Monsieur de Montagu*'.[103] Charles was apparently also satisfied with the conversation - the French ambassador informed his royal master that Charles regularly went through the going to bed ceremony at Whitehall, and when his gentlemen and servants had left, got up, dressed and stole off to St. James's Palace, where he arrived after the Duchess's card parties were over, and did not return until five in the morning. In May '*The duke of York has bought a new built house of Lord Windsor in St. James's Park and given it to Madam Mazarin to live in as long as she continues here. She supt about ten days ago with Lady Harvey who is her intimatest friend, and the King cam in and surprised them*'.[104] The King seems to have found strong-minded women particularly alluring. (Even after Louise had replaced Barbara Palmer as his principal mistress the latter was able to exercise considerable sway over him by force of personality). Perhaps Charles wondered what might have been had Cardinal Mazarin consented in 1659 to the marriage between him and his niece. Hortense also proved to be a great hit with King's eldest daughter by Barbara, the countess of Sussex. Courtin reported that the young Countess (she was about fourteen years old and had been married two years before) saw Hortense as a heroine of romance because of her exciting past, and on November 23 1676 wrote that '*Madam Mazarin, after piously attending Mass on Sunday, dined with me and played the rest of the afternoon in my withdrawing room, at battledore and shuttlecock, with Lady Sussex*'. Conveniently for Hortense, Lady Sussex occupied the apartments in Whitehall that her mother had used when in favour, which were directly above the King's cabinet, and which he could access by a private staircase without being seen.

The two friends also had more unusual pastimes: '*they went down into St. James's Park the other day with drawne swords under their night gowns, which they drew out and made successful fine passes with, much to the admiration of severall men that was lookers-on in the Park*'.[105] Hortense didn't undermine the political strength of either Barbara or Louise but the King provided for her with a pension of £4,000 a year

[101] E. Hamilton *The illustrious lady : a biography of Barbara Villiers, Countess of Castlemaine and Duchess of Cleveland* (London 1980) p.163
[102] CA 117, f.14
[103] CA 119, f15
[104] Lady Chaworth to her brother Lord Roos, Belvoir Mss, II p.67
[105] Ibid. p.34

(prompting the poet Andrew Marvell to complain '*That the King should send for another French whore When one already had made him so poor*'). Since Charles shared his favours amongst many women, Hortense saw no reason why she shouldn't share hers so when the handsome Prince of Monaco came to London in October 1676 she allowed herself to be worn down by his pleading. Charles, of course, was not amused. Edmund Waller wrote of the rivalry between Louise and Hortense in "The Triple Combat":

When thro' the world fair Mazarin had run,
Bright as her fellow-traveller the sun,
Hither at length the Roman eagle flies,
As the last triumph of her conqu'ring eyes...
But Portsmouth, springing from the antient race
Of Britons, which the Saxon here did chase,
As they great Caesar did oppose, makes head,
And does against this new invader lead

Hortense attracted the admiration of another strong willed woman, Aphra Behn, a spy and one of the first professional female writers. Aphra dedicated "The History of the Nun or the Fair Vow-breaker" to her in 1688, affirming '*how infinitely one of your own sex adores you*'. Ralph's sister also attracted literary praise -the poet La Fontaine (whose patron was Hortense's sister Marianne Mancini) included a verse portrait of her in his Fables, as Le Renard Anglais (the English Fox). '*You are such a good companion, with a good heart, and a hundred qualities too numerous to summarise, a talent to promote business and people. A frank and free manner, and all the qualities that make you a good friend, regardless of Jupiter himself, and the current stormy times*'. Interestingly le renard is usually seen as male, and La Fontaine did not refer to the main attribute usually attributed to the fox – its cunning. Jupiter is doubtless a reference to Charles.

A letter written by the French ambassador (Courtin) on 23 November 1675 makes reference to '*Mrs Middleton...she is the sweetest woman I ever came across in any foreign country. She is beautiful, has an air of high breeding, is full of talent and yet modest and unassuming*'. The thirty-year old Jane was the wife of an impoverished younger son of Sir Thomas Middleton of Chirk Castle, and it was said that they and their young daughter depended on the generosity of her lovers. Like Ralph's wife, her portrait had been painted by Lely to hang as one of a set of ten at Windsor Castle of women considered by the duchess of York to be the most beautiful at Court. There are several intimations linking her name with Ralph's, not least by the comte de Grammont who knew him well, and was apparently a rival for her favours. He described her *'one of the handsomest women in town, and so much of the coquette as to discourage no one'*. He declared that Ralph was *'no very dangerous rival on account of his person, but very much to be feared for his assiduity, the acuteness of his wit, and some other talents, which are of importance, when a man is permitted to display them'*. Courtin recounted an anecdote that brought all these formidable and beautiful ladies together. Meeting them at the theatre, he wrote that Lady Harvey and Mrs Middleton proposed supper at his house three days later. The duchesses of Portsmouth and Mazarin promised to join them, as did Lady Beauclerc, though she and Lady Harvey were at daggers drawn and could not endure each other. It was the first time that Portsmouth & Mazarin had met and it was thought that, as rivals for the King's favour, there would be a spat. Courtin locked them in the same room, until eventually they came out hand in hand. Louise pushed the spirit of conciliation so far as to ask Mazarin to dinner, and then took her to the Mall in her coach, to the astonishment of all the gentry, who were no less thunderstruck when Lady Harvey appeared in the same company. The friendship between the two mistresses may have been more politic than real. On July 2 1676 Courtin wrote to Pomponne: *'Madame Mazarin is coming to dine with me today with the Countess of Sussex. Near me dwells Madame de Middleton, who is the most beautiful woman in England. Poor St. Evremond has fallen passionately in love with her in his dotage. In the afternoon I take (three friends) to her house, and then I meet her again with them towards eleven o'clock in the evening at St. James's Park, where I also meet the poor Portuguese ambassador, who is dying for love of Madame Mazarin. Mr de Montagu who had a mind to conduct an intrigue for the King with her has fallen himself into her toils, and malicious tongues here say that he is being unfaithful to the beautiful Madame de Middleton, with whom he is said to have been in love for a long time'*.[106] By this time Ralph had been married for three years.

---

[106] CA 119 f.15

Chapter 3
Danby 1676- July 1678

In August 1676 Ralph Montagu was once more named as ambassador to France, but the appointment did not provide an opportunity to renew his friendly official relationship with Lord Arlington. 1672 had proved to be the highlight of the latter's career. He had supported the Stop on the Exchequer, and Charles's Declaration of Indulgence of religious liberty in the spring, and had been rewarded with an earldom and the Garter before cementing his ties with the King by betrothing his four year old daughter and heir to Charles's illegitimate son by Barbara, the nine year old earl of Euston. Then fortune ceased to smile upon Arlington's enterprises. His visit with Buckingham to William of Orange to agree terms for an end to the Third Anglo-Dutch War was a failure – one of his great flaws was his arrogance, a trait William detested, which made his dealings with diplomats difficult. Worse still a fellow member of the Cabal[107] (Clifford) was appointed Lord Treasurer in November. This was the prime post Arlington coveted. (Whilst he was one of Charles's most talented ministers he was much underestimated by his jealous contemporaries, as he has often been by later historians). In the same month Parliament, worried by the navy's failure (and the financial cost of its upkeep), the consequences of potential French victories, and the threat from the new alliance, had refused to vote funds to continue the war. Public opinion had been inflamed by a flood of Dutch printed pamphlets, many written by Ralph's former secretary du Moulin, which claimed that Charles intended (in concert with Louis) to make England Catholic again. People took the duke of York's resignation as Lord High Admiral and marriage to the Catholic Mary of Modena with Charles's consent as an indication (quite rightly) that the heir to the throne had converted to Catholicism. Since the King was now extremely unlikely to have a legitimate child, the next ruler, the next head of the Church of England, would be a Roman Catholic. Charles must have known, and been advised of, the fears this would raise yet ignored them: royal marriages, like foreign affairs and the right to wage war, were part of the royal prerogative (something for which his father had preferred to sacrifice his life than give up).

1673 had seen more reverses – Arlington encouraged Charles to allow referral of the Declaration of Indulgence to the House of Lords, where it was declared illegal. This was followed in the autumn by the Test Act under which anyone filling civil or military office had to swear an oath which included denial of transubstantiation and an undertaking to take the

---

[107] The Cabal consisted of Clifford, Arlington, Buckingham, Ashley and Lauderdale and was a grouping that had come to prominence after the fall of Clarendon in 1667. They would Charles's main advisers until 1672.

Anglican sacrament of communion within three months. Whilst this had the beneficial effect (in Arlington's eyes) of removing the Roman Catholic Clifford, who resigned as Lord Treasurer rather than take the oath, Charles still didn't promote him to the vacant post. It was given to Thomas Osborne and the King said that this was because Arlington wasn't fit for it. Both reverses to royal policy had been political necessities, but backing them hadn't make Arlington popular with his monarch. Having clearly lost the King's support, Arlington finally came out as pro-Dutch, but this availed him nothing when, the day before the House of Commons tried to impeach him for corruption, popery and betrayal of trust (on 15 January 1674), Buckingham publicly accused him of being the chief mover behind a pro-French, anti Protestant foreign policy. The attack on him in the Commons was led by his brother-in-law, Lord Ossory. Nine months later, unable to recover support, he sold his office as Secretary of State for the South to Sir Joseph Williamson and accepted the ceremonial role of Lord Steward from Charles. There is an intriguing record of a rumour that Ralph might have had the coveted Secretaryship back in March.[108] Arlington did not give up on his attempts to regain influence, as his encouragement of the duchess of Mazarin in 1676 shows, but Ralph would have realised that, for the moment at least, other patrons should be sought.

The obvious choice was Osborne (soon made earl of Danby), now occupying the central post in government. They were related, having a common grandfather in the 1st Lord Montagu. This hadn't stopped Ralph from writing to Arlington in May 1669 that he wished *'my Lord Duke of Buckingham would not give as much credit to Sr Thomas Osborne as he does for I am confident of something I have heard by a brother-in-law of his that went by here that he betrays all to my Lord Keeper.'* Danby owed his rise to Buckingham, Ralph's enemy, but by 1674 had broken with him. An excellent administrator, his experience as Treasurer of the navy had demonstrated his flair for accountancy. To restore royal credit he now arranged to pay the bankers who had suffered from the Stop of the Exchequer £77,000 in interest and then negotiated lower interest rates on loans. He also increased some existing taxes and thus greatly benefitted Charles's income. This put him in a position to tell Charles an uncomfortable truth – that he would continue to have problems unless he went along with the views of his subjects. They were becoming increasingly anti-Catholic, so rather than pursuing an unfruitful alliance with the Catholic dictator Louis XIV he would be better advised to approach his natural ally, his fervently Protestant nephew William of Orange. Danby himself, a dour Yorkshireman, was a committed Anglican

---

[108] Verney Mss mic M636/27 Sir Ralph Verney to Edmund Verney March 5 1674: *'Tis reported Arlington shall quit his place as Secretary and be Lord Chamberlain and that either Ralph Montagu or the Speaker shall be Secretary.'*

opposed to religious toleration on moral grounds. Charles agreed to issue royal proclamations reinforcing laws against non-conformists and stringent penalties on Englishmen attending mass, even in foreign embassy chapels, which had previously been safe havens. Danby was able to use Dutch money to bribe biddable MPs. So when Parliament reconvened after a fourteen month suspension in April 1675 the King was able hypocritically to state that his actions showed his zeal for the Church of England, and that any wavering from this position that had been perceived previously was down to ill-intentioned ministers. He then asked for more money for the navy. Members were not convinced. They demanded the recall of the troops that Charles had offered France and the impeachment of Lauderdale, who ruled Scotland with an iron fist. When that was refused they turned on Danby, who they claimed had violated ancient practice in his methods of increasing tax revenues and believed that royal proclamation could supersede parliamentary law. Danby and the King had hoped to get an amendment to the Test Act passed that any applicant for public office would not "endeavour any alteration of the Protestant religion now established in the Church of England, nor will I endeavour any alteration in the government or state as it is by law established." The first half of the clause would have pleased MPs but the second could be used to construe any opposition to the King as a violation of this oath. The earl of Shaftesbury, Lord Chancellor, who had used his great powers of oratory in the defence of royal policy two years before, saw this clause for what it was and had it pulled down in the Lords, showing that it would be a further step along the road to arbitrary government, the strengthening of royal power. Charles prorogued Parliament. Danby realised that he needed to further consolidate support by appealing to an Anglican cavalier mentality in MPs while branding the opposition as dissenters and republicans. He used propaganda and bribery but the attempt to create a court party inevitably led to the creation of a more organised 'country' party to oppose it and make further accusations of arbitrary government.

Danby may have held the Montagus in some regard, for in April 1676 Lord Montagu wrote to him from Boughton giving profuse thanks for the appointment of his brother William to the post of Chief Baron of the Exchequer.[109] This made William head of the equity court, a post he would fill for the next decade. Nonetheless Ralph's new embassy is more likely due to lobbying on his behalf by the duchess of Mazarin than to Danby. Bishop Burnet, in his "History of My Own Time"[110] states that Ralph told

---

[109] Thomas Osborne, *Copies and Extracts of some Letters written to and from the Earl of Danby, (now Duke of Leeds,) in the years 1676, 1677, and 1678, with particular remarks upon some of them.* (London 1710)
[110] O. Airy ed., *History of my own time* (Oxford 1897)

Sir William Temple that he intended to be ambassador again. Asked how that could be, since he knew the King didn't love him and Buckingham hated him, he replied *'That's true, but they shall do, as if they loved me'*. Which, Sir William told the bishop, he soon brought about *'by means of the ladies, who were always his best friends, for some secret perfections, that were hid from the rest of the world'*. Given their future relationship it is interesting that it was known that Ralph was not liked by Charles. Nonetheless Charles may have wanted to keep Ralph on side so that he could provide for another of his bastards by marrying him to Ralph's stepdaughter Betty, the Percy heiress. Ralph knew about his embassy at least a month before the official announcement: amongst all the entries in Hooke's diary relating to the building of Montagu House there is one for Saturday July 8 *'Resolved...to goe into France with Mr. Montacue'* and another of September 21: *'To Mr. Montacue's. With him to Bloomsbury. Pleased with chimneys, cupelos over gateways &c. He promised me French Academy books. Took his last leave alone'*. Ralph also took with him as his chaplain Dr Thomas Blomer of Canterbury, who would draw the profits of his canonry whilst enjoying the pleasures of Paris.[111] On the 24th Ralph and his wife left for France.[112] The lure of becoming ambassador once more (despite the many complaints he had made about lack of recompense for his previous embassy, both financial and in honours), was clearly enough to draw him away from his incomplete house. (On 11 February 1676 his wife had written to her sister: *'If our house went up as fast as we have models made, we should be in it before you get to yours, for we have no less than three that are big enough for Miss Ann* [his daughter] *to walk in'*).[113]

A letter from John Brisbane to Secretary Coventry dated December 6 1676 reports that *'yesterday I waited with others on my lord Ambassador to St. Germains, where he had an audience with the King in our presence, another by himself, and after noon of the Queen, Monsieur le Dauphin, Monsieur, Madame and Madamoiselle... my lord Ambassador and I perusing together yesternight a copy which I have of the Earl of Sandwich his treaty, we do not find the security of enemy's goods plainly enough provided for. Sure I am that it was provided for in the treaty of Breda'.* [114] Ralph's own preserved letters to Danby from France do not start until January 8 when he wrote to add his thanks to his father's for royal permission to deforest Geddington Wood (i.e. cut down and sell the timber, and then plough the land for agricultural use) which Lord Montagu stated *'would bee a greate conveynyance and pleasure to my seat'*. Ralph

---

[111] Cal SP Dom August 15
[112] HMC Rutland Lady Chaworth to Lord Roos September 23 1676
[113] M. Caygill & C. Date *Building the British Museum* (CUP, 1999)
[114] HMC Lindsey Mss p.18/19

goes on to tell Danby that Louis had at last consented to the Marine Treaty, so it should be possible to have it signed before Parliament meets. '*I wish it may have soe goode an influence upon them as to dispose them to doe all things that are necessary to put our master at ease in his affairs, and your Lordship more quiet and satisfaction in the great employment you are in*'. Danby replied that he was pleased at the progress and that, with Ralph's permission, he had proposed another treaty to Charles, namely the marriage of Ralph's stepdaughter to Charles FitzCharles, earl of Plymouth (the King's son by Catherine Pegge, one of his mistresses in exile). '*You may remember I then told your Excellency and I still find that the King would rather that match could bee had for my Lord Northumberland, and I perceive hee is informed that the Dutchesse of Cleaveland and your Lady are upon so good tearmes with one another that he believes the motion might perhaps now bee agreeable to your Lady, though itt have not been so formerly, and hee has commanded mee...to learne your opinion in this particular. But if yet the same difficulties remaine I find his Majestie will look upon it as a good service if your Excellency can procure itt for my Lord Plymouth [who] will shortly bee att Paris in his way for England, and I have hinted to him his obligation to your Excellency, though I have not acquainted him with the particular. I know his Lordship will need no recommendation of your Excellencies care whilst hee is att Paris*'. Clearly Lady Cleveland's lobbying Charles for her eleven year old son George carried greater clout than providing for the twenty-one year old Plymouth. (He would be married off the next year to one of Danby's three daughters, and die of dysentery in 1680 during the siege of Tangier). It is clear from the letter to Williamson just after Ralph's marriage that George's name had been in the frame for three years although many others had been put forward – at Christmas Betty's uncle was told that the duke of Somerset was being considered.[115]

Ralph's wife may have felt insulted that, only three years after her first husband had died, Charles gave his ancient title of earl of Northumberland to one of his bastards. If she did, it was impolitic to say so and Ralph's reply to Danby on March 1 demonstrates his diplomacy. '*I should not have bin soe long as I have bin without returning an answer to your Lordship's letter, but that two dayes after I had received it my wife fell extreame ill, and has not till now bin in a condition to speak of many things that must needs concern her soe much as what relates to the marriage of her daughter, my Lady Betty Percy. I shoed her your Lordship's lettar, and will tell you as neere as I can her answer, that you may give his Majesty the better an account how this affaire stands, and at the same time of doeing me the goode office of assuring his Majesty of the utmost of my*

[115] HMC Rutland ibid December 25 1676

endeavours in it, whenever it shall be a proper and seasonable time to put it on foot.

But as yet my wife sayes she does think it will be very improper and very prejudiciable to the interest she ought by nature, and though it be given from her by the rigour of the law, dos yet expect to have in the disposal of her daughter, if she should entertaine any proposition, for it is by that argument of how fitt and just it is that the child should be of yeares to choose for herself before she be engaged that she keepes my old Lady Northumberland from disposing of her as yet where she would perhaps be miserable and unhappy all her life, though I find by her letters to my wife she is extreamly set upon marrying her to my Lord Ogle, and sayes that the Duke of Newcastle has the King's leave for his pretensions, as she may easily believe by the marques of honour his Majesty has conferred on him since the death of his father. I find my wife extreame avers too this match, in which the grandmother can doe nothing these two yeares, the child being but ten yeares old; and then I believe there will be that disagreement betweene the grandmother and mother that it must naturally come before the King and Councell, and then it will be the time of serving his Majesty, for I will make noe doubt but that the daughter will declare for marrying wher the mother pleases and not where the grandmother desires, which she has alwaise bin soe positive in, though she is soe young, that whenever she is with her mother, though her grandmother be present, she declares she will never marry but where her mother will have her. As for what you please to take notice in your letter concerning my wife and my Lady Dutchess of Cleavland being upon goode terms, it is that which was not heretofore, for they now visit pretty often; but my Lady Dutchesse has never named yet this matter either to my wife or me. I confesse her uncle, Mr. Ned Villars, did to me, and rejoiced soe extreamly at theire visiting one another that I think but for me he would have had the discretion to have proposed the match upon their second meeting; and I find by him that all the family doe reckon that the King has engaged himself to my Lady Dutchess of Cleavland to doe all he can to procure this match for my Lord Northumberland, whoe himself is already cunning enough to be enquiring of me after my Lady Betty Percy, and has taken such an aversion to my Lord Ogle about the report, that when they meet at my house he is alwaise ready to laugh or make mouthes at him, soe that the gouvernour now will never scarce let them meet'.

Ralph's wife had something else to occupy her mind: '*I am glad to be confirmed that my Lady Northumberland is breeding. Its said, when she went to wait upon the Queen of France, never such a concourse of people was seen upon such an occasion as then [came] to view her*' (William Montagu, February 22). The correspondence between Ambassador Montagu and his master Danby deals with business henceforward. On 24

February 1677 Ralph and de Pomponne had concluded the Marine Treaty. This left Ralph free to plan other measures. On April 4 he encloses a letter which *'if your Lordship thinks it proper after you have reade it you may shoe to the King or burn it, and be pleased to doe me that justice as to interpret aright my intentions in it, not to set up for a politician but to play into your hands a businesse of soe much advantage as this may be to the King, and which I am sure without complement you will manage better than anyone els'.* Ralph then sets out an idea which he must have known that Charles would find very attractive. The towns Louis has taken in Flanders *'he owes them more to our master than to his owne army that takes them, for there is not one of these townes which you see soe easily taken that if they were encouraged by a declaration of the King for them would not hold out long enough to ruine the best army in Fraunce before they yielded. I am sure there is not a man in Fraunce, except those French ministers that know the contrary, that doe not conclude that our master for his newtrality has every year subsidies to the valew of at least three or foure millions…I was the other day discoursing something of this kind with Monsieur le Tellier, and I demonstrated to him that Cambray, Valenciennes and St. Omers tooke away nine millions of livers from the Spanyards and gave it to the French, which he allowed to be true; and I will be answerable you will find it as true that whenever our master shall think fitt to insist upon it he may have from the French money or moneys worth to put him considerably at ease in his owne affaires'.* Having floated the concept of taking French money to aid Charles's desired freedom of parliaments, Ralph then promotes another in respect of the peace negotiations between the French and Dutch that had commenced at Nijmegen the previous year. *'It is my part, my Lord, to tell you what may be; but for the advising part I submit it to those of a better understanding than myself. Only one thing I hope you will not think me impertinent for giving my opinion in. I am sure your Lordship is informed of the difficulties were made at Nimeguen of giving our master the title of mediatour, which I think was very disrespectfull to soe greate a king, and in it his Majesty knows the French ministers did not behave themselfes so well as might have bin expected from them. I would therefore end that dispute of being stiled the mediatour, if I were in his Majesty's place, recall all my plenipotentiaries from Nimeguen, and make all the parties concerned send their ambassadours and treate at London, or els fight dogg fight beare.*

The King will by this, if the treaty [negotiations], *as it may doe, last two yeares, save at least fifty thousand that his ambassadours and ministers cost him there, and draw a greate deale of wealth into his owne kingdom, by the expence of soe many forreigne ministers as must attend the treaty at London. I am sure the French will hope to have an advantage by it by the partiality they think the King has for them, and the Confederates will be fooles enough to think they shall find theirs by the partiality of the people'*. The rest of the letter praises Charles's knowledge of foreign affairs which would enable him to make an advantageous peace on the spot, and ends with the postscript *'I beseech your Lordship not to let this be seene at the Committee of Forreigne Affaires'* which wouldn't welcome Ralph's meddling.

Danby didn't burn the letter but it is likely he didn't show it to the King. At exactly this time he wrote memoranda in which he told Charles that the reason for the government's recent success in Parliament was because he had convinced it of the King's commitment to Protestantism and determination to withstand France. Fear of French aggrandisement had reached such a pitch that only an open declaration of opposition would calm the situation and open the Commons' purse-strings. It would help in negotiating desired commercial concessions from Spain and Holland, which would also go down well in the Commons. That body would then vote the money to raise an army and strengthen the fleet, and this would help the King to be more independent of Parliament. At worst he could then ask for more money, including sufficient revenue for the future, if that body insisted on the army being disbanded later on. This seemed to be the only practicable way of ensuring Charles could cease to *'depend rather on his subjects than they upon him'*.[116] Danby's arguments are weak but the nation's interests and Charles personal ones were at such variance he had to use what he could. He made no real attempt to suggest that the two interests should be identical, and regarded Parliament as a third interest that couldn't be identified with either. Charles was prepared to go along with this but wanted to see the colour of Parliament's money and on April 11 sent a message to the Commons saying that he needed supply to make war preparations. The problem was that he wasn't trusted to use the money for that purpose. There was fear of a "pickpocket war".[117]

On June 21 1677 Ralph wrote directly to Charles. He reminded him of his royal annoyance at the intemperate reaction of Ruvigny, the French ambassador, to the news of England's separate peace with Holland: *'att an intertainment made for you by my Lord Lindsay att Chelsey you were pleased to call mee to you and command mee because of my friendship and acquaintance with him to advise him to change his language and behaviour'*. Ralph did so, adding that the French were lucky Charles hadn't chosen to join the confederates (in alliance against France). *'When I delivered him your Majesties message I found him extreamly surprised and frighted, which I improved on as much as I could. All hee had to say to*

---

[116] A. Browning, *Thomas Osborne, Earl of Danby & Duke of Leeds 1632-1712* (Glasgow 1951)
[117] HMC Essex Papers, ii.110

mee was that after such great sums of money as his master had paid into England itt was hard to bee left so. I told him, that as for the sumes of money, they were not so great as to regret the payment of them; that to my knowledge the Crowne of France paid to the Crowne of Sweden two millions and an halfe to be neuters…and that your Majestie, who was so great and so powerful a king, had but three millions of livers for so vast a fleet as you putt to sea, and for some ten thousand of your subjects that you lett passe over into the French service'. Ralph told the King briefly of his words with Ruvigny but when, in accordance with royal command, he informed Arlington in more detail and added that he was sure that if the ambassador was 'well managed' the three million Charles had from the French during the war he could continue to be paid to be neutral, Arlington 'answered mee that I was out of play and no longer ambassador, and that you would not take itt well, he was sure, my medling any more in businesse'.

Ralph had clearly felt aggrieved at this slap down for acting, as he saw it, in the King's best interests. So when a few days later Ruvigny came back to him he felt justified in undermining Arlington. Ruvigny said that all Charles's ministers were turning against France, Arlington in particular, and he needed Ralph's advice on what he should do to keep Charles on-side. 'Whereupon I told him my Lord Arlington (as hee was pleased to say to me) was going out of play, that my Lord Treasurer was the man you now trusted, and in my opinion (if your Majestie would accept of itt) the best way was to offer the continuation of the three millions during the war for your neutrality, car dans ce monde on ne fait rien pour rien'. (In this world no-one does anything for nothing). Three months later Ruvigny thanked Ralph for his good advice and said his royal master was obliged to him, leading Ralph to think that he had done Charles a good service in getting him so much money. However he had discovered that he was deluded when he came back to Paris as ambassador and started chatting again with Ruvigny, who revealed that Charles had accepted far less. As a Huguenot Protestant the man was clearly feeling sidelined. 'Ruvigny, who partly with age and partly with discontent att his ill usage att Court is the most broke that can bee…finding him alwaies complaining of his ill usage after the great and good services hee had done, I flattered his discontent as much as I could to get out of him the great services I found hee so much talked of, and att last hee confessed to mee that when I advised him to offer your Majestie the continuance of the three millions that hee proposed itt att this Court, that they consented to itt,…that he had done itt so well as to bring your Majestie to bee content with an hundred thousand pounds.'

Ralph now returns to his great idea, one that he perhaps anticipated would render Charles so grateful to him for bringing about that the King couldn't help but reward him with at least the earldom he wanted for his father. '*I am sure the greatnesse of the King of France is supported only by your Majesties connivance att what hee does and the good will Christendome sees you have for him. The advantages he has by itt, even in the point of revenue by his conquests, do amount to five times the summe you now have from him, and though after-games are hard to play I thinke I understand this Court so well, and if you care to have itt done I am confident I could get you by agreement a million of livers a year to bee paid whilst the war shall last, and foure millions six months after the peace shall be made. I meane, Sir, over and above what you have from France now, and if you approve of my proposition bee pleased to write me five or six lines with your commands and directions, and I doubt not but to give you a good account of itt.*

Since I do not know which of your ministers you are most willing to trust, I have taken the boldnesse to give yourself this trouble, and if you trust any I had rather itt were my Lord Treasurer, because I think hee is the best judge of such an affaire; and except you shall thinke itt for your service that hee sees this letter, I humbly beg my sister may see itt burnt, because Monsieur de Ruvigny is concerned in itt, whose utter ruine the story I have told you might bee, and your Majestie is so wise and just that I in no manner doubt of your secrecy. I have prepared everything for the execution of your commands in this matter, and if you lay it upon mee it must be soone, for the conjecture makes a great deale, which towards the winter may not bee so favourable. Your Majestie will excuse this trouble from the zeale I have for your service'.

Charles did indeed think it fit that Danby should see the letter, and the Lord Treasurer drafted a reply just over a fortnight later telling Ralph that he had royal permission to proceed, but only on condition that he can secure both payments (the annual one during the war, and the single one six months after the peace). Metzger states that the reason Ralph put Danby's name in the frame was so that, if any of this came to the notice of the Commons, it would be Danby who would suffer the consequences. This statement employs the benefit of hindsight. Ralph's name was on the letter proposing that he negotiate a bribe from the French to keep Charles, and therefore the nation, on their side when the nation was generally anti-French. He was as likely, if not more so, to suffer any consequences. It is more likely that Ralph wanted to ensure that if the King chose not to tell Danby, but he later heard of it, Ralph couldn't be blamed for the secrecy.

Danby was under no illusion that '*the very receiving money from them (were itt known here) would bee highly prejudiciall to him,* [the King] *because itt would presently bee construed a bribe to keepe off the meeting of Parliament*'. He didn't believe the French promises of money would be kept but, in case they were, Mr. Chiffinch had been appointed to receive the cash. (William Chiffinch was an unofficial secretary to Charles, whose rooms on the backstairs of the palace adjoined the King's bedroom. This allowed those who Charles wanted to entertain there some anonymity. He had been the receiver of the "small treasure" that the French had previously paid, and over fifty payments of English secret service money passed through his hands during Charles's and James's reigns). *'I am very glad of itt, being truly desirous to have as little to do with them in any kind as I can, unlesse itt were to cudgel them out of that contempt they have not only for our nation but the very person of the King, although hee bee so unhappy as not to believe it'*. Danby then mentions that he had passed on Ralph's suggestion (of which he approved) that the Nijmegen negotiations be moved to London, but that the King said he had agreed to the location so couldn't now change his mind. The French were negotiating a separate treaty of commerce with the Dutch at Nijmegen, but denying it to Ralph in Paris. What Ralph didn't know was that while Danby and Temple were courting William of Orange, Charles had people in Nijmegen courting Louis. *'The King would heare from you about the money matter as soon as you possibly can."* [*"Tis fitt you should know Monsieur Courtin hath made an offer to give his Majestie 600,000 crowns to bee paid betwixt this time and Christmas next'*. This sentence was struck out by Danby]. *'The Parliament mett this day and is adjourned to the 3rd of December next'*. The King was so keen to hear about the money that he wrote separately to Ralph on July 18: *'I have directed my lord Treasurer to tell you my minde in answer to your letter, and would have you follow those directions, so as I have nothing more to add but to thanke you for the industry with which you serve me in the station where you are, and to assure you that I will always be your assured friend'*.

It wasn't until August 7 1677 that Ralph wrote again. *'I could not dispatch this messenger sooner, because that Monsieur de Pomponne desired me to retain him till he had an answer from Monsieur Courtin, from whome he did hope to hear that the King our master would be satisyfed with the 600,000 crowns'*. But since that answer hadn't arrived Ralph had given it on Charles's behalf, telling the French Secretary of State for Foreign Affairs *'that it would be impossible for the King my master to subsist and support his government with a lesse summe then 200,000 pound sterling whilst the war shall last, and to commence from the first of August, which was the day I proposed it. And for the reasons your Lordship was pleased to give me I have insisted with his Christian Majesty for the payment...during the war rather than any summe six months after the peace, considering how hard it is to secure it, and of what greater advantage the encrease of the summe at present will be to our masters affaires'*.

Five days later Ralph wrote to say that he had been at Versailles for two days waiting for Louis to give consent to the payment, *'taking it for granted that Monsieur Courtins answer must be come back'* that Charles backed the proposal. *'But Monsieur de Pomponne tells me this morning that Monsieur Courtin has agreede this matter with the King my master and in your Lordship's presence, and that his Majesty will be contented with two millions of livres a year only during the war, which I confesse surprised me extreamly, considering the necessity of his Majesty's condition and the positivenesse of his commands to me by your Lordship to insist upon 200,000 pounds sterling, which I had done very effectually and must have succeeded in, considering the reasonablenesse of the demand, except the generosity of the King our masters nature, who values money so little'.* Ralph must have been piqued that, after all his efforts, Charles and Danby had again gone behind his back and agreed to accept less, not least because he might well have thought that this would undermine him in the eyes of the French court – it showed that either he wasn't trusted by his masters or was kept insufficiently informed. Charles valued money greatly of course, especially if he could get it from a source other than Parliament. He may have considered, (given his own practise), that the greater the royal promise, the greater the gap between it and delivery. And as Ralph later pointed out (on August 30), by agreeing a sum in French currency rather than sterling, £12,000 would be lost through exchange. Worse still for Ralph is that he had used the same method of lobbying as he had during his previous embassy to enable Charles being released from a clause committing him to raise and maintain troops for French service *'which I very luckeleye did, saving his Majesty, besides the other inconveniencys, above a hundred thousand pound a year for a present of 2,000 pistoles'.* In other words he had again bribed the Secretary for War's mistress with an amount proportionate to the large sum he hoped to extract from the French for Charles. This letter was intended for Danby to show to the King, as is apparent by an accompanying letter of the same date. It congratulates the Lord Treasurer for having made Chiffinch the receiver of the French monies: *'That office can never doe you any goode, and may doe you hurt. You may be confident of my secrecye about this whole affaire, both for the Kings, your Lordships, and my owne sake, for it would be no popular nor creditable thing if it were known'.* Danby replied that he knew nothing of Charles's acceptance of a lesser sum, despite what Ralph had heard.

Having now fully realised that the Lord Treasurer wasn't involved in the change of plan, Ralph wrote to him on August 30 outlining his activities. Through the bribe he had elicited the information that the dukes of Bavaria and of Hanover had also been receiving cash from Louis, and that though both were of less importance than Charles, the former at least was receiving as much as Ralph was asking for. The same informant also told Ralph that the French conquests would bring six million livres in annual revenue. Ralph still hopes that he can use this information to negotiate for the larger sum. '*Pray, my Lord, let me have your directions at large and as soone as you can, for I doe tell you very frankly, and I hope the King will pardon me since it is out of zeale for his service, that if he has not 200,000 pound sterling it is his owne fault, and if he has condescended to two millions I can, I am confident, bring on my first proposition of foure millions after the peace...I goe to-morrow to Fountainbleau, and leave directions behind that any commands of yours may be brought to me'.* Danby replied on September 3 that he had been able to talk to the King after his return from Plymouth and reported that Charles and the duke of York hadn't realised that the sum they had agreed upon with the French ambassador was half what Danby said the King would need. (In other words either the King hadn't sufficiently thought the matter through before agreeing to something in the absence of his chief minister, or he was being economical with the truth). The King wasn't willing to approach the matter again with the French ambassador but commanded Ralph to insist on the original sum. Since ambassador Courtin was about to return to France, confident in his agreement with Charles, '*you are to expect that difficulty and contend with itt as well as you can*'.

On September 22 Ralph left Paris for Fontainebleau to try to accomplish a task which Charles had made even harder. He took advantage of Monmouth's return to England from the French Court three days later to send a letter with him to the King his father. Ralph had pointed out to Louis that, whilst he professed himself to always be available for a quiet word, he nonetheless insisted that beforehand the relevant minister be apprised of it. This was because in the past '*he had given his word in things which, when he afterwards weighed and advised with his ministers, he could not without greate incoveniency keepe. This I told him was your Majesty's case, for if Monsieur Courtin had consulted with my Lord Treasurer, without whome noe king in the world can tell what money is necessary to support his affaires, these mistakes would not have happened, and you would not soe easilye have condescended to what proves soe inconvenient to you, your Majesty not then considering the breach that may happen with Spayne, the fall of your Customes by the merchants not daring to venture to trade, and the encrease of your expence by your being obliged perhaps to give them convoies; that it was alsoe partly my fault by keeping the courier you sent me here with positive orders to insist upon 200,000 pound sterling, which I did, but ought not to have done, though the King here desired it, for it exposed your Majesty, whoe is of soe generous nature as not to love the discourse or dispute of money matters, to the solicitation of Monsieur Courtin whoe, as all goode servants are, must spare their masters purse as much as they can...All these things considered I hoped he would supply you with the summe first insisted on'*. Neither Louis nor his ministers were able to gainsay Ralph's argument but requested he wait for a reply until after Courtin had arrived and reported. He warned Charles that the opportunity would probably be taken by the new ambassador to get the King to confirm that he really was happy with the lower sum, and that it was only Ralph that was aiming for more.

Ralph sent a letter of the same date, and with much the same content, to Danby but added '*And besides which I would have you doe that which none if the Kings ministers have yet had the adresse to doe, which is to take an ascendant over France, which... you say you have a mind to doe, which is to cudgel them into a better behaviour and more respect to our master. And this is the time of doeing it, for by this we shall judg of our strength, which as yet we are ignorant of...I had forgot to tell you that I find heere Monsieur Courtin negociated this matter of contenting the King with two millions privately at Mr. Chiffings his lodging, and I conclude without your participation, for Monsieur de Pomponne, in the heate he was to convince me the affaire was concluded, shoed me Monsieur Courtins letter, where he sayes as much, but was sorry after he had shoed it; soe that by this you may see how they endeavour to surprise the King'.*

The time taken for letters to get to and from London and Paris meant that it wasn't until October 12 that Ralph could give Charles news of progress: '*the business is brought to this that yesterday, after I had had a long audience and discourse about the matter, I was desired to stay for my answer till after Councell, and then Monsieur Pompone brought me word, Monsieur de Barillon, finira l'affaire avec le Grand Tresorier en Angleterre, soe that you may reckon upon it as done, for I alwaise told you, Sir, that my pressing heere would be looked upon as a superofficious zeale to doe you a goode service, except I had the assistance of one whome you trust soe much in your affaires as you doe my Lord Treasurer, and whose office as well as his ability puts him in a capacity of representing to Monsieur de Barillon, as I have done heere, the reasonablenesse and indispensable necessity of such a supplye. I have fixed the payments according to the instructions of my Lord Treasurer, which you order me to follow, to begin from this Michelmas after the rate of 200,000 pound sterling, and to continue till the peace be made'.* When Danby later published the Montagu correspondence he suppressed this passage (amongst others) which clearly shows that, whilst the French subsidy may not have been his preferred policy, he played a full part in it. Again, Ralph has been accused of ensuring that Danby was fully implicated in case anything went wrong. But whilst there may have been an element of insurance on Ralph's part the deal could not have been struck without Danby's cooperation. Ralph's letter continues: '*I have not bin mealy-mouthed in this occasion, and have told them plainly that your Majesty understands very well the advantage the Crowne of France must receive by this war, both of encrease of power and revenew, and that it was not reasonable, if you did not get your share, you should be a loser'*. Danby then suppressed: *'Monsieur de Pompone desired to know of me whether, in case his master should agree to pay from Michaelmas next till a peace be concluded the summe of 200,000 pound, you would not promise to have the meeting of your Parliament deferred till then also'*. Ralph closes by asking leave to come to England for a fortnight, both so that he can communicate other things in person and because of *'some little domestique affaires of my owne which are in disorder by the death of a servant that manageth all my wife's estate'*.

There also survives a rare (if short) letter from Ralph to a relative, his *'deare cozen'* Charles Bertie, who he says he will seek out before anyone else when he gets to London. Danby and Ralph's 'cozenage' with Bertie was through the 1st Lord Montagu, Bertie's great-grandfather, but Bertie was more closely related to Danby through the latter's marriage to Bertie's sister. As a consequence, when Danby had been appointed as Lord High Treasurer in 1673, he made his brother-in-law Secretary to the Treasury. Ralph's desire to see him is likely to be less out of affection, (even if he does sign off as *'Your most obedient faithfull servant and kinsman'*), than to seek repayment of the bribe he had paid to du Louvois's mistress amongst other debts.

The exact dates for Ralph's visit to London are unclear (Hatton wrote on October 23 that he was expected) but since his last letter to Danby from Paris was on November 3 he would have missed the great rejoicing in England over the marriage next day of the twenty-seven year old Prince William of Orange to Charles's niece, the fifteen year old Princess Mary. The King may have thought that this match would give him greater influence over his nephew, particularly with regard to a settlement with France, whilst the marriage of the second in line to the throne to the Dutch Protestant prince would mitigate the deleterious effect of her father's marriage to a Catholic. Louis saw it differently, reputedly taking the news *'as he would have done to the loss of an army'*.[118] Certainly Ralph was in London on November 14 when Sir Robert Southwell wrote to the duke of Ormond that *'The Lord Feversham is gone for France, Mr. Montagu having prayed to be excused for some little time'*. The same correspondence tells us that he was back in Paris on December 22nd.[119] He may have wished to stay in London until after the new French ambassador made his public entry. Having experienced so many problems with regard to his own public entry in Paris he would have relished ambassador Barrillon's quandry: *'On Thursday last Monsieur Barrillon made his*

---

[118] O. Airy vol.I p.132
[119] HMC Letters of Sir Robert Southwell to 1st Duke of Ormonde

public entry, and being advertised the night before that what had been lately practised at Paris in giving precedency of the coaches belonging to the princes of the blood to those of our two late ambassadors ... the like rule was now intended by His Majesty, who appointed the coaches of the Duke and of the Prince, to follow next immediately after his own. This message put the ambassador to his wits end. He would have an entry without it, and would have no entry with it; and in this contention and uncertainty he remained even until the next morning. What was affirmed therein ...could not appease him, till he understood that His Majesty was firm in the matter' (December 4 1677). [120]

Since there is a lengthy set of instructions issued in the King's name to Ralph on 4 December 1677 [121] it is quite likely that he took these back to Paris with him. These were to be followed in promoting the peace treaty negotiations. *'That we had press'd the Prince of Orange to the utmost in order to his agreement to a Peace...That without Valancionns, Tournay, Conde, as well as Charleroy, Roth, Cortreeth and Oudenard, the Prince doth not conceive Flanders can be in any possibility of defence, and is therefore sure the States can never go lower then that...That we desired to know the Most Christian Kings mind upon these terms by Lord Feversham, but he hath brought us back no answer in general. That the Propositions are no way receiveable, which doth very much suprize us, when we consider how nakedly we by him stated the case to his Most Christian Majesty'*.

Williamson wrote to the ambassador in the Hague the same day: *'His Majesty has commanded Mr Montagu forthwith to return to Paris and with utmost instance to press France anew to accept of the Propositions sent by the Earl of Feversham'*. In the next surviving letter to Danby, from the court at St. Germain on December 27, Ralph reports that he has *'lost soe much time by being stopped at Dover by contrary winds that I was forced to come away post as soon as I landed'*. This short missive was probably to explain why he had not brought Danby's son and heir Lord Dunblane with him (he would arrive in Paris next day). Metzger suggests that he was sent to keep an eye on Montagu for his father. Perhaps, but it was doubtless also so that the young man could enjoy Paris at a time when he would be shown great respect at the French court, obtain some French finesse and learn lessons in diplomacy. In a letter from Ralph to Dunblane's father of 29 December the ambassador promised Danby that once the holidays were over he will *'put him into the best methode I can of learning all there is to be learnt heere'* and suggested that enrolment in an academy would perfect his knowledge of the French language and get him out of English company. In the event Dunblane had little time to spy or

---

[120] Ibid.
[121] BL Add Mss 25119 f.3

learn – his father instructed that he should be at Calais in mid January to meet the yacht sent to carry him home, and Ralph was asked to help him on his way. *'I am afraid hee will be willing to loiter if hee can'*. Ralph responded: *'I am sorry your Lordship will have my lord Dunblane come away soe soone, but I can say nothing against the reason you doe it for, not to have his Majesty loose a vote in Parliament. But a yeare heere would doe him the most goode in the world, for I never knew a more ingenious young man, or one that is better inclined to all things that should make an honest homme'*.

These were diversions from the serious business at hand. Ralph went to St. Germain to try to persuade Louis to accept the terms of the peace treaty as outlined in his instructions. He first met with de Pomponne, the foreign minister, who said that he hoped that the Prince of Orange would, in light of the honour shown to him in being permitted to marry the King's niece, be prevailed upon to *'recede from such high terms as are proposed'*. Next was du Louvois, the war minister, who started off by asking Ralph "Monsieur, have you brought us good news?" Ralph replied that he had none other than that which Lord Durras had already brought. After the usual compliments *'He presently fell upon the suddaine calling of the Parlament, and saide that was the greatest signe that could be of your Majesty's intending to declare against them; told mee that for Valenciennes, Conde and Tourney, he knew the King his master would make warr a hundred years rather than part with them; if he lost them by war there was no dishonour in it, but if he should give them up without defending them his people would reproach him'*. Ralph replied that it would be a greater blemish to Louis's honour if he refused to accept Charles's arbitration, particularly since he had given his word to do so when persuading Charles to accept the French "progress" into Flanders. French concern was further shown when du Louvois suggested that *'if the calling of the Parlament soe soone was an effect of your Majesty's great want of money, there was noe summe you could desire that he did not believe his master, even to the engaging of his jewells, which are to soe vast a value, would not furnish you with, provided you would not let the Parlament draw you into a war against France, that if you could stop theire mouths would procure a generall truce for a yeare, and in that time manage the Prince of Orenge soe as to not insist upon these three places for which your majesty should be paide for as much as if those places were yours and you sold them...such a summe of money as this would be hard to returne, but it should be put into wedges of gold, and soe put into bales of silk and sent over in a yacht; and as for my Lord Treasurer, whome they looked upon as a greate adviser in this affaire, if I would but doe them the kindnesse heere as to sound him, there is noething they would not give him to make his fortune; it should be given him in diamonds and pearles, that noebody could ever know it, and I myself should not be forgot if I would propose it to him'.* Ralph replied that Danby would not be bribed away from his master's interest, and that currently lay in the peace treaty and Louis restoring the three towns, which would content Parliament. The war minister responded, since he couldn't induce Ralph to make a proposal to Charles, ambassador Barillon would be told to do so. The next day (December 29) Ralph had an audience privately with the King himself, who called for a map and showed the consequences if he gave the towns up, which he would not do, though a breach with his cousin Charles was the thing he feared most in the world. Ralph's analysis of Louis's attitude was that if there was to be war with England, in the first year little could be achieved and after that Parliament would be weary of it. Ralph had tried to disabuse him and suggested to Charles that he should propose a year's truce to William of Orange whilst he took stock of the views of Spain, Holland and Parliament *'and you shall hearken to any propositions of money made to you by the French, I humbly advise it may be with all the secrecy imaginable, and that whatever summe you shall insist upon you would let my Lord Treasurer manage with Monsieur de Barillon in England and by me with the King heere. When I know your mind, I know soe much of theirs that I am sure I shall make a better bargain then you can for yourself'.*

The news Ralph now sent to London was not good. 29 December 1677: *'His Majesty has this night declared Dr. Sancroft Archbishop of Canterbury, and just now is arrived an express from Mr. Montagu signifying that the King of France does on Monday next march at the head of his troops towards Flanders, and that he declared his resolution for keeping his Court at Brussels, so that now no man doubts but that we must enter into a speedy war'.* [122] Negotiations began over the truce while Louis continued to prepare his army. Ralph wrote again to the King, on January 5 1678, to tell him that in light of this he had requested an audience with Louis at St. Germain so that he could express *'what ill consequence it would be to your Majesty's affairs in England, just upon the meeting of your Parlament, the noyse of his attempting anything that should tend to any farther conquest in Flanders'.* Louis offered to hold off for five days and Ralph countered by asking for a month. Finally Louis agreed to wait until he had heard from his royal cousin. Ralph believed that once Louis started the campaign Ghent, Mons and Ypres would fall with three weeks, and that whilst the ministers of finance and foreign affairs were for peace, and Louis not averse, the minister for war (unsurprisingly) wished to press on. Charles asked for a two month respite during which he could consult with Vienna and Madrid. Ralph wrote to Charles again, on January 10, to say that he had talked with Louis after a council meeting and the French

---

[122] HMC Ormonde letters p.391

King had only accepted, if Parliament was put off until the end of February, to hand back any towns he would capture if a truce was agreed. Ralph had responded that the Spanish were unlikely to consent to a year's truce when their best towns were lost at the beginning and that if Louis had to give them back he would have expended men and money to no purpose. *'This would appeare a practise soe contrary to his conduct that did not use to doe things to no purpose, that the world would thinke their was some misterye at the bottom they could not dive into'.* Perhaps Ralph was implying that Louis's promise would not be believed. He also suggests that if there was a truce and then a war, which led to worse peace terms for France than they currently had, du Louvois would lay the blame on Colbert *'and disgrace him by it'.* The people Ralph had talked to be believed that Charles only insisted on the restitution of Tournai *'out of a kindnesse to your nephew the Prince of Orenge'.* But if he didn't insist, the proposed marriage of the Dauphin was not so advanced that he could not instead be married to Charles's niece (Madame's daughter) and so make her Queen of France one day.[123]

Ralph sent an accompanying letter to Danby in which his language is blunter. *'Your Lordship will see by the King's letter the ridiculous proposition that is made of putting off the Parliament, and the restoreing any places that shall be taken in Flanders before ratification of the suspension of armes shall be delivered. I cannot imagine from whence this resolution should arise, except it be from the opinion they have in this Court (and indeed till now they have had reason enough for it) that they aught to have us do what they please, and never do anything wee desire. Besides I am confident some of the discontented Parliament men have been intrigueing with the French ambassador; for I saw a letter of his to Monsieur Courtin...where he says...that the King cannot do what he will with his Parliament...I wish your Lordship would let me know freely the Kings intentions as to a war or a peace; for if it were to a war, I might perhaps doe him a service I dare not venture to name by a letter, and if to a peace, give you some termes that would be very advantageous'.* Further evidence of Louis's approaches to MPs as well as to Charles came in a letter next day informing Danby of *'the reasons of Monsieur de Ruvignys sonnes journy into England, whoe will be there perhaps as soone as this lettar. If his fathers age would have permitted it, I believe they would have sent him...and the particular freindship which father and sonne have with Mr. William Russell, he is to be introduced into a greate commerce with the malcontented members of Parliament, and insinuate what they shall thinke fitt to crosse your measures at Court, if they shall proove disagreeable to them heere, whilst Monsieur de Barillon goes on in his*

---

[123] An interesting concept – that the value of a town and its people could be equated with an advantageous marriage. Since the Dauphin died before his wife she did not become queen.

smooth civill way...They are heere in greate paine till it be knowne what will become of the Parliament, and doe not stick to say. If that be put off for a moneth, they doubt not of a peace'. Ralph clearly did not feel bound by kinship to protect his brother-in-law Russell's reputation. One easily forgets, when reading this flow of letters, the problems there could be in delivery. Ralph's letter sent to Danby from Paris on Wednesday, January 12 1678 (unusually marked with the time: ten at night) finishes: '*I have now two couriers at London that attend to bring me any commands that require haste'.* But the Channel had to be crossed and, as we have seen from Ralph's personal experiences, weather could intervene. His next letter of January 18: '*I heard just now from Calais that two expresses that I sent were both yet there, and could not passe for the contrary winds, which I am extreamly troubled at because of the consequence it is to his Majestys affaires to have bin sooner acquainted with theire resolutions heere'.* Ralph goes on to say that he has twice conversed with a close friend of Colbert's, who believed Charles should benefit from Louis's gains in the war but that de Louvois opposed him. The French ambassador wasn't to be trusted since he was a "creature" of the war minister.

Ralph had also taken the somewhat unusual step of negotiating the recruitment of a French general into Charles's service. Knowing '*how unprovided we are of goode officers in England in case we should have a war, I thought I could not doe his Majesty a better service then to engage some of the best they have in this country to come and serve him, and I have engaged one of the best they have, whoe is willing to leave Fraunce and end his dayes in our masters service, and I believe will bring with him severall goode officers...The king will guess whoe I meane but I will name noebody'.* This person expected the same rank and rewards as he presently enjoyed: £4,000 a year, a dukedom for his life, an earldom for his eldest son and, after his death, £1,000 per annum for that son and £500 for his youngest. No-one was to know of the deal, not even the duke of York. Danby's annotation shows that the reference was to the Friederich Schomberg, a career soldier who, though German, had become a French subject and a marshal. He may already have felt that his talents (demonstrated in the victories he had won for Louis in Spain) were being overlooked because he was Protestant. Nothing came of Ralph's attempts at recruitment.[124] Danby had responded to Ralph's letters stating that he couldn't see how, if Louis set out for Flanders, war could be avoided, and that Charles was angry with his royal cousin at his precipitate action (January 9). That anger had been heated by the payment of only £18,000 of the £50,000 due to Charles from the French in December, even though the

---

[124] Ultimately he would join William of Orange in 1688, receive the title of duke of Schomberg K.G., and be killed at the Battle of the Boyne.

French ambassador had admitted to having the money in his possession. He followed this with one on the 14th: '*Upon that part of your letter to the King which speakes of money hee told mee hee should be glad of theire money, provided the Confederates might have such a peace as would satisfy them, and if things shall att any time come to that pass you need not feare but your advice of secrecy will bee taken. The management of itt will also as certainly fall to your share, both for the reasons given by yourselfe to the king, and that I shall very unwillingly enter into a matter which first I beleeve they will not performe, and if they should may perhaps do the King more hurt than good*'. Although endorsed by Danby that this letter '*shows his* [Ralph] *being the proposer of money to the King*' it was, ironically, Danby himself who would later be hurt by it. On the 17th he reported the conversation he'd had with young de Ruvigny. The latter had asked him to persuade the King to overrule the Prince of Orange and allow Louis to keep Tournai. The unlikelihood of this, and the duke of York growing daily more inclined for war, made Danby despair.

On the 26th Ralph sent an express letter to inform Danby that Louis had resolved to set out for Metz in eight days and that it was likely he would take a town or two along the way. He had that very morning told Louis any war would lie at his door. When a copy of Charles's speech to Parliament arrived Ralph had it translated into French and some copies distributed. '*I never saw a greater consternation in my life than it makes in people here...I have had with me one of Monsieur de Louvoy's intimate friends, who told me we had taken an ill way with the King of France to have the towns we asked for... My answer was that our master had trusted to fair words too long, and from hence forward would goe upon surer grounds*' (February 12 1678). Danby sent a letter the previous day to the effect that Charles was secretly asking William of Orange if he would be willing to see Louis give up another town of consequence rather than Tournai. Ralph responded that Louis had gone to Sedan (the site of a humiliating French defeat two centuries later) and feared that the weakness of Namur would mean that he wouldn't be able to resist capturing it, thus complicating matters further. Louis took Ghent instead and when the news reached the Commons on February 22 a motion to remove evil councillors (i.e. Danby) was only narrowly defeated, whilst one calling for war with France was passed. Danby had to oppose this, despite it being what he had wanted for years. He was losing the trust of both the King and the Commons. The latter hadn't voted supply for the war and by stopping the import of goods from the French enemy had also caused a great drop in customs revenues, so Charles was the more eager for French financial help.

Ralph now wrote some letters which do not quite fit with the view of some authors that he was plotting Danby's ruin. '*There came with me into England one Monsieur de la Tolade, whome I left sick of the gout. He was formerly a great acquaintance of the Duke of Buckingamm, and being in England was much with him. You know, my Lord, how freely he speakes his mind; and he told this man that he did not doubt of ruining you, and being better with the King than ever, and in order to ruine you he had consulted with his friends whether he has best make up with you or noe, and that he was advised not to...and therefore desired the King, who offered to make you friends, not to doe it...This same man tells me that young Ruvigny, by orders from the King of Fraunce, has made Monsieur Barillon strike up a league with him, that they meet often privately, and that Monsieur de Barillon is much guided by him. The Duke of Buckingamm, I find, reckons that he has the greatest part of the court with him, and ownes the having a promise of being very soone again a gentleman of the bedchamber. I have had from severall hands an overture of reconcilement; if not, I am to be one of the proscribed, and I intend to doe with him what he resolves to doe with your Lordship, that is not make up. And if I might be worthy to advise, were I in your Lordships place I would doe so to, for I am confident you will find his friendship as troublesome as his ill will can be dangerous'.* (March 12). This isn't information that he needed to share with his master. One might wonder if he was playing a double game, but we also have a letter from him of the 29th to Charles Bertie (Lady Danby's brother) on similar lines. It is worth quoting, not least because Ralph mentions the post he desires: *'soe many things come betweene the cup and the lip, especially at Court, that till things are done one must never despaire, noe more then I doe of being Secretary of State, if my Lady Danby continues her favour to me and can work of Sir William Temple. I know for certaine that there is a greate cabal to bring in Mr. Hide, and that Nelly* [Gwynn] *and the Duke of Buckingam are in it purposely that noe friend of my Lord Treasurer may be in the place. And they have engaged Mr. Secretary Coventry by Harry Savell, whoe writ a lettar last post to my Lady Cleavland, that his fortune depended on her coming over, for that he had engaged his unkle, the Secretary, for Mr. Hide, upon condition he should have Mr. Hide's place of the Robes, which he could never compasse money to buye, except she got the Kings leave for him to sell his bedchamber place, and some additionall money to help. You may let my Lord Treasurer and Lady Danby know of this, but it must be kept very secret, for els it would hinder me knowing many things that may be for theire service....For my part I care not for the place except I come in with his favour and kindnesse. I have tried no other waies to compasse it, neither will I... Pray put my Lord Treasurer and my Lady Danby in mind of me, with the assurances that they have noe servant truer to them then myself, nore more intirely, Deare Cozen...'*

So Ralph was concerned that there was a plot to get the Secretaryship he coveted for Lord Hyde, Clarendon's son, and that the duchess of Cleveland's services were being engaged to that end. Lady Danby might not have been the best person for him to rely on. *'She had certainly great defects in her brain...She was always dressed in a very odd manner...Most frequently she had fits of raving and her passions were unlimited, and I have been often witness of it, but the worst part of her was the itch she had to meddle with public affairs...I knew her to be most capable of taking whatever was offered'.* [125] Cousin Bertie sent back news and Ralph replied on April 11: *'I am glad to heare there is such a rubb in Sir William Temples way. Mr. Secretary Coventry consented to me myself the endeavoring for his place, provided he had ten thousand pound, which I will lay downe whenever the King gives me his consent to come in. But I would neither venture my money nor give myself the trouble were anybody but my Lord Treasurer in the favour and credit he is with the King. I know all men make professions to get their ends, but my Lord Treasurer has a very goode pawne for the security of my firmnesse to him, since besides the tye of kindred and honour I venture my owne money, and anybody that did that, and were at a difference with him, would have layde out his money very ill'.* [126]

A problem for Ralph was that Danby both had a long standing friendship with Temple (they had travelled on the Continent together when young) and trusted him. Additionally, Danby was close to Temple's wife, Dorothy Osborne. She was Danby's cousin and he had wooed her, but though her family thought he was the better match, she and Temple had fallen in love at the age of nineteen and held out until they were able to marry eight years later. Temple shared Danby's view that the Protestant powers should be aligned against French aggression (he had been ambassador to the Netherlands twice). So it was natural for Danby to prefer to wait until the Secretaryship could be obtained for his trusted friend rather than Ralph. The latter, of course, thought differently. Temple could have had the Secretaryship in 1674 when Arlington resigned. Ironically Ralph had even offered to loan him the money needed. Now the King was prepared to help but Temple still refused – why wouldn't Danby accept this and allow Ralph to achieve his ambition? Was it because he preferred not to advance someone who clearly had initiative, intellect and daring, and who might well in time (having entrenched himself politically as Secretary) become chief minister?

On March 25 1678 a list of the ten Flanders towns that were to be returned to Spain by France at the peace (Conde and Ypres marked *'not'*

[125] HMC 15th Report, *The Mss of the Duke of Somerset, the Marquis of Ailesbury, and the Revd. Sir T H G Puleston, Bart.* (London 1898) Ailesbury Memoirs
[126] BL Add Mss 39757 f.105

by Ralph) were sent to him by Danby, enclosed with a letter that would ultimately serve to cause the Lord Treasurer's ruin. '*That you may know from whence the nicety of this affaire proceeds, it is necessary to informe you that for feare of its being ill resented by the Parliament here the King will not make any proposal at all of peace, unlesse hee shall bee presst to itt by the Confederates....I am comanded by his Majestie to lett you know that you are to make the propositions inclosed to the King of France, and to tell him the King will undertake for the seeing of them made good on the part of Spaine and Holland in case they shall bee accepted by him. And in your answer you must write the same thing to the Secretary by way only of haveing felt the King's pulse, which you must do to the King as a full answer from the King of France, and such a one as the King may depend upon, whatever that shall bee. For the most dextrous management of this matter the King is advised to shew these proposal to Monsieur Barillon, but not to give him a coppy, so that by strength of memory itt is expected hee shall write to his master, and by that meanes only are wee to hope for an answer to a matter of this vast importance; and consequently you may imagine what a satisfaction wee are like to reape from itt when itt comes. I doubt not but that by your conduct itt will bee brought to a speedier issue, which is of as great importance as the thing ittselfe, there being no condition worse for his Majestie then his standing unresolved betwixt peace and war.*

I find by Monsieur Barillon that tis like some places, which are dependencies upon greater townes, may be demanded by the King of France; but if hee intend the peace (which you will do very well to know his mind fully in), you may justly say you hope hee will neither stand upon one single place (though a fortified on), nor upon any place unfortified which is a dependant upon those which are to be restored to Spaine. And if anything should bee mentioned about Sicily to remaine in the French hands...you are only to say you are not impowred to say anything upon itt...

In case the condition of the peace shall bee accepted, the King expects to have six millions of livers a yeare for three yeares from the time that this agreement shall bee signed betwixt his Majestie and the King of France, because itt will bee tow or three yeares before the Parliament will bee in humour to give him any supplys after the making of and peace with France, and the embassador here has alwaies agreed to that sume, but not for so long a time. If you find the peace will not bee accepted, you are not to mention the money att all, where for the most part wee hear in ten daies after of anything that is communicated to the French ministers.

I must againe repeate to you that whatever you write upon this subject to the Secretary (to whom you must not mention a syllable of the money) you must say only as a thing you believe they would consent to, if you had power formally to make those propositions. Pray informe yourself to the bottome of what is to bee expected from France, and assure them that you believe that this will bee the last time that you shall receive any propositions of a peace, if these bee rejected (as indeed I believe itt will), so that you may take your owne measures as well as the Kings upon itt'.

Ralph responded on April 9 that he had received the letter but could do nothing until the next evening at the earliest because it was Easter. He met Louis twice and spent over two hours debating the proposals with him, who after a long council meeting was particularly insistent on keeping Conde and Ypres, pointing out on a map how strategically important they were to him. Ralph replied that if Charles agreed that those towns and Ghent were retained England would feel that Louis had given up nothing, whereas the French felt that giving up any of them would be like giving up everything. De Louvois had only insisted on the retention of Conde in his discussions with Ralph. The minister and his royal master were both very inquisitive as to whether, if a peace was agreed, Charles would prorogue Parliament, and whilst Ralph had to say that he didn't know he was able to use this opportunity to remind them that they would need to pay Charles the six million for three years if there was a peace. He was also able to report that he had been told by one of the greatest men at the court that Louis might well give up Ghent and Ypres if the peace truly depended on it, but would *'chicanne as long as they could'*. Ralph finished his report to Danby by expressing his hope that the messenger made good time in its delivery since he was writing as soon as he could after leaving Louis – there was a constant concern that Barillon received news in London before Ralph's got there, and would use the time-lag to France's advantage. When Ralph next spoke with Louis *'hee grew mighty hot and passionate upon the subject of Ipres, rather like one that was angry and displeased that he was obliged to part with a thing he had a mind to keepe'.*

Parliament was recalled on 29 April in the hope that it would vote the money for the troops that Charles had been forced to raise, but the attacks on Danby were so fierce that it only sat for two weeks before being prorogued again for a month. Danby asked Ralph to find out what ships were in the major ports, particularly the naval ports of Brest and Toulon, and whether they were being readied for war (April 4). Ralph replied on May 16 that he had hired two cashiered naval officers and sent one to the ports of Normandy and Brittany, and the other to La Rochelle and the Charente. Whilst he wasn't sure if they could be trusted they would be accepted in those ports whereas an Englishman would be taken as a spy. A cessation of hostilities was agreed from 1 July to 6 August which put Parliament *'upon warme debates att this instant whither to support the army for some time longer, or to desire of the King that they may be disbanded immediately...That which was this day required by the King from the House of Commons was that they would provide some further supply for the army, the last being almost expended; and the House (which is but just risen when I had writt thus far) have in answer to that demand desired the Secretaries of State to bee informed from his Majestie whither hee would have itt in order to the war or a peace, because the proportion of theire supply must bee suitable to itt. But in their debates they have shewed all the desire imaginable to a war, although both Spaine and Holland should go out of it'* (Danby, 27 May). More worrying for the Lord Treasurer was that he had heard of *'divers private negotiations betwixt his Majestie and Monsieur Barillon which have not been communicated either to myself or any other'.* Danby later endorsed this with the words *'This was projected by French agents to bring the King into want and destroy my power, and Lady Portsmouth was in this design'.*

Only one letter is preserved for June 1678, and that from early in the month, on the 4th. Ralph may have heard that Temple wasn't as much in favour as he had been and so it could now be possible for Ralph to advance his ambition. *'When I was in England I took the liberty to propose to your Lordship my coming into Mr. Secretary Coventry's place; but finding you lay then under some obligation to Sir William Temple, I wholly submitted my pretension to your Lordships pleasure, not caring or believing it was, or is, possible to compass it without your good liking. I presume the measure Sir William Temple may have given his Majesty of late in the politicks may have a little worked off that engagement which I am sure your favour only made the King think he had to him; and without flattering your wisdom, you have shewed yourself too good a Lord Treasurer to advise the King to give ten thousand pounds for Sir William Temple, so that now his chief merit is your Lordship's great nicety of your word... Mr. Secretary Coventry is willing to resign to me, if the King will consent; and I will lay down ten thousand pounds to satisfie him, without the King's being at any charge'.* It may have been in order to further argue his case, as well as report in person, that Ralph asked leave to come over, but he was to be disappointed: *'I am extreamly ashamed that your Lordship should have given yourself the least trouble in the explaining of the reasons why at that time the King did not consent to my coming over...I should not have made use of it till I had seen this difficulty of surrendering the towns over... I am very unlucky that your Lordship's engagements to Sir William Temple are like to deprive me of your protection and assistance in my pretensions, it being at thing in which I am confident his Majesty will be so wholly directed by you in that it will be in vain for me to make the least step in it'.* But another letter to Danby of the same date (July 1) shows he was clearly imminently expecting permission to come for a few days to *'acquaint his Majesty with what I dare not doe by letters'* which may allude to what Danby wrote to Ralph that day of *'so sudden a change of all affaires betwixt us and France that I know not whither wee are not nearer a war then ever, att a time when I thought everything had been established beyond the possibility of a rupture...It was intended to have sent my Lord Sunderland...but that intention is changed for the present, and I suppose that whatever can bee done in that Court will bee more effectually done by your hand then any other'.* Ralph was seemingly still in Paris on July 5, when he followed up a lost letter to his sister with another enclosing a draft which he recommended the King used as a model for writing to his wife concerning Betty's marriage. This needed to be done before Ralph left Paris *'that shee may not think I had a hand in it'.* He thought that it would be best that his sister should see Danby and have him show it to Charles, rather than have her approach the King direct. *'Besides I am so much obligd to my Lord Treasurer that I would have him have all the share that may bee in a thing that will be so agreeable to the King; and besides my wife will like the businesse the better if my Lord Treasurer is interested in it, because she has so good an opinion if him'.* Clearly Ralph was still trying to curry royal favour by furthering the marriage of his step-daughter to one of Charles's sons, and was willing to share some of that favour with Danby.

Yet on Monday July 8, at nine at night, Ralph was in London asking for Danby's protection against the threat of being sent to the Tower of London once more.

Chapter 4
How are the Mighty Fallen 1677 - 1678

Whilst much diplomatic correspondence between Ralph and Danby survives, little evidence exists of his life in Paris. His wife Elizabeth was there with him and would have been a welcome help in running the household and entertaining when she was well. She was not always so and John Locke treated her on return from his sojourn in southern France (where the climate was good for his asthma) in June 1677. They seem to have met when he paid his first visit to France five years before.[127] He sent three letters to his friend Dr. Mapletoft (the same man that had been given care of the young Betty Percy) in November 1677. *'I have not had a more unwelcome occasion of writing to you than now'*, he said in the first, written at ten o'clock on a Saturday morning, *'believing I can scarce send you more unacceptable news than that of the illness of a person whom not only you & I, but all the world, have so great reason to esteem and admire. On Thursday night last, I was sent for to my lady ambassadress, whom I found in a fit of such violent and exquisite torment that (though she be, as you know, a person of extraordinary temper – and I have seen her even in the course of this distemper endure very great pain with a patience that seemed to feel nothing) it forced her to such cries and shrieks as you would expect from one upon the rack, to which I believe hers was of equal torment, which extended itself all over the right side of her face and mouth. When the fit came, there was, to use My Lady's expression of it, as it were a flash of fire all of a suddaine shot into all those parts, and at every one of those twitches made her shreek out, her mouth was constantly drawn on the right side towards her right eare by repeated convulsive motions...These violent fits terminated on a suddaine, and then My Lady seemed perfectly well...Speaking was apt to put her into these fits; sometime opening her mouth to take anything, or touching her gums, especially in places where she used to finde these throbbings; pressing the side of her face by lying on it were also apt to put her into these fits. These fits sometime lasted longer, sometimes shorter...at intervals between them not halfe an hower, commonly much shorter'.* They were so bad that Locke thought it must be a far worse illness than trigeminal neuralgia (which had only been first described six years before). *'I wish, with all my heart, you were here'* he wrote in his last paragraph, both to assist and so that he did not have to bear the burden of treating such an illustrious person alone. She had little success with the French physicians in Paris that summer when she had also been ill, and for eight days they had been unable to administer any relief. *'I beg your opinion, and of whoever else the ablest of*

---

[127] Locke's Travels to France 1675-1679 as related in his journals (Cambridge 1953) p.184

our physicians you shall think fit to consult with; but I wish much more for your company... I beg your pardon for writing. It is in haste and fear'.

That letter was followed by another, written in the afternoon of the same day, describing progress in the intervening hours, and by a further one written on Sunday evening reporting that Lady Northumberland was very much better. *'I believe the drawing of those two teeth, especially the last, hath injur'd some nerve, and so makes it very apt to be provoked, and draws its neighbours into consent; yet by what My Lady informed me, since the violence of her pain has been over, I have reason to suspect there is an ancienter fault in the nerves on that side'.* Every entry in Locke's diary for the first fortnight in December is about the case.[128] When she was ill she would have been able to call upon the help of her sister-in-law, Lady Betty Harvey, to run the household. (She was in Paris from late August 1677 until April the following year).[129]

Barbara, duchess of Cleveland, was also in Paris. She had moved there in March 1676 with her three sons, in order to live more economically and practise her religion more freely.[130] Her daughter Lady Sussex was also there, her conduct continuing to upset her mother who consequently sent her to a convent. In April 1678 Cleveland made a visit to London (as did Lady Harvey) apparently to see whether the earl of Sussex would have his wife back, or would prefer her to become a nun.[131] On her return to Paris in June she continued her campaign, on behalf of her son, of persuading Ralph's wife to back his marriage to her daughter. (The King himself wrote from Whitehall to her on 10 February applying for her hand for "my son George"). Rumour had it that she now hoped *'to get the King to break her son the Duke of Grafton's marriage to Lord Arlington's daughter, and then hopes to make a match between him and Lady Percy, and her son Northumberland and Miss Anne Mountagu, which double marriage they say Lady Northumberland and her husband approve'.*[132] The Arlington marriage, though economically sound, was apparently less attractive to the Duchess now that Arlington had lost his power. If rumour had become fact Ralph's daughter and step-daughter would both have been married to the King's sons.

If one judges by what Ralph wrote, he had befriended Barbara and promoted her interests. He asked her to take to London a present from Paris for Henry Sidney to whom he wrote on May 11 that he had sent *'a fine embroydered cloake by my lady Duchesse of Cleavland whome I have*

[128] H.R.Fox Bourne, *The Life of John Locke* (London 1876) vol. 1, p.383. Case notes preserved at Royal College of Physicians "Dr Locke's case of the tic douloureux in the Countess of Northumberland" Ms405

[129] Thomas Osborne, Letters of 1710; Montagu Correspondence, p. 375

[130] Cal SP Dom 1676 p.25

[131] HMC Rutland

[132] HMC Rutland 1677 Dec. 18 Lady Chaworth to her brother lord Roos

bin soe much obliged to heere, that I desire you will waite of her from me, & acknowledg all her favours & desire the continuance of them, in her good offices to his maiesty; if you have a mind to part with your jewels your mother left you, I told her of it, & believe she will give you more for it than any body; & methinks the wisest thing you can doe is to sell it'. Sidney apparently sent Ralph thanks for his gift and news, for Ralph replied that *'I am glad to hear my Lady Cleveland looked so well. I do not wonder at it – I will always lay on her side against everybody. I am a little scandalised you have been but once to see her – pray make your court oftener for my sake, for no man can be more obliged to another than I am to her on all occasions, and tell her I say so and, as my Lord Berkeley says, give her a pat from me. If you keep your word to come in June, I fancy you will come together, and I shall not be ill pleased to see the two people in the world of both sexes I love and esteem the most'.*[133] If one takes this at face value then what the Duchess was about to do to Ralph would be all the more outrageous, but another letter to Sidney that survives from June 11 gives a different slant: *'Having had some experience in my life of what jades and bitches women are, Madame Vernon whoe is come to town estant de le nombre la as Bussy sayes & she & Mrs Kerk eternally railing at me, as if I woud have hinderd the match...I desire you will have an eye upon Sr William Temple and if you learn any thing that can conduce to the great designe to let my sister know of it, for if that affaire were once done my friends woud not be the worse nor ones enemies the better for it. I thank you for your civilitie to her Grace of Cleavland who is yet a greater jade than if she were of the family of the Kerks. But sometimes it is necessary to dissemble, therefore until she be gon do as you did for reasons you shall know when we meete. Pray think of that affaire of your nephew Pelham & believe me yours. I am of opinion it is goode for me to come over. But I must be cautious not to do it but on a goode opportunity'.* One must assume that the "great design" was Ralph's ambition to be a Secretary of State.

Besides concerning herself with the future of her children in Paris, the Duchess continued her affair with the 25 year old marquis de Chatillon, a poor handsome captain in Monsieur's guard (Barbara was in her 38th year). Lady Sussex had taken advantage of her mother's London trip to move from the convent at Conflans north-west of Paris, to that of the Holy Sepulchre, Belle Chase. Here the sixteen year old was able to come and go as she pleased. Unsurprisingly she preferred to spend most of her time in her mother's vacated house (rather than in the convent) where she was much visited by Ralph and by his wife. A little while after her return to Paris the Duchess wrote to the King about their daughter that *'I was never so surprised in my whole life-time as I was at my coming hither, to find my*

---

[133] BL Add Mss 3280 f.36. Paris, May 27th 1678 to Henry Sidney

Lady Sussex gone from ... monastery where I left her, and this letter from her, which I here send you the copy of. I never in my whole life-time heard of such government of herself as she has had since I went into England. She has never been in the monastery two days together, but every day gone out with the Ambassador, and has often lain four days together at my house, and sent for her meat to the Ambassador; he being always with her till five o'clock in the morning, they two shut up together alone, and would not let my maitre d'hôtel wait, nor any of my servants, only the Ambassador's. This has made so great a noise at Paris, that she is now the whole discourse. I am so much afflicted that I can hardly write this for crying, to see a child, that I doted on as I did on her, should make me so ill a return, and join with the worst of men to ruin me'.

Bishop Burnet added his own colour: *'Montagu, that was a man of pleasure, was in a lewd intrigue with the duchess of Cleveland, who was quite cast off by the king and was then at Paris. The king had ordered him to find out an astrologer, of whom no wonder he had a good opinion, for he had long before his restoration foretold he should enter London on the 29th of May, 60. He was yet alive, and Montagu found him, and saw he was a man capable of being corrupted. So he resolved to prompt him to send the king such hints as should serve his own ends, and he was so bewitched with Cleveland, that he trusted her with this secret. But she growing jealous of a new amour, took all the ways she could think on to ruin him, reserving this astrologer for her last shift; and by it she encompassed her ends, for the king looked on this as such a piece of treachery and folly that Montagu was entirely lost upon it, and was recalled'.* Interestingly Burnet makes no mention of Lady Sussex. If she had been the "new amour" he surely would have said so.

We are fortunate to have a rare letter from Ralph's wife to her husband, sent just after he had left for London, which shows the young woman had been staying with her. *'Since I sealed up my letter, Mr. Brisbane has been here to speak with me. His business was about Lady Sussex, to let me know that (by order) he was last night to wait upon Lady Cleveland, who he found very positive about her going to Port Royal [convent] and she had the king on her side, and that he thought that...it was fit for him to persuade her to it, since if she should disobey the king it would be mightily to her prejudice, and it would be thought the advice of others. So I told him, as for disobeying the king, I thought it very unfit for her to do it, and could I pretend to advise (which I did not) I should persuade her...but since Mr. Montagu was no more here, and that the poor woman was really ill and taking physic for her health'* she might be given time to recover before re-entering a convent *'since a strange monastery, where she knew nobody, was but a melancholy place to do it in; but that I had nothing to say in it, but that as she was in my house and I did believe her innocent of all was said of you, so my house was at her service so long as she thought fit, provided she lived as she ought to do in it. Perhaps you may think me a little impertinent in troubling you with this strife, but it is now so public a thing that I thought it not amiss to let you know all that passes about it, and to receive your orders about what I shall do or say further in it. Surely there was never a more vexatious business...Pray God send we may meet quickly, Yours for ever...* ' [134] This personal letter shows her true belief in Ralph's innocence, at least so far as Lady Sussex was concerned. It can only have got into Danby's hands via Ralph, who must have hoped it would prove his innocence to the Lord Treasurer and so to the King. (Interestingly the same Mr Brisbane, a government marine agent, later gave information that *'My Lady Cleavland says that Mr. Montagu hath long designd my Lord Treasurers ruine, and would have putt her upon itt'.* Her version of events was clearly disseminated widely).[135]

King Charles may well have been sceptical about the Duchess's story that both she and her daughter had been having affairs with Ralph, but there was more poison in her letters that was personal to him. *'For he has no conscience nor honour, and has several times told me, that in his hart he despised you and yr Brother; and that for his part he wished with all his hart the Parliament wd send you both to travell, for you were a dull governable fool, and the Duke a wilful Fool. So that it was yet better to have you than him, and that you allwais chose a greater beast than yrself to govern you...And in the mean time, because I will try to get Secretary Coventry's place, when he had a mind to part with it, but not to Sir Willm Temple, because he is the Treasurer's creature, and he hates the Treasurer; and I have already employed my sister to talk with Mr. Cook, and to send him to engage Mr. Coventry not to part with it as yet, and he has assured my Lady Harvey he will not. And my Ld Treasurer's lady and Mr. Bertie are both of them desirous I shd have it. And wn I have it, I will be damn'd if I do not quickly get to be Lord Treasurer; and then you and yr children shall find such a friend as never was. And for the King, I will find a way to furnish him so easily with money for his pocket and his wenches, that he will quickly out Bab May and lead the King by the nose'.* (Baptist or "Bab" May was Groom of the Bedchamber and one of Charles's most trusted servants). Cleveland also told the King *'that he could not imagine that you ought to be so angry, or indeed be at all concerned; for that all the World knew, that now all things of Gallantry were at an end with you and I; that being so, and so publick, he did not see why you shd be offended at my Loveing any body...I promise you, that for my conduct it shall be such, as that you nor nobody shall have occasion to blame me; and I hope you will be just to what you said to me, which was at*

---

[134] A.Browning, *Thomas Osborne*
[135] Lindsey Mss p.399

my House, when you told me you had letters of mine; you said 'Madam, all that I ask of you, for your own sake is, live so for the future as to make the least noise you can, and I care not who you love'. The letter shows how, even though she now lived abroad, and Charles had a new maitresse en titre, she was so accustomed to bullying the king through self-interest that it did not occur to her that he would resist. Due to his susceptibility for strong women, he did not. News of Ralph's problems had already reached London by 2 July. Henry Savile told Lord Rochester: *'There are terrible doings at Paris betwixt my Lady Cleveland and her daughter Sussex. As I am a friend of the family, till the story be more complete, I will not venture at sending you the whole relation, but whilst the mother was in England, the daughter was debauched by our Ambassador, Mr. Montagu, who has lived with her in most open scandal, to the wonder of the French Court and the high displeasure of this, the king being very angry with the Ambassador, and his friends and enemies now struggling at Court to support or ruin him, the latter, as I think, the likeliest'.* Clearly even those who should be last to cast a stone love relating scandal, but it was a politic line on Savile's part, since he was about to be sent to Paris to reconcile the Duchess and her daughter. On the 6th Sir Robert Southwell wrote more fully to the duke of Ormond: *'tis not unlikely but this Lord may soon be planted as Ambassador in that Court, for Mr. Montagu is in some tribulation and under a cloud. My Lady Cleveland having done his errand for what has passed between him and my Lady Sussex, which makes up a loud and dangerous intrigue, sometimes of love and sometimes of jealousy. And who else is concerned and who not I cannot tell; but Mr. Montagu is expected this night, some say to fight a duel with a certain Frenchman, but he comes without leave and had been soon commanded home if he had not'.* Who was the Frenchman Ralph was to fight?

Even Mary Hatton, in a French nunnery, heard the story at the start of July 1678 and wrote to her brother: *'What I have to aquaint you withal of Paris news is our cosin Montagues being gon last Monday post towards Ingland...which they say my Lady Cleavland has intrigued, out of revenge to the ambass for being soe jealous of her for one Chevalier Chatillon as to wright it where he thought it might do her most prejudice, which she being advised of, and attributing to it the cold reception she found when she was lately in Ingland, has, as they say, accused him of not being faithfull to his master in the imployment he gave him here; too which there is anither particular that dus much aggravate her, and that is that, whilst she was in Ingland, the ambassador was every day with her daughter Sussex, which as occasioned such jealousy of all sides that, for the safety of my Lady Sussex, it is reported the ambassador advised her to a nunnery, and made choice of Belles Chase fore her, wher she is at present and will not see her mother. The Chevalier Chatillon is a person of quality, young and handsome, but no estate, and therefore pour la bigitte, si elle ne puet courrir, quell trotte'.* [136]

None of this could serve as the official reason for Ralph's disgrace, so the one given was that he had left Paris without having waited to receive the recall papers dated 3 July.[137] He arrived in London on the 13th and two days later *'His Majesty, in Council, did order Mr. Montagu's name to be struck out of the Council-books, and I think it was the only reason why the Council met, since both Houses were to sit the same afternoon. Thus the badges of honour drop away; for the Embassy of France is granted to my Lord Sunderland, and the more material things are already in the general rumour disposed of, namely, the Wardrobe to the Earl of Plymouth, and the Mastership of the Horse to the Lord Latimore – some say to the Lord Dunblane. His Majesty did, as it were casually, meet at my Lord Treasurer's with Mr. Montagu, who, beginning to enter on the story of my Lady Cleveland, His Majesty told him he knew already too much of that, and bade him declare what affair of state it was that made him quit France without leave. In which point, having nothing to answer, he was thenceforth forbidden His Majesty's presence and the Court. And he is loaded by the women to have done many heinous things – as not only without order to have proposed a match between the Dauphin and Mademoiselle, the King's niece, but to have spoken treason to the Duchess of Cleveland, and contemptuously to have acted His majesty in ridicule among the French. But where the women engage there is no bounds to wrath, and, therefore, as he himself tells the story, it is thus: That long time past my Lord Treasurer did, by the King's command, commit to his care and industry the compassing of a match between the Lord Northumberland and Lady Percy. That the Lady Cleveland was herein ordered to act her part with more complacency and visiting of his Lady, which at length improved into some sort of friendship. But his Lady being (on a visit to the Duchess) forbid admission because Monsieur Chattillean was with her, she returned in high resentment, so that he, seeing the designed marriage in danger, took on him to expostulate very roundly with the Duchess for her licentious course of life with the said Monsieur, which the whole town and country rung of, and brought disgrace to the children His Majesty had by her. The Duchess not enduring this doctrine, and from such a hand, returned all upon him with rage and contempt, and 'twas his only care to get well home. The war being thus begun, and Mr. Montagu contriving how to get some witnesses to speak for him, did so prevail with a nun who conveyed all the amorous letters between the Monsieur and her Grace that he got six of them into his hands, whereof some abounded with gross and unseemly things in the trade of love; some with disrespect to His*

---

[136] Hatton correspondence p.168
[137] Cal SP Dom May 27, 1679

Majesty, and some to a project to marry the Dauphin unto Madamoiselle. By some chink or other the duke of Orleans had a hint of this project, and to purge himself from any part therein came to remonstrate his innocence to his brother the king, who, it seems, till that time had not heard thereof...the news coming to Mr. Montagu's ears persuaded him also to a compurgation of himself. And so he went to assure his Most Christian Majesty that he was not the author of that intrigue, but had discovered it in the letters aforesaid, which His Majesty desiring to see he gave him copies, having (as he said) sent the originals into England. And this, he says, is the whole scope of this affair...And as to any foul play between him and the Lady Sussex he says that at her coming to Paris the Duchess imparted to him her condition, which was so bad in point of disease that he found out both the chirurgeon [surgeon] and the doctor that took her into cure, and that she was so sensible of his respects that she refused to take part in the following war that her mother made against him. And to prevent her mother's severity hereupon she resolved to remove into another convent, unto which removal he gave his humble assistance and that was all'.

'Yesterday the Parliament was prorogued to the first of August next, with intimation that the state of peace or war was so uncertain that his Majesty would not have the meeting of this Parliament at too great a distance.... Yesterday His Majesty spoke to the Queen to discharge Mr. Montagu of her service; she made answer that Mr. Montagu having not given her any offence it would be hard for her to punish him, but if he were criminal to His Majesty he had full power to do what he thought fit. This was all which then passed, but everybody concludes that Mr. Montagu will lose that station at least. Mr. Savile is restored to grace, having kissed the King's hand, and is departing in quality of mediator to compose matters between the Duchess of Cleveland and the Countess of Sussex'. [138]

Can support for Ralph be read into the Queen's reply? It is interesting that Cleveland made no mention of the astrologer (and Burnet none of Lady Sussex). Perhaps the Duchess saved that story as a coup de grace when she met the King in person. Ralph may well have thought that an astrological prediction that implied he should be made Secretary of State could help him achieve his frustrated ambition. The reported comments about his views of the King and duke of York have the ring of truth – views that were shared by most of his contemporaries. It is impossible to tell whether Ralph was guilty of any or all of the things that Cleveland accused him of but history shows her to have been a bitter enemy. Ralph had clearly committed a serious error of judgement by telling the King of her affair in Paris, since he should have known that she would hear of it and that he would come off worst in any exchange. Even if he feared that

---

[138] Ormonde Mss IV July 16

her behaviour would jeopardise the prospective double marriage of their children his diplomatic skills should have enabled him to handle the matter better. He must have looked back across the ruins of his career, at the King's unfulfilled promise to make his father an earl and his failed attempt to gain the Garter, at the enormous costs he had incurred as Charles's ambassador to France, his efforts to extract money from Louis so that Charles could achieve his aim and live without being dependent on Parliament, the fall of Arlington (with whom he seems to have enjoyed a warm working relationship) and the rise of Danby (with whom he did not) who he had supported (outwardly at least). If Danby had backed him in his aim to be a Secretary of State he might not have come to this pass. Nor had Danby supported him in the face of Cleveland's allegations. It now seemed unlikely he would ever achieve great office or rank. Some men would consider that it was best to accept fate, retire to one's estate and concentrate on being a power in the county. But Ralph's father was still filling that role in Northamptonshire and, in any case, that doesn't seem to have been his nature. The alternative was to live in his fine new town house and strike back, dangerous though that would be. He had decided on the latter course by late October when the French ambassador wrote to his master that he and Ralph had discussed the matter. The latter's spin was that he had earned Danby's enmity for refusing to press Louis hard on the subsidy to keep England out of the war, and that Louis himself was reluctant to help his cousin avoid Parliament. The best way to mitigate the dangers of his intended action was to become a Member of Parliament and so gain protection. Whilst Danby concerned himself with the marriage of his daughter Bridget to the earl of Portsmouth in the autumn of 1678, Ralph set about getting himself elected.

It might have expected that he would try for a constituency in the Montagu heartland of Northamptonshire but he had to go wherever a vacancy beckoned. He first tried for East Grinstead, without success.[139] But then fortuitously Lord Ilbracken, one of the M.Ps for Northampton died. His son Donogh (who happened to be Danby's son-in-law) was put forward but he was considered too young at fifteen (and his mother refused to allow him to stand).[140] So Danby decided to put up Ralph's rival for the Secretaryship Sir William Temple, who had married Donogh's mother, the widowed Lady O'Brien, earlier in the year. A contemporary report exists of the election: *'I was last week at Northampton, for not having taken the air for some time I made use of that opportunity to meet Sir Nicholas L'Estrange. I found all things in a merry posture. Mr. Montague was that day there, and it was a holiday. They were very busy about the election of a burgess, there are four that stand, my Lord O'Bryon, Sir George Norris,*

[139] BL Add Mss 28044 f.33
[140] Carte Mss. 103, f.236

Mr. Montague, and of late Sir William Temple. Mr. Montague is the only man who treateth, and they say it hath cost him £1,000 in ale, let who will believe it, but certain is, as the townsmen themselves say, both he and his father spend £100 per week, but they say to no purpose, for whomsoever the King will recommend they are resolved to choose, and there coming a letter in favour of Sir William Temple, he, it is thought, will be the man'.
141 & 142

Although Temple lost, the sheriff (doubtless under pressure) announced him the winner. Ralph had to petition the Commons against the return on November 6. The Whigs acted promptly: it was heard at the bar of the House to save time and to gain more publicity (rather than being referred to committee). On November 12 *'another part of the time was employed in examining at the bar the irregularity of returning Sir William Temple burgess for Northampton, for which the High Sheriff was laid by the heels, and Mr. Montagu presently voted in with so united a cry as made it very legible what inclinations they bear to the patron of the first, whom they reckon the adversary of the latter'.* [143] Five days later he was declared as duly elected and the sheriff was arrested for making an improper return (the mayor had signed Ralph's indenture and affixed the town's seal. Neither signature nor seal were on Temple's). The fact that Danby was unable to get his man elected was an indication of the difficulty he was having in managing the Commons. But until he was implicated in the move to arbitrary government which the opposition believed was happening he could still exert great authority in the House through bribery, patronage, adjournment and, if necessary, prorogation. Ralph was now in a position to be able to take his revenge and do more than just implicate Danby.

The political temperature had already been raised greatly by what became known as the Popish Plot. Presaged by three solar and two lunar eclipses, it was the creation of one of those singularly unpleasant characters that crop up in history who seem to have no morals or redeeming features. Titus Oates had a flat face like a dish, with snub nose and sunken eyes. Half his face was taken up with his chin. Expelled from school and a Cambridge college, he was later dismissed from a church living for incompetence and from a naval chaplaincy for sodomy. Deciding to become a Catholic, he went to the seminary in Valladolid, from which he was thrown out for lack of qualifications. In June 1678 he was expelled

---

[141] Egmont Mss vol II pp.76/7. John Percival to Sir Robert Southwell, October 17 1678,

[142] In Northamptonshire a handful of landowning families – the Spencers, Berties, Cecils, Finches, Hattons, Ishams and Montagus – excercised real political power. If they had been able to agree on the candidates for elections the freeholders of the county would never have been able to exercise their vote. The electorate of the town of Northampton grew from 60 in 1604 to around 1,000 by 1641, hence the cost to the Montagus of beer.

[143] Ormonde ibid p.471

from his teaching post at the Jesuit school in St. Omer and returned to London with a burning hatred for the Jesuits. Here he became reacquainted with Israel Tonge, a Puritan clergyman who was convinced that the Jesuits had started the Great Fire (in which his church was destroyed and so his living lost). Oates told him of a Catholic plot to kill the King and other important figures (including Tonge himself of course) and raise a false rebellion to oppose James. The French army would be brought in to crush it and restore both James and Catholicism. If two named Catholics (one a Jesuit lay brother) did not succeed in shooting Charles, the Queen's doctor would poison him. He hid a document with further details in the wainscot of a room in a nobleman's house for Tonge to discover.

On the evening of August 13 Tonge managed to get an audience with the King who, whilst disinclined to believe the story, left it to Danby to deal with whilst he went off to Windsor. Danby told Tonge he needed more facts, so Oates obligingly forged five letters addressed to the duke of York's Jesuit confessor. These were not intercepted as had been intended, but the confessor handed them over to the Duke who considered them to be part of a campaign by the Parliamentary opposition to discredit him and his fellow Catholics. He therefore insisted that the Privy Council conduct an investigation. This was a foolish move, for the air of publicity allowed the Plot to grow. Fearing that Oates would desert him, Tonge prevailed on him to swear the truth of his allegations before a magistrate on September 6. Sir Edmund Berry Godfrey, one of the few City merchants who had stayed in London during the Great Plague to oversee mass burials and was much esteemed as a result, reluctantly took the depositions of the two men. Then Charles, in Council, began the investigation. The letters were dismissed as fake and Tonge's performance was so shambolic that Charles dismissed him and left for Newmarket races with his brother. Charles's laziness and impatience with business would now cause more problems. After lunch the councillors remaining examined Oates. He used his eloquence to answer questions and spin further plot lines. Of course the handwriting in the letters differed from that usually used by the correspondents he said - Jesuits always disguised their script thus, as was natural for born plotters. Over several hours he spun his web of lies and drew the councillors in until they felt that it was very likely that London would be burned again, the King killed, and 20,000 Catholics would slit the throats of 100,000 Protestants. Those Oates had named were rounded up and the King had to return from the races to chair the meeting next morning.

Charles caught out Oates on some details and those arrested answered well, but Oates now testified against Edward Colman, once secretary to the duke and duchess of York (who Oates didn't actually know). On September 29 Colman's residence was searched and all his papers removed before he was examined in council next day. Oates didn't recognise him, further damaging his credibility. His accusations may ultimately have come to nothing, but when the Council read Colman's letters on 4 October it was shocked. Much of the language was open to interpretation, and so the worst could be read into them. They certainly talked of bribing MPs and removing the need for a Parliament. It was apparent that some had been written at the duke of York's instigation and in one Colman had written that the Duke had been *'converted to such a degree of zeal and piety as not to regard anything in the world in comparison with God's Almighty glory...and the conversion of our kingdom which has a long time been oppressed and miserably harassed with heresy and schism'.* This appeared to give independent confirmation of the essence of Oates' accusations and put the Duke in the midst of them, not least when Colman insisted that he had authorised most of what had been written. On October 12 Sir Edmund Berry Godfrey disappeared. Five days later his body was found in a ditch on Parliament Hill. He had been strangled with his cravat and his own sword thrust into him. The death of this respected figure caused uproar amongst the London populace. [144]

Charles summoned Parliament. The investigation picked up again and now Oates accused five Catholic lords, who the Commons had arrested and sent to the Tower. On November 5 Guy Fawkes' effigy was replaced by the Pope's on the annual bonfires. Later that month Oates accused the Queen of planning to poison her husband and Charles, having once again caught him lying, had him arrested. But Parliament forced his release and he was now riding so high that he asked the College of Arms to trace his "noble" lineage. The Plot was reinforced by informers or suspects who named others when interrogated. (Three Catholic priests would be hanged on Primrose Hill for Godfrey's murder on information given by one of the Queen's servants, who recanted three times before sticking to his original evidence). Ten days after Ralph's election as M.P. Colman was tried. His papers had shown his wish for French money so that Charles wouldn't need an anti-Catholic parliament, expressed through letters to Louis XIV's Jesuit confessors. Oates swore that he had carried treasonable letters from Colman, who had known of the plot to poison the King. Though Oates put up a poor performance, Colman's letters were considered enough to

---

[144] The identity of Sir Edmund's murderers remained a mystery. One candidate is the 7th earl of Pembroke who had been prosecuted for murder by Godfrey in April. Pembroke had married the duchess of Portsmouth's sister and in January 1678 (having nearly killed a man in a duel the year before) was sent to the Tower for a few days by Charles for "horrid and blasphemous words". Shortly after his release he killed a man in a tavern brawl and was found guilty of manslaughter. He claimed privilege of peerage and was released. Two years later he would kill a night watchman after a drunken evening in Turnham Green. Although he couldn't claim privilege of peerage a second time his fellow peers petitioned the King, who pardoned him. He died aged 31.

convict him of treason and on Tuesday December 3 he was hung, drawn and quartered. The five Catholic lords were found guilty the same day.

It was against this background that Ralph was preparing to act. He is likely to have spent the month after his election further preparing the ground, briefly potential allies and distributing French gold to the waverers. Louis had decided that, in addition to emasculating Charles through encouraging opposition to him in Parliament, it was time to remove Danby from the scene, as someone who would never truly favour the French side. Ambassador Barillon talked to Sidney and Ralph about the secret parts of the Treaty of Dover, and on November 24 had given Ralph papers concerning the secret treaty of May 1678 which agreed the increased subsidy from France in return for English neutrality and disbanding of the army. They are likely to have leaked information to others to get them on side and so Danby came to hear something of what was afoot. He wrote to Temple in The Hague on the 19th of the '*ill practises of Mr Montagu...since his coming to the House. I have heard more of his ill practises of other kinds, and some of them particularly against yourself, which I am hunting as well as I can to find out. And I hear, that Mr Olivecrans can tell us of some things, if he pleases, of Mr Montagu, which would both spoil his Plots, and his seat in Parliament*'.[145]
(Olivencranz was the Swedish ambassador at The Hague). The next day he noted that Sidney, Ralph and others were preparing to attack him and that Sidney's nephew Halifax '*was most bitter against me*'. [146] Another nephew, Sunderland, was also being briefed. A further letter to Temple of the 22nd indicates what Danby was hoping to use against Ralph: '*As to what concerns Mr Montagu, I perceive his Majesty knows nothing of his Conferences with the Pope's Nuncio; And for what Mr Olivecrans supposes might have been the occasion of those conferences viz a treaty of marriage between the King of Spain and the Duke of Orleans daughter, his Majesty says he never entered into any such treaty, nor ever gave Mr Montagu any instructions about it. You say also in your letter that in 12 or 15 days Mr Olivecrans would probably be able, both to tell the time of these conferences more precisely...which gives us great impatience till we hear again*'.[147] On December 17 '*There went last night a rumour about as if this day there would break forth in the House something like an impeachment against my Lord Treasurer. Others spoke as if he meant frankly to throw up his staff, which, I suppose, was a great mistake; and so many other tales that are whispered as great secrets. One of which is that Mr. Montagu, who is become a declared enemy to his Lordship, has exposed to the view of several members (who lifted him by a very summary*

---

[145] Letters of Earl of Danby 1676-1676
[146] Browning vol 2, p.9
[147] Letters of Earl of Danby

proceeding into the House) some letters received by him while at Paris from his Lordship, which contain great matters in them – I know not what, but such as the learned in the law do think contain in them matters for impeachment of a great strain, Whether there be any foundation of truth herein time will show'. [148] Danby seems to have decided on a pre-emptive strike on Ralph, hoping to take advantage of the hysteria surrounding the Popish Plot and link him to it. The Privy Council ordered that Ralph's papers be seized in order to obtain material that would incriminate him, and perhaps to add to what was found or remove items unfavourable to Danby or the King. Ralph had taken the precaution to ensure that the latter, at least, were in a safe place. So the Council's action not only failed in its main intent but worse still inflamed the temper of the Commons.

On Thursday, December 19 the Chancellor of the Exchequer, Sir John Ernly, waited until the House was about to adjourn at one o'clock to deliver a message to the Commons from the King: *'That his Majesty, having received Information, that his late Ambassador in France, Mr. Montagu, a Member of this House, has held several private Conferences with the Pope's Nuncio there, has to this end that he may discover the truth of the matter, given order for the seizing of Mr. Montagu's papers'.* It is clear that the House too had the Plot in mind. Mr Maynard responded: *'Colman had time to sort his papers, and this diligence would have prevented it...The charge against Mr. Montagu...borders on treason very near; at least it looks that way. Correspondence of this nature may sometimes be justifiable'.* The violent response to the accusation that Danby had hoped for didn't happen – MPs were more balanced in their reactions, probably because they had been expecting it. *'Possibly he may have had it for the good of the nation, and possibly to destroy the kingdom. You cannot do your Member less than right to hear him'* (Mr. Vaughan). When Ernly repeated part of the charge Mr. Powle gave a more robust response, reminding his colleagues of Charles I's actions which had ultimately led to civil war: *'No man can defend an Ambassador's having Correspondence, or Conferences, with the Pope's Nuncio. Montagu is a Member of Parliament; and it is an old rule that, in Treason, no private man, nor Member's person, can be seized, before the accusation be given in upon oath: If not any Member may be taken from Parliament...This was a fatal case in the last King's time, of seizing members and their papers. I hope never to see the like again. If a great Minister has a quarrel against a Gentleman, and one go and tell the King a story of him to his prejudice, and his Papers thereupon be seized, I know not wither that will go. In the first place, I would be instructed from Ernly, who brought the Message from the King, whether there be any legal Information against your Member? And, if there be not, then you may consider what to do'.* Ernly

---

[148] Ormonde ibid p.490

repeated the King's message in full, this time he reportedly added the words '*contrary to instructions*' to '*private conferences.*' Sir Thomas Clarges responded: '*I am glad to hear that the Ambassador had instructions not to correspond with the Pope's Nuncio. I am very glad to hear it indeed* (Jeering). *Sir William Godolphin, the Spanish Ambassador, is accused of High Treason by Mr. Oates, and yet we hear nothing of him*' and asked the question again whether the information was on oath. Ernly replied that he had delivered the message as commanded, adding that he hadn't said '*contrary to any instructions*' but '*without any instructions*'. Mr. Powle now revealed that he had indeed been fully briefed by Ralph: '*Correspondence with the Pope's Nuncio, or his Internuncio, as Colman had at Brussels, is as much Treason. I shall acquaint you from Mr. Montagu, that he will deliver all his own Papers himself; else Papers for his own private defence may be embezzled. He will resign them to any hand this House shall appoint*'. Mr. Bennet worried that: '*If his Papers are seized, Papers may be put into his Cabinet, as well as taken out, to his great prejudice*' and Powle added: '*Five or six Gentlemen, from Whitehall, have seized all the passages to Mr. Montagu's house, and his Lady has sent him a letter of it*', which is particularly interesting as indicating that Ralph was not at home. Had he sought refuge elsewhere in case there was an attempt to seize him as well as his papers? Colonel Birch seems not to have been briefed: '*This is a mighty mystery, and the greatest business I have heard here. I should be very loth to make a wrong step in it here. I have always taken it for granted, that no Member's Papers can be seized. I know not what haste they are in, in this matter, nor where it will end. Forty more Members papers may be seized, as this rate, and the House garbled; and then the game is up...The Kingdom of France is in Secretary Coventry's province; and I would have Members go to his Office, to search the Minutes for Ambassador Montagu's Instructions, when he was sent into France*'. Sir Thomas Lee proposed an Address to the King asking whether the information was on oath and Colonel Titus, in seconding, added that if it wasn't then the act of seizing Ralph's papers was a Breach of Privilege.

Sir William Coventry, in the same vein, added (from experience) that: '*An Ambassador has nothing for his justification, but his Papers; and his neck may go for it, if he has not his Papers to justify him...I had rather my shirt, than my Papers, taken from me. Montagu desires only the sorting of his papers, and that he may mark them, and set them in order, to make his defence the better*'. The Speaker kept a stricter line: '*The thing is of great moment, and the King has told you why...and Montagu has told you* "He has received a letter from his Lady, that his house is guarded &c" *but they are not to be seized until Montagu comes to his house to sort the Papers. You concern yourselves not in matters of State, but matters of Privilege.*

Till you know that his charge is not upon oath, you ought to believe that the matter is upon oath. It is a nice thing, and I know the stress and consequence of it'. Sir Robert Howard, backed by Colonel Titus, wanted the King to be asked the nature of Ralph's purported conferences with the Nuncio (such things being sometimes part of an ambassador's duties). Other MPs put forward their views, in the same vein. Sir William Coventry however was against asking the King or enquiring if the accusation was under oath and repeated his points about papers being a person's defence. *'I believe that there are persons that put the King upon this...and I believe it is not Treason he is charged with, because they have not seized Mr. Montagu's person, as well as his Papers'.*

There seems to have been a break in the Commons' proceedings, perhaps for dinner. Mr. Harbord then reported that he had gone to Montagu House and found that Ralph's cabinets had been seized and moved to a room near the Council-chamber in Whitehall, but were not to be opened until he was present. Ralph now makes his dramatic first appearance: *'I believe, that the seizing of my Cabinets and Papers was to get into their hands some Letters of great consequence, that I have to produce, of the designs of a Great Minister of State'.* Harbord raised the tension: *'This has been intended three of four days, but, I believe, they have missed of their aims; and I would not for £40,000 they had those Papers. And, freely, this was my great inducement to stir so much to make Mr. Montagu a Member of this House. In due time you will see what these papers are. They will open your eyes, and though too late to cure the evil, yet they will tell you who to proceed against, as the authors of our misfortunes. I desire that some persons of honour and worth may be present at the opening of these Cabinets, lest some of the Letters should be there. For they are of the greatest consequence that ever you saw'.* Sir Gilbert Garrard wanted to ask the King to have the cabinets delivered, unopened, to the House next day. Sir Nicholas Carew disagreed, saying the House should sit on so that they could examine the papers *'and if they concern any man, under the King himself, I would prosecute the thing now. I know not whether we shall be here tomorrow morning, or no. It may be, we shall all be clapped up'* (i.e. imprisoned). Sir John Lowther agreed, but thought Ralph shouldn't be sent to collect them for fear of assassination: *'For ought I know, Montagu may be served as Sir Edmundbury Godfrey was'.* Sir Henry Capel concurred, adding that he now understood why the Sheriff of Northampton had made a false return for the election there - to keep Ralph from gaining Parliamentary protection. Lord Cavendish couldn't resist raising the temperature still further (and arguably stealing some of Ralph's thunder) by announcing that: *'I believe, it will appear by those Papers, that the War with France was pretended, for the sake of an Army, and that a great man carried on the interest of an Army and*

Popery'. Lord Russell (Ralph's brother-in-law): '*Montagu has imparted some of the contents of those Papers to me; and I was required by him not to impart them to anybody; but now it is no secret*'. Mr. Harbord and some others were ordered to recover a box of Ralph's papers from where he told them they could be found. Unfortunately the key to the box was locked in the seized cabinets, so they had to send for a locksmith to break it open.

Whilst they waited Ralph played the innocent and told the Commons that this wasn't what he had intended: '*I am sorry that so great a Minister has brought this guilt upon himself. It was my intention (making reflections upon your apprehension of a standing Army) to have acquainted Mr. Secretary Coventry with the Papers. I will only now tell you, that the king has been as much deluded as the Dutch or Spain; and you have been deluded to by this great Minister. This I should not have done, out of duty and respect to the King, but by command of the House*'. The box was duly opened and Ralph extracted two letters which he passed to the Speaker, one of January 16 1677/8 and the other of March 25 1678. It was deemed that the thrust of the letters was contained in these words: '*In case the conditions of Peace shall be accepted, the King expects to have six millions of livres [£300,000] yearly, for three years, from the time that this agreement shall be signed by his Majesty and the King of France; because it will be two or three years before he can hope to find his Parliament in humour to give him supply, after your having made any Peace with France*'. Subscribed '*Danby*'. And '*To the Secretary you must not mention one syllable of the money*' (thus exonerating Coventry). The Speaker also told the House that the letter bore the addition of '*This Letter is writ by my Order. CR*'. Since the King could not be attacked directly, this defence did little to protect Danby who was made culpable of a treasonous act for carrying out royal orders which were contrary to his own inclinations. The House will have been well aware that on March 20 they had voted money at Charles's request to fight France. Here was a letter that showed the Lord Treasurer was trying to get French money to keep out of such a war at the same time as he was asking for English money to prosecute it.

The Commons seem to have been stunned. Mr. Bennet, one of Shaftesbury's men, spoke first: '*I wonder the house sits so silent when they see themselves sold for six millions of livres to the French. Some things come home to Treason in construction. I would have the lawyers tell you, whether this you have heard is not worthy of impeaching the Treasurer of Treason. Now we see who has played all this game; who has repeated all the sharp Answers to our Addresses, and raised an Army for no War. You know now who passes by the Secretaries of State. I would impeach the Treasurer of High Treason*'. In answer to a question, Ralph assured the House that the letters were in Danby's hand. Mr. Harbord then made a statement full of wild imaginings: '*I hope now Gentlemens eyes are*

121

opened by the design on foot to destroy the Government and our Liberties. I believe, if the house would command Mr. Montagu, he will tell you more now. But I would not press it now upon him, because poisoning and stabbing are in use...let him reserve himself till the matter comes to Tryal before the Lords. As to the danger of the King's person...I am afraid the King will be murdered...poisons both in liquid and in powders'. Sir Henry Godrick tried to defend Danby by stating that he had defended Protestantism but was shouted down by Mr. Bennet who repeated the accusation of treason. Sir John Knight summed up the feeling of many: *'This Army was raised for a French War, and so many hundred thousand pounds given for that purpose, and yet we had no War! Money given to disband the Army, and that not done! The Popish Plot discovered at that time! And all runs parallel. Take such evil counsellors from the King, that have done these things, and he...and we all shall flourish; else we shall be destroyed. I move for Impeachment'*. Sir Thomas Higgins suggested that royal attempts to extract money from France had happened before in English history, and that an honourable peace was being negotiated, so there was no treason. But members knew that these letters proved Parliament was being prorogued or adjourned effectively at Louis's behest – this was not just arbitrary government, but the delivery of that government to a foreign, Catholic power intent on dominating western Europe.

Ralph's ally Mr. Powle stated that the matter should be fully debated by the House and suggested that Danby's crime was *'encroaching upon Royal Power. When one, two or three Counsellors undertake the management of all affairs, without communicating them to the rest of the Lords of the Council, it was the treason of ...Richard II's time. And then in the Parliament of those times, it was so adjudged... Now there is a Treaty with a foreign Prince for peace, whilst Parliament was giving money for an actual War with that Prince, and a Treaty, for which he makes a bargain of six million...consider whether that could be for our advantage, and the French King pays so dear for it, and concludes, that this money was "that the King might not meet the Parliament."'* Colonel Titus expressed similar views but the Chancellor defended Danby, saying that he opposed France and that it was the allies that wanted a peace, not the King. They had pressed for the army to be maintained in case it was needed to defend Flanders. He suggested that Ralph's replies to the letters should be seen. Ralph responded that Danby had copies of his replies in which *'you will find, that if my advice had been followed, the Army had not been raised, and a better Peace made. And I aver, that the French King offered our King some money, and more towns, than when we were in conjunction with France...I was for Peace, because I saw no intention of our Ministers for War, and so would have had no Army. I brought the conditions so far* as that the French should deliver Valenciennes and Conde to the Spaniards; far better conditions than they now have...If I have done ill in this, impeach me for it'. Danby's son Dumblane rewarded Ralph's hospitality in Paris by telling the Commons that he heard him say that 'the House of Commons has a company of logger-heads and boobies in it'.

The opposition outmanoeuvred Danby's supporters through their preparedness, eloquence and effrontery. After several other contributions to the debate the House voted at ten at night on whether there was sufficient in the letters to impeach Danby. 179 were in favour and 116 against. This was an unusually large majority and showed that Danby's laboriously constructed Court Party was no more.

Next day the Speaker announced that Danby had sent him two letters written by Ralph, the first of which mentioned a trip of young de Ruvigny to London 'and his practise among the Malcontents' and the other de Ruvigny senior's belief that, before the French could achieve anything in England, Danby's standing needed to be diminished. Lord Russell was named as one of the chief men to be worked on but the ranks of others who were doubtless "malcontents" closed to protect him. Ralph said that his wife had written to her sister to warn her of this attempt to bribe her husband, and that all that ambassadors write as news wasn't always the truth. 'My wife and family at Paris were laughing at Ruvigny's project of doing France any service by his relation to that noble Lord' (not something he had reported to Danby). Sir Henry Capel said there was no harm in trusting Russell with anything to do with France and Lord Cavendish that 'These Letters, that the Treasurer has produced, are either to recriminate upon Montagu, or to justify himself'. Russell himself made a dishonest denial.

It is interesting that when the duke of York wrote to his son-in-law the Prince of Orange next day he ascribed Ralph's motives to the accusation of his having had treasonable conversations with the Papal Nuncio rather than to the duchess of Cleveland's attack. 'I believe you will be surprised to hear what Mr Montagu has done; for being yesterday accused in council of having had secret conferences with the Pope's Nuncio at Paris, he to revenge himself of that, produces letters written to him by the Lord Treasurer by his Majesty's command, when he was ambassador in France, and shows them to the Commons, who upon it ordered an impeachment to be drawn up against the Lord Treasurer. I am confident there was never so abominable an action as this of Mr Montagu's, and so offensive to the King, in revealing what he was trusted with when he was employed by his Majesty. All honest men abhor him for it'.[149] He doesn't reflect on the difficulty of finding an honest man at Court.

---

[149] London December 20 1678. Dalrymple vol.1 p.260

On Saturday 21 December Sir Edmund Jennings, doubtless briefed by Danby, observed that there was another letter Ralph had sent in which he stated that de Ruvigny had come over to detach England from her allies using French gold, and that Ralph believed he could extract twice as much. He had told Danby that only the King should know of it. This letter predated those from Danby shown to the House. '*If it be a crime to transact affairs without acquainting the Secretaries, it is no less a crime in Montagu. And if six millions be a crime in the treasurer, it is also a crime in Montagu to get twelve.*' Ralph wriggled out of the first point by replying that he could show the House an earlier order of Danby's insisting on secrecy. Whilst the second point was true it hadn't been Ralph who had asked Parliament for money to raise an army that wasn't to be used. The Lords debated the matter next day. Danby still had a majority there. '*I send your Grace the articles against my Lord Treasurer, upon presenting of which there arose the last night a long and warm debate, but so much in my Lord Treasurer's favour that it was ordered that he should not withdraw during the debates. The rest was adjourned until Tuesday, so as there seems little disposition to comply with the Commons in the imprisonment desired, and how they will resent it will prove a question, The King puts all his faculties to work and everything at stake and risk to serve that great Lord. Mr. Montagu was this morning writ unto to attend, or somebody from him, the opening of his papers at a Council to meet again this afternoon; but he wrote to the Clerk of the Council that for fear the House would deem it a consenting to the breach of privilege he would first ask their permission; with which answer His Majesty was so little satisfied that he opened one of the four cabinets and examined several papers, but being very late he went no farther*'. [150] The fact that Charles was willingly to risk furthering upsetting the Commons by opening the cabinet when, on the 19th, that House had indicated that would be a breach of privilege, shows the desperate point that the King had reached.

The same day Charles sent the Commons two letters further intended to tar Ralph with treason. The first was from Nijmegen and suitably dated November 5 1678. It reported that the Swedish ambassador there was reflecting on the Popish Plot and said that he "doubted" Ralph because eighteen months before he had been told by his colleague in Paris that Ralph had held several conferences with the Papal Nuncio. Another of December 3 said that the '*Abbe de Sures had a Conference three or four days with Montagu*'. Ralph replied that '*If ever I was in the Abbe de Sure's house in all my life, I will forfeit my head. He is a common news-monger. I protest, I was never alone in a room with the Pope's Nuncio in my life...I desire that my Boxes and Cabinets may be opened, and my Papers viewed, and I will submit to his Majesty's pleasure*'. Bishop Burnet recorded that

---

[150] Ormonde ibid p.491

Danby had told Jenkins, at Nijmegen, to send him such letters. It is also clear from Danby's papers that he wanted to remove Ralph from his post as Keeper of the Wardrobe, or at the least stop the revenue he had from it, and had him suspended from the office on August 13.[151] It seems that on the morning of the day that Ralph revealed Danby's letters to the Commons there had been an '*Extraordinary Council. King communicates a letter from Sir L Jenkins of 5 Nov to the Lord treasurer. Olivencrantz told him Mr Montagu, while ambassador in France, had had several private conferences at night with the Pope's Nuncio. The Swedes minister had writ this to Olivencrantz and the master of the house had told this to that minister. Asked, if with the King's knowledge, well. If not, of dangerous consequence &s. Knows nothing of the matter. As to the time, in May and June, 77 that the information had not come by letter or writing to him. Lord Treasurer writ back to Sir Leoline that the King knew nothing of Mr Montagu's conferences with the Nuncio nor anything of what Olivencrantz supposes of a marriage between the King of Spain and the Emperor's daughter. Sir L Jenkins second letter of 3 Dec. that he had spoken with Olivencrantz, but he as yet could say nothing more to the matter. As to the time, when Cambray was besieged. At the Abbot Siri's (?) house. Three conferences in 15 days. Might possibly know more, but the correspondent asked for a cipher, and it was sent 8 days before. King suspects one Falaiseour (?) Mr Montagu's secretary'*. These are Williamson's notes preserved in the Calendar of State Papers. Danby's spin on Ralph's unbidden return from his ambassadorship without royal leave was that it was a very high misdemeanour for which in centuries past he might have been hauled before the Star Chamber, and could now be fined by the Kings Bench, thus further weakening him financially. [152]

At the same time as wishing to impeach Danby, the Commons were unwilling to see any money voted for disbanding the army go to the Exchequer (controlled by Danby), and would only do so if it went to the Chamber of London. They also wanted a militia in case of a Catholic uprising. Charles of course was not prepared to allow a precedent of money raised going anywhere other than to the Exchequer. Hence there was deadlock between the opposition majority in the Commons and Danby's allies in the Lords, who when reading the articles of Danby's impeachment sent up to them on December 23 were not even prepared to expel him from their House. (Shaftesbury, one of the opposition's chief leaders there, had always recognised that he would not be able to prevail in the Lords but thought that, if he was appointed to great office by the King in order that supply would then be voted through, the office-holding peers, who usually supported the ministers, whoever they were, would swing

---

[151] Cal SP Dom
[152] BL Add Mss 38849 f. 188

125

behind him. Danby could then be prosecuted). Charles could not endure this deadlock – the result would be no vote of supply, the possibility of further awkward secrets being revealed in the dispute between Ralph and the Lord Treasurer, and a further increase of tension in a London already inflamed by the Plot. On the last day of December: *'After the Council rose His Majesty went and prorogued the Parliament...The thing was very surprising unto all, and, as is usual in such cases and very natural too many melancholy, ill-boding things were heard, and some much more angry and malicious than the thing would bear. Many lies were also presently dispersed, as if the guards were looking out for Mr. Montagu and some other member; that Oates was fled, etc'.* [153]

Although Danby had clearly proved unable to manage the opposition, (they had also monopolised the investigation in the Plot), there was no obvious candidate to replace him as chief minister, and Charles needed his dedication and financial skills. Danby might even think the unthinkable and blackmail Charles over the negotiations with France, something even Ralph had shied away from. So the King and Danby approached a group of moderate opposition MPs who promised that if Charles dissolved Parliament and summoned a new one they would, on return, be willing to see Danby resign. A supply to disband the army would be voted through. There was also a promise from the King to limit the life of a parliament to three years (he had managed to have the Triennial Act repealed in 1664, thereby enabling him to call, prorogue or dissolve a parliament at will). Charles prevaricated. It may only have been the news that the City was planning a closer alliance with the opposition, particularly in relation to the prosecution of Danby, that prompted him to dissolve the Long Parliament on January 24 1679. It had sat for almost eighteen years since May 1661 (the longest Parliamentary session of all time). The royal proclamation contained no reference to the promises of disbanding the army or limiting the life of parliament. The new parliament would not sit until 6 March. Ralph's protecting parliamentary privilege vanished.

Ralph apparently knew of the impending dissolution, or anticipated it, and so feared arrest. He decided to leave England, but was caught in flight. A great deal of detail about what happened survives. The Calendar of State Papers contains a letter of January 20 from Williamson to the Mayor of Dover: *'I have received yours of this evening by express concerning your having stayed Mr Montagu as he was passing beyond the seas, and am commanded to signify his Majesty's pleasure that you continue to make stay of him till his further pleasure be sent you'.* (A letter commanding that Ralph be ordered to appear before the King in Council was not sent). Mayor Coventry replied: *'I will observe your order as to the stay of Mr. Montagu; he has been treated with respect and seems satisfied, except with*

---

[153] Ormonde Mss. IV p.494. Sir Cyril Wyche to Ormond

the guard, civil men of the town, placed in the house where he is. I dare not release him on parole, though he earnestly presses it. I enclose two affidavits relating to his seizure. I have promised a reward to the two seamen that made the discovery.

Deposition of Francis Bastinck, clerk of the passage at Dover, Simon Conyet, postmaster, and James Lingoe, master of a packet-boat that on the mayor's being informed on Sunday 19th by 2 mariners that they were hired for a large reward to transport a gentleman by night to a French shallop that was come into Dover Road, for his transportation beyond the seas, he sent for Bastinck, who took the other deponents to his assistance, and they, lurking near where the gentleman was to be carried off, intercepted him with another and took them before the mayor who threatened to send them to the common gaol, whereupon one confessed himself to be Mr. Montagu, late ambassador to France, and the other Baker, his servant.

Deposition of John Lodwick, commissioner of the passage. He had gone with the mayor the next day to the inn where Mr Montagu was confined, who pressed the mayor to take off the guard and to take his parole, which the mayor refused. The shallop to carry him over was a hired vessel of Dover, belonging to Richard Browne and the master of the inn had prepared it to carry Mr Montagu over'. Ralph's bravado apparently hadn't completely deserted him - the Mayor writing again three days later: '*I have parted with Mr Montagu by order of Council, on his bond of 1,000l not to depart the kingdom; he threatened me for keeping a guard on him, and has left a bill of 6l or 7l at his inn, which the guard drank, for the constable to pay, which I pay myself, rather than an officer should be discouraged. If the contrivers of his intended transportation escape, there will be little hope to stay others in future*'.

In the letters which Danby had printed in 1710 to vindicate his conduct at this time there is a long account by John Brisbane of Ralph's fears and attempted flight. '*Upon the news and heats that were in the House, about seizing Mr Mountagu's papers at his house, my Lady Harvey first told me, her brother was very much afraid of being sent to the Tower. I told her I thought not, the Parliament sitting. She replied, my Lord Danby would cause a dissolution or prorogation, and he would then be snapt, And therefore desired me... that I would be as quick among all my friends and companies as I could possible, to make the first discovery if such a thing were intended, and to be always every day about the House; and if I got the least inckling of it, to send for him out, and clap a cloak about him (which I was enjoin'd not to be without) and carry him away by water into London, or where else I thought fit; his resolving to trust himself, his life and all he had, with me, before any body about or that belonged to himself, they being (as she term'd them) all fools and knaves... He himself spoke to* me to the same purpose, and swore he had no mind to eat meat of others dressing, where he must eat either poison, or starve.

The Parliament broke up on a Monday morning. He had notice of it, and did not come to the House. I waited there, got what intelligence I could, and made what observations I could and went to him to a house in Fleet Street, where he had withdrawn himself. From thence I took him ... to a friend of mine in Lime Street, where I kept him about two or three and twenty days; in which time I privately carried several of his friends to him, amongst other, Mr Barillon. The night being then long and dark, we went often out to some tavern, or private house of my acquaintance, where the French Ambassador, and others of his friends, several times met him.

The visits at that time from the Ambassadors, were very frequent to Lady Harvey, who never failed once a day to bring him the result of them, or what else she had. After he had been thus secreted about ten or twelve days, he told me, he was resolved if he must be a prisoner, it should be at large. He would go overseas, and asked me if I could securely hire a vessel on the Exchange, and would go with him? I told him I could, and would wait upon him wherever he pleased. The next day I gave him an account, that a stout ship of Dort of 130 tuns, should be ready for him in two days... Having resolved at last (for he was very irresolute and fearful) that he would go, and the time, I ordered the Master to wait for us, with his boat's crew, at a certain place below the block-houses at night. In the morning we took coach, and at the Half-Way house to Deptford met with Sir Thomas Armstrong, who waited for us, with another Gentleman, a groom, and two spare horses with arms for us two. We got on board well that evening, immediately weighed, and stood as far as we could that tide. Next day we got into Margate Road; the wind chopt upon us, and in the night it proved a great storm. We lost our boat adrift about midnight, which frighted him much... I told him, we had good anchors and cables, and could ride out without any danger in the world. He would not, but told me, he would rather I would throw him into the sea, than keep him in that condition, for he was very sick. I would have gone for Holland, for we could have done it, but he would not, so we run back that night into Queenborough-water, where it was very quiet. He then had a mind to go ashore to sleep a night, and in the morning would go by land to Dover. I promised to secure him thither, but could not there, because I thought he was well known. He had a thousand resolutions, I left him at Canterbury, and rode that night to Dover, and hired a small boat to put us over at Calais or Bologne... which was to have taken us on board the next night at twelve from the beach. I fetched him from Canterbury at the time; and as we were stepping into the boat, were seized by officers that lay in wait for us, we having been before discovered by one of the boat's crew, were made prisoners there about six days, till orders came from Court. We *gave security to a writ ... and came for London, but just at the Towns-end, were frighted again by a note from his sister, that told him if he were yet at liberty, he would do well to take care, and keep himself so; for resolutions had been taken at Court the night before, to make him close prisoner.*

This made him leave his coach and servants just at Kent-street End privately. That but one or two of them knew of it, and through the gardens I carried him to Redriff, crossed the water to Wapping, and by that time he believed himself safe again.

I brought him to Aldgate in the evening, took coach, and went with him to Bloomsbury Square. He sat in the coach whilst I went to my Lord Russel's, and to his own house, to give his Lady an account that he was well and safe. I lodged him that and the Sunday night in Lombard Street, and on the Monday morning he went home. He was suddenly afterwards chosen at Huntingdon, and now all was well again, the family very quiet, full of joy and good humour'.

Brisbane, who had worked with Ralph in Paris from 1676, seems to have decided after the event that it was best to assist Danby rather than his old master.[154] Nonetheless the main elements of Brisbane's narrative are likely to be accurate, even though words like *'fearful'* and *'frighted'* could be colouring to discredit Ralph (having crossed the Channel so many times, often in bad weather, it is strange that this trip was exceptional). The letters were published the year after Ralph died, so he was unable to challenge them. On Tuesday, January 28 1679: *'Mr. Montagu is at his own house under £2,000 bail; 'tis said that he is to appear tomorrow at the Council Board and his papers to be read'*. [155]

---

[154] Samuel Pepys, who had been Secretary to the Admiralty until accused of criminal correspondence with the French and imprisoned in the Tower, had asked Brisbane to help investigate the case against him in Paris. But the penurious Scotsman was offered Pepys's old job, which created a conflict of interest. (The only silver lining for Pepys was that William Harbord, his persecutor, had wanted it). [154] He was eventually promoted to the post of secretary at the embassy

[155] Letters of Sir Robert Southwell to 1st Duke of Ormond p.312. Mr. Mulys to Earl of Ossory

Chapter 5
Exclusion 1679 - 1682

Despite his vulnerability until Parliament sat again, the Crown did not act against Ralph even though it could have harnessed the febrile mood of the public created by the Popish Plot to do so. Perhaps the evidence against him with regard to meetings with the Papal Nuncio was considered too weak, or it was feared that he would reveal more damaging information on Charles's relations with Louis. It is certainly the case that many in the opposition party (and therefore allies of Ralph) were supporting and using the prosecution of the Plot for their ultimate aim of excluding the duke of York from the throne.

Mr. Mulys informed the earl of Ossory on February 1 1679 that: '*On Wednesday last, in the morning, Mr. Montagu was with Mr. Secretary Coventry, and appeared with Captain Titus that morning in the gallery; at night he appeared but was not called for by the Council. In Northamptonshire he stands for Knight of the Shire...The idle people of the town is full of the discourse of Sir Edmund Godfrey's ghost appearing when the Queen was at High Mass at Somerset House*'.[156]   Perhaps to make sure that he would not be elected for Northampton, Ralph was sent a letter at Boughton commanding him to appear before the Privy Council in London.   But he didn't receive it– he had gone to Huntingdon, where the extended Montagu family also exercised great electoral influence as landowners, and been chosen M.P. there. (The heirs of the earls of Manchester and Sandwich were both under age and so weren't eligible). When Ralph did appear before the Council in mid February he was asked why he had left Paris before receiving the order for his return. He replied that he knew he had been so ordered, even if the formal paper had not arrived, and since he owed £8,000 spent on the King's account, and feared arrest for debt, he went to Calais to collect the paper there. Then he was asked about corresponding with the Nuncio, which he denied. Finally he was asked for the keys to his cabinet which had been seized '*(which it seems they had not opened, though seized you know when)*' but he cheekily replied that he couldn't remember where he had hidden them. He was dismissed with the request that he should send them when he found them.[157]

Unsurprisingly the new House of Commons was even less easy to manage than the old one and Danby, seeing himself still in danger, persuaded the King that the duke of York had to go, to lower the temperature. He even drafted the letter in which Charles commanded his

---

[156] Ormonde correspondence
[157] HMC 13th report Appendix, pt. VI, 14

brother to travel abroad. On March 22 the King addressed both Houses of Parliament and told them that the letters Ralph had produced in the Commons had been written at his command; Danby had his confidence and would always be pardoned, but had been dismissed from both Court and Council. (Whatever satisfaction the opposition may have taken from this was undermined by the fact that Danby had been promised a marquisate and large pension). The Commons took no notice, pressing on to impeach Danby and questioning the royal prerogative to pardon in such cases – their mood had not been improved when the Speaker they had elected was rejected by the King. Royal confirmation of the election was usually a formality but the proposed Speaker and Danby loathed each other. Though the Lords would not accept impeachment, the Commons kept up their demand for Danby's incarceration in the Tower. Charles tried to get him to flee, but he refused even though the Lords transformed the Commons bill of attainder into one of banishment. For a fortnight there was deadlock between the two Houses until on April 15 the Lords, by a narrow vote, followed the Commons. Next day Danby was in the Tower, where he would remain for almost five years.

Ralph's contributions to this session are recorded in Gray's Debates. On Thursday, April 10 the Commons discussed a petition from Dr John Nelson denying that he'd published a book of "Letters from a Jesuit at Paris" but that Danby, having got a copy of it, had it printed. Ralph commented that '*I am against discharging him till Lord Danby be tried. One of the Articles against Danby is "That he is a favourer of Popery", and so against the Church of England; and this man, by his encouragement, has written this Book*'.[158] In the 6 May debate on an address to the King for the removal of the duke of Lauderdale: '*Out of duty to the King, and not from disrespect to the Duke of Lauderdale, I shall second the Motion. When I see the Duke of Lauderdale and others added to the Privy Council, I cannot but think that this last project (the new Council) was to save themselves, and not for the good of the Nation; and what good can we expect from it? It is to put new wine into old bottles, and new cloth to piece up an old garment; and this, I fear, will be the consequence of the new Council. You have been shown how dangerous a person he is, of what a nauseous tongue, &c. His intolerance to Lord Cavendish, who deserves it not from any man, but for having the Duke's ill will. I will not advise to impeach him, there are such delays in Impeachments. Nothing is more ancient nor parliamentary than Addresses, and I second the motion to address*'.[159] Finally, on Saturday May 17 1679:

---

[158] A. Grey *Debates of the House of Commons, from 1667 to 1694, collected by the Honble Anchitell Grey* (London 1769) vol 7 p.104
[159] Ibid p.189

'I have been silent in this matter of Lord Danby, out of respect to the House, lest it should look like private pique against him, &c. But since, by his Pardon, I have made observation that the Justice of the Nation will be stopped, and that by his ambition he may be on the same foot still, to the ruin of the Nation, I would not proceed to the Tryal of the other Lords till this be over'. It is always difficult to judge whether Ralph's words are truly meant, or are merely politic, but Ralph's friends (and enemies) must have smiled when they heard the words *'lest it should look like private pique'.*[160]

As so often, Charles was bombarded with contradictory advice: James and Danby wanted him to stand by them (his father, after all, had not been saved by the sacrifice of Strafford and Laud), whilst Portsmouth, Sunderland, Temple and others suggested conciliation with the opposition. Charles appeared to agree with the latter and the new Privy Council appointed in late April to direct all domestic and foreign affairs contained men who the Commons could trust. Charles did not, however, go so far as to invite Ralph. Its President was the earl of Shaftesbury. He was Temple's brother-in-law, had fought on both sides in the Civil War, and sat on the Council of State under Cromwell but had been one of the MPs who had travelled to Holland to invite Charles to return. His reward was to be made Chancellor of the Exchequer, a post he held for eleven years and as Lord Ashley he had been the second A in Charles's Cabal. Later, as a supporter of religious dissenters and opponent of what he saw as Danby's move towards arbitrary government, he moved into opposition. For a year (from February 1677) he had been imprisoned for suggesting that, because Parliament hadn't met the previous year, it had been dissolved. This was an attack on the royal prerogative, which jealously guarded its right to determine whether Parliament should meet or not. He had sat on the committees to combat the Popish Plot and had finally decided that the duke of York should be excluded from the crown, preferring to see the duke of Monmouth as heir. He saw his appointment as President as grudging royal acceptance, at the very least, of the validity of his views and set about trying to promote them. Charles may have thought that the large salary attached to the post would buy him off. Whatever the case, Charles had no intention of allowing the new Council members to achieve anything. He knew that their appointments would split them from those in opposition who were still "out" such as Ralph. When he did appear to concede something, for example when the Council wanted to ensure all Justices of the Peace (JPs) were true Protestants, he then worked behind the scenes to water down its effects. On April 30 the Commons heard his offer of limitations on any future Catholic king: he would only fill major offices in Church and State after consulting Parliament. As intended this

---

[160] Ibid p.294

split the opposition further – some favoured it but the majority still pressed for James's exclusion. The mood of the country in many ways reflected that of Parliament – it was probably more divided than it had been at any time since Charles's restoration. The Habeas Corpus Act was passed, making it less easy for the government to imprison opponents without trial. Charles had at least been able to get a grant of supply for the army, since the Commons had decided its consequent disbandment was better than living with the fear that it might be used against them, but supply for the fleet was denied. Charles realised he had little to gain by keeping a recalcitrant Commons in session and prorogued it on May 27 1679. He didn't bother to consult his Privy Council before doing so.

It seems that Charles still didn't know what to do for the best. His room to manoeuvre was limited. So he sought the easiest way out and appealed to Louis through Barillon for more French money, suggesting that the Commons wanted to control the government and would then declare war on France. But Barillon, and Louis, were happier to see England paralysed and found it cheaper to pay Ralph and the opposition to keep it so than give millions to Charles. Neither did they trust Charles's word, especially after the Treaty of Nijmegen was finally signed in September. Louis considered that the terms of the peace were humiliating, because he didn't get all he had wanted. Charles continued to live in hope, and eventually that hope was fulfilled: once Louis had decided that he would ignore the Treaty a subsidy of a million livres per annum (some £75,000) for three years was agreed. In return Charles was not to conclude any alliance, or maintain any treaty, contrary to Louis's interests. If he did call Parliament it was to do nothing to oppose France. Ultimately Charles did not go through with it – he may well have feared what would happen if such secret negotiations came to light, as they as had previously done through Ralph's revelations. (It would become clear to Charles that Barillon was not to be trusted – the ambassador sent a letter to his colleague in the Netherlands telling him that Charles was opposing a French-Dutch alliance because he was negotiating for an English-French one. The recipient then showed it to the English ambassador). To save money the army was disbanded, court expenditure reduced and pensions left unpaid. (The duchess of Cleveland, of course, was not impressed by this attempt at economy. Edward Pickering wrote to his relative Lord Montagu on July 31 1679: '*The Duchess...will shortly to Windsor, if not already. His Majesty gave the Commissioners of the treasury fair warning to look to themselves, for that she would have a bout with them for money, having lately lost £20,000 in money and jewels in one night at play. Nell Guin's mother was found drowned in a ditch near Westminster*').

Now for the first time a Papist Plot trial at which Oates gave evidence returned a not guilty verdict. Whilst this caused many to claim that the judge must have been bribed to acquit Sir George Wakeman, the Queen's physician, it encouraged doubts about the Plot in the minds of others. Henry Sidney had recorded on July 17 that he had discussed with Temple *'how ill Lord Chumleigh, Mr. Montague and Sir Wm. Carr behave themselves, what mischief they are because they are not uppermost'* and three days later that *'At night Mr. Montague was with me and told me how glad he was of Wakeman's being acquitted, "for" saith he "it is much better for us mutineers" (the name given to the most violent of the popular party). He gave me great charge to remember his pills'* (Sidney was about to leave for Holland).[161] Charles decided that the tide was turning, and it was time to dissolve Parliament and elect another, believing it would be more favourable towards him. When Shaftesbury protested that the King had said he wouldn't do anything without consulting the Council, of which he was President, Charles simply responded that dissolution, like prorogation, was a royal prerogative.

On August 11 Ralph wrote to his 'friend' Sidney: *'You are, I presume, so much taken up with politics, that a letter from a man that is out of them, and is in town when the Court is at Windsor, cannot be of much use to you. My wife is well brought to bed of a son, and I am going into the country to be chosen if I can of the new parliament where your brother Algernon is already chosen* [for Guildford], *but upon a double return...The King, when he heard he was chosen, said that he did not believe Mr. Algernon Sidney would prove an honest man'.* (Ralph's first son, named after him, had been born on the 7th). A week later Ralph's ally in the House, Harbord, wrote to Sidney that *'our friend Mr. Montagu is now at Newport on his way to Northampton to be chosen there wch he will without the least difficulty or opposition; & indeed without any considerable expence, wch added to the favour his Lady hath lately donne him makes him happy enough'.*[162]

The MPs elected in late August were no more malleable - there was no-one in government able to coordinate the election of the greater number of loyal members the King hoped for. Charles fell seriously ill (he may have had a stroke) and fear of his death led to panic. Some Privy Councillors, concerned at what Buckingham and Monmouth might do if that happened, recalled the duke of York who was encouraged by the generally good reception he received. When Charles recovered the Duke was able to build on this to insist that, though he was prepared to go away again to ease the King's relations with the new Commons, he would go to Scotland rather than abroad, and that Monmouth should go to the continent. Nonetheless, when they both left London it was Monmouth who was cheered. The duke of York wrote to his son-in-law the Prince of Orange from Windsor on September 16 1679 that Monmouth was leaving because he *'has not*

---

[161] Sidney correspondence
[162] BL Add 32095 f.79

behaved himself as became him to his Majesty, for he has kept very ill company in London, and not followed his Majesty's orders in having no more to do with such kind of men. Mr Montagu is one of his state counsellors, and all the Presbyterians and dissenting people flock to him'. [163] Many believed that if Charles had died in August 1679 there would have been civil war.

In the autumn Ralph pressed for the money he had been promised for engineering Danby's fall. He wrote to one of Louis's ministers on October 26 1679

'Although I know you are often importuned on my account, I cannot, Sir, dispense with importuning you myself; I am pressed in so strange a manner, and have such interested persons to deal with, that I am in an embarrassment, from which I cannot draw myself without your help. You know, Sir, there are nearly eight months run since I absolutely fulfilled what I engaged myself for; and if you will be at the trouble of reading over the letters from this country between the 15th and 25th October 1678, you will see there is not the least difficulty in my affair and that the event has even gone beyond my hopes. The person whom the King employs here has been a witness to my conduct. He knows, that to perform the engagement I entered into with him for refusing all proposals which might be made to me, however advantageous they might be, has cost me sixty thousand crowns, without reckoning what I lost before, and have lost these six weeks...I am persecuted on all sides, and if the King is not so good to me as to give orders to extricate me from the trouble I am in, I am upon the point of being reduced to the necessity either of losing my credit and my reputation, or of selling my estates to disengage the promises I gave upon the promise of the King. There is not a day but I am exposed to persecutions, the more disagreeable as the people who make them have a right to do it. The affair in question is so trifling that I cannot doubt of its being speedily finished, if you will do me the favour to represent to the King what I have wrote... I ask pardon for the trouble I give you, and the manner in which I write, but you know, Sir, the reasons I have to act thus, and the danger I should put myself in if I wrote this with my own hand'. [164] This letter suggests that Ralph had handed out money to stiffen the resolve of those opposed to Danby and that offers had been made to him to drop his own opposition.

The French Ambassador had, of course, also been asked for the payment. In a long letter to Louis dated December 14 1679 he talks of how he was still "managing" Lord Hollis and Messrs Lyttelton, Harbord,

---

[163] J. Dalrymple, *Memoirs of Great Britain and Ireland. From the dissolution of the last Parliament of Charles II till the capture of the French and Spanish Fleets in Vigo* 3 vols. (London 1790) vol.1, p.239
[164] Ibid

135

Sidney and Powle. (Of the latter: '*He was put into the council when the persons who opposed the court were put there...He is a man fit to fill one of the first posts in England; he is very eloquent and able; our first correspondence came through Mr Montagu's means; but I have since kept it by my own, and very secretly*'). The letter also clearly shows that Ralph was also being "managed". '*I ought to give your Majesty an account of what regards Mr Montagu separate from the others, being engaged as he is in your Majesty's interests by particular considerations. I have had trouble enough to defend myself for these six months against his solicitations for the payment of the sums which was promised him for the ruin of the high Treasurer. He alleges that the condition is fulfilled on his part. I have always endeavoured to make him understand that it was an affair not entirely finished, and that being fully assured of what had been promised to him, he ought not to make himself uneasy whether the payment be made a little sooner than later. He does not give way to my reasons*'. Ralph had apparently sent a servant twice to France for the purpose, but without success, and he would have gone himself as the Ambassador related: '*if he could have left England at this time when affairs are in so great commotion, and in which he has acted so great a part. Your Majesty will remember, if you please, that Mr Montagu spoke to me in the month of January last, to try if you would favour the Duke of Monmouth's pretensions. It was the principal motive of his journey to France when he was seized at Dover. Mr Montagu knew well afterwards by the reservedness with which I spoke to him upon that affair, that your Majesty was not disposed to support so unjust a design, and which then appeared very chimerical. However, upon other affairs we have always had a good correspondence, and have preserved the greatest union. He has often spoken to me of getting Lord Shaftesbury into your Majesty's interests, and alleges it would not be impossible if a considerable sum were employed. I don't know if your Majesty will judge it useful to your service to endeavour at it at present; it would be a very proper means to stir up new embarrassments to the King of England, and Lord Shaftesbury would be still more bold if he found himself secretly supported by your Majesty. But it will be difficult to turn him from his engagements against the duke of York, and prevent him bestirring himself for the elevation of the Duke of Monmouth, or for that of the Prince of Orange; for his designs are difficult enough to penetrate. And perhaps his principal end is to endeavour the establishment of a republic, of which he would aim at being chief.*

If your Majesty will give me leave to say what I think ought to be done at present with regard to Mr Montagu, I think you might command me to give him positive assurances of the payment of what was promised him, and that a certain time be named on which this payment shall be actually made. If after this your Majesty will, by his means and those of Mrs

Hervey his sister, gain any members of parliament, I can answer that two persons cannot be found more proper to traverse all the designs of the court. It was by an intrigue of Mrs. Hervey that I caused to be continued in Brussels a certain person named Bulstrode[165] who, as Monsieur de Louvois at that time informed me, was useful to your Majesty's service'. [166]

Ralph's continued political scheming is shown by entries for November 1679 in Sidney's diary: *'Mr Montagu was with me; he told me his opinion of Lord Essex, Lord Halifax and my brother Algernon'* (2nd); *'I went with Sir Henry Capell to Mr Montagu'* (11th); *'Mr Montagu was with me to propose some expedient for uniting; I proposed my Lord Shaftesbury being of the Treasury; he said he would do all he could to persuade him'* (12th); *'I was with Mr Pelham: met Sir Wm Jones, dined with Mr Montagu, who told me Lord Shaftesbury would not accept of being Commissioner of the Treasury; Sir Stephen Fox thought of'* (13th): *'I was with Mr Hide and my Lord of Essex: he is horribly vext; told me the story of the plot, and thinks we shall all be undone; he bids me tell the Prince that they are endeavouring to get witnesses to swear the King was married to the Duke of Monmouth's mother'* (14th). On the other side of Europe the English ambassador to Istanbul was hearing Ralph praised by the French ambassador, who *'knew Mr Montagu to be a man of parts, extolled to the skies his lady, and said his sister was a masculine wit and was an H-'.*[167]

Even proroguing a difficult Commons didn't stop those who wanted to complain about arbitrary government, and/or exclude the duke of York, from pressing their case through the press and petitions, and it further raised the temperature. When Shaftesbury protested that the Duke should not have been allowed to stay in the kingdom he was removed from the Privy Council. He may well have encouraged Monmouth's unauthorised return from Holland, much to Charles's anger. Perhaps as a consequence the duke of York was allowed back from Scotland. Ralph's brother-in-law Lord Russell, Powle, and Cavendish resigned from the Council, and the City elections in December 1679 saw an increased number of oppositionists on its council. All would have had in mind the events of 1641-1642 when the City of London moved against Charles's father. This period saw the growth of a loyal grouping that has often been considered as the forerunner of Tories to fight against the opposition or Whigs. (Both names came from insults thrown at them – the former were Irish Catholic bandits and the latter strict Scottish Presbyterians. In practise these groupings had no unchallenged leader or common party agenda (other than exclusion and the independence of Parliament), both of which would later be engendered by annual parliaments and regular elections, to allow us to

---

[165] Sir Richard Bulstrode, English agent in Brussels
[166] Ibid pp.337/341
[167] HMC Finch vol ii, p.155

consider them as "political parties" in the modern understanding of that term). Charles made some changes in the judiciary, exploiting his power to ensure loyalty to the Crown through appointing and dismissing JPs and judges, but he erred on the side of caution, hoping that this might signal his intent and not further provoke the opposition. And he continued to prevent Parliament from meeting. Ralph and the exclusionists carried on with their own plans. In the spring of 1680 rumours were spread that Bishop Cosin of Durham had left a sealed paper in a black box to his son-in-law which was only to be opened after the King's death. Nonetheless it had recently been opened and proved that Cosin had married Charles to Monmouth's mother. Some thought Shaftesbury responsible for the rumour, but K.D.H. Haley in his biography of the Earl thinks it might well have been Ralph.

Shaftesbury tried to keep the members of the opposition 'grouping' focussed on the issues that he thought mattered, in particular York's exclusion and their self-preservation, and so keep them united. At the same time he may have been jealous of the influence of potential rivals like Ralph - on March 22 1680 Dorothy Sidney wrote to her brother: '*My Lord Shaftesbury says, he never had anything to do with Mr. Montague, nor never will*'. Yet Ralph suggested to Barillon that he could get Shaftesbury to favour France and to Sidney that he would try to persuade the earl to be Lord Treasurer, so it is difficult to discern the true relationship between the two men. This rivalry indicates that had exclusion ever been achieved the opposition might have fragmented into the groups indentified by J.R. Jones in "The First Whigs" (1961): "the 'old Presbyterians' zealous for religious reform and Protestant unity, led by Wharton in the Lords; the 'country Opposition' representing the nation against the corrupt Court, was the largest group, and had many independently minded (and electorally independent) members, and many who came from royalist families; the radicals, derived from levellers and republicans, who though rarely elected to parliament, assisted greatly in the organisation of support for the party in the cities, where they were concentrated; Monmouth and his circle – usually young, fashionable and dissolute like the Duke, and the adventurers, which overlapped the latter group". Jones defines the adventurers as "opportunists who attacked ministers in order first to supplant, and then to imitate them. Power and money were their real objectives. (Men from this group provided Barillon with most of his agents and contacts). The group among the Whigs included some outstandingly able men, notably Ralph Montagu, William Harbord, and Sir Francis Winnington. Apart from their greater unscrupulousness they were marked off from the majority of their colleagues by the fact that most of them had held office at one time and were accustomed to life at Court. By vigorous denunciations of ministers, by constantly advocating the most extreme measure, they tried to efface these facts – with some success, especially in 1680 when for a time they dominated proceedings in the Commons, and even tried to wrest the leadership and direction of policy from Shaftesbury. But it was impossible for them wholly to overcome the justified suspicions, felt by many of the Whig rank and file, that they were thinking primarily of themselves and would, if given encouragement, desert to the Court." Jones's "adventurers" matches Ralph's description of his colleagues as "us mutineers". Their activities were monitored: *'to tell you that Lord Russell & Mr Montagu were yesterday at Lord Shaftesbury's, and that Mr Montagu is today gone out of town with the duke of Monmouth (it is given out) to Moor Park, and that the Duke goes Saturday for Hampshire'.* [168] [169]

Whilst Henry Sidney's diary provides valuable information on Ralph's activities in November 1679, for the early part of 1680 much of the little we know comes from his sister Dorothy's letters. Dorothy, dowager countess of Sunderland, was one of fifteen children of Robert, earl of Leicester by Elizabeth Cavendish, daughter of the 1st duke of Newcastle. These letters mix family matters and gossip with political information. The first, from January 6, makes reference to Ralph's sister Lady Harvey: *'she cannot forebear comedy; the last subject was her daughter ... thinking her husband handsome. She says, three heads and ten noses could not be uglier than he is...My Lady Harvey says, to hear him (*Lord de Lisle*) and you talk 'tis a wonder you should disagree in anything. As to the other brother (*Algernon*), she wonders nobody shoots him'. 'I suppose now the most factious people will not say the Dutch have agreed with France and broke with us; within these two days Tom Pelham and Montague believed it, so as to make me angry. They, instead of improving by Sir Wm Jones, will be quite spoiled; there is not a lie out of any mutinous shop in town, but that they believe it. I think I have almost ended our marriage treaty (*with her sister*). He is not more ill-favoured than Montague, and his wife kisses him all day, and calls him her pretty dear'* (January 23). The marriage treaty was between Gervase Pierpoint, grandson of the 1st earl of Kingston, and Lucy, daughter of Sir John Pelham by Lucy Sidney (daughter of Robert, earl of Leicester) and so sister to Thomas (later 1st Lord) Pelham mentioned above. (Tom's first wife was Sir William Jones's daughter, and his second would be the daughter of the 3rd earl of Clare by Grace Pierpoint. His son would inherit his uncle's estate and become the great duke of Newcastle). Ralph's presence at the wedding shows how close the Sidney connection was to his family, even though the blood connection was fairly distant (his great-great-grandmother was a Sidney). It was also a demonstrable reminder of the family connections between

---

[168] Moor Park was the Duke's magnificent country mansion, near Rickmansworth in Hertfordshire.
[169] Cal SP Dom 29 September 1680

political allies. Another letter, from March 12, has more about the wedding which had taken place two days before: '*I will let Mr Pierpoint know your willingness to favour him; he was gone out of town before I had your letter. He & his mistress, Montague & his wife, went down to Holland with Sir John.*[170] *Next week they are to be married. Tomorrow Tom Pelham goes, but not his wife, because she is with child... Mr Ogle does prove the saddest creature of all kinds that could have been found fit to be named for my Lady Percy, as ugly as any thing young can be... After our wedding at Holland, I had a letter from Mr. Mountague that made me fear that Mr. Pierpoint was not liked; but he is, I doubt, a little malicious...Mr. Mountague goes no more to Madame Mazarin; the town says he is forbid; whether his love or his politics were too pressing, I know not. I hear he has lately endeavoured to make his peace at court; but it will not be, and he is reduced to spend much of his time at my Lady Oxford's. Perhaps you will think I express it ill, but no matter for that. The Duchess of Modena may be come, but I do not know it; I do know that nobody will go to her, nor to the Duchess when she is with her.*[171] *I heard last night the council had sat twice yesterday about information given of a design the apprentices had to rise, & that some were got together, but all is very quiet; & my intelligence must ever be late, for I write in the morning & see nobody but in the afternoon*' (March 22). Dorothy's final letter that Spring: '*Tomorrow our new married couple will be her; all I hear from thence is satisfaction, he very fond, & Mr. Montague writ to me that her kindness might be called so too*' (April 6). This correspondence provides a useful reminder that, beneath the flow of high politics on which history books usually concentrate, the constant undercurrent of daily life continued.

The summer passed with Ralph and his colleagues continuing to keep the opposition grouping together through conversation and counsel. Henry Sidney dined with Ralph on June 5 '*& came from Windsor with Lord Sunderland & Mr. Godolphin, & went to the Duke of Monmouth. He said he was pleased with the Alliance*' and again on September 15 '*& heard all his designs. I went to Sir Wm. Jones & informed him of all the good designs we had*'. In July and August his sister Dorothy wrote some surviving letters to Lord Halifax, her son-in-law. '*It is something like what Mr. Montague said, when many of his acquaintances were taken into the Council, and he left. A pox on them! If he had thought they would have gone without him he would never have brought out my Lord Danby's letter*'; '*Lord* [Shaftesbury] *&, I think, the Duke of Monmouth, dined with Mr. Montague to rejoice*' (at York's discomfort); '*My brother* [Lord Leicester] *is come from Tunbridge, not well. Mr. Montague and Jones are*

---

[170] Halland was the ancient seat of the Pelhams in Sussex, near Glyndebourne. Tom Pelham was moderate Whig MP and Dorothy's cousin

[171] A reference to the visit of the duke of York's mother-in-law

there now. He looks after his own health, but poor Lady Northumberland! the talk of a cure for her is at an end, and never the journey intended for that'; *'This wet weather has not driven everybody from the Wells. Sir Jones is there too, and Mr Montague, two great friends. If Jones is wise and obstinate, sure Montague cannot have so great a power over him as many believe'*.

By the autumn of 1680 it seemed as if the opposition to the duke of York's succession was prevailing and Charles thought it advisable to send him back to Scotland – even the duchess of Portsmouth considered it now in her best interests to encourage the move. Dr. Burnet believed, from his later conversations with Ralph, that it was he who had persuaded her to support exclusion.[172] Henry Sidney arrived from the Netherlands on September 16 and spent his first days in London with his associates of the previous June, Ralph & Sir William Jones, and on the19th conferred with Temple & Capel. As a result Capel proposed to the exclusionists that James be banished to Audley End, and Parliament take what measures to protect the church on accession it saw fit. Sidney made further entries in his diary on events in October: *'Mr. Hyde spoke to me of the Prince's coming, & is very angry. I went to my Lord President & to my Lord Chancellor, & spoke to them both freely. I dined with Mr. Montague, & found he had a great mind to be taken in'* (5th); *'I brought my Lord Sunderland & Mr. Montague together. I dined at Lord Mulgrave's'* (15th); *'I was with Sir Harry Capel & brother Algernon. An extraordinary council was called, & there the king resolved to send his brother into Scotland. The king told the Duke all his people were out of heart. I was with Mr. Montague in the park'* (16th); *'Harbord told me he suspected Montague was for the Duke of Monmouth, & some others. Lord Halifax of the same mind'* (17th). This correspondence is of particular interest in indicating that Ralph still yearned to be in office, rather than in opposition, and that it wasn't clear to everyone how close Ralph was to Monmouth, being one of those pushing him towards the throne.

When Parliament finally met, on October 21, it was in a highly excitable atmosphere. Charles only asked for money to protect Tangier (which his wife had brought him as part of her dowry) and promised to do anything necessary to preserve the Church of England as long as the succession wasn't interfered with. The Commons' response was as expected – the King's speech was not his own, but his foolish councillors'. Hansard reports Ralph's speech in the House on October 26

'Sir, you have heard what an influence the Popish party hath had in the management of all our affairs of greatest importance, almost since his maj.'s happy Restoration; how the making of peace or war, or foreign alliances, hath been over-ruled by that party, to the great danger of the

---

[172] O.Airy ed.,*"History of my own time* vol. 2 p.367,

nation, and Protestant Religion both at home and abroad: insomuch as it may be justly feared, that there is a general design to root out that religion from the face of the earth; which may not be difficult to be done, if by establishing Popery here, assistance to the Protestants abroad may be prevented; or by destroying the Protestants abroad (which are so many bulwarks to us) we should be left to resist alone. You have also heard how that party hath influenced the resolutions made touching parliaments and affairs here at home. The truth is, sir, that interest is crept into our court, and hath a great power in our councils; it is crept into our courts of justice, and hath a great command in our army, our navy, our forts, and our castles, and into all the places upon which our security depends. And it is impossible that it should be otherwise as long as we have a Popish Successor, and that party the hopes of a Popish king. And I humbly conceive it is very obvious, that as long as that party hath such a power, not only our religion, but the life of his majesty, and the whole government, is in danger. And therefore I think we cannot better comply with our duty to our king and country, than in resolving to use our utmost endeavours to extirpate Popery, and prevent a Popish Successor; and therefore I would desire you would be pleased to put the question'. It was then resolved, nem. con. 'That it is the opinion of this house, that they ought to proceed effectually to suppress Popery, and prevent a Popish Successor' and 'That an Address be made to his majesty, declaring that the Resolution of this house, to preserve and support the king's Person and Government, and the Protestant Religion at home and abroad'. [173]

Ambassador Barillon reported to King Louis on October 31 1680 that

'Mr Montagu says, the Duke of Monmouth at present has no other design than that of procuring the good and advantage of all the nation by the Duke of York's exclusion...I have kept myself very reserved with Mr Montagu upon the subject...I have endeavoured to make him understand that your Majesty's interest is confined to preventing the parliament from granting money to the King wherewith to support his alliances, but that your Majesty could not enter into other affairs entirely separate from what is at present in agitation; that I perceived your Majesty was far from favouring the Prince of Orange's party, and that you even judged it very important for your service to prevent him from establishing himself on the Duke of York's ruin; that in this it appeared to me the Duke of Monmouth would find a great advantage...I thought, Sire, I ought to speak in this manner to Mr Montagu to prevent the Duke of Monmouth from losing altogether the hopes of having your Majesty's protection; for this would facilitate his reconciliation with the Prince of Orange....

---

[173] T.C. Hansard *Parliamentary History of England from the Earliest period to the year 1803* Vol iv

Yesterday evening I saw Mr Montagu; he did not conceal from me that the Duke of Monmouth was reconciled with Lady Portsmouth and Lord Sunderland, and that various proposals were making for the future, and that there would be great changes at court'. [174]

The Commons spent the first fortnight of the new sitting discussing and complaining about official obstruction to the prosecution of the Plot and the frequent prorogations which prevented them from conducting business. They reminded Charles that when he had been invited to return to England he had in his response stated that he looked upon Parliament as a vital part of the Nation. The Triennial Act, consented to by Charles I in 1641, had affirmed that it would meet for at least fifty days every three years. If the King did not issue writs for elections the Lords could meet and do so. In 1664 a trusting House had allowed this provision to be removed. They now greatly regretted it - the majority in the Commons were greatly annoyed at misgovernment and worried about the future. Colonel Titus suggested that they should proceed in just the same way as they had in the last session, to show that prorogations achieved nothing. Backed by Jones and the others, each vote of the previous House was read and passed without opposition. The Exclusion Bill now became part of the Common's main grievances, rather than a side issue. When first read on November 4 the debate was opened by Sir Leoline Jenkins, a Court supporter, stating that Parliament could not disinherit the heir to the throne. Ralph responded: *'The honourable Member that spoke last, may understand very much of the Laws of other Countries, and foreign Affairs; but I am apt to think, not much of the Laws of this Nation; or else he would not argue, that this is a Popish Bill, when it is the only thing that can save his King, the Kingdom, and the Protestant Religion; which I hope will never come to that Extremity, as to need any thing that is Popish to save it. For my part, I am so far from thinking that this Bill is so unreasonable as hath been argued, that I think this House of Commons will get as much Credit by passing of this Bill, as that in 1660 did, by passing that which brought home the King. For as the one restored him; so the other may preserve him, and nothing less. And therefore, I think, Sir, you ought not to delay the giving it a second reading, but appoint a speedy day for it'.* In another debate, again in response to Jenkins: *'The other day, this worthy Member told you of the Laws abroad in relation to Succession, and now he says,* "This is a Popish Bill." *I observe, that his knowledge of the Laws and Divinity abroad is more than at home. If any man thinks that the Duke, &c. is not in the Plot, nor a Papist, let him give his Vote against the Bill: I am satisfied in both, and therefore do desire the Bill may have a second reading. Till this Bill be passed, the King is exposed to the malice of the Papists, and importunities of solicitations from the Duke's friends; and I hope this*

---

[174] Dalrymple pp.346/50

Parliament will give as good testimony of their duty for preservation of the King's Person, and the Protestant Religion, as the last did. Saving the King from the malice of Rome is as great service as bringing him from Brussels. This Bill saves the King's Prerogative and Religion, and two good things it saves besides, the King's Life and his Authority; and I am for a second reading'.

The Bill was passed on November 11. The mood was caught by Colonel Titus: *'I am come hither to do my duty, & to speak plain. Were there any place left for moderation or expedient, I would run to it. To act moderately, that is to act with reason, immoderately is with passion. No man advises you to love your wife & children moderately, or to serve God moderately'.*[175] The Commons hoped and believed (based on past experience) that Charles would bow to pressure. The Lords, led by the earl of Halifax, threw the Bill out on the 15th (the King was present in the House until they did so) and when, two days later, the annual pope-burning procession was attended by some 100,000 Londoners, there was much fear of public disorder though it passed without rioting.   Ralph's next contribution was to press for the removal of Halifax from the Council: *'It was not for want of zeal that I did not trouble you the last Debate. I am sensible of the miseries we lie under through the loss of our Bill in the Lords House – it has been always the Privilege of the House of Commons to use Common Fame as an Information of things, the best of Parliaments have done it, and the best of Kings have granted it. Common Fame says "that Lord Halifax advised", and... he has owned the Dissolution of the last Parliament. I think therefore, that in justice you can do no less than vote him an Enemy to the King and Kingdom'* (November 18).[176] Halifax's mother-in-law Dorothy Sidney: *'my Lord of Shaftesbury & Mr. Montague have singled him out of a herd of sixty-three that were of his mind, to desire to remove him from the King, having given no reason yet but that common fame said he had been for proroguing the Parliament, & having very great parts, which made him the more dangerous. Your friend, Mr. Herbert, said, other Lords had been of the mind for Parliaments, but they had given satisfaction, as it was begun by Montagu'.* The next month, on the 15th, Ralph spoke again: *'I believe there is great expectation, both without and within doors, of the Day's Debate, which I wish may be to the satisfaction of every body. The Order of the Day is, "To consider how to prevent Popery and Arbitrary Power." Ever since the Parliament sat, we have been about that – Some time has been taken up in the Bill of excluding the Duke, and Tryal of a popish Lord, and another thing, in punishing those who hindered the Subject from petitioning for Parliaments. These three are all I can recollect; none more against Popery*

---

[175] Grey ibid, p.396
[176] Ibid. p.21

than the two first, nor for our Safety and Property than the rest, &c. you were told, upon the Debate upon the Bill of excluding the Duke, "That though it did pass, there was a Loyal Party, that would stick to the Duke." Now if there be not a Protestant Party, who will stick to themselves, and a Couragious Party, that will stick to that Bill, we must trust to God's Providence; and I hope some skilful Persons will bring about this Bill, if not, something else, to secure us against Popery and Arbitrary Power'. Lord Cavendish suggested that Parliament should draw up a Form of Association agreeing that all should support a Protestant heir to the Crown. When, in debate, alternatives were suggested, Ralph responded that *'My opinion is that this alone will not do your business. When a house is on fire, and buckets of water are not sufficient to quench it, the engine must be made use of. Our only security is Lord Cavendish's Motion; an Association'.*

Determined leadership was arising in the House which was more radical than Shaftesbury wished. On November 25 1680 Dorothy Sidney wrote that *'My Lord Shaftesbury disowns having anything to do in it*['s proceedings], *and my Lord Russell. I heard 'twas Montague and the two lawyers Jones and Winnington, who show their profession. I wish with all my heart the bill had passed, that they might not make that excuse for doing nothing for the King; but I fear that it will soon appear that those persons who have now most power would leave the King none. Some think theirs will not be very lasting. My Lord Shaftesbury says he does no more understand the House of Commons than he does the Court. He does lose ground. Montague was so ashamed, he did not say one word when the second debate was about carrying the address against my Lord Halifax, or laying it aside... One asked, what shall we charge him with? Montague said:* 'With being an enemy to his King and Country' ". These three were joined by a third lawyer, Sir John Maynard (a man in his seventies who had prosecuted Strafford, Laud and later Dr. Coleman; he had opposed Shaftesbury's release from prison), and by Colonel Titus. All had, in their time, been great supporters of the Crown but Charles's actions had led them to becoming its greatest opponents.

Ralph continued to try to get Louis's backing for Monmouth, as Barillon told him on December 5 1680. The letter shows that French money was still being spent on MPs. *'I send your Majesty, in a memorial apart, the names of the members of parliament whom I have engaged in your interests The foundation of all these engagements is, that the parliament shall not enter into any alliance made with Spain, nor those that may be proposed with the States General, the Emperor...nor give any money to his Britannic Majesty to support them, the greatest part of these connections could not be made by myself; few were to be found who would treat directly with, or have any commerce with me, by which they might have exposed their fortunes and their lives. I have made use of Mr Montagu and Mrs Hervey his sister; of Mr Harbord, Algernon Sidney and the Sieur Beber ...*

The interests of those with whom I am in commerce are very different and very opposite. Mr Montagu would willingly be well with the court, and have a great place if it were possible; he would be very glad to go ambassador extraordinary to France for some time. He has declared himself openly against the Duke of York, and is entered into an intimate confidence with the Duke of Monmouth; he is also united with Lord Russell and Lord Shaftesbury. Although Mr Montagu has been in your Majesty's interests a long time, and the sum of which he expects the payment is alone sufficient to prevent his taking any contrary step, he wishes that I would enter farther into the Duke of Monmouth's affair, and the reserve which he observes in me upon that has, makes him sometimes suspect that your Majesty supports the Duke of York, and that you will protect him hereafter. I make him easy by telling him that the resolution to support such a pretension as the Duke of Monmouth's is not lightly to be take; that it ought to suffice that the Prince of Orange is his greatest enemy, as he is of France; that your Majesty will determine according to what you think most proper, when the crown of England shall be disposed among many pretenders; but in the interim it is not your province to meddle with the domestic affairs of England, except to prevent any steps being taken with regard to foreign ones, which might be contrary to your interest... That with regard to the King of Great Britain, all he has done for some years past would put it out of your Majesty's thoughts to assist him in augmenting his authority, and governing absolutely...All I said did not persuade Mr Montagu, but the money I paid him by your Majesty's order makes his mind very easy. I believe it will be necessary to make him a second payment of fifty thousand livres, for the excuse of bills of exchange not coming fast enough is not sufficient, and in the present conjunction he may be of great use to me in your Majesty's affairs. Mrs Hervey his sister, is as deep as he in all the intrigues; she is a woman of a bold and enterprising spirit, and has interest and connections with a great number of people of the court and parliament. It was through her I engaged Mr Hamden and Mr Harbord, who are two of the most considerable members of parliament...Mr Harbord is the same whom I engaged in the affair of the high Treasurer; he is a friend of Mr Montagu's but he has not the same connections with the Duke of Monmouth; on the contrary he appears to be in the prince of Orange's interest. Through him I have engaged many persons if great credit in parliament and in London. He is an active vigilant man, from whom I have very good information, and who has a great desire to make his fortune by means of France. Mr Montagu knows only a part of the connections which we have'. [177]

On December 23 the King again remonstrated with the House for its concentration on Exclusion. Ralph's response was: '*Mr. Speaker, Sir, the truth is, we committed a great Error in the Beginning of this Session; when we went about to look into the Popish Plot, we went into the Tower, whereas we should have gone to the Court; for it is plain, that the Duke's Friends which are there, do still carry on the Plot against the Protestant Religion, as much as ever the Lord Bellasis, Powis, or any of those Lords in the Tower did. And we may reasonably conclude by the little Success we have had against Popery this Session, that until we can remove that Interest from about the King, we take pains to no purpose*'.

It seems possible that, during the Christmas holiday, some of the opposition again urged the King, through Sunderland and Portsmouth, to accept exclusion in return for supply. The duke of York suggested that '*many of the heads of the party, like the prudent Steward in the Gospel, had the grace not to forget themselves*', expecting office as part of the settlement. The group seems to have been known as the Southamptons, from Ralph and Russell's houses in Southampton Place. Rumour suggested that Russell would command the key garrison at Portsmouth, Jones would be Lord Chief Justice, and Colonel Titus one of the secretaries of state, with Ralph presumably the other, since it was the office he had so long wanted. The information was relayed by both the French and Dutch ambassadors to their royal masters. Since Shaftesbury hadn't been told, it is possible that Charles encouraged the rumours to sow dissension. Knowing better than to exclude him, it had been thought he would consent if made Lord Treasurer, but he was angry on discovering the plans at being sidelined. There must have been concerns as to whether anything could be achieved by them taking up office unless the King allowed them to govern (which he had not allowed the Council Shaftesbury had been part of the previous year). The Commons reconvened on December 30 when there were motions to prevent MPs accepting office without the House's consent. Many MPs rightly thought that if colleagues did accept office they would not be able to achieve anything without compromising their political principles. '*Lead us not into temptation*' said Colonel Titus piously.[178] Barillon was now at last prepared to back Charles's plea to Louis for help for fear that, if he did not do so, a republic might be brought into being – Louis would have remembered that republican Cromwellian England had been a far more formidable force in Europe than it was ever to be in Charles's reign.

---

[177] Dalrymple p.355
[178] K.H.D. Haley, *The First Earl of Shaftesbury* (Oxford 1968)

The Commons was furious with frustration and continued to bluster but an increasingly number of MPs came to realise that only exclusion would legitimise resistance to a Catholic king. Consequently they fell back again on their only legal sanction and refused, point blank, to supply the King with money until he agreed to exclude his brother. Thus when invited by the King to reconsider the Bill they refused, on January 7, stating that it had been thoroughly debated and settled, and no good reason had been given as to why they should withdraw it. Ralph summed it all up in the Commons that day: *'we sat so many weeks, and made so many requests, without any satisfactory Answer. I believe, there was never more Loyalty to a King of England from his Subjects; but not to have one Bill pass, nor a kind Answer to our Addresses! Therefore I expect not much good from Bills we are like to pass. We have nothing left us but Votes. When the King recommended the Plot to our consideration, we, like honest Country Gentlemen, looked for it in the Tower, but it was not there; let us look into Whitehall, and we shall find those more guilty of it than Lord Powis, and the rest of the Lords. He that goes to War with Armour not proof, had rather have none; nothing can secure us but the Bill of Exclusion, &c – We see those in the Lords House, who were for the Bill, put out of Office, as here and those put into Office who were against it. I am of opinion, that both Tangier and Flanders are in danger of being lost; but I had rather see the French in Flanders, and the Moors in Tangier, than the Pope in England; and I would give no money till the Bill of Exclusion be passed, as the only security we have, &c'.*[179] Ralph and his colleagues believed they had a policy of managed confrontation, having their hands on the two extra-parliamentary sources of money: from the City and Louis. Next day members found that Parliament was, once again, dissolved. They condemned the move as treasonable.

Charles commanded that Parliament should meet again at Oxford late in March 1681. The fear of riot in London, though not realised the previous year, still existed and Oxford was reliably royalist (it had been Charles I's headquarters during the Civil War). Electors were asked by the opposition to return the same MPs, to show that this Parliament would pursue the same course as the last. That came to pass – the same Bills were discussed and passed. Once again there was a crisis of popery and arbitrary government, and many of those sitting in Parliament had been alive when there had been such a crisis in 1641, and knew how that had played out. It was on the 26th that Ralph, now an MP for Northampton, suggested in the House that Charles's refusal of exclusion meant that *'The Security of the Protestant Religion, and the Safety of the King's Person, are things of so great a weight, that we should not have stayed so long as this day, to take into consideration the Exclusion of the duke of York from inheriting the*

---

[179] Grey p.262

148

Crown, &c. I am sorry to hear of the King's giving us Expedients to secure the Protestant Religion: I am sorry to hear that language. This is not to be used as an English Parliament, but a French, to be told in the King's Speech, what we are to do, and what not. The greatest Arbitrary Power that can be used in England, is to cow a Parliament, and, it may be, that was the design in bringing us hither. But be we called to York, or all England over, we shall, I believe, be the same men, both as we are here and were at Westminster, in our opinions. When Lord Danby dissolved the Long Parliament, he said, "He had spoiled the old Rooks, and had taken away their false dice." Soon after him, started in new Ministers of State, and they shuffle and cut the cards again, and will dissolve and prorogue Parliaments, till they can get one for their turn; and in this condition we are – As for the Bill of disinheriting the duke of York, were my Brother or my Son like to ruin my Family, I would disinherit them, and turn away servants that would ruin me. If the Bishops, and the Counsellors had spoken plain English to the King, things would not have been in this condition... But neither these Ministers of the Gospel have endeavoured the preservation of the Protestant Religion, nor the Ministers of State the Government, both acting against Religion, and the Preservation of the King's Person. And seeing no Expedient can serve us, but the Bill for excluding the Duke, &c. therefore I move for it'. [180] Shaftesbury suggested to Charles that exclusion could be avoided by determining that if James became king power would be given to Monmouth. When the King replied that would be contrary to his conscience and the law Shaftesbury responded that the law could be changed. On March 28 the Commons gave the first reading to a new Exclusion Bill.

Shortly before arriving at Oxford Charles had been offered a subsidy by Louis: two million livres for the first year, one and a half million for the next two. Perhaps Louis had had a rare pang of conscience about encouraging republicans to exclude his Catholic cousin James. Consequently, seeing that the Commons were intransigent, Charles responded to the new reading of the Exclusion Bill by summoning them to the Lords the same day. The latter had been meeting in the hall of Christ Church College, and the Commons arrived in some excitement, expecting at the least the announcement of concessions. The King suddenly appeared in the hall wearing the crown and robes of state and dissolved Parliament, which had only sat for a week. He had decided that he was now financially able to do without it, so long as he had no active foreign policy (with his usual fecklessness he even felt able to grant the duchess of Portsmouth £100,000 out of the French monies). The opposition was left shocked and disorientated, even though they could not know that they would no longer be able to counter Charles's policies through Parliament,

---

[180] Ibid p.310

since he would not call it again for the four years remaining of his reign. The government media campaign included a broadsheet of "A Dialogue between ghosts of the last two Parliaments at their late interview" in which the ghost of the Westminster parliament tells the ghost of Oxford that '*No freedom of debate was left to you, When all was mov'd and managed by a few, Your leading M- J- and W- As if all Wisdom was in them alone, A House of Commons crumbl'd into Three*'. Presumably the letters stood for Montagu (though M could also stand for Maynard), Jones and Winnington.

Charles took advantage of this by strengthening his position. His supporters had learnt from the opposition's exploitation of the media and produced a flood of pamphlets, plays and poems. The laws against Dissenters, who were often for the opposition, were more actively enforced and there was increasing pressure on town and city corporations to surrender their charters in favour of new ones. These might contain additional privileges but also specifically allowed the King to remove "disaffected" councillors. Shaftesbury was removed as far as the Tower on July 2, accused of treason. Monmouth visited him there on the night of his arrest and a few days later went to Tunbridge Wells for a month to drink the waters, accompanied by Ralph and Armstrong. If things improved for Charles they were unlikely to be beneficial to Ralph, as one of the malcontents. He spent part of the autumn dreaming up a scheme to benefit Louis (and himself).

Ambassador Barillon was approached by Ralph on September 20: '*after a long discourse upon the service he says he has done your Majesty, he told me he was at present in a capacity to do you as considerable a service as he had done in accusing the high Treasurer; that he would do it with a great deal of zeal, but could not engage in any new affair till the first was finished, and till he saw himself certain of entire and complete payment...what he had to say to me was to put you in a condition not to be hurt by England for a long time... for such a recompense as you might think he deserved... But he stuck fast to having positive assurances of being paid what was due to him, and that without it he could not again hazard his fortune and his head. I pressed him much to open himself further, but it was impossible for me to get any thing more from him, except that when he was sure of his entire payment, your Majesty would find he was not an imposture...*

I had at first some suspicion that Mr Montagu wanted to discover... whether your Majesty had made alliances with the King of England that could hinder him from taking any other measure; but it has appeared since to me that he has something solid to propose which might tend to destroy the cabals and intrigues of the Prince of Orange, and prevent their being in the end powerful enough to give law to the King of England and the Duke of York.

Your Majesty will judge what is convenient to your service; it is not hazarding much to advance the payment of what remains to Mr Montagu. It may be thought that if he should be entirely paid, he would be less zealous to act, and would not care to expose himself for your Majesty's interest; but on the other hand, I do not see a possibility to make him act without satisfying him, and I believe he will not find his advantage in abandoning your Majesty's interests, from whom he will always expect powerful protection, and new advantages when he does new services.

I could not help entering into Mr Montagu's proposition, and discussing it with him, otherwise he might have believed me entirely engaged with the court. I ... pressed him strongly to be more explicit; but he told me he should wait for the orders which your Majesty should give me, and if he was well treated I should see what he was capable of doing.

I endeavoured to penetrate, through Mrs Hervey, into what Mr Montagu had to propose, but by what she said, I find he did not trust her with the matter, I plainly see it aims at hindering something important which the Prince of Orange wants to attempt, when it is the least expected, and this may probably be a project of reunion of all the cabals, and a general amnesty, by which the catholic lords, and Danby and Shaftesbury may get out of prison, and the King of England offer on his part to forget all, provided the parliament on theirs will change its conduct with regard to him...

In waiting for the receipt of your Majesty's orders upon what Mr Montagu said to me, I shall endeavour to manage his spirit, and draw from him something more than he has yet told me. He is a man who may be of very great help, and by whom I can do more than many others. To speak the truth, he is not contented, and thinks he has been neglected; but all this may be removed if your Majesty gives order for the payment of what is due to him'. [181]

The political ferment is well demonstrated by entries in the Calendar of State Papers concerning the election at the end of 1681 of a Recorder for Northampton. '*Since the bailment of the E(arl) of S(haftesbury) that party are grown insolent and troublesome. I shall now only tell you what has passed in that most base and ungrateful corporation of Northampton. About a month since Mr. Ralph Montagu promised the town 500l., since which the recordership thereof is void by the death of the Earl of Northampton. The present mayor, a loyal and true servant to his Majesty, finding the whole factious gentlemen of the county in the town soliciting, who had by fear, promises or threats gained the greatest number of votes, and that Mr. Montagu's 500l. and other great promises biased them so that no other interest could prevail, advising with his Majesty's friends, it was thought fit, as a means to divert them from that choice, and telling*

---

[181] Dalrymple. Barillon to Louis Sept 22 1681

them that it was a way to prevent all differences and animosities between them and other gentlemen that might appear on either side, to beseech his Majesty to nominate one, that so their choice might not be disagreeable to him, but the faction was so prevailing and violent, that it became tumultuous in the assembly of the corporation, on which the mayor endeavoured to break up the assembly, but by force was kept in for some time, but at last took his mace and went out, but with affronts and blows to him and his friends, after which the factious party continued and after some hours' debate elected (without the Mayor) Lord Montagu recorder and will present it for his Majesty's approbation. I need not acquaint you with the great disadvantage it will be to his Majesty's service and encouragement to his enemies'. [182] It is very interesting to note that it was Ralph's father whose name was being put forward, not Ralph himself - their interests were apparently not thought to be different. The furore caused by this local election of a town official, and the appeal to the Crown, indicates how politically important such posts were considered to be.

Another version of events gives more detail: *'The cause of the uproar was because the Mayor would not put Lord Montagu in competition with his Majesty. They were animated to this by 16 or 17 of the country gentlemen, who with some few who live in the town meet in a cabal every Saturday, and several of them went from house to house amongst the 48 burgesses, who are of the meanest sort of people admitted into the corporation, and with threats and promises procured from most of them a promise to vote for nobody but Lord Montagu. The Mayor, consulting the charter again as to the clauses relating to nominating a recorder...found that in strictness we could not nominate any but an honest and discreet man learned in the laws...proposed nominating Serjeant Bugby for his Majesty's approbation. For his recommendation the Mayor & six more aldermen with most of the Bayliffs and some few of the 48 burgesses, 27 in all, voted but the rest of the 48 with five of the Aldermen and some few of the Bayliffs voted for Lord Montagu, having bound themselves at the instigation of the said cabal to do so and no otherwise. This cabal consists of most of the Justices lately put out and some others, who on all occasions have expresses great disaffection to his Majesty, some of whom were in arms at the very taking of Lambert in our country and were beholden to the Act of pardon for their lives. This cabal is looked upon as persons who abet the thing called an association and is esteemed as dangerous a meeting as most in England'.* [183] The Mayor's insistence that the charter stated that only a lawyer should be appointed as recorder must have

---

[182] Cal SP Dom. Sir Roger Norwich to Secretary Jenkins, Brampton Dec. 20 1681, p.633
[183] Cal SP Dom. Major John Willoughby to Edward Griffin at Dingley. Northampton, Dec. 23. p.640

sounded rather empty since all knew that the previous post-holder was the earl of Northampton. Griffin dutifully wrote to the King the following day: '*I thought it my duty to let your Majesty know...Thither come many of our best freeholders for the love of drinking free of cost, and the poison they suck in from the discourses they hear against your Majesty and the government, have their hearts so alienated that I much fear, that, when you call a Parliament, we shall not be able to send men suitable to our desires or your service...hope that you will not approve the riotous election of Lord Montagu, who is introduced by that factious party only to make sure of his son's election there and whoever else he thinks fit, and besides it will influence the whole county a great deal*'.

Whilst Ralph was fully occupied with politics his pregnant wife had domestic turbulence to contend with. In November 1681 her widowed fourteen year old daughter Betty Percy, Lady Ogle, disappeared. A letter to the duke of Albemarle sent on the 14th gives full details. '*The extraordinary news with which the Town was filled this morning, and is now become the discourse of the Coffee houses...is that the Lady Ogle is gone from her grandmother from Northumberland House, without giving any account whither, and as yet not anybody can tell what has become of her. The manner was thus: Yesterday morning about nine a clock the Lady Ogle dressed herself to go abroad as she said to Lombard Street, to buy some plate and other things at a goldsmith's. She took her own coach and footmen along with her, but instead of going to Lombard Street she went into the old Exchange, and left the coachman and footmen below stairs, telling them they should not stir from thence till she sent them order; and having only her page with her, she feigned a pretence of sending him on some errand, bidding him return to her when he had done, but when he came back he could not find his Lady. However, all the servants stayed at the Exchange till eleven a clock at night, and then thought fit to go home; which when the old Lady was informed of...she sent everywhere to enquire, but could hear no news of her; upon which Capt. Brett went to the King, and told him she had been married some time ago to Mr. Thyn; to which the King made no other return but this, that if she was married to him she had been betrayed by those who pretended and ought to have been her best friends.*

The old Lady Northumberland could hear no news of her till this morning, when the young Lady's chambermaid brought her a letter written with her own hand, which she left with her, but charged her not to deliver it till the next day, in which she did own her marriage in some measure to Mr. Thyn, but not fully, and that now she could not endure him, and therefore could not think of living with him, and therefore was gone away, but would not let her know where nor with whom. She had also sent a ring which Mr. Thynn had presented her, to be returned to him; at which Mr.

Thynn storms and rages to extravagancy in his passion, and owns his marriage, but says not that he has bedded her...tis said that Sir William Temple's Lady and Mrs. Stanhop her woman were with her at the Exchange, and are gone in her company, most believe to Holland. The Lord Poorescott[184] gave her in marriage, and his Lady and Capt. Brett and his Lady were by when 'twas done, which cannot be very lately, for the Lady Katherine Brett has been dead at least six weeks... 'twas said she was gone along with the Count Coningsmarke, but that is only a report'. A month later, on the 15th, Ralph's uncle William wrote to Lord Montagu *'I can write nothing to your Lordship of Lady Ogle, but that her mother writ to her, if she was married, it was best to come live with her husband. My Lady herself hath been ill this two or three days and kept her bed, but I hope is in no way of miscarrying'.*

The Calendar of State Papers Domestic contains a remarkably frank exchange between the earl of Anglesey (in the guise of a friend of her grandfather's) and Lady Ogle. Having read how the Earl deplored her conduct, she replied at equal length and asked *'why nobody should believe it feasible for Mr. Bret to get money by selling me as by robbing on the highway'.* She considered that *'of two evils the least is to be chosen, for I think there may be more sin and shame in people living together than in parting.'* An even more perspicacious comment, especially for someone of her age, was *'I may...with plainness tell you that Mr. Thynne may if he pleases, trouble himself and me and we may make both our fortunes a prey to lawyers and seven years hence be where we are (except so much older and poorer). If he like it, I am content, for in all probability myself and my purse may hold out as long as his'.* Tom Thynne of Longleat was one of the richest commoners in England. M.P. for Wiltshire, he was close to Monmouth and supported his aspirations which would have made him close to Ralph. Whilst Lady Ogle's first husband had been of similar age, Thynne was thirty-three years old to her fourteen. Exactly what her relationship was with the twenty-two year old Swedish mercenary Count Konigsmark was probably as unclear to contemporaries as it is now. He seems to have been rejected as a suitable match by Lady Betty's guardians, if not by her. Late in the evening of Sunday February 28 1682 Thynne's coach dropped off Monmouth and continued along Pall Mall on the way to old Lady Northumberland's. Three horsemen hired by the Count emerged from the darkness and one of them shot Thynne, mortally wounding him.[185] Lady Ogle was a widow once more and the Count travelled to

---

[184] This is probably a reference to the Irish peer Lord Powerscourt.

[185] The assassins were tried, condemned and hanged in Pall Mall. Konigsmark was apprehended at Gravesend trying to flee, denied complicity and was released after trial. Charles may have welcomed the removal of Thynne, considering him to be a baleful influence on his son. He certainly stopped Lords Cavendish and Mordaunt travelling abroad to challenge the Count. Konigsmark was killed in 1686 fighting the Turks in Greece. His

Holland, though there is no evidence of an attempt to persuade her to marry him. Another suitor was apparently already on his way in the person of Henry Sidney. Perhaps he wasn't considered a suitable match either, even though his mother was a Percy, because in April 1682 the countess of Rutland was told by her mother that '*Lord Northumberland is to marry Lady Ogle, and that my Lady Cleveland comes over this week about it, and that Ralph Montague will be made a Marquis'.*[186] This was a revival of the marriage planned five years before. Was a much coveted title sufficient for Ralph to forgive Cleveland? Did he hope that the King might do the same and allow him to return to Court? In the event Betty Percy married the 6th duke of Somerset the following month (brother to the Duke who it had been suggested she might marry in December 1676 – he had been shot dead at the age of 20 by a Genoese whose wife he was said to have insulted).

At the start of 1682 the duke of York suspected that Halifax was negotiating with Ralph and Shaftesbury against him,[187] but things were so much improved by the spring that he was allowed to return home. Encouraged, Charles moved against Shaftesbury. In July he was accused of having conspired to wage war against the King at the time of the Oxford Parliament. Ralph was one of those who offered themselves as sureties for his good conduct. The trial began on November 24. As witnesses gave evidence against him they were heckled by spectators, encouraged by Ralph, Monmouth and Russell.[188] Ralph and Russell had managed to get themselves chosen as members of the grand jury, which unsurprisingly announced there was insufficient evidence to proceed. There was widespread rejoicing in the City: it, at least, remained in opposition hands. The duke of Monmouth remained popular, even though the King would have nothing to do with him. He had been forbidden the Court in December 1681 and though he made qualified overtures to his father, he wouldn't abandon Shaftesbury and the opposition. When he made visits to English towns there were disorders, and Charles ordered his arrest. Monmouth questioned the warrant's legality and, at first, refused to agree to keep the peace, which further infuriated the King.

In late 1682 Shaftesbury, fearing that strengthening court influence in the City might lead to his own arrest, fled to Holland, where he died a few months later. But for this he would doubtless have been implicated in the Rye House Plot to assassinate Charles and James on their return from

---

brother Philip disappeared in 1694 – he had been the lover of Sophia Dorothea, wife of the future King George I. His sister Aurora went to Dresden to get help in her search for him from the Elector of Saxony and became his mistress.

[186] HMC Rutland 1682 April Viscountess Campden to her daughter
[187] J.P. Kenyon, *Robert Spencer, Earl of Sunderland, 1641- 1702* (Westport, 1975) p.79
[188] J. Miller, *Charles II* (London 1991) p.359

Newmarket, which came to light in June 1683. It is hard to decide at this distance what had been merely idle chat among frustrated radicals and what had been intent. Monmouth and Essex would never have agreed to kill the King, whilst Ralph's brother-in-law Russell may simply have discussed whether the right of resistance should go that far. Charles considered that there was so much evidence, of the discussion of rebellion at the least, that the balance of probability permitted his drastic actions. Even if Russell didn't support the death of the King, he knew of the plot and did not reveal it and was therefore executed for treason on July 21. Another of Ralph's relatives, the republican Sir Algernon Sidney, and Sir Henry Vane were also executed. Essex killed himself in the Tower. There would not have been enough evidence of treason to convince a modern jury to convict, but Charles considered that if he did not take their lives they would ultimately take his and his brother's. Ralph was extremely lucky not to have met the same fate, according to the French ambassador. ('*I found, in Barillon's correspondence, that infinite pains were taken in England to fix...that conspiracy upon him, but in vain*').[189] Even flight abroad might not have been enough to save him – Sir Thomas Armstrong, who had helped him at Deptford at the start of 1679 when he was trying to get to France, and had drunk the Wells water with him in July 1681, was captured in Rotterdam in June 1684, brought back and then hung, drawn and quartered. [190]

Ralph was still forbidden the Court when in 1683 he wrote to Sir Leoline Jenkins, Secretary of State:

Being so unfortunate as not to have the hour of coming into his Majesty's presence, I desire you to present this petition to him. Your station and the relation my petition has to your office, I hope will excuse my giving you this trouble, nor would I do it now under the circumstances I lie under of his Majesty's displeasure, but that I know his goodness to be such that, though one loses his favour, yet one has never reason to despair of his justice.

Ralph Montagu to the King. Petition stating that the petitioner was twice ambassador to France, the first of which embassies, determining about April 1672, 1,300l was then due to him for his ordinary entertainment, as appears by a tally then given him for the same, but that tally was not then satisfied, nor much pressed by the petitioner, the Commissioners of the Treasury then telling him that he had a good security in his hands for the said sum, meaning the plate which he had on

[189] Dalrymple ibid vol.2 p.256
[190] Until the early 20th century the Rising Sun, a Tudor tavern on Wych Street, north of St. Clement Danes church, housed one of Armstrong's bones, taken from the quarter set up on nearby Temple Bar.

his bond from the Jewel House for his use in that employ, that the same plate without alteration or addition served the petitioner again in his second embassy, from being which recalled 3 July 1678, there was then further due to him 22,000l as appears by certificate from the Secretary of State and Sir Robert Howard, that the petitioner is called on by the Master of the Jewel House to answer his said bond either by restoring the plate received from thence or the value of it and that the petitioner's departure from Paris and the determination if his last embassy was so sudden that, having a little before advanced all his ready money at his Majesty's desire to bring the English troops out of France, who were then in great necessity, he wanted wherewithal to pay his debts there and to provide for his family and servants remaining behind, and was thereby forced to sell his own plate as well as that he had out of the Jewel House, and therefore praying that his Majesty will direct that the value of the said plate may be allowed to him for so much due to him and that the Master of the Jewel House may be ordered to deliver him his bond for the same, and for the rest remaining due to him he shall wait till his majesty's convenience. [191]

The attitude of historians towards Ralph has usually been formed primarily from his central part in Danby's fall and his prominent role in what has become known as "the Exclusion Crisis". It is particularly critical of his negotiations for French money for both Charles and himself, reflected against a view of history drawn with the benefit of hindsight and a belief that the Revolution of 1688 was indeed Glorious. It takes little account of the retributive justice of Danby's fall in light of his work to bring down Clarendon, and his acquiescence in a foreign policy which he knew to be wrong and considered not to be in the best interests of his country. There is an alternative view to that held by most historians. The Restoration was backed by the concept of returning the nation to the happy days before everything had gone awry under Charles I. Unfortunately the same concerns about royal policy towards religion, foreign relations and parliament came to the fore under Charles's son. There was again a Scottish rising, an impeachment of the first minister (Danby) modelled on that of Strafford, and a popish plot. (From a modern viewpoint much of the Popish Plot looks like hysteria, but those living through it felt surrounded by a resurgent Catholicism, with Ireland to the west and the continent to the east. On November 17 1679, the anniversary of Queen Elizabeth's accession and always a celebration of Protestantism and her golden reign, there was a procession of some 150,000 people in London - almost a third of the city's population). The fear was that "arbitrary government", that is government without the participation (through parliament) of the people, would not only lead to absolutism but also to popery. Indeed, since England had a Protestant political elite, that was the only way in which

---

[191] Cal SP Dom January 22 1683

popery could be introduced to land. As we have seen, being an MP meant expense, not just at election time, but during attendance in London. Members often had to travel long distances to get to London but they did this as a duty and/or to maintain their status in society, so the *'prorogations, the dissolutions, the cutting short of Parliaments, not suffering them to have time or opportunity to look into anything'* mentioned by Shaftesbury in a Lords speech of 1680 were galling from this point of view as well as what it indicated of Charles's attitude towards the nation's representatives. Ralph's former doctor, John Locke, published a polemic in the same period showing that this was a way of dissolving governments from within.

It might be said that Charles's dependence on parliaments he could not control over the period 1678-1681 arose from his attempts to carry through exactly what ambassador Ralph had advised the King to do – raise the price Louis was prepared to pay him. The dynastic union between William and Mary in 1677 had created a potential threat to Louis who responded by destroying both Danby, arranger of the match, and the political quiet (in part by using Ralph as his agent). Louis was quite aware of the game Charles was playing and decided to punish his cousin for his temerity by not paying up the amount that had been promised in the agreement of May 1678. Once more the existing political structures could not cope with the problems and polarisation began to occur in parliament and the City. But this time Charles II's more adroit handling of things, not least through exploiting the nation's fear and memory of civil war and the Commonwealth led to a different conclusion. Whereas the opposition in 1678 - 1680 had heightened fears of a hellish and bloody plot by Jesuits to kill the King, introduce popery and arbitrary government, leading to many executions for treason, the loyalists who gained the upper hand in 1681-1683 accused the group Ralph was associated with of a most horrid plot to kill the King, destroy the church and bring in arbitrary government. Ralph was very lucky not to have been in the second group of treason victims, whose trials were consciously modelled on the first.

Chapter 6
Exile, Restoration & Revolution 1683-1690

Ralph decided to go to France and be out of the dangerous limelight of English politics. He left after his brother-in-law's execution and arrived in the middle of September.[192] (John Locke similarly thought it wise to leave England for Holland).The following letter from Lord Preston, ambassador in Paris, to Lord Halifax (the man that Ralph had tried to have voted as an "enemy to the kingdom" in the Commons three years before), provides a little more information.

Since my last to your Lordship, I had some more lights concerning Mr Montagu, and I have them from an original hand, and I dare assure your Lordship of the truth of them. He did twice, during his stay here, desire to see this King in private, and twice it was refused him, he being told the last time, that his most Christian Majesty did not think fit to see him at this time, when he had so good a correspondence with the King, our master, and when he, Mr Montagu, was so ill to him. When he could not obtain an audience, he then, by the same hand, desired to know if he might not expect some money as a gratification, he having at this time occasion for it. He was denied that also, which made him more haste away than he designed to do at his arrival here. I am told he intends to leave my Lady Northumberland at Monpellier, and to pass the winter himself in Italy; at least he pretends this. I remember I took particular notice of the word gratification when this thing was told me, and I desired to know if that was the term he used, and the person who told me assured me a second time that it was. I need not observe to your Lordship, that gratification pre-supposeth service. *I have, since I had this account, considered why Mr Montagu should have been treated worse than Dr. Burnet,[193] and I can only think of these reasons for it. First, he cannot be so useful at this time as the doctor, who, if he be gone into England, may continue his former practises with the discontented party. In the next place, if Mr Montagu had had a reception, it could not have been excused to the King, our master, as that of Dr Burnet was by his most Christian Majesty, pretending not to know his character and circumstances. Or, perhaps, another reason might be the scarcity of money here, where they are begun to retrench themselves in all sorts of expences. It is a question now often asked at this court in confidence, whether there has been really any such thing as a late*

---

[192] BL Add 70119 Robert Watson to Robert Harley, 15 September 1683. *'Dr. Burnett is safely arrived in Paris...as also Mr Montagu'.*
[193] The Dr. Burnet referred to was Gilbert Burnet, a Scottish theologian. He had defended Russell after his arrest, and decided that it was politic to leave England afterwards. He also talked extensively to Ralph and so has been quoted earlier in this book.

conspiracy in England? Which I take to be one effect of the doctor's late conversation here. November 5 1683 [194]

Comparatively little is known about the years Ralph spent in France. He had been there for less than a year when his father died at the age of 68 on January 10 1684. (Ralph thus became the 3rd Lord Montagu of Boughton). One of the rare personal insights we have of his wife Elizabeth's life is a letter sent some years before from Ralph Winwood to his brother-in-law Lord Edward, which shows her making family visits. He sends some Ditton grapes by the coach that has brought her and her children to Boughton, regrets his Lordship's indisposition, and mentions the remedies and diet which he himself has adopted. Another letter alarmingly mentions that she *'has got over the accident to her arm by the pricking of an artery'.* [195]

There is no evidence of a trip by Ralph to Italy, but we do know that by the summer of 1684 he was with his wife in Montpellier. The latter was known to the English as Mompey and long had a small English community. Some visited because the southern climate was beneficial to their health, others as a congenial place to settle whilst out of favour with the current political climate at home (and less expensive than Paris), or simply as a place to draw breath before continuing south to Italy or Spain. The town was also fashionable with the French, so there was usually a sprinkling of deputies of the States General and nobility whose society could be enjoyed. On May 7 Elizabeth replied to a letter from her sister Lady Russell that had clearly reflected on the execution of the latter's husband the previous July. The reply not only gives precious information on life at Montpellier but also on Elizabeth Montagu's personality. *'It is the saddest thing, my dearest sister, in the world to read your letter, by which one finds your affliction, if it be possible, daily to increase; but for God's sake, do not add to it by making reflections when it is too late, but as you say afterwards, consider it was God's will it should be so ... and it ought to be a great comfort to you that you left nothing undone, either as to your advice or other endeavours, to hinder that fatal stroke. For my part, when I give myself leave to think of your misfortunes (which I confess I do as little as I can, finding it but too uneasy for me) I cannot but look upon it as the immediate work of God, that chose him out to undergo those severe trials for his glory; for certainly never man suffered with more Christian patience the injustice of his enemies, by which he left an immortal fame here below, and without doubt gained a crown of glory in the kingdom of heaven, which ought to be your comfort. I am mighty glad your dear children are so well and prosper ...*

---

[194] Dalrymple
[195] The manuscripts of Lord Montagu of Beaulieu H.M.C. 1900

As for our coming to England, we have not yet the least thoughts of it; this air, thank God agrees perfectly well with me and the children, so that I am very well to continue in it; and as for my Lord, he is so really affected with your misfortune that I think it has given him a dislike to his country, as to hinder him from returning till our healths are so established that we might continue our journey together. He is your very real humble servant. We now have the finest weather that ever was seen, which you will believe when I tell you that for these ten days I have not seen one spark of fire, only one little vine faggot morning and night to air my linen, and the sun is now so hot that I cannot bear going out in the coach till four o'clock, and in a little time I believe must leave it quite, for there is no shade in the country... My dearest sister, farewell! Pray God preserve you and support you that you may not sink under your affliction. Yours with all passion...' [196]

Just over a year after Lord Edward died King Charles followed him, on February 6 1685. His brother James succeeded, as Charles had always intended. Ralph could not have expected that the new king would welcome him back to court, since he had been so active in trying to prevent James's accession to the throne. However James made it clear that he was prepared to forget the past in return for future loyalty from his subjects. Perhaps Ralph had become aware of this when he wrote to Lawrence Hyde, Clarendon's son and so the new king's brother-in-law, two months after Charles's death. *'I would not have been so long without congratulating you with the honour his Majesty has done you in making you Lord High Treasurer of England, but that the news of it came to me as I was upon my journey hither; and had I not been stopped by an indisposition...I intend, my Lord, to pay my attendance at his Majesty's coronation. I know not how unfortunate I may be as to lie under his Majesty's displeasure, but I know the generosity of his nature to be such, that Louis Duke of Orleans, when he came to the Crown of France, said that it was not for a King of France to remember the quarrels and grudges of a Duke of Orleans, so I hope his Majesty will be pleased to think the King is not to remember any thing that has passed in relation to the Duke of York; for whatever my opinions were when I delivered them, being trusted by the public, they are altered now I am become his subject, knowing myself obliged, by the laws of God and man, to hazard life and fortune in the defence of his sacred person, crown and dignity. I hope my coming can give no offence, since it is out of no other end but to do my duty and submission, as it is fit for a subject to do, and to enjoy that protection and justice under his Majesty's Government, which I am confident he will refuse to no man who resolves to be so loyal and respectful to him in all things as I do. I beg of your*

---

[196] *Letters of Rachel, Lady Russell* (London 1853)

Lordship, when the occasion offers, to afford me your good offices, which shall always be acknowledged as the greatest obligation in the world'. [197]

There seems to be no record of Hyde's response, but Luttrell states on May 8 1685 *'it is reported that the lords Mountague and Lovelace were to wait upon his majestie and kisse his hand, but were not admitted to that favour',* an indication that James was indeed not ready to receive him.[198] It is interesting that Ralph is here bracketed with Lovelace, who had been implicated in the Rye House Plot. Parliament was due to meet on May 19 and Ralph might have hoped to take up his new place in the Lords. We know that he was certainly in England the previous month through a letter dated April 15 from Edward Scawen to Mr Warner: *'My lord intends to be at Boughton next Tewsday, being Easter tewsday, wherefore he desires yt you would take care & get some beife and veale and mutton, & such provisions as ye country will afford & let Lawrance take some bread & speak to him to aire my Lds bedding, & all other things & to make ye chamber very clean. By Kettering coach on Saturday will come down a Dutch Gardiner. You must appoint him a chamber, & take care of him till my Lord gives you further order. Pray send to Mr Cartledine ye cook & if he be not engagd in a servit, my Lord would have him be at Boughton for 4 or 5 days yt he shall stay there'.* [199] Perhaps after this mark of royal disfavour he decided that his best course was to go out of town, deal with business at Boughton and then go back to France.

Ralph's protégé Monmouth had also been preparing to return, in rather different circumstances. He had been meeting with English and Scots exiles in the Low Countries and by late February it had been agreed that he would raise an insurrection against his uncle in England whilst the duke of Argyll would do the same in Scotland. There is no evidence, or even rumour, that Monmouth had been in contact with Ralph. Given how close they had been in the late 1670s, this is a little strange but, if they had corresponded, experience of the Rye House Plot would have shown the wisdom of destroying papers. It may have been fortunate for Ralph's future that he had gone to France rather than the Netherlands. On June 11 1685 Monmouth landed at Lyme Regis and raised his standard. Just over a month later, having been defeated at Sedgemoor, he was executed. Ralph remained in France even though life there had become increasingly uncomfortable for Protestants. Between 1679 and 1684 they had been successively excluded from one profession after another until none were left open to them. Schools, chapels, colleges, hospitals were closed and

---

[197] H.Hyde, *The Correspondence of H. H., Earl of Clarendon, and of his brother, Laurence Hyde, Earl of Rochester; with the Diary of Lord Clarendon from 1687 to 1690* (London 1828) p.114

[198] N.Luttrell, *A brief historical relation of state affairs from September, 1678 to April 1714* (Oxford 1857) vol.1, p.341

[199] Montagu correspondence Letter 97, vol. 7

their finances taken over. Calvinists were tortured. Soldiers were quartered on Protestant households with instructions to be brutal. Finally in October 1685 Louis revoked the Edict of Nantes by which his grandfather had allowed Protestants freedom of worship. Protestant priests had to leave France and all children were henceforth to be baptised as Catholics. As a result hundreds of thousands of Huguenots, many of them skilled, emigrated. In November Lady Montagu sent her sister a letter from Paris: '*She writes as every body that has humane affections must, and says that of 1,800,000 there is not more than 10,000 esteemed to be left in France, and they, I guess, will soon be converted by the dragoons or perish. So that next to two millions of poor souls, made of the same clay as himself* [Louis], *have felt the rigour of that savage man'*. Even the English ambassador to France was told in June 1686 that the Huguenot servants who had come with him from England would not be allowed to return there. James ordered them all to return. Louis was surprised by his fellow Catholic's action but condescended to allow them to leave. Whilst Louis saw the revocation as a purely domestic matter it helped to raise concerns in both England and Holland that James both approved of it (though he seems to have been ambivalent) and would similarly aim for the ultimate goal of making his own realm wholly Catholic.

We know from a brief comment in Roger Morrice's "Entring Book" dated January 1686 that Ralph and his family not only saw the effects but felt them too (despite their rank): '*The Countess of Northumberland, wife to my Lord Montagu, obtained to have her woman that lately dyed to be buryed privately like a Protestant, and the people were so full of rage that they did open the grave and caused her flesh pulled to pieces I think by dogs and used with all possible contempt and scorn'*.[200] Morrice also records a great calamity happening that month to Montagu House: '*On Tuesday night the 19th instant after midnight a fire broke out in it, and has consumed and burnt down the great room, and most of the body of the house, the wings scaped pretty well, and my Lord Devonshire saved a pretty deale of his household goods that were very valuable. My Lord Montagu reserved a wardrobe in that house to his own use, and his servants aired it that evening, and it is commonly said that the house was set on fire by negligence of those servants and so Lord Montagu must bear it.*

The damage is thought to be 30,000l or a great deal more. It is said my Lord Devonshire had offered Lord Montagu 15,000l for the house'. [201]

Lady Russell, living next door, witnessed the fire and wrote to her chaplain: '*You will easily believe Tuesday night was not a quiet one with*

---

[200] R. Morrice, *The Entring Book of Roger Morrice 1677-1691* (Woodbridge 2007/9) vol. iii p.78

[201] Ibid vol. iii p.91

us. About one o'clock in the night I heard a great noise in the square…I called up a servant, and sent her down to learn the occasion. She brought up a very sad one, that Montagu House was on fire, and it was so indeed: it burnt with so great violence, the whole house was consumed by five o'clock. The wind blew strong this way, so that we lay under fire a great part of the time, the sparks and flames continually covering the house, and filling the court. My boy awaked, and said he was almost stifled with smoke, but being told the reason, would see it, and so was satisfied without fear; took a strange bedfellow very willingly, Lady Devonshire's youngest boy, whom his nurse had brought wrapped up in a blanket'. Ellis gives further details: *'On Wednesday, at one in the morning, a sad fire happened at Montague House in Bloomsbury, occasioned by a steward airing some hangings etc in expectation of my Lord Montague's return home, & sending afterwards a woman to see that the fire-pans with charcoal were removed, which she told him she had done, though she never came there. The loss that my Lord Montague has sustained by this accident is estimated at 40,000., besides 6,000l in plate'.* [202]

Despite the fact that Ralph's servants were commonly being spoken of as the cause of the fire, he nonetheless attempted to sue the earl of Devonshire. (Whilst the first fire insurance office had been founded in 1680 Ralph doesn't seem to have subscribed). Clearly the fact that they had been colleagues during the exclusion crisis (when Devonshire, having not yet inherited, was Lord Cavendish) was not allowed to get in the way of business. The following year Morrice reported: *'The Earl of Devonshire and the Lord Montagu have a Tryall at Bar about the fiering of Montagu House this term, a jury out of the County of Middlesex of knights and esquires is summoned to appear. It is very likely…that they two [will not] outlive to see the last Tryall if the matter be not amicably compromised betweene them which is more unlikely every day than other'.* [203] The understandable antagonism aroused by the case can be seen in a surviving letter from the Earl dated May 15th 1686: *'if your Ladp continue your resolution to sue me about the burning of your house, I hope you will not command me to observe other methods then what my Councell shall think most proper for my defence'* but in April 1687 Ralph finally conceded that he would not win: *'they proved that my Lord Montagu's steward ordered a fire that evening in the upper Garrats that were reserved to the Lord Montagu's own use out of the Earle's lease. That the Lord's servant that made fire went out of the house and said he locked the Garrat door after him before ten that night. They proved that the fire broke out at the windows and top of the Garrat about midnight or a little later. The servants carried goods out of the lower rooms an hour or two longer*

[202] G.J.W.A. Ellis, *The Ellis Correspondence* (London 1829)
[203] Morrice vol. iv p.16

before any fire was in any of the rooms below staires and this evidence was very full and plain. The Lord Montagu had 20 witnesses or more ready to be sworn but they were many of them his own servants or interested in the matter. Therefore the Lord sent a complement to the Earle, that he was so satisfied that he would Non suit himself (it may be to mollify the Earl that he may bring no action against him for his goods that were burnt)'. [204]

In June 1686 Ralph finally received royal permission to return to England. He had clearly had further correspondence with the Hydes. Ellis reports the rumours on March 30: *'Lord Montague is coming from France, some whisper to be again intrusted, & what honour shall be given to the man that will propagare fidem'.* And on April 17 *'I hear little of Lord Montague, but I know long conferences are between Sunderland & Lady Northumberland, lately come from France. Much work upon the anvil'.* [205] It seems as if Ralph's wife returned to London before her husband to ensure that it was, at least, safe for him to do so. She apparently then went back to husband and family. Lady Russell wrote on July 11 *'I hear by my sister Montagu that she found a sickly family at Paris, her daughter in a languishing condition, worn to almost nothing with a fever, which has hung about her for these last six weeks; the doctors apprehended a hectic, but youth, I hope, will overcome it'*. A newsletter of the 21st recorded that: *'Lord Mountague landed at Dover last week. As he was at sea two French men of war gave them a gun, forced them to come a-lee and searched for French Protestant fugitives and found three whom they by force took & carried back to France'.* [206] Later that month he was at Windsor to kiss the King's hand *'and has been severall times there since his return'*. It was said that *'It is very likely the lord Montagu will be both in great favour and great place at court'* and these rumours reached as far as Paris from whence Henry Hyde wrote to his brother Rochester on August 3 *'Every packet from England brings some entertainment or other, the last, which was of the 17th past, says (at least I have seen mention of it in two or three letters hither), that my Lord Montagu was extraordinarily well received by the King, and that the general opinion was, that he should be secretary of state in the place of Lord Middleton, though it is not said that the Lord is in disgrace, or that he is to be advanced to a higher station: if that be so, I will only say, miracles are not yet ceased'*. Ellis had recorded more detail on July 26: *'The Chancellor of Scotland stays here to take Lord Middleton down with him President of the Council of that kingdom; poor Middleton hangs back, thinking of Cleveland's judgment, & of Cain's doom. The chief reason is to admit Lord Montague in his room,*

---

[204] Ibid vol. iv p.25
[205] Ellis pp.88,105
[206] Cal.SP Dom

who is come in with the Jesuits & will be Secretary'. [207] This is Ellis's second implication that Ralph was thought to be favouring Catholicism. If a Secretaryship really wasn't possible his ambassadorial experience might be called upon again: *'Lord Montague is much at Court, & goes Ambassador extraordinary into France, if Sir Wm Trumball will accept the Turkish embassy...Mr. Fielding tells me this evening that Lord Montague shall remove Sir William Trumbul'* (August 7). [208] Perhaps if he had converted he would have finally attained the great office he had long aimed for. It was becoming increasingly clear that conversion was the only way to power – in late November 1686 the King held a small conference of Catholic and Protestant divines in his chamber in an attempt to persuade Lord Treasurer Hyde, his brother-in-law, to convert. Hyde would not and was dismissed, as was his brother from his post as Lord Lieutenant of Ireland. James believed that *'no man must be at the head of his affairs that was not of his opinion'* and the removal of two men so closely related to the royal family would be noted as another marker of the direction the King was taking.[209]

In this climate it is unsurprising that rather than receive an appointment Ralph was removed without recompense from the only post he did hold, the Mastership of the Great Wardrobe, which was given to the same Lord Preston who had sent back a report of his activities in Paris. Since Ralph had paid a great deal of money for the office, which provided considerable income, this was a serious blow. Although not a good omen Ralph may still have been hopeful since: *'The Countess of Northumberland is very often at court, and playes much with the Queene, who seems to be very well pleased with her attendance. Some think that the Lord Montagu her husband will have some considerable preferment. The Countess is a woman of good sense and not easily imposed upon, but her quality and education do incline her strongly to a court life'* (December 11 1686).[210]

Ralph would have attended Parliament, though now in the Lords rather than the Commons, when it was commanded to meet in November. The persecution of Protestants in France, the expansion of the army, and the appointment of Catholic officers to it were all causing concern. Lord Halifax, who had led the opposition to his uncle Shaftesbury's attempt to pass an Exclusion Bill in the Lords, and had been retained on the council by James, expressed this concern and refused to support the King's wish to repeal the Test and Habeas Corpus Acts. He was dismissed and the other councillors warned that they could expect the same treatment if they were

---

[207] Ellis p.154
[208] Ellis pp.157, 159
[209] J.H. Parker ed., *The Autobiography of Symon Patrick, Bishop of Ely* (Oxford 1829) p.116
[210] Morrice vol. iii pp. 149, 165, 200,320

not compliant. The zealots were gaining ground. James asked Parliament for money to support the army and stated that he was happy with the loyalty of Catholic officers. The Commons were not and voted, by a majority of one, to discuss the officers before supply. Worse still, despite James's presence in the House, the Lords stressed the need to preserve the country against Popery. The next day he prorogued Parliament which, though loyal, was not prepared to be subservient and vote against their sense of self-preservation by providing money for a Catholic led army.

A heavier blow than the loss of the Wardrobe fell on Ralph in February 1687 when his eldest son died. The boy's aunt, Lady Russell, wrote of her sister on February 9: '*it has been the will of God to take the life of her eldest son after lying ill of a fever eight days. I believe she takes it heavily, for truly I have not seen her since the child died on Sunday morning, and her Lord and herself went on Saturday night to Lady Harveys. She gave me her girl to take home to me; the other boy being then feverish also, continues in the house. Now my own sad trials making me know how mean a comforter I can be, I think my best service is to take some care of her two children, who are both well now, and hope God will be pleased to keep them so, and teach her to be content*'. Nine days later: '*My sister continues still at Lady Harveys, much afflicted at her loss; it seems as if they would not return again at this time to Montagu House, but take some house near Windsor. Her daughter is still with me, but the boy at Montagu House: though now very well, he is not suffered to go further than the next room; the present terror upon the loss of the other has occasioned more care of him than was necessary. This is a fine lively child; I hope God will spare it to them to their comfort*'. (Despite the fire a year before part, at least, of Montagu House was clearly still habitable). Further letters of October 1687, and January and July 1688 indicate that Lady Northumberland spent much time in the house at Windsor (sometimes visited by her sister), and the October letter shows that Ralph was certainly with her at that time, since Lady Russell refers to his frequent visits from thence to London. In June 1688 Ralph's wife was apparently pregnant ('*Miss Montagu is with me. I hope breeding prevents me from seeing my sister*').[211]

The earl of Sunderland had slowly edged out Lord Treasurer Hyde from his position as chief minister by manipulating the King and offering policies designed to appeal to him. According to Kenyon's book on Sunderland he was engaged in mysterious negotiations with Ralph in expectation of a consequent ministerial reshuffle. The cessation of Catholic persecution had caused no outcry but James wanted more – there should be legal toleration too. In April 1687 he issued the Declaration of Indulgence formally suspending the penal religious laws. He seems to have been genuinely convinced that liberty of conscience bred peace and

---

[211] Letters of Rachel, Lady Russell

harmony. However the use of the royal prerogative to suspend penal laws in religious matters had been declared illegal by the Commons in 1663 and 1673, and on the latter occasion Charles had tacitly accepted this view by cancelling his declaration. Ralph seems to have let it be believed that he supported the King in this.[212] James began to insist that Oxford and Cambridge universities agree to give fellowships and positions to Catholics (having previously suspended the need for dons and undergraduates to attend prayers or take oaths). He thought that, if there could be balanced debate amongst academics and those preparing for ordination, many would see the light and convert to the true faith. The statutes of Sidney Sussex, the Montagus' favoured college, laid down that Catholics were ineligible for admission, but James insisted that they took a Catholic as the new master. When the fellows of Magdalen College, Oxford opposed a similar appointment and installed their own choice James deprived them of their fellowships and declared them ineligible to hold office. Also in 1687 Judge Jeffreys, on instructions from the Privy Council, implemented the King's wish that Catholics (if suitably qualified by ancestry & property) should share with Protestants the honour & responsibility of being JPs. The next year many Protestant squires were purged as JPs and replaced by Catholics and others alleged to be unqualified because of their dissenting views on religion, shady political pasts, or inferior estates and families. The result of political revolutions in the localities would be a counter-revolution, in which the majority of the purged would demonstrate their anger at indiscriminate interference with their local status by acquiescing in James's removal.

The great magnates began to absent themselves from court, leaving apolitical civil servants who did not offer the King advice and extremist Catholics who unfortunately did. They told him what he wanted to hear and Sunderland, though aware of the truth, could do no more than try to delay or modify since he wasn't prepared to relinquish power by upsetting his royal master. James began preparations for parliamentary elections which he hoped would return a House of Commons more amenable to his views. All MPs, JPs and those holding office were asked whether they would vote for the repeal of the Test Acts if elected to Parliament, or would support those that would do so. About half of the lords lieutenant refused even to pose the question to the gentry in their counties, and were dismissed. A majority of JPs were also hostile. Secure in his conviction that his intentions were honourable and in the best interests of the nation, James could not believe that the majority of his subjects were unable to comprehend and share his views. It is clear from what he wrote later to his son while in exile that he truly believed (as his brother had done) in liberty

---

[212] BL Add 34526 f. 48-56; Haley *A list of English pe*ers p. 304; Hosford *The Peerage and the Test Act* p. 118

of conscience and resolved that the boy should be brought up in the spirit of toleration.[213] He would later insist that Anglicans and Dissenters at his exiled court of St. Germain should be treated no differently to Catholics, and when it was reported in the summer of 1694 that Louis might allow them to worship he resolved to encourage him. Yet he had shown his subjects, by the removal of Hyde and Clarendon, that he was not willing to take advice even from members of his own family that were not of his faith. The tragedy of James's life is that his lack of skill as a politician, his mindset and the inability of most of his subjects to conceive that toleration could be beneficial both to their consciences and the good of the nation, made his efforts to bring it about doomed from the start.

Protestant resentment was stiffened by William and Mary's public opposition to the removal of the Test Acts, which didn't improve their relationship with James. William finally found himself able to access the finance necessary to improve his country's navy and army. This was represented to James by his (Irish Catholic) ambassador as a threat and Barillon, of course, reinforced that view. William, in turn, feared his father-in-law might alter the succession to secure a Catholic heir, call a Catholic Parliament or, at the least, support Louis in another land grab. Out of the political mainstream, Ralph apparently spent time supervising the rebuilding and refurbishing of Montagu House.[214] His wife and children seem to have gone to France for a while, since Morrice's Entring Book has the curious entry for February 1688: '*There is a yacht sent to Dipe to fetch over the Lady Montagu and her children, they say (but I think falsely) they are all turned Papists.*' (p237)

In May James ordered all Anglican clergy to read his Declaration of Indulgence in their churches. Archbishop Sancroft and six of his episcopal brethren presented the King with a petition pointing out that it had been previously accepted that he could not use his dispensing power in this way. James was shocked and furious. He was even angrier when the Dissenters supported the bishops – they hated Catholics more than they desired toleration. He foolishly decided to have the bishops tried, so that he could then show magnanimity in pardoning them after conviction. They were sent to the Tower on June 1, blessing the cheering crowds as they passed. Ten days later the Queen gave birth to a son. It was so providential for James that many Protestants believed that the child had been smuggled into the Queen's bed in a warming-pan. Even Princess Anne seemed to believe that he was not her brother, despite many people witnessing the birth. James could have used the occasion as a reason to pardon the bishops. He did not and they came to trial at the end of the month in front of a partisan crowd – when Sunderland gave evidence he was hissed so

---

[213] E. Corp *The Last Years of James II* "History Today" Sept 2001
[214] Luttrell entry for March 20th, 1686/7, p.397

loudly he could hardly be heard. His recent politic conversion to Catholicism had not improved his popularity. Next day the jury found the bishops not guilty, prompting far greater demonstrations of joy than the birth of the Prince of Wales had done. James's attempts to act against those who lit celebratory bonfires met with opposition: it was clear that, though not rebellious, James's subjects would do little to help him if he was attacked. The earls of Danby, Devonshire and Shrewsbury, Lord Lumley, the Bishop of London, Edward Russell and Henry Sidney met and wrote an invitation to William asking for his help and assuring him that an invasion would be successful. In late September William informed the Dutch States General of his intention to accept this invitation to save the English from slavery and Popery. He would not usurp James but ensure that an independent Parliament was elected. Louis believed that his own stated intention to give James French aid if required would defuse the situation but it only confirmed in Dutch minds that there was indeed a secret alliance between England and France against the Netherlands. When Louis went off with his army to attack yet another Alsatian fortress William knew the French would be unable to go to James's aid.

James and Sunderland did little by way of defensive preparation. It was late in the year for a naval expedition, most intelligence was coming from the French who were suspected of wanting to pull England into a war with the Dutch, and James could not imagine his daughter agreeing to her husband making war on her father. Furthermore James's navy was about twice the size of, and army was equal to, William's and would be fighting on home soil. Fear nonetheless made him announce his intention to call a Parliament in late November. There was no likelihood of a 'loyal' Commons without extensive gerrymandering, and even if that was achieved James's insistence that the Test Acts still had to be repealed showed how out of touch he was with political reality. When William launched an invasion fleet in late October it was blown back to port by a bad storm: God had given James a sign of his approval. Sunderland was dismissed for trying to hold back James's political agenda. But divine providence now swung behind William, bringing an easterly wind that blew his fleet down the Channel (whilst keeping James's trapped in the Thames estuary) and ensuring that he landed safely at Torbay on the propitious 5th of November.

James did not know whether to remain in control of London (and protect the Catholics) thus allowing William time to gather support and undermine the morale of James's army, or to march against him. When he eventually decided on the latter course he was reminded of how difficult it was to move and supply an army in winter, a difficulty which became the greater if one could not locate the enemy and force his army to fight. Good intelligence was hard to come by and rumour was constantly unsettling.

The King continued to do what he was good at – micromanage whilst being unable to grasp and attempt to shape the big picture – and exhausted himself doing so. His generals advised him to return to London. As he did so two of them – the duke of Grafton (James's nephew and Arlington's son-in-law) and John Churchill (who owed his rise to the duchess of Cleveland's favours) - defected with officers and men, followed by Prince George of Denmark, Princess Anne's husband. The Princess soon joined him, persuaded by her confidante Sarah Churchill to turn against her father. There were more defections, and rumours of Catholic risings, of French invasion, of rioting. James's advisers were split between those who insisted he should seek accommodation with William, (who was stressing he only wanted a free Parliament and help against France, and not the deposition of his father-in-law), and the Catholics who pointed out that accommodation would harm the monarchy (and themselves of course). Neither course was palatable to James, who had in mind his father's attempts to come to an agreement with his subjects when weakened. On December 3 the earl of Feversham told him that he could no longer assure the army's loyalty. When James received William's demands (which could have formed the basis for a settlement) on the evening of the 10th he said that he would give an answer next day. That night he fled from London, with just two Catholic servants.

The earl of Rochester and Bishop Turner of Ely had had the prescience to draw up an emergency plan of action should the King leave the capital without naming a regent. There was to be a provisional government composed of the peers present in the city, many of whom had backed Rochester's attempts to negotiate between James and William. It was to provide a focus for law and order, and maintain James's kingship. The plan had been cleared with the Archbishop and letters prepared to send to the peers if needed. When the King's flight became known the turbulence that followed showed the necessity of such a plan.

The discovery of the journal of this provisional government not so many years ago provided a great deal of additional information about how events developed in the Glorious Revolution of 1688 as it has become known, and showed that the outcome was not as inevitable as many earlier historians had thought.[215] Twenty-seven peers met at the Guildhall in the city of London on the 11th and were welcomed by the Lord Mayor and Aldermen, who promised support. James's supporters (Rochester and the six bishops) could rely on the support of some two-thirds of those present but were opposed by the 'violent' Whigs such as Ralph, Wharton and Dorset. Archbishop Sancroft, who would usually have been expected to preside, realised how difficult the task of resolution would be and so,

---

[215] R. Beddard, *A Kingdom without a King: the journal of the provisional government in the revolution of 1688* (Oxford 1988)

pleading old age and deafness, proposed Rochester. Having ensured that James had left no orders with the Secretaries of State, the peers issued orders to the Lord Lieutenant of Middlesex, General Feversham and Admiral Dartmouth, and replaced the unpopular and pro French Governor of the Tower. Rochester and a few colleagues prepared a draft statement stating that the group proposed to negotiate with William on the basis of his Declaration which stated that his objective was to uphold the law through a free parliament and the resumption of government by the absent monarch, having 'brought the King home again with honour and safety'. Ralph and Wharton vehemently opposed this and managed to have the clauses most favourable to James taken out, even that calling for his return with honour and safety. In order to present political unanimity to the fearful populace the loyalist majority was forced to agree a shorter and blander statement. Thus Ralph's intervention helped both to prolong, and improve, the opportunity to ensure James did not return. The Guildhall Declaration of November 12 1688 did not issue an invitation to William to come and take up the government of the nation as Burnet later claimed. It thanked William for coming to rescue the country *from the imminent dangers of Popery and slavery*', pledged assistance in calling a free parliament, and used the well-worn method of blaming misgovernment on misguided ministers rather than the monarch. Even James's flight was blamed on *'the pernicious counsels'* of Papists. A copy of the Declaration was sent to William, and another to the Lord Mayor and Alderman who then sent an address to the Prince, asking for his protection and urging him to come to London. William was happy with the latter but not with the Declaration, even as amended. Rochester's brother told one of the emissaries that William would now only be content with the crown.

When news of James's flight became public on the 11th it led to a night of riot and arson. Catholic chapels were sacked and set on fire, as was the house of the Spanish ambassador, though Spain was an ally of Holland. Ironically only the French ambassador's residence was safe – he, unlike his diplomatic colleagues, ensured that tradesmen were regularly paid. News came from Rochester that it was on fire too. The magistracy ordered Catholics to give up their arms, thus leaving them defenceless. There were fears that armed bands of Irish Catholics from James's disbanded force would arrive in towns and villages at any moment and massacre the inhabitants: Feversham was criticised for having disbanded the army without first disarming and paying them off. The publication of the Declaration next day helped steady the nerves of magistrates. The Foot Guards were called out to disperse the large mob who had gathered at Whitehall, cavalry sent to Somerset House to guard Queen Catherine, and troops arrived at St. James's just in time to stop the plundering and burning of the chapel there. The peers met in the Council Chamber at Whitehall and summoned James's Privy Councillors to join them. Six did so and Halifax presided. The numbers attending over the next few days fluctuated between twenty-two and thirty-eight. Ralph and two others were sent to seal the King's Closet and so secure James's papers. In the early hours of the 13th a rumour swept the city that a great number of Irish had burned Uxbridge and massacred the inhabitants, and were now marching on London. All the houses in the city were lit and the populace prepared to flee. Ten peers met, put the military on stand-by, sent out messengers and discovered that it was a false alarm. They reassured the Lord Mayor and city, and people began to return to their beds at four in the morning. During the disturbances an officer of the militia had been killed by the rabble in the Haymarket and Ralph was one of the eight peers who signed an order *'to quell and disperse the said rabble; and, in the case of necessity, to use force and fire upon them with bullet'*. Later that morning a letter arrived, relating how the King had been stopped on the Isle of Sheppey by sailors looking for Catholic priests fleeing from London. Halifax, perhaps not knowing how best to act to secure his own political future, did not tell his fellow peers. But one received the news from another source and, when Halifax tried to adjourn the provisional government, told his colleagues. Four loyal peers were sent to James but Halifax hedged by stressing that they could only speak on their own authority. Meanwhile there was daily business to attend to – Ralph and a few other peers authorised the searching of ships in St. Katherine's dock and next day, the 14th, authorised the discharge of the Hopewell, a ship which had been seized.

The King returned to London and was well received by the citizens. Although he was irritated by the provisional government – "You were all kings when I left London" – the fact that the loyalists had overcome the opposition mollified him. He summoned the Council, and heard mass but privately still felt very insecure. Ralph, Halifax and others 'that had ventured for the Prince' fled to Windsor 'for fear of being apprehended' on charges of treason. Ralph dined with William there on Sunday November 16.[216] William was extremely annoyed at James's return, which upset his plans. He had sent a message to the King when he heard that he had been stopped on Sheppey, telling him to stay in Rochester, but it had not arrived in time. He was even more annoyed at the provisional government for sending peers to encourage the King to return, when he thought they had submitted their authority to his. Howard and Powle, both Exclusionists and the latter a close colleague of Ralph's, had been with the Prince at Windsor and were sent to the City with his letter stating that the King's return was without his authority, and promising he would be with them in two days. An attempt to vote an address of congratulation to James on his return was

---

[216] Morrice p.398

defeated by only one vote, showing how finely balanced things were. The Recorder said that he couldn't see how the aldermen could both invite the Prince and congratulate James, and pointedly wondered what the rabble would think of such a vote. The Aldermen took the hint and said nothing.

Whilst James had recovered some of his standing by returning, he had thrown much away by fleeing in the first place, making no provision for law and order, and hindering the proposed new parliament by destroying most of the electoral writs and throwing the Great Seal into the Thames so that new ones could not be issued. And he no longer had an army. Feversham was arrested on William's orders, which further unsettled him. James was ordered by the Prince to go to Ham House. When Clarendon asked William why the King couldn't go to Hampton Court or Windsor, as being more suitable, Lord Delamere replied that *'he did not look upon him as his King'*. William instructed Halifax to tell James this news, ensuring that the peer would finally come down on the Prince's side. The King was woken at one in the morning to be told that it was *'for the greater quiet of the City and the greater safety of his person'*. Earlier that night the guard he had posted was replaced by Dutch soldiers. James may now have feared assassination but he knew that if he left London again he would hand control over to William entirely. He offered to put himself in the hands of two wealthy Whig merchants he knew, until he had satisfied his subjects in all things relating to liberty and religion. This was put to the City's Common Council but blocked by Exclusionists there – they knew that William would not want this. James gave in, and suggested that Rochester would be more convenient for him to go to, as a place where he had his own guards. On the morning of the 18th he said farewell to those still loyal to him, made it clear that he left under duress, and took a boat down river. At three that afternoon William took up residence at St. James's Palace.

Ralph was one of the many signatories on the Prince's summons to meet at St. James's on the 21st in the Queen's Presence Chamber to give advice on the best way to achieve his objectives. The House of Lords met the following day. The principal matter was *'to consider a way to have a parliament'*. The difficulty was that the monarch was not in the position of being able to call one. They passed to an easier task: *'that the most ready and most effectual way to remove the Papists out of town be considered of'*. Ralph stated that *'to the best of his memory the Proclamation Caroli Secundi used to mention Papists and repute Papists'* and this proclamation was reissued. Only twelve Catholics had licence to remain in the capital – one being Ralph's old friend the Duchess of Mazarin. James in Rochester decided it was time to leave, despite his supporters telling him that they could not imagine his life was in danger. He replied that if he stayed he would be sent to the Tower *'and no King ever went out of that place but to his grave'*, so he slipped away.

Seventy-three peers met at the House of Lords on Christmas Eve, now aware that there was no monarch in the kingdom. There were notable divisions on how to go forward between those still loyal to James, led by his brothers-in-law Clarendon and Rochester, and the Williamites, led by Ralph, Wharton and Devonshire. When mention was made of a letter James had sent to the earl of Middleton, (which it was believed gave his reasons for leaving), and it was suggested that its contents should be shared with the House, Ralph objected (perhaps concerned that it would increase sympathy for James) and said *'That the letter or anything should not direct the business of the day. If the letter was of a publick nature, his Lordship would bring it to them'*. Lord Paget proposed that Mary be declared Queen. As soon as she was proclaimed a parliament could be called. Ralph suggested that the procedure embodied in the old Exclusion Bill should be adopted. Nottingham reiterated the common belief that the kingdom *'cannot come to have a parliament but by the King'* and that King was James. The fact that the 'non-contents' prevailed showed that the majority present wanted to distance themselves from James. (Sheffield thought it *'the first proof of the Lords intention of excluding their King, 'tho many divisions arose among them afterwards about the best way of doing it'*). They then pressed their advantage, pointing out that they were caught in an interregnum for which there was no legal or historical precedent. The very fact of their meeting, without the King's consent, was proof legal government no longer existed in England. Devonshire asked whether James's withdrawal from government wasn't a demise in law, knowing that this was an idea formulated by Halifax when he had been at Windsor (the same Halifax who was now chairing this meeting). Ralph put to the House the blatantly Whig proposal: *'Whether you will refer it to the advice of the lawyers, or determine it by your own prudence?'* suggesting that the Exclusion Bill might provide methods worth consideration. Although these revolutionary sentiments were put as suggestions and questions, not a single loyal peer responded. Before the 23rd the Williamites were inhibited by the continuing presence of the King in his kingdom from speaking treason. Now, by contrast, the loyalists were inhibited by the presence of the Prince (and his troops) at St. James's, across the Park from where they were meeting. The only agreement the peers could reach was to ask William to issue letters to the constituencies for electing a Convention (which side stepped the problem of how to call a parliament when there was no monarch to call it). When they met again at two in the afternoon of Christmas Day itself they called on William to take up the reins of government until the Convention met, so avoiding defining the status of James who had landed in France that morning. On Boxing Day a meeting called by William of all the surviving MPs, the Lord Mayor and Aldermen, and fifty representatives of London's Common Council echoed this request.

The experiences of the past decade had left the Whigs as a shattered force (if the term Whigs is used to cover those who had opposed arbitrary government and the advance of popery under Charles and James). In the election just after the start of James's reign in 1685 only 57 of the 525 MPS elected had been Whigs. They had lost their hold over the middle ground in politics. It has been argued that James had built on his brother's successes against the 'opposition' and tried to create a modern, absolutist state. His Catholicism did not include loyalty to the Pope – like his cousin Louis he wanted to be master of the church in his own domain and the Jesuits he supported disagreed with the papacy on two counts. Like them he believed that there were no earthly limits on monarchs, who could demand active as well as passive obedience, and that heresy was an act of human will which may need to be broken to be corrected. This looking to France had dovetailed with English Catholics long suggesting that the monarchical religion there could be seen as an acceptable middle way between papal and Protestant fanaticism. Indeed, fifteen years earlier the duchess of Cleveland's husband had written a work that put forward the Edict of Nantes as a demonstration of just this middle way.[217] The Revocation of the Edict by Louis, his persecution of Huguenots, and his military expansionistic policies served to throw this suggestion back into the faces of English recusants. Whilst James was politician enough to realise that compromise was needed to achieve his ends, he still believed there was only one true church. Despite some statements and other indications of his belief in toleration, the man appointed as his son's tutor, John Betham, stated that God would not tolerate those who would not accept the blessings of the true faith. *'God will not have patience to expect their natural death, but will hurry them away without the least warning'.* Looking at Louis's successes, James and his advisers promoted a modern bureaucratic state, with an efficient standing army, a first rate navy and an overseas empire to provide the means. Town and city corporations were being moulded into loyal instruments of local politics, and the press used to disseminate the official view, whilst the law was used in attempts to silence dissent. Hindsight allows us to believe that James's regime was brief and weak. Those living through it would have thought differently – like Ralph they would have believed that they had to co-operate with it to survive politically and financially. James's opponents believed that a strong modern state was better achieved through political participation rather than absolutism, and more tolerance than French Catholicism afforded, with greater emphasis on promoting home manufacture than empire. They looked to the Netherlands, not France for their model.

---

[217] Earl of Castlemaine, "A Full Answer and Confutation of a Scandalous Pamphlet" 1673

William's arrival from that country and declared intent to '*retrieve and promote the Reformed interest and religion here and abroad, and to repress the tyranny of France*' was manna from heaven for the Whigs. It is likely that those who went to meet William encouraged him down the path to the throne, and he came to realise that they, rather than the loyalist Tories, would be his best allies not only in helping establish his rule in England but also in prosecuting a war against France. The greatest symbol of this turnaround was the release of Titus Oates, creator of the Popish Plot. Ralph had called for this as early as December 12 (he may have also thought it would please the mob) but Oates had to wait until the 28th before he had 'libertie to go abroad'. The views of many (though not of all) were expressed by one of Locke's correspondents at the close of 1688: '*I know you can be no stranger to the wonderful successe which God Almighty hath given to the Prince of Orange in his late undertaking to deliver our miserable and distressed kingdoms from popery and slavery, which mercy we in England esteem no less then the Israelites deliverance from Egypt by the hand of Moses*'. [218]

The Convention opened on January 22 1689 and Ralph took his seat in the Lords. A week later the Commons passed a resolution that James had tried to subvert the Constitution and had vacated the throne by leaving the kingdom. Nottingham denounced the idea and Bishop Turner exposed its inconsistencies. Ralph, Mordaunt and Delamere retorted by reminding the Lords of the threat James's actions had posed to English liberties. On the 31st, during a debate on the state of the crown, Ralph stated that he was '*so perfectly satisfied that the throne was vacant, that he had a dispensation within him, without the help of one from my Lord Jeffries or Sir Edward Harbart [judges] and therefore did declare, that from this day he looked upon himself to be absolved from all allegiance to King James*'.[219] He voted in favour of declaring the Prince and Princess of Orange king and queen, and entered his dissent when the Lords resolved not to agree with the Commons. Around February 3 William sent for a handful of leading peers including Halifax and Ralph's old enemy Danby, the chief supporter of Mary's independent claim to the monarchy. He informed them he wasn't prepared to be merely a consort of his wife, or regent. Of course he would share the monarchy with Mary and allow Anne to succeed rather than any offspring he might have from a second marriage – he would still rule and be able to achieve what he wanted. If this was not accepted he might well return to Holland with his army. Whilst the Whigs had to concede the word "desertion" rather than "abdication" in describing James's action, the majority who had rejected a "vacancy" in the throne dropped from fourteen votes to one. Ralph was prominent amongst

[218] J. Hoppit, *A Land of Liberty? England 1689-1727* (Oxford 2000) p.49
[219] *The Correspondence of Henry Hyde, earl of Clarendon* ed S W Singer (1828) ii, p.257

William's supporters in persuading and pressurising those who supported James or Mary to the exclusion of William to either absent themselves from the divisions or concede. On February 4 a full House of Lords (109 members) debated a vote from the Commons to the effect that the throne had been "abdicated" and was thereby "vacant". When the Lower House had used the word in their vote of January 28 the Lords had substituted the softer word "deserted" and removed the reference to a vacancy, but the Commons had reinstated the words. Two days later Ralph voted again for "abdication" and "desertion". [220] When put to the vote, the majority of the Lords refused to back down but Ralph was one of 34 peers who agreed with the Commons. On the 12th Ralph was in the House when the "Declaration concerning the oppressive and illegal Measures of the late King; and for the Prince and Princess of Orange to be King and Queen" was read. The words insisted upon by the Commons (and Ralph) formed part of it. The importance of these debates is indicated by the earl of Thanet's comment that he thought *we had done ill in admitting the monarchy to be elective.*' [221] Many involved in the French Revolution a century later acknowledged a debt to the events Ralph was involved in. Dalrymple, talking of 1688 debates about the vacancy in crown, mentions *'Lord Montagu, beyond others, displaying that spirit of intrigue, which in a former reign, had been so fatal to Lord Danby'.* [222]

What were Ralph's prime motives behind his support of William and hence of the so-called Glorious Revolution that would have such a profound effect on the nation's future? Given his experience of kings Charles, James and Louis he might well have been committed to the concept of limited monarchy. Cleveland had told Charles *'that in his hart he despised you and yr Brother; and that for his part he wished with all his hart the Parliament wd send you both to travell'.* If he had truly said this it might indicate that, despite his co-operation as ambassador in Charles's designs, he nonetheless had inherited a streak of Montagu parliamentarianism. Had Ralph absorbed political ideas from his one-time physician John Locke, the Father of Liberalism, during conversations in Paris?[223] Locke wrote that human nature was characterised by reason and tolerance. Defence of the Protestant religion may have been a secondary consideration – nothing survives in Ralph's extensive correspondence to indicate he was a religious man (unlike his wife). He probably led a conventionally observant Christian life, albeit that his faith was firm

---

[220] Wilts RO, Ailesbury Mss 1300/856

[221] Ibid p.261

[222] Dalrymple vol.2 p.256

[223] Locke's influence on the Founding Fathers of the United States was so strong that the Declaration of Independence quotes a passage from one of his works. His belief that all men had a natural right to defend their life, health, liberty and possessions was the basis of the Declaration's phrase "Life, liberty and the pursuit of happiness".

enough to resist the temptation to convert to Catholicism and so win favour and office from James.

Did he join Shaftesbury, Russell and Sidney in opposing Charles in the early 1680s because he shared their views or simply because he cast himself into opposition? If he did have convictions about the way in which his country could best be governed to ensure its future political and economic health they were surely mixed with self-interest. With the majority of his class he must have felt increasingly denied his natural place in the ruling caste by James's actions. It would have been difficult for Ralph to see a flourishing future for himself and his posterity early in 1688. Any expectation that he may have had of favour from James had proved to be misplaced, whereas pushing William's claim to rule equally with his wife could have been in hope of reward from a grateful King, despite that latter's disapproval of his actions as ambassador.

That reward was duly given. Ralph was appointed to the Privy Council on the February 14 and soon after, on April 5, he finally achieved the elevation he had long desired – the new monarchs created him earl of Montagu, and viscount Monthermer. (The viscountcy would be born by his son as a courtesy title). Many other supporters were recognised at the same time: John Churchill was made earl of Marlborough for example. Six days later Ralph would have attended the coronation, giving an opportunity to relish his elevation (particularly in the procession "by order of rank" to the Abbey). At last the senior branch of the Montagu family which he represented had been raised so that it was no longer junior in rank. Perhaps the choice of titles can be seen as pointing this up – rather than a city or county name being taken, for example, Montagu was retained and added to it was that of the other illustrious line from which the family claimed descent, the Monthermers.[224] (Ralph's coat of arms showed both lines). At about this time he had six full length paintings of his ancestors made by Jeremiah van der Eyden, to be hung in the Drawing Room at Montagu House. Three were of his grandfather (1st Lord Montagu), and the latter's father Sir Edward (died 1602) and grandfather Lord Chief Justice Montagu (died 1557), both in legal robes. The others of William de Montacute, 1st earl of Salisbury (wearing a Garter cloak, though he died four years before the Order was founded), his second son Sir John (through whom Ralph's family claimed the Montagu name), and Ralph de Monthermer, earl of Gloucester (whose marriage to King Edward I's daughter brought royal blood to the line), all depicted in armour. No-one who visited Ralph Montagu would be left in any doubt as to his illustrious and ancient lineage of both robe and sword.

---

[224] This reminder of descent, although unusual, was not unique. George Monck, the son of a poor country gentleman, chose the title of Albermarle as a deliberate reference to distant Plantagenet origins.

As part of Ralph's revived career in politics he was named as a member of some 14 Lords committees over the late spring and summer of 1689 (including one to reverse the attainder of his executed colleague Algernon Sidney).[225] There were suggestions that even greater things could be expected by Ralph: a letter survives at Boughton from May 1689 which shows that he came near to achieving his ultimate political ambition. *'You have no doubt heard by now that my Lord is no longer Secretary of State. Its true all of London believed he was, and apparently he would have remained so if the King hadn't found it necessary to give the post to a man who had done all he could against his Majesty in Parliament. My Lord has returned to his role, and it is to be of the Privy Council, but that is all '.*[226] The *"man"* must be Nottingham. Nonetheless hope remained. *'There is a very good understanding like to be brought about between the Earl of Monmouth and the Lord Montagu. It is highly probable as the Lord Montagu will be a great figure in the house of Lords this session. So that he will also be set at some great Post at court'* (October 1689). [227] Monmouth (later earl of Peterborough) had been appointed as first lord of the Treasury on April 8, but lasted less than a year in the post.[228] Nonetheless Ralph's hopes must have remained high that he would finally achieve office – in April and in November 1690 it was rumoured that the earl of Nottingham would resign his place as Secretary of State and that Ralph was likely to succeed him.[229]   He was certainly now amongst the most influential men in the country. On Thursday, December 5 1689, Morrice mentions that, with Mr. William Stockdale (MP for Knaresborough), Ralph dined with the duke of Bolton *'they had little but mixt common discourse, it may be some what how the king might borrow money and on what terms.'* Ralph's only known political activity that year was sitting in the Lords occasionally from April, and mid to late November. (On November 23, when debating the Succession to the Crown and Rights of the Subject, Bills, Ralph again was with the minority (of twelve) siding with the Commons, this time supporting the concept that a royal pardon on impeachment was only valid if both Houses agreed – no doubt memories of the failure of the attempted impeachment of Danby a decade earlier came flooding back). This would become a regular pattern of activity for the next decade – Parliament usually sat from November until late April (although it 1698 it sat during May and June as well). In

---

[225] Lords Journal xiv. 174, 189, 192, 222, 227, 231, 235, 245, 258, 265, 279-80, 284, 301, 308-9
[226] HMC Buccleuch p.349
[227] Morrice p.194
[228] Viscount Mordaunt's opposition to James, as duke of York and then as King, had led to his exile in Holland where, in 1686, he had urged invasion of England. He had sailed with William to Torbay and was made Earl of Monmouth.
[229] BL Add. 70014, ff.322,361

July his sister-in-law recommended to her regular correspondent Dr. John FitzWilliam (formerly chaplain to her father and character witness at the trail of her husband) that his '*power and good-will*' could be useful to the cleric with regard to the problem he was experiencing over his refusal to take the oath of allegiance to the new monarchs. (The nonjurors felt legally bound by their oath to James II. Ironically five of the nonjuring bishops were amongst those tried by that king for refusing to read the Act of Indulgence). If FitzWilliam did approach Ralph, it availed him nothing, since he was deprived of his living for refusing the oath.

The end of the year saw the passing of the Bill of Rights, which restated in legal form the Declaration of Right which Parliament had presented to William and Mary as part of the invitation to them to become joint sovereigns. This "*Act Declaring the Rights and Liberties of the Subject...*" asserted the right to petition the monarch and addressed other sources of conflict that had arisen between the people and crown during Charles's and James's reigns, such as the constitutional requirement for the monarch to seek the consent of his subjects, as represented in parliament. Many of the concepts it contains had first been explored in print by Ralph's former physician, John Locke. It is still one of the main documents that form the uncodified British constitution. On January 23 1690 the Lords considered a Bill to restore town corporations to their ancient rights, which James and Charles had interfered with. In a House of 84 peers Ralph was one of only nine unhappy with the removal of certain words, the omission of which '*seems to be the justifying of the most horrid Action that King James was guilty of during His Reign and, we humbly conceive, a denying the chiefest Grievance mentioned in King William's Declaration*'.

Ralph's other main recorded activity at this time was the pursuit of Lord Preston for the income lost due to his deprivation of the Mastership of the Great Wardrobe from 1685-88. Although he didn't regain the post until after the Revolution, on March 15 1687 Ellis had recorded '*Lord Montague very nigh disrobing poor Count Preston*', a rumour showing how uncertain Ralph's position had been under James, often expectant but ultimately yielding nothing.[230] He certainly pursued the matter with vigour - Morrice records that in October '*Lord Preston was beset by 30 Bayliffs at the Lord Montagu's suit to arrest him, but he begged protection from the Court*'.[231] Preston had foolishly accepted a patent of peerage from King James at St.Germain on 22 January. This led to a debate in the Lords about its validity in November, (since it had been given during the interregnum), which resulted in Preston being sent to the Tower for his rashness. A year later Ralph was awarded £1,300 damages for his loss. It was only a fraction of the true figure but it is likely that Preston was not a wealthy man.

---

[230] Ellis p.259
[231] Ibid p.211

Chapter 7
Ralph Montagu, Emperor of China
1690- 1701

The portentous events of 1688 occurred after Ralph had seen to the marriage of his daughter Anne. She had been married on May 25 to Alexander Popham with a dowry from her father of £12,000. The Pophams of Littlecote had extensive lands in Wiltshire which they acquired through an ancestor who had made a fortune through the law, at the same time as Sir Edward Montagu had done. Edward and Alexander Popham, grandsons of Lord Justice Popham, had distinguished careers in the navy and parliament respectively, such that Cromwell attended Edward's state funeral in Westminster Abbey. Anne's husband was the grandson of Colonel Alexander and, as seems usual after young aristocrats married, he soon left his wife and went abroad to further his education. Letters survive which show that Ralph was fully involved in this. *'We are at Boughton with the same company that we had at Windsor...What I can't avoid doing is to tell you on behalf of my Lord that, after you have had a good look at Venice, to return to Geneva (and you might as well pass by Turin). After all, Mr Popham is perfecting his riding, shooting, speaking French etc. He should be very happy that he isn't in England at this time, because with the King in Ireland, and all the young men of quality travelling, he wouldn't be able to avoid going there. My Lord thinks Mr Popham would do well, when in Geneva, to buy saddlehorses rather than a carriage. This would much better suit a young man, which he will not be for very long, and is more commodious for taking the air and learning to shoot from horseback. Please give the enclosed to Mr Popham'.*[232] Popham's family had substantial influence at Chippenham and in 1690 he was elected there, probably under Ralph's tutelage (his own father having died when Alexander was a boy). A draft letter of thanks to the electors of 1690 is in Ralph's hand.[233] Later in the year, at the behest of his father-in-law and Wharton, Popham helped the Hon. Thomas Tollemache gain the other seat for Chippenham in a by-election and in March 1691 competed unsuccessfully for the post of vice-chamberlain to the Queen. Despite his wife's infidelity with Henry Sidney, Lord Romney in the late 1690s he seems to have stayed within the family circle, becoming MP for Bath in 1698 (where his father had sat) so that Edward Montagu, a great-grandson of the 1st duke of Manchester and another Wiltshire man, could have the

---

[232] HMC Buccleuch p.349
[233] HMC report. See also F.W.Leyborne-Popham. F W Popham "A West country family" 1976

Chippenham seat.[234] Alexander would die aged 33 leaving a young daughter to inherit his wealth.[235]

Ralph's joy in being created an earl in 1689 was followed by sadness at the death of his wife Elizabeth on September 19 the next year. There is little evidence for the nature of their relationship after the time of Elizabeth's support for him in Paris during the Cleveland scandal in 1678, but the fact that she accompanied him into exile in 1683 and was still giving birth to their children almost twenty years after they had met, indicates at least a certain degree of 'togetherness'. References to her in the Montagu letters and elsewhere always give the impression of a respected woman, considerate of others. An example is given in a letter to Ralph's father from his brother William: '*My son...waited upon my Lady Northumberland, saw her and the children very well...It was very kindly done of my Lady...to do my daughter the honour to dine there. My son tells she commended the place much, and the dinner not a little*' (October 3 1681). The cause of her death on March 29 at Boughton may have been the after effects of giving birth to a third son, John. Perhaps the couple thought it was wise to have a 'spare' in case anything happened to their heir Winwood (who had been born c.1682). Certainly in July 1689 there had been a further scare over the children's health – their aunt Lady Russell wrote: '*I received a letter from my sister, which I have just read; she says her son is well recovered of the measles, but is very lean, and her daughter very pale; that she is going in a few days to Boughton. I believe country air will be to their advantage. I pray God spare them to her, poor woman*'. The usual cause of death after childbirth was puerperal fever, which occurs during the first ten days after birth (it killed Queens Jane Seymour and Catherine Parr). Elizabeth had given birth to at least five children before John, but she was about 44 years old at the time of his birth. Lady Russell wrote to her son-in-law Lord Cavendish of her death: '*The separation of friends is grievous. My sister Montagu was one I loved tenderly.*' The last of the few letters from Elizabeth to her sister that survive, sent from Boughton the previous Christmas, indicates the care they had for each other: '*I am very sorry, my dear sister, to find by yours, which I received by the last post, that your thoughts have been so much disturb'd with what*

---

[234] Edward's father had married an heiress of the Hungerford family through whom descended land at Chippenham. Edward was a protégé of Charles Montagu, earl of Halifax who was an MP 1689-1700. Halifax's brother Christopher sat for Northampton 1695-1702 and brother James for Tregony 1695-8, Bere Alston 1698-1700 and Carlisle 1705-13. Charles, son of the 1st earl of Sandwich sat for Durham 1695-7, 1695-1700 and his brother Sidney Wortley for Huntingdon or Peterborough at various dates 1679-1726. More than twenty Montagus sat in the Commons from the Restoration to the death of Queen Anne.
[235] The House of Commons, 1660-1690, ed B D Henning; 1690-1715 eds D W Hayton, E C Cruickshanks and S N Handley

I thought ought to have some contrary effect.[236] *'Tis very true what is once taken from us, in that nature, cane never be returned; all that remains of comfort (according to my temper) is a bringing to punishment those who were so wickedly and unjustly the cause of it. I confess, it was a great satisfaction to me to hear that was a publick care, it being so much to the honour, as well as what in justice was due to your dead Lord, that I do not doubt, when your sad thoughts will give you leave to recollect, you will find comfort. I heartily pray God you may, and that you may never have the addition of any other loss, which is and ever shall be the prayers of your entirely affectionate E Montague'.*

On April 23 1691 the King honoured Ralph by coming to dine at Montagu House which *'occasions great discourse'.*[237] A week later, on May 1, the widow of Ralph's cousin Richard died and the whole of the Winwood estate was inherited by him, including Ditton. This was a fine house (albeit smaller than Boughton) which was particularly convenient as a base when the King and Queen were at Hampton Court, just a mile or so upriver. It came with an estate worth some £2,500 pa., but despite this inheritance, the considerable dowry which Elizabeth had brought him, and his ancestral property, Ralph was living at a rate which outstripped his income. Though its outer court and shell had survived the fire, Montagu House had had to be completely refitted internally whilst Ralph was also remodelling Boughton with a fashionable French façade, to make the old house look as if it was a coherent whole. Ditton needed similar treatment. Ralph was in need of another wife with money and set his sights on the richest single woman in the kingdom. There was, however, a major impediment – she was insane. Furthermore some suggested that the cause of her madness was furor uterinus (nymphomania), considered to be an infectious disease.[238]

Elizabeth Cavendish was born in 1654, the eldest of the five daughters of the 2nd duke of Newcastle, and sister of Henry, Lord Ogle, who had been married to Ralph's stepdaughter, Betty Percy. Ogle had died at the age of 21 in 1680 and so Elizabeth and her sisters would expect to inherit their father's wealth. She had married Christopher, son and heir of George Monck, duke of Albemarle, on December 30 1669 in the Duke's bedchamber where he lay dying of dropsy (he died four days later). Christopher's mother Anne Clarges was dying next door. As General Monck, the Duke had been in charge of the Parliamentarian army in Scotland. Just as Sandwich had been of great assistance in bringing over the fleet to Charles II at the Restoration, Monck had done the same with

---

[236] This is probably a reference to the Commons committee to examine who were the advisers and promoters of Lord Russell's execution
[237] BL Add Mss 70015 ff57,59 April 23 1691
[238] Bodleian Ms. Carte 79, f.455

the army, and had been far more handsomely rewarded. When the army was disbanded only his regiment, the Coldstream Guards, survived. His wife had been his seamstress and, supposedly, his mistress. Burnet describes her as a *mean, contemptible creature'*. Christopher had been proposed for Anne Scott, duchess of Buccleuch in her own right, but her ambitious mother aimed for royal blood and she was married to Monmouth at the age of twelve (her husband was fourteen). Three weeks after the duke of Albemarle's state funeral at Westminster Abbey King Charles had signed the Treaty of Dover. Christopher is supposed to have been left £60,000 in cash and an income of £15,000 pa (only the dukes of Ormonde, with some £22,000 pa, and Buckingham, with £19,000 pa, were richer). The Albemarles must have lived in great splendour -when he came of age in 1675 he paid £25,000 for Clarendon House, one of the finest in London - but, as with Ralph, his great income was less than he spent. In 1682, only seven years after the purchase, he had to sell the house to cut down on his expenses and reduced his wife's allowance to £1,000 pa (though she had brought him a dowry of £20,000). By the summer of that year she was showing signs of mental instability and in the autumn, when she was at Welbeck (her family's country seat), her father wrote to Danby (then in the Tower): *'my Daughter Albermarle was here. She was not madd, but there was a great consternation upon her, I suppose caused by her own folley and Pride, and Mallis of others who noe doubt has indeavored her ruen a long time and sure never woman has been so deafe to good council as she has been, nor did ever Parents doe so much for a Daughter as we have done for her'.*[239] Although her physician Dr. Barwick said that she was incapable of judging what she said or did, she was sufficiently well to take part in James II's coronation on St. George's Day, 1685.

A few letters from the Duchess to her husband survive from June and July 1685 when he was with the army opposing Monmouth's rebellion. *'My Deare Lord, I am exstremley troubled at ye difarant storryes I heare but that which disturbs me most to find soe many roueman catholecks gon to you for God sake find a way to have them retourn for feare of loseing your interest. Hevn spare your life for I have lived in such pane since you went that tis imposable for my Deare master to emagin, Yours for ever most Dutyfully, E Albemarle'. 'My Deare Lord, I beg to heare very often if you hope I shall ever sleep from any boddy about you. To heare you're alivee is some satisfackion but when I consider ye dangare your in ye worst friend I have will pitty me. This last nuse which is com covers me with continuall feares of foul play which all most gives me a despare of never seeing you more if that sad fate seseis me I pray to God to have such merse for his poore servant... I am full of a troubled tendernes and have*

---

[239] Leeds Mss

good reson apon a thesthen skores which I doe not dout but you will allways beleve you affectionate dutyfull wife, E Albemarle'.

These letters give no proof of madness (despite the idiosyncratic spelling). She is indignant in someone about the King thinking it fit 'to put those above you you have formerly commanded' (Feversham and Churchill) and they are full of affection. *'Your kind letter was very welcome to me, and Jo. Fontane came here today to tell me my dear love is well, but no certainty of being blessed with your presence.'* The Duchess certainly had her wits about her when she was trying to persuade her husband to change the deed he had signed in 1681 making the earl of Bath his heir (Bath had been promised his cousin General Monck's title by the King if his line failed) and enlarge her marriage settlement even though it already gave her £8,000 pa and the country house at Newhall in Essex for her life if she was widowed. The Duke duly signed a new will in 1687, but his actions may indicate duress: the original deed said it could only be revoked by another signed by six witnesses, three of whom had to be peers, and in the revocation sixpence must change hands. The 1687 deed only had three witnesses (none peers), and no money changed hands. At the same time she was unsuccessfully petitioning her father for a larger part of his estate than her four sisters were to have, since she was the eldest.

Despite the Duke showing a signal lack of his father's military prowess when in charge of troops in 1685, the next year James II came to stay with him and his spouse at Newhall. (Built by Henry VIII as the palace in which he and his new wife Anne Boleyn would bring up their family). Shortly afterwards the Duke was appointed Governor of Jamaica, an island that had been taken by England only thirty years before. (Slaves comprised some 50% of the population there (it would be over 90% by 1722) and the island was a favourite haunt of pirates). He sailed out of Portsmouth on September 19 1687 with his wife and his doctor, Hans Sloane, and they arrived in Port Royal (having stopped for ten days in Barbados) on December 19. Not long afterwards fortune shone on them: the Duke's share in the treasure recovered from a sunken galleon weighed in at 26 tons and was worth some £150,000.[240] But that was the end of their luck – less than a year after they had arrived, on October 6, the Duke died at the age of 36 (doubtless exhausted by the climate and Sloane's ministrations). The Duchess only arrived back at the end of May, after a very difficult journey during which the crew of the accompanying frigate had deserted,

---

[240] . William Phips, who had salvaged the Concepcion, brought James II's share to England and in return was knighted and was later made the first governor of Massachusetts under its new royal charter. He created the court that held the Salem witchcraft trials and eventuality closed it down and pardoned the condemned who had yet to be executed. In 1978 the stern of the Concepcion was found (Phips had salvaged the bow) and the treasure recovered was appraised at some $13 million.

intending to go over to the exiled James II. On board with her, in addition to the Duke's embalmed corpse, and the treasure, had been a seven foot snake, a crocodile and an iguana. The latter jumped overboard and was drowned, the crocodile died of natural causes, and the snake escaped and was shot by the Duchess's alarmed servant. The plants and fruits that Sloane had collected fared better, including the cacao beans. Although these were considered on the island to be good for the digestion, the doctor found them oily, nauseous and "hard of digestion" but much improved when a drink was made with them.

The voyage could not have helped the Duchess's nerves and in February 1691 her father declared she *'was not capable of managing any estate'*.[241] Later that year her mother wrote to Lady Thanet that *'Your sister Albemarle is incapable of anything'*. Despite (or perhaps because of) this, she was left to the care of her women, the two Wright sisters, and Elizabeth, wife of Sir Thomas Stamp, and of her physician Dr. Sloane. One assumes that at some time in 1692 Ralph determined to marry her and so improve his finances. He was still living in the highest style – on St. George's Day, 1691 *'His majestie without any guards went in the lord Sidney's coach to the earl of Montagu's house...and dined there: these lords dined there also – duke of Ormond, earls of Dorset, Shrewsbury, Monmouth, Marlborough, Portland; the lords Newport, Sidney, Godolphin and Cornwallis'*.[242] These ten peers were the governing elite of the moment.[243] Ralph had managed to persuade Elizabeth Wriothesley, the heiress daughter of one earl and widow of another to marry below herself, to plain Mr. Montagu, son and heir of a baron. He was now an earl and so might be able in the ordinary way of things to persuade Elizabeth Cavendish, the heiress daughter and widow of a duke, to do the same. But in her insanity she decided that she was only willing to marry again if it was to someone above her social standing. As a duchess the only way to do that was for her to marry royalty. Since there were no eligible Stuart males remarriage was therefore out of the question. Even if there had been a royal suitor he may have balked at wedding a thirty-six year old mad woman who had proved incapable of giving her late husband a child. The Duchess's madness had not discouraged other suitors, such as Harry Saville, (who had also pursued Ralph's first wife), and another who, in annoyance at losing her to Ralph, wrote:

> Insulting rival, never boast
> Thy conquest lately won;

---

[241] Welbeck Mss
[242] Luttrell p.215
[243] Cornwallis had married Anne Scott, duchess of Buccleuch, widow of James, duke of Monmouth

No wonder if her heart was lost
Her senses first were gone.

From one that's under Bedlam's laws
What glory can be had?
For love of thee was not the cause,
It proves that she was mad.[244]

There had been previous Montagu links with the Monck family – in January 1671 Albermarle had written to Ralph's father in answer to a letter which Lord Montagu had sent begging a £500 dowry for Betty Pride (second cousin to Christopher, in whose household she had lived until she was sixteen). The Duke said that he could *spare nothing from my ordinary expenses, but something I owe her, which shall be paid when I come of age*. When he removed his uncle Sir Thomas Clarges as a trustee, the latter in turn sought reinstatement through Lord Montagu's influence. Ralph was more direct in achieving his aim of marrying the widowed Duchess – he seems to have prepared the way by making 'gifts' to Sloane[245] and her waiting women. (This was not uncommon - in 1685 a Mrs. Potter had sued Tom Thynne's executors for redemption of the £500 promissory note he had given her for her assistance when he had wooed her mistress, Ralph's step-daughter Betty).[246] The story that passed into family legend tells of Ralph wooing her in the guise of the Emperor of China, ensuring that he and the servants accompanying him were suitably dressed. Dazzled by the prospect of becoming an Empress, she married him on Thursday September 8, 1692, probably in Newcastle House, Clerkenwell.[247] She supposedly insisted on being served on bended knee for the rest of her long life Although contemporary evidence for this story doesn't seem to exist, repetition has given it the status of fact. Whilst Ralph is likely to have been discrete about the nature of his courtship it was hard to keep a secret in London. On the day of the wedding there was an appropriate portent of the trouble this marriage would cause him. Richard Lapthorne wrote to his friend Richard Coffin, of Bideford, Devon: *'I perceive by your letter you felt not the Earthquake in your parts. It was*

---

[244] A.W. Ward, A.R. Waller eds. *Cambridge History of Literature* Vol. II, (CUP 1912) attributed to a Lord Roos or Ross of whom I can find no trace
[245] Ralph was well acquainted with Sloane – there survives a letter he sent the doctor from Beaulieu on July 26th the previous year: "*Sr, I received the favour of your letter about the french wine your brother had provided, for which I am obliged to you & him. But I found two peeces of claret and one of white heere, & with what I have at london that will do my business I hope, till the seas are cleere. Pray give him many thanks from me.*"
[246] Vernon to Shrewsbury letters p.161
[247] NCRO Montagu papers vol.189 contains a paper dated 29 November 1697 in which William Wing of Bewley, clerk, swears on oath that he performed the marriage in Clerkenwell parish.

felt...at Amsterdam and Ostend, and in most places within 60 miles and further about London'.[248] Three months before an earthquake had destroyed Port Royal, Jamaica (described at the time as one of the wickedest places on earth) where the Duchess had previously lived. Lord Thanet wrote a diplomatic letter to his new brother-in-law on 16 September: *'The news of your Lordship's marriage was not more surprising to me than pleasing to me since I am certain it will on all accounts be extremely to the satisfaction of my Lady Duchess'.* He adds that her father, always desirous of a grandson, had urged her to marry again, that she might have children. Given the view that her father had of her, and his knowledge of her poor mental health, this seems to be politeness.[249] Certainly the Duchess's other brothers-in-law had different views: *'News of the Duchess of Albemarle's marriage to my Lord Montagu, who are furnishing Montagu house in a most sumptuous manner in order to their reception, and I hear my Lord Bath is in great disorder with the match, as I believe my Lord Clare will be too'.*[250] They had clearly calculated on her wealth being distributed amongst them when she died. Lady Russell's reaction was rather more down to earth: *'For the chat of the town, as the successor to my poor sister, I will not venture to hurt my eyes for it'.*[251] Metzger states that 'Montagu became a godsend to comedy'. He repeats an assertion made by F.E. Budd in his book on the dramatic works of William Burnaby that the latter's play "The Ladies Visiting Day" alludes to Ralph's courtship in its plot. Lady Lovetoy is far more interested in exotic gentlemen than in Englishmen and so Courtine woes her as Alexander, a Muscovite prince. She had seen the real prince as he passed by: *'He had the finest foreign Face and Bezarr Equipage'.* On their marriage Courtine pulls off his whiskers to reveal himself. Nor is Lady Lovetoy mad – she is eloquent in her reasons for her preference: *'I hate a home-bred Fellow; he smells of the Chimney Corner'.* Foreigners have experience of life and the world she feels, and so are of far greater interest. *'To have all the Fellows in Town striving and toasting one's health, is to live indeed. A Woman's character is not compleat before she has been in a Lampoon, and had a Fellow or two kill'd for her, but to have A Prince fight for one is a fine thing. I shall be talk'd of all the world over'.* Metzger states that Courtine is a portrayal of Ralph, but the play was not written until nine years after his marriage, in 1701, and so whilst some in the audience may have known of, and remembered, that event, it doesn't seem current enough to have served a direct allusion. There is, however,

---

[248] R.J. Kerr & I.C. Duncan eds., *Portledge Papers : being extracts from the letters of Richard Lapthorne to Richard Coffin* (London 1928)

[249] E.F. Ward, *Christopher Monck Duke of Albemarle* (London 1915) p. 343, drawing on Welbeck Mss

[250] Finch Mss vol 4 p.457 Marquess of Carmarthen to his daughter Lady Leominster

[251] Letter from Rachel, Lady Russell, to Dr. FitzWilliam, 19th Sept. 1692

mention of Montagu House. Captain Strut challenges Sir Toby Dolt to a duel in the fields behind. He also states that Colley Cibber used the courtship as a basis for "The Double Gallant", produced in 1707. In fact Cibber took some of Barnaby's work, and also made free with Mrs Centlivre's "Love at a venture", when putting together his own play. If the plot is supposed to refer to Ralph it is well disguised: Careless falls for Lady Dainty with £2,000 a year who is *'for any thing that comes from beyond sea...and she's is love with nothing o'this side the line'*. So he woes her as Prince Alexander and reveals his true identity after they marry.

It is clear that Ralph intended to gain as much from his marriage as possible – only five days after the ceremony the gossip was that he *'resolves to have a suit of law with my Lord Clare for a share of the Duke of Newcastle's estate.'*[252] At the end of 1693 a lawsuit began to determine whether Duke Christopher's new will was a true one, enabling Ralph to have the management of the greater part of the Albemarle inheritance. The earl of Bath argued that it was not true and the case went to the Lords. On the first day of the hearing Sir Thomas Higgins dropped down dead after giving evidence.[253] Not a good omen. On Friday December 22 the lord chief justices gave their first judgement for Bath. Six days later Ralph appealed. The Thames froze over. Luttrell wrote presciently on February 19 *'tis likely to be some time before it will be determined.'* It would be almost five years. Ralph's appeal was narrowly dismissed, 28 peers being for him and 30 against. In November there was another hearing which continued overnight until nine in the morning. (Hearings were commonly held at night). Ralph lost again. Then there was a complication – Albermarle's Pride cousins sought to prove that he was the son of Anne Clarges' first husband and not of the 1st Duke. If that could not be proved there was still the rumour that Anne's first husband was still alive when she remarried and so Duke Christopher was illegitimate. If either was true the 1st Duke's estate would go to the Prides. So whilst Ralph and Bath were opposing each other in some hearings, they joined in court to oppose the Prides' claims. The case was the subject of a good deal of discussion. In March 1695 Ralph's neighbour Lord Spencer wrote to the duke of Newcastle that *'My Lord Montagu, who I believe has it in his nature never to be quiet, has again petitioned the House today...that he may have another trial with Lord Bath'* but a few days later he told the Duchess *'I can send you the good news of Lord Montagu's petition being yesterday rejected by the House.'* [254] On June 18 1696, after a hearing which had lasted from nine in the morning until noon next day, Ralph defeated Bath, who then had eleven of Ralph's witnesses indicted for perjury. *'Tis said*

[252] BL Add Mss 70116
[253] Portledge Papers p.125
[254] HMC Portland vol. 2 p.172

the latter will indict ten of the earl of Baths witnesses for the like crime'.[255]
It took almost a year for this claim to be heard. One of Ralph's witnesses, Harris (a schoolmaster), had sworn that Sir John Coplestone *'who was witness to the duke of Albermarles deed of gift, was not then in London, but in Somersetshire: it was proved plainly, by records and other evidence, that Sir John was in London when the deed was signed...the lord chief justice summ'd up the evidence, and left it to the jury to consider whether to lord Montagu's witness was not mistaken, or whether guilty of wilfull and corrupt perjury'.*[256] The witness had stated that Coplestone was at the Wells assizes on June 22 1681 and read from an entry in his almanac to that effect. Unfortunately a lawyer remembered that the assizes had been held at Bath that year. When the almanac was examined it was found that the relevant page had been sewn into it. It was suspected that the entry was for the Wells assizes on June 22 1682 but, although the witness had brought other almanacs into court to show that he regularly kept them, the one for 1682 was missing. He was found guilty of perjury, as was Duke, a farmer, a few days later. Bath's council then moved to try the next witness but was told *'there could be no more this term, because the judges were not able to sit up another night'.*[257] Two more witnesses, Melling and Greipe, were eventually convicted, and Bath also acted against a Mr. Osborn and Mr. Lambert *'who promised to some persons that they should be well paid if they would swear to such and such things'* (apparently that Ralph had made £2,000 available for the purpose).[258] Lambert had been Ralph's chaplain but had recently (and unexpectedly) made an advantageous marriage. Despite this Luttrell records on Saturday May 28 1698 that *'the tryall at the common pleas bar between the Earls of Bath and Montagu...which commenced on Thursday morning, held til Fryday noon, when the jury, after a quarter of an hours withdrawing, brought in a verdict for the latter'.*[259] The previous year Sir Francis Pemberton, one of Ralph's counsel, had died *'of a cold he got in Westminster Hall the last time he sat up all night, as the custom is, in the case between the Earls of Bath & Montagu. He was 75 years old'.*[260] Finally, on Thursday October 25: *'The earls of Bath and Montagu, who have been many years in law, and spent vast sums of money about the late duke of Albemarle's estate, have now at last agreed the same'.*[261] Such was the fame of the case that the next year *'the House of Lords had under consideration the exorbitant fees of the lawyers, occasioned by the late very expensive trials between*

---

[255] Luttrell p.78
[256] Ibid
[257] Ibid p.223
[258] Ibid p.242
[259] Ibid p.385
[260] Cal SP Dom June 11 1697
[261] Luttrell p.443

the Earls of Bath & Montagu, and they appointed a committee' which achieved nothing.[262] The Prides hadn't given up however, and eventually the main Pride claimants were bought off, Bath purchasing various properties for £8,500 from one and Ralph the Honour of Clitheroe from Mrs Sherwin – the same Betty Pride for whom his father had begged a marriage portion. Proceedings were finally stopped by the Lord Chancellor on June 28 1709, three months after Ralph's death. The agreement that Ralph and Bath came to was that the latter relinquished all rights to the Duchess's estates during her life. She would outlive Ralph by twenty-five years.

It is interesting that Boyer, in his obituary of Ralph, states that during William and Mary's reign he *'intermedled not much with public affairs'*. Whilst his name might not have been on the public's lips when politics were discussed, he was still very much involved. (Indeed in both April and November 1690 Ralph's name was in the frame to replace Nottingham as a Secretary of State).[263] At the start of William's rule he decided that since men of various political colours had invited him over, and supported him, there should be a mixed ministry. Whilst laudable in its aim, a mixed ministry led to mixed advice. William had no truck with the republican aims of the younger Whigs - autocratic Stuart blood ran in his veins. So Danby and Nottingham were preferred to even moderate Whigs and when Parliament met in March 1690 there was a Tory majority. Slowly however they came to believe that they had only replace one unpopular Stuart with another who gave wealth and positions to his foreign friends and had lumbered the country with a very expensive war. In July London received the news of the defeat of the Anglo-Dutch fleet by the French off Beachy Head on the 10th sparking fears that the victorious enemy would sail up the Thames. William had gone to Ireland the previous month to oppose King James and the troops he had raised there. Marlborough brought Queen Mary an offer from Shrewsbury, Godolphin, Wharton and Ralph to raise twelve hundred men at their own expense to help oppose any invasion. They asked to be reimbursed with the cost in due course and didn't want their names to be made public. She wrote to William from Whitehall:

'Last night lord Marlborough came to me, and made me an offer from Lord Shrewsbury, Lord Montagu, Lord Goldolphin, Mr Wharton and Mr Jepson, to raise 1200 men immediately at their own charges, so I would but give my word they would be reimbursed when it was convenient'. She decided that by the time they were raised William would be back, so just thanked them. Mary says she knew William would trust anything Shrewsbury did, *'yet I did not know if all else might be employed. I confess I do not like Lord Montague, so indeed he said there were persons he*

---

[262] Cal SP Dom Jan 18 1698
[263] BL Add Mss 70014 ff.322, 361

believed you would mistrust, and named him'.[264] Ralph hadn't improved his image in her eyes by his behaviour on the 10th – the Queen told the King that Nottingham had arrested Lord Ross and the privy council had agreed, but when it came to signing the warrant Bolton refused *'and hindered Lord Devonshire by a whisper, and his son by a nod; Lord Montagu would not sign either'.*[265] A few days later the news of William's victory at the Boyne arrived in London, and the need to raise troops disappeared. Mary also mentioned to her husband that a loan of £5,000 from Ralph had been accepted on June 12 – part of the £18,500 lent by a group of noblemen to the Crown. This is a large sum, especially in light of the claim he had made to the Collector of Taxes a year before that he had debts of over £20,000.[266] [267] It may have been royal antipathy that continued to kept Ralph from office- in February 1692 it was rumoured that he would join Sir Edward Seymour and Sir William Trumbal to act as the Lord Lieutenant of Ireland.[268] Two months later the post of Lord Privy Seal was being mentioned.[269] Neither came to pass. Ralph continued to keep up his contacts – in August he is recorded as having dined at Pontack's famous tavern in Lombard Street with Shrewbury, Marlborough and Sidney Godolphin.[270] Nonetheless he sometimes considered it more important to support a neighbour rather than the Whig position and so in January 1693 he voted against the bill to permit the 7th duke of Norfolk to divorce his wife for adultery. Duchess Mary had not given her husband an heir and had been having an affair with Sir John Germain (reputedly the illegitimate brother of the King), As heiress to her father the earl of Peterborough she owned the Drayton estate near Boughton.[271]

Next year the earl of Sunderland was allowed to return to England, having abandoned his Catholicism with as much insouciance as he had abandoned the Protestant faith years before. By the summer of 1693 he was back in politics, using his skills to persuade the King that a Whig ministry might do more for him if given power, and so remove the

---

[264] Dalrymple vol. 3 p.99

[265] Cal SP Dom

[266] In reply to a circular letter addressed on behalf of the Marquess of Halifax, Lord Privy Seal, by Thomas Medhurst, Collector of Taxes, to 100 Peers, requiring a return of their personal estate with a view to the payment of tax in accordance with the terms of the Act for a General Aid to Their Majesties.

[267] Devonshire Mss., Chatsworth, Halifax Collection , Group B/10.

[268] BL Add Mss 70119 Feb 4 1691/2

[269] Cal SP Dom 1694 p.349

[270] Bodleian Ms. Carte 79, f.223

[271] Norfolk had been a Catholic but was now a Protestant. Mary had been a Protestant but was now a Catholic. Both had committed adultery but Norfolk wanted to keep his wife's inheritance. He finally got his divorce in April 1701, having agreed to return his wife's dowry. Exactly a year later he died, unmarried, and his Catholic nephew succeeded him.

difficulties they were throwing up in opposition. On August 24th the Whig leaders met at Sunderland's house at Althorp: Shrewsbury, Devonshire, Wharton, Admiral Russell and Charles Montagu (Ralph's second cousin), together with Godolphin and Marlborough. It seems that Ralph was kept at a distance by his neighbour: Shrewsbury wrote afterwards to his friend Wharton that he hadn't visited him because to do so would rob him of his excuse (usually ill health) for not visiting Ralph at Boughton (a short ride from Althorp), but that the true reason was that if he went to see Ralph then Sunderland would be "disobliged".[272] Yet Montagu was apparently too influential a Whig to ignore. Fortunately there is a record of what followed the Althorp conference because a Mr. Dolben decided to reveal its secrets to Nottingham in a letter of September 3. '*On Wednesday last I waited on my Lord Montague at Boughton, four miles from this place. There I found Mr Hampden the younger with whom I have been for some years well acquainted. He told me, had I come two days sooner, I should have seen much company there, and named Lords Marlborough and Godolphin, Mr. Russell and Mr. Felton; that they came from Althrop (my Lord Sunderland's) on Saturday night, and left Boughton on Munday afternoon to go to Mr. Wharton's in Buckinghamshire. This gave me curiosity to ask whether it was a progress of diversion or of business? He said, of extraordinary business. That a scheme was formed at Althrop of several considerable alterations in the ministry, but the principal and most immediate endeavour was to remove your Lordship and place Lord Sunderland in your station, who (said Hampden) is infinitely desirous of the preferment and has gained many solicitors (particularly of the house of Bedford) by professing himself to be a very good Whig, to which party his courtship is so universal and incessant that he leaves not the most minute member of either house unapply'd to, whose inclinations bend that way, and whom he can possibly reach by himself or his agents. That the visit was to work upon Lord Montague, and that the finishing stroke will be at the Comptroller's, where the final measures in order to the effecting this grand design will be concluded and established. Much to the same purpose fell from this gentleman...I confess I am in doubt whether every particular he says may be relied upon as a true report, probably your Lordship may know the character of the man, his violence in discourse, and his proneness to affirm at random. My distrust of him prompted me to get what I could out of lord Mountague, who told me very frankly that the business of this itinerant cabal was to contrive in favour of Lord Sunderland. Some of them shewed great zeal and promised to themselves success, others, particularly Lord Godolphin, were cold in the matter, and*

---

[272] D.H. Somerville *The King of Hearts. Charles Talbot, Duke of Shrewsbury* (London 1962) p.85

194

if I would know his opinion, twas in plain terms, that Lord Sunderland deserved rather to be impeached than to be preferred'.[273]

The conference bore some fruit: Nottingham was dismissed and Russell put at the head of the admiralty. Ralph again failed to achieve office. It had apparently been proposed that Godolphin should be Lord Treasurer, Sunderland the President of the Council and Ralph Lord Privy Seal. *'These proposals tis said Lord Sidney is gone over with the King and if he will accept it...will give him 4 hundred thousand pounds.'*[274] Shrewsbury, much trusted by William as a moderate, was reluctant to take up office. His view was that the *'toil and torture of so much business is a good bargain to none but those who are fond either of ambition, experience or money'*. It is interesting that in the same draft letter he says that a Secretaryship was worth £10,000 pa. The official salary was only £1,850 but it is generally agreed that the perquisites were worth far more. If asked, Ralph might have responded that he had wanted a Secretaryship for all three reasons mentioned by Shrewsbury. William's reluctance to pass the Triennial Act that many Whigs wanted meant that few of those needed to form a new administration would put themselves forward.[275] The King finally agreed the Bill in the following year, and then Shrewsbury and Trenchard were appointed Secretaries, Charles Montagu Chancellor, Somers Lord Keeper. Though Danby was still President of the Council he was left with little power and influence. (To placate him he was made duke of Leeds). Ralph's disappointment at lack of preferment didn't stop him from working on behalf of the Whigs. The death of Anthony Parker, the MP for Clitheroe, led to a by-election in late 1693 when one of the candidates was John Allen *'put up by Lord Montagu'*[276] who was clearly exercising the influence he had gained in the area through his recent marriage. However the earl of Macclesfield was a Lancashire man and managed to get his second son elected.

William was desperate for more money to prosecute the wars against France, and hoped that the Whigs would be able to provide it. Charles Montagu revived an idea of William Paterson, a Scottish banker, to found a private institution called the Bank of England. This was set up to raise loans that could be advanced to the government. More than a million pounds was raised in under two weeks and half the money was loaned to

---

[273] Finch Mss vol. 5 pt 1 p.243

[274] Verney Mss mic M636/47 Anne Nicholas to John Verney Aug 31 1693

[275] The new Act went further than reinstating the 1641 Act that required Parliament to meet for at least a 50 day session once every three years, whether the King agreed or not (the mechanism employed to cope with the latter eventuality was repealed in 1664) by ordering that it should meet annually and that elections should be held every three years. It was thought that this would prevent resumption of the arbitrary government of Charles II and James II.

[276] Ibid Nov 11th 1693

help rebuild the navy. For some reason Ralph was minded to be one of only seven peers who voted on February 24 1694 against the part of the Tunnage Bill that incorporated the Bank. (The Bank proved a far more successful scheme that Paterson's project for a colony in Panama a few years later – the Darien Scheme – which financially wrecked the Scottish kingdom and so helped remove resistance to the Act of Union with England in 1707). He was certainly willing to avail himself of one opportunity which the Bank presented – four months after it opened he secured a loan of £2,000 (on November 22). On January 12 following he borrowed a further £4,000, this time secured on three pearl necklaces, and a diamond one with a diamond cross. There are very few loans in the Bank's books in these early years, and this security is most unusual. Perhaps Ralph asked his cousin Charles to exert his influence.

On May 18 1694 Ralph had written to the King:

Sir   I did not think it very good manners to trouble your Majesty in the middle of so great affairs as you had at your going away, else I should have made it my humble request that you would have been so gracious to have done my family the same honour you have done to my Lord Clare, Bedford and others. This request had been made to you by the old Duke of Schomberg, who thought himself under some obligation to me for the encouragement I gave him to attend you in your expedition to England, but that I did not think it reasonable to ask that being put over the Duke of Schomberg's head; but now, Sir, that you have given him that rank which the greatness of his family and personal merit has deserved, I may, by your Majesty's grace and favour, pretend to the same dignity as well as any of the families you have promoted, being myself the head of a family that many years ago had great honour and dignities, when I am sure these had none; and we have lost them by the civil wars between York and Lancaster. I am now below the two younger branches, my Lords Manchester and Sandwich. I have to add to my pretension the having married the Duke of Newcastle's oldest daughter; and it has been the practise of all your predecessors, whenever they were so gracious to keep up the honour of a family by the female line, to bestow it upon those who married the eldest, without there were some personal prejudice to the person who had that claim.

I may add, Sir, another pretension, which is the same for which you have given a Dukedom to the Bedford family; the having been one of the first, and held out till the last, in that cause which, for the happiness of England, brought you to the crown. I hope it will not be thought a less merit to be alive and ready on all occasions to venture all again for your service, than if I had lost my head when my Lord Russel did. I could not then have had the opportunity of doing the nation the service I did, when there was such opposition made by the Jacobite party, in bringing my Lord

Huntington, the bishop of Durham, and my Lord Ashley, to vote against the Regency, and for your having the crown; which was carried by those three voices and my own. I should not put you in mind of this, but hoping that so fortunate and so seasonable a service as this, may supply all my other wants of merit; and which, since you were pleased to promise me in your bed-chamber at St. James's before you were King, never to forget, you will not now that you are so great and so gracious a one. The Duke of Shrewsbury can further satisfy you what persecution I suffered, and what losses I sustained in the two last reigns, which must make the mortification greater if his humble suit be refused to...&c [277]

Dalrymple, who prints this letter, comments: '*This letter is singular in several respects. First it assumes that Lord Russel's conspiracy had been agreeable to the Prince of Orange. Secondly, it insinuates that Lord Montagu had been a party to it, whereas it was certain he was not. I found, in Barillon's correspondence, that infinite pains were taken in England to fix...that conspiracy upon him, but in vain.*' [278]

Metzger is far more critical: '*The letter is a masterpiece of self-styled importance ...composed of one convinced of his exaggerated self-worth...presumptuous at best*'. [279] He doesn't consider whether Ralph may have thought that, if his branch of the family had received the earldom so frequently talked of, promised (and lobbied for) in the reign of Charles II, he could have received a further elevation when William came to the throne and so reasserted his branch's precedence over those of the earls of Manchester and Sandwich. (In procession he would have been far behind his kinsmen, since order of precedence was by rank and then by date of creation). Certainly his distant cousin Halifax recognised that he headed '*the Chief Branch of our Family*'.[280] As recently as 1692 there was apparently gossip about his further elevation: '*The earle of Mountague, 'tis said will be made a marquis*', but this was to be yet another unfulfilled hope. [281]

The importance placed on precedence and descent in Ralph's letter was shared by his class and seems a long way from the modern world. Algernon Sidney may have been a republican but he had railed against recently ennobled Tories: '*Nothing can be more absurd, than to give a prerogative of birth to Craven, Tufton, Hyde, Bennet, Osborn and others, before the Cliftons, Hampdens, Courtneys, Pelhams...and many others...I forbear to mention the sordid ways of attaining to titles in our days...Whatever the ancient noblemen of England were, we are sure they*

[277] Cal SP Dom 1694 p.138
[278] Dalrymple vol.2 p.284
[279] E. C. Metzger, *Ralph, First Duke of Montagu, 1638-1709* (New York 1987) p.310
[280] BL Add Mss 70028 Aug 30 1711
[281] Luttrell vol. 2 p.574, 1692, Sept 25

were not such as these.' [282] When Harley created nine peers on January 1 1712 the letters patent had to be both dated and timed to avoid disputes over precedence amongst them. Its importance was voiced when there was an attempt to add lustre to the duke of Marlborough's name in 1708 by giving him precedence over other dukes. The idea worried even his friends since it *'would raise more envy and hatred in our ancient nobles than the thing would be worth. For none are so jealous of their dignities and pre-eminence as those that have nothing else to value themselves upon...And the ill humour and resentment of those peers that would be disobliged by it would run through all their families and relations.'* [283] The value first of Ralph's barony and then of his earldom had been diluted by the creation of so many peers over the century. The fifty at Elizabeth's death had grown to one hundred and thirty by 1628, and there were a further hundred creations between the Restoration and 1714.

Metzger also does not consider why Ralph broached the subject with the King at this time, despite the mention in his letter of Clare's elevation. John Holles, 4th earl of Clare, was Ralph's brother-in-law, having married Margaret Cavendish, and so someone Ralph doubtless knew well. (He was also Sir Tom Pelham's brother-in-law). On May 16 1694 he was made duke of Newcastle, two days before Ralph wrote the letter. As he mentions, it had been past practise when recreating a title to do so for whoever had married the eldest daughter. That person was Ralph, not Clare. Just as wounding to Ralph's pride must have been the elevation of his old enemy Danby to the dukedom of Leeds. This happened only a fortnight before. In fact at the end of April the King had had patents drawn up for the creation of five dukedoms: the earls of Devonshire and Shrewsbury were also elevated. In doing this he changed the nature of ducal rank. Historically dukedoms had only rarely been conferred on aristocrats who were not members of the extended royal family (so when Richard II made his favourite duke of Ireland in 1386, and James I made George Villiers duke of Buckingham in 1623 it was an unwelcome signal to others that these individuals were being given quasi-royal status). Charles II created more dukedoms than any other monarch but only four (Albermarle, Newcastle, Beaufort and Ormonde) were not for his mistresses and children. In five years William created eight dukes and only one of those was for a member of the royal family – no wonder Ralph felt left out. He does, however, put his finger on the reason he was overlooked: *'without there were some personal prejudice to the person who had that claim'.* It surely must have been this royal prejudice that kept him from ever attaining this or any of the political offices he was tipped for.

---

[282] Algernon Sidney, *Discourses concerning government* (1698)
[283] BL Add Mss 61459 ff.155-7

What is most striking is his manifest belief in the Montagus' close connection with their distant medieval relations, and the idea that "honours and dignities" had been lost during the Wars of the Roses. The last Montagu earl of Salisbury died at the Siege of Orleans in 1428, long before the civil war began. His title and wealth passed through the daughter he had by Alice Chaucer (the poet's granddaughter) to Richard Neville, one of the main protagonists of the Wars. So the main Montagu line died out, rather than being cut down by war. It might be that this invocation of ancestry was simply a way of pointing out that, since Ralph was descended from such an ancient family, his expectations of honours were more justified than those showered on parvenus such as the Russells (who with the Wriothesleys, Cecils, Cavendishs and, indeed, the Montagus were amongst many other noble families who owed their initial rise to serving the Tudors). But it is even more likely that Ralph had been brought up to believe that truly was the case: in 1621 Ralph's grandfather the 1st Lord Montagu wrote to Ralph's father '*You are discended of worthy auncestors. I accomted them allways my greatest Glory. So do you. And as you possesse there landes, so Imitate there vertues, and you shall be the crowne of them*'. This instruction Ralph's father may well have passed on to him. If he was also given the rest of it, he didn't heed it: '*Travyle not too much to be Rich...He that is greedy of gayne trobleth his owne soule...In your marriage look after goodness rathe than goodes; yet disparage not your selfe, nether match higher than your owne degree*'.

On March 2 1605 Sir Edward (made 1st Lord Montagu in 1621) had been called to an Earl Marshal's court at Whitehall to hear a petition from Viscount Mountague against him on the grounds that he had no right to bear the Montagu arms.[284] This was a very ancient coat, of three red conjoined lozenges on a silver ground (quartered with the green griffin on a gold ground of the Monthermers).[285] He told the Earl Marshal that his ancestors had borne this coat, with the difference of a black border, from time out of mind.[286] Asked to provide by October a family tree showing his entitlement, Sir Edward Montagu did not, since the '*same remains obscure and full of difficulty*' and '*the Commissioners much disliked the neglect or rather contempt of the said Sir Edward Montague in this behalf*' yet

---

[284] The Montagu archive contains an undated agreement by William Camden, the famous antiquarian and herald, to do some work for £50 and also simplified Montagu pedigrees in the hand of Camden's rival Ralph Brook, York Herald. (Rival because Brook accused Camden in 1602 of granting arms to "mean men" such as Shakespeare's father).
[285] The red lozenges may be a rebus for monte acuto (pointed mount). A Richard de Montagu gave land to Montacute Priory in Somerset. There was a steep mound nearby, once fortified.
[286] G.E.Cockayne, *The Complete Peerage of England, Scotland, Ireland* (London 1910) vol. ix app D

seemingly never forbade him to continue using the coat.[287] It must be significant that 1694 is the date of John Tillotson's genealogy rectifying this "difficulty" that traces the Montagu descent from Simon, brother to John, 1st earl of Salisbury, through Thomas, John, William, Richard of Hennington, Thomas, & Lord Chief Justice Sir Edward. It shows all the branches of the family extant at that time.[288] This belief in an ancient lineage was further reinforced and displayed to all by van der Eyden's six paintings of Montagu ancestors.[289] King William probably saw them when he went to Montagu House for dinner, and when he visited Boughton he would have seen the overmantel in the Little Hall which showed by means of many coats of arms Ralph's descent from the first King William, the Conqueror. (There still exists a sketch showing that it was originally intended to go right back to the Emperor Charlemagne. Perhaps this was thought to be going too far, in both senses). The Montagus may have felt a need to display and reiterate their noble descent to combat the comments of men like Francis Lane. In the 1670s Ralph's father had brought an action of slander against him for having stated several times in 1666 that he was an enemy of the King, and in 1669 having told one of the secretaries of state that he was a disloyal and disaffected nobleman. Several witnesses gave testimony that he had described Lord Montagu as *'a mongrel and not a Montagu and that his true name was Ladds and that his ancestors changed their name and arrogated to themselves the name of Montagu'*. Lane clearly hated the whole clan and *'hoped that he should see in a short time never a Montagu in England have their heads upon their shoulders'*.[290] Although two centuries had passed since Richard Ladde had adopted his father-in-law's surname there were clearly still some who knew of it.

Letters asking the monarch for a sign of honour were by no means uncommon: Ralph's grand-daughters would petition for their husbands' elevations sixty years later. At least Ralph didn't sulk at the disappointment as Lord Clare had done in 1691 when he asked William for the Newcastle dukedom only a few months after the death of his father-in-law. The King *'was pleased to say he would consider it, which Clare took as refusal and desired leave to retire, which the King granted. He laid down commission as lord lieutenant of Middlesex. Lords Stamford and Mountague are talked of it'*.[291] Rather he continued to put himself forward. On June15 Shrewsbury wrote to the King: *'Some time after I had*

---

[287] NCRO Montagu papers vol. 189

[288] Ibid

[289] The portraits could not have been painted much later than 1694, when Ralph wrote his letter, since the artist died in the following year. He had settled in Northamptonshire and also painted a series of ancestors for the earls of Rutland at Belvoir.

[290] History of Parliament Trust

[291] Luttrell p.301; *Honour, Interest & Power* (2011) p. 188

returned you answer to Lord Montagu, upon Lord Falkland's death, he came to me to offer himself if he could be useful to you in Holland. I found he meant it as a compliment, and proof that he was ready in any capacity to serve you. I promised him to acquaint you with it'.[292]

The timing of Ralph's request for a dukedom could have been better: William had gone to the Hague and was worrying about keeping the Danes and Swedes in the alliance. And though the Whigs had been holding sway since late in 1693, the Queen detested Sunderland and the King thoroughly disliked Russell, Wharton and Ralph's relative Charles Montagu. Yet they had achieved office and Ralph had not. Perhaps he was disliked even more and his Whig colleagues feared his ambition. Did he believe that what he had done to help to secure the throne for William should outweigh his betrayal of the Stuarts in the Danby affair, followed by his attempt to exclude Mary's father from the throne and to encourage Monmouth's designs on it? Perhaps he thought that William would accede to his request as a further means of placating the Whigs without giving him office. Since no reply survives we have no idea of the King's thoughts on the matter. Metzger further castigates Ralph's pretension in having a 'bed cover woven at the Mortlake Tapestry works with his ducal coat of arms' in 1684, as well as on a mirror and table.[293] In fact we know that in 1695 a tapestry woven in the 1680s with Ralph's monogram had an earl's coronet inserted (at a cost of £6). There is no evidence from surviving items at Boughton that Ralph presumed so far as to pretend to a rank he had not been granted. Tapestries dating from before he inherited his father's title have a coronet of roses over his monogram rather than a baronial one.

The Triennial Bill became law on December 18. Ten days later Queen Mary died of smallpox at the age of thirty-two. Ralph would have been present at her funeral in Westminster Abbey on the evening of March 5, 1695 (he had been sitting in the Lords that day). The two Houses followed the hearse, the Lords in scarlet and ermine and the Commons in black. No previous sovereign had been followed to their grave by a Parliament since the two were deemed to expire at the same time, pointing up the uniqueness of William and Mary's dual monarchy. Ralph would then have sat in his damp robes after the procession through the sleet and heard Purcell's sublime anthems written for the occasion. His step-daughter Betty, the Duchess of Somerset, was chief mourner (as she would be for Queen Anne).

March also saw the removal of Sir John Trevor as Speaker of the Commons – the cross-eyed Welshman was found guilty of accepting a large bribe from the City to assist in passing a bill, but was not forced to

---

[292] Cal SP Dom
[293] Metzger, p.330

disgorge it.[294] Fellow Tories Danby and Sir Edward Seymour were strongly linked to similar offences and effectively compulsorily retired – Danby wasn't made a regent in William's absence later that year. In May 1695 Parliament was prorogued. The King went abroad to his army and had a successful campaign, so when he returned to London in mid October he was welcomed with more enthusiasm than usual. He agreed to Whig requests for election of a new Parliament, and also to a three week royal progress whilst awaiting the results. This required the King to make a special effort since he found the presence of a lot of strangers uncomfortable, and having to be polite to and interested in those he had no time for he found irksome. His health, always far from robust, was also declining. Lord Spencer wrote to let the duke of Newcastle know that *The King will be with you by the end of next week, intending to take a progress northward in this idle time til the Parliament meets. He intends to set out on Thursday for Newmarket, and from thence will go to Althorp on Monday, where he will stay til Friday, and from thence will go to Nottingham intending to hunt in Sherwood Forest. It is so sudden a resolution that it will be very troublesome to everybody to whose house he goes. The people that go with him are the duke of Shrewsbury, Lord Portland, Lord Godolphin, Tom Wharton, Mr Montagu, the duke of St. Albans.'* [295] From Sunderland's house at Althorp he went to dine at Castle Ashby and could hardly refuse an invitation from Ralph to dine at Boughton. This occurred on Saturday October 23 1695 (the visit was not for fifteen days, as suggested by Metzger). It would be nice to imagine royal approval being given in particular to the fine set of state rooms that can be seen, little changed, at Boughton today. Yet it seems that they were far from being completed. Roger Davis was paid that year for *'helping the Upholsterer to putt up Hangings and take them down again when the King was at Boughton'* and the elaborate parquet flooring (the first use of parquet in England) which was the work of the joiner Peter Rieuset (paid the incredible sum of £5,000 for his work here and at Montagu House) doesn't seem to have been laid until the next year, when he was paid *'to go to Boughton with my man 8 days work.'* This honour was added to by royal recognition of his place in the ruling class when he was appointed as one of the Commissioners for the new naval hospital at Greenwich that year.

The King's visit to Northamptonshire prior to the elections made little difference to the outcome. Government still depended on the Whigs, plus those who still hankered after James's return, the 'country' opposition and four statesmen of indeterminate political allegiance (who some thought of as opportunists), namely Godolphin, Marlborough, Sunderland and

---

[294] This is a different Sir John Trevor to the one mentioned earlier in this book, Secretary of State for the North, 1668-72
[295] HMC Portland vol.2 p174

Shrewsbury. Despite the fluidity of the political scene, the town of Northampton duly elected a Whig (Christopher Montagu, brother of Charles) and a Tory (Justinian Isham – who had voted against William and Mary being offered the crown) just as it usually did.

The new Parliament met on November 22 and Ralph was there. The next day he made his response to Bath's latest complaint in the Albermarle will case, saying that he could not *but wonder much at the petitioner's troubling your lordships with a petition of this nature...seeing your petitioner is so unstable in his own thoughts not to be at certainty with himself.* [296] Though the Whig ministry continued, it couldn't be sure of a majority in the Commons, not least due to the number of independently minded 'country' members whose main aims were the end of the war and consequent reduction of tax on their land. The main matter to be considered was the state of the coinage – most of the silver in circulation was heavily clipped – and a hard choice had to be made between devaluation and inflation. Charles Montagu, and the City interest, won the battle for recoinage and devaluation (the cost of which would be met by a Window Tax). As ever lack of funds was William's greatest worry (for all public services as well as the war) and he wrote to Shrewsbury in mid-July 1696 *'If you cannot devise expedients to send contributions or procure credit all is lost and I must go to the Indies'*. The Tories tried to set up a rival to the Bank of England in order to raise cash for the King and gain his favour but failed. The Bank reluctantly advanced a further £200,000. The public knew comparatively little of such politics but great national excitement had been created by the discovery of an assassination plot in February. Sir John Fenwick had been hatching such schemes for years (it has been suggested that he had once been reprimanded by William when serving under him). The details were unclear, but James II's illegitimate son the duke of Berwick was in the country plotting for his father's return when it was discovered, James himself went to the French coast, and three hundred transport ships sailed from Dunkirk for Calais. The failure of the plot and the presence of the Navy prevented any planned invasion. James would not get Louis's backing again and the scare boosted loyalty to William.

In the Commons it led to an Association to defend the person of the 'rightful & lawful' King and if necessary to avenge his death. It was then promoted at assizes and quarter sessions by MPs and others in a display of conspicuous loyalty. The leaders were quick to see that it provided an opportunity to expose men whose commitment to the Revolution was equivocal, since the phrase 'rightful and lawful' was unacceptable to those

---

[296] Parliamentary Archives HL/PO/10/1/485/1066d History of Parliament Trust, London, unpublished article on Ralph Montagu, duke of Montagu, for House of Lords 1660-1832 section by Robin Eagles

who, while agreeing that William was King *de facto*, still believed that the 'rightful & lawful' King was in exile. On April 21 1696 the Act for the Security of the Crown made subscription to the Association obligatory for all office-holders. Nine days later, the Privy Council required every *custos rotulorum*[297] to forward the names of JPs who refused. Lords-lieutenant had given similar instructions with regard to defaulting deputy-lieutenants & militia officers. A nationwide regulation of local officials was thus underway, and as returns came in between July 1696 and March 1697 the Council issued orders to Lord Chancellor Somers to put 156 specified gentlemen out of 33 county commissions of the peace.

This was the first centrally controlled revision of the peace on a large scale since the Revolution. However, it was a cumbersome administrative operation: inconsistent, haphazard and, above all, slow. There were several reasons for this. The most obvious is that the remodelling was conducted by the unwieldy Privy Council, not by Somers or the Secretaries of State. The King was doubtless reluctant to give the Whig politicians a free hand in a purge of their political opponents. He evidently preferred to invoke the traditional authority of the Council where decisions were recorded; but it proved incapable of speedy action. It is not clear whether it even appointed a committee to deal with the returns. When, in November, some tardy magnates had to be reminded that the Council was expecting lists of non-subscribers, the letters were signed by a small group of nine Councillors (including Ralph). The earl of Pembroke, one of the nine, signed letters to defaulting lords-lieutenant and *custodes* which were identical to those he had himself received in respect of his own neglected duties in Cardiganshire & Breconshire. Not a sign of efficiency.[298]

There is evidence from this period that Ralph continued to exercise his political influence when opportunity offered. On December 30 1696 there was to be a by-election caused by the death of one of the two MPs for Buckinghamshire. The other seat had been held by Wharton for seventeen years until the Tory Lord Newhaven (a cousin of Ralph's wife) took it in February. Two letters of December 6 state that Ralph backing was being sought by the candidates, that he opposed Wharton's interest and that it was rumoured he might back John Hampden, who he had supported previously. (Hampden had been arrested with Russell and Sidney over the Rye House Plot in 1683 but was spared execution. He had held the seat from 1679 – 1681 when he swapped with his father Richard for one of the two family seats at Wendover. Father and son held the latter together from 1689 – 1690). But a fortnight before the election Hampden killed himself. Sir John Verney had already written to Ralph (amongst others) seeking

---

[297] The keeper of the rolls, the highest civil officer in a county
[298] L.K.J. Glassey, *Politics & the appointment of Justices of the Peace, 1675-1720* (Oxford 1979) p.120

support: *'knowing your honour hath a great interest as well as Estate in that county emboldens me (tho unknown to your lordship) to desire the honour of your countenance in that affair. And this being a Post night it maybe your honour may command your servants both in the Chilterns and in the Vale to act as your Lordship thinks fitting. I was in hopes my Lady Stamp had made my name and thoughts known to your honour, but as soon as I can stir out I'll attend your Lordship, begging your Lordship's interest for me'.*[299] The letter only just stops short of asking Ralph to order those voters over whom he could exercise influence to Vote Verney. More remarkable is the fact that Verney was a Tory but nonetheless hoped that in the absence of anyone else Ralph might be inclined to support him rather than Wharton's candidate. He did not get elected.

Good news came late next year – the French suddenly agreed to make peace, recognise William as King of England, and restore Luxembourg with its fortifications intact. The Treaty of Rijswijk signed in September 1697 was a substantial victory for the allies – the French disgorged much of what they had captured, a humiliation for Louis. The wars had financially exhausted all the protagonists but William had been able to make political capital out of the fact that he had been rebuilding his palaces at het Loo and Kensington, and extending Hampton Court, whilst Louis had been forced to stop work on Versailles. On Tuesday November 16 there was a great procession of the nobility in their coaches, followed by the King, through the City to Whitehall. And in the month before the procession: *'Thurs October 7 ... 'tis generally discoursed that the duke of Devon and earl of Montague will goe ambassadors extraordinary to that court'* (France).[300] Perhaps the dispute over the fire at Montagu House hadn't too badly affected their relationship.

In April it had been rumoured that Ralph had been appointed to replace the earl of Monmouth as Lord Lieutenant of Northamptonshire (Monmouth had been implicated in Fenwick's conspiracy).[301] The post only ever went to the great magnates of the localities, and enabled them to exercise patronage as heads of the county militias. It also provides an important link between central and local government, particularly through the lord lieutenants recommendations of who might serve as JPs. They in their turn exercised much of the hard work of county government, providing the links between county, boroughs and parishes. Being a JP added status to one's reputation amongst the gentry, such that being removed might well be a matter of distress or even dishonour. In 1689 William had replaced 32 of the 42 lord lieutenants. The post proved to be yet another which eluded Ralph.

[299] Verney Mss mic M636/49 6 & 12 Dec 1696
[300] Luttrell, p.289
[301] Luttrell vol 2, p.205

The Whigs ability to supply the King with money through the Bank of England kept them in the ascendant. Sunderland, though still much disliked for his abilities (and for being even more untrustworthy than most politicians – a man of neither party or principle), had been made Lord Chamberlain in the spring of 1697, and Somers made Lord Chief Justice. Admiral Russell was created Earl of Orford, and Charles Montagu went to the Treasury. If one looks up the Montagu name in any records of the 1690s it is Charles who will have the most entries, achieving the political success Ralph dreamed of. Only Shrewsbury seemed able to keep these disparate characters working together, and he constantly asked to resign his Secretaryship due to ill health. Sunderland used his influence with the King to get his own people into vacant government offices but resented the fact that the rest of the ministry didn't show proper gratitude to him for all he did. Many in the Commons still saw him as James II's servant, not William's, and the Whig members of the House wouldn't defend him when he was attacked by the opposition. In a fit of pique (and goaded by his wife) he resigned at the end of the year.

William was not pleased with the display of party politics and individual ambition, in the House and by his ministers. He now consulted them infrequently and took advice which he liked, from whatever source, and then dictated it to the Cabinet. Methuen wrote to Lord Galway in April 1698: *'I confess it is not very proper to speak of the Ministers here since there are not properly any that at present ought to be so called. But when I use the word I mean...*[Somers, Montagu, Orford and Wharton]*...who are the only persons that are at present in the management of Affairs, if it may be said that anything is managed'.*[302] William was doubtless happy to slip away to the continent on August 1 to attempt the easier task of concluding a treaty with France partitioning Spanish possessions when Carlos II died (something that monarch resolutely refused to do, despite being weak all his life). By the close of 1698 the Whig ministry had begun to crumble away. Shrewsbury and Somers were unwell, Orford weary, and Charles Montagu, seeing the way that the wind was blowing, had made his brother auditor to the Exchequer to keep the place warm for him if he was dismissed as Chancellor (as happened next year). The grandees' continuing suspicion of Sunderland, who might have held together the administration, kept him from office and ultimately the ministry became filled with men of various alliances and little talent.

In the summer of 1699 William indicated that he wanted (as ever) a moderate ministry that was prepared to use Sunderland's abilities. Shrewsbury visited the latter to see what might be done and a meeting of the chief Whig politicians was called for August 11 at Boughton. The location showed that Ralph clearly still had a part to play as a Whig

---

[302] S.B. Baxter *William III* p.362

grandee, and his house was conveniently near Althorp and Deene. (Shrewsbury's relations the Brudenells lived at Deene. He had been invited to visit in August the previous year when Charles Montagu wrote that *'Lord Montagu has a design of inviting your Grace to go from thence (*Newmarket*) to Boughton. I have promised to be of the party, in hopes, since you are so idle, you will go on a ramble, to see his water-works'.*[303] Shrewsbury wrote to Orford and Wharton asking to meet them at Boughton on the 9th alone *'so that we private people might spend two or three days well enough before the great scene opens'*, but they refused, as did Somers. Henry Guy, who often acted as Sunderland's right-hand man, was at Althorp and hoped to bring Robert Harley, a rising politician, and his cousin Foley into the discussion (it seems from a letter from Guy to Harley, dated August 19, that Harley may have been at the meeting).[304] In the end only Godolphin, Marlborough, Charles Montagu and Harley's friend Henry Boyle joined Shrewsbury at Boughton. Sunderland had agreed that the latter could negotiate on his behalf but, although the meeting was extended two days, without the other leaders it could be no more than an enjoyable social occasion. It broke up on 18 August, and Charles Montagu and Shrewsbury went off to talk with Wharton about a new ministry. They met with no positive response, and on arriving in London on the 23rd they found Somers had rushed off to Tunbridge Wells. When Vernon talked to Shrewsbury he was amazed to discover that *'These meetings that were thought to be big with intrigue, have produced nothing'*. Shrewsbury and Ralph cornered Lord Chancellor Somers at the Wells and he now seemed amenable, whilst Wharton was indifferent at worst, so it seemed Shrewsbury's engaging personality and prestige might pull a government together but on September 8 he fell ill. The proposed ministry fell with him.[305] Ralph alluded to these negotiations when he wrote to Christopher Hatton on September 4: *'I am to beg your lordship pardon for goeing out of the countrye without waiting of you, & returning my thanks for the honour you did me. But some businesse calls me to London sooner than I intended; this I hope will make my excuse & not be thought want of respect'.*[306] (Hatton lived at Holdenby, not far from Boughton). There seems to have been another attempt at holding a meeting at Boughton to form a ministry the following year, when Somers wrote to Shrewsbury on July 25 1700 that, having expressed uncertainty about going there, Charles Montagu had told him *'that my lord Montagu would not only be disobliged, but would downright quarrel with him, should I fail to be at the meeting...it is with the utmost reluctance that I think of going*

[303] Shrewsbury Correspondence pt.3, chap.7, p.551
[304] Portland Mss III, 607
[305] J.P. Kenyon *Sunderland* p.312
[306] BL Add Mss 29549 f.93

into a throng'..[307] Another writer recorded in August that *'my Lord Montagu's is still the seat of politics and this night a consult is to be held there, which is to model a new settlement to break country politics and to do other wonders.'* [308]

Hatred of the King's influential foreign friends and of the wealth and titles given to them by a tax-burdened people was at its height. Danby, now completely out of office, vented his spite by spreading rumours that William had more than a business relationship with Arnout Keppel, a handsome Dutchman nineteen years his junior. Like Robert Kerr, James I's favourite, Arnout had come to the King's notice by displaying great courage when he broke his leg (no doubt hunting – William spent a good part of the day in that pursuit and then worked late into the night). Both William and Keppel had a mistress (though William had parted from Betty Villiers after Queen Mary's death), and that Keppel also spent a lot of time with other women, but that wasn't allowed to get in the way of a good rumour.[309] Robert Harley (later earl of Oxford), one of the most able of the younger politicians, was able to lead a trenchant opposition in Parliament which insisted in getting back the forfeited Irish lands of Jacobites which King William had given his personal supporters (most of them foreign, but also including his mistress) before they would vote through supply. The King was furious at what he saw both as ingratitude for ridding the country of James, and as a personal attack, and considered proroguing Parliament and refusing royal assent, as his uncles would have done but wiser councils prevailed and he gave way. The Commons, triumphant, could not prevent itself from adding further insult to injury by proposing an address for removing "foreigners" from all the King's counsels. William's sensible desires to reform the calendar, and have an Act of Union between England and Scotland, were ignored in all the party point scoring.

1700 witnessed two deaths that would have a significant effect on English history. On 28 July Princess Anne's son William died at the age of eleven. Of Anne's eighteen pregnancies, only four live babies had been delivered, and only William had lived beyond his second year. King William wanted to ensure a Protestant succession, and so rule out any possibility of James II or his son coming back to England, indebted to Louis XIV. He had discussed with Sophia of Hanover, granddaughter of James I, the prospect that she should inherit and that after her death the crown should pass to her son George. (There had apparently been some discussion about it going to her daughter Sophia Charlotte and so through

---

[307] Shrewsbury correspondence, pt.3, chap .7

[308] BL Add Mss 72498 f.20

[309] Keppel nearly caused a scandal by trying to seduce the Elector of Bavaria's mistress. Danby had once bribed a youth to testify that Buckingham had tried to seduce him, another illustration of how intimations of homosexuality were used politically.

her marriage to the Hohenzollen family in the person of Frederick of Brandenburg (William's nephew), but William had fought alongside Sophia's husband and her son). Once she had agreed to put aside her Jacobite sympathies they came to an agreement.

An even more significant death, in political terms, was that of Carlos II of Spain. In the last few days of his life he had made a will in favour of a grandson of Louis XIV. That king hoped to take the whole of the Spanish inheritance without a war, not least since the allies were unsure what outcome they wanted, and most people (and their politicians) did not want the return of the higher taxes that would be needed to fund it. In England the Commons wouldn't fund a war until Louis had made himself the aggressor and by that time the Netherlands would have been overrun. Fortunately the French made sufficient provocative acts that the allies began to regroup and prepare. In September 1701 James II died and Louis recognised his son as King of England, thus persuading the English to back William, not least by electing a Whig majority to the Commons at the end of the year. But a few months later, on February 21 whilst William was trying out a new horse in Richmond Park, his mount stumbled and fell. The King's collar-bone was broken. A fortnight later he became cold and feverish, and on March 8 1702 he died at the age of 51. The horse he had been riding was White Sorrell, one of the possessions of Sir John Fenwick confiscated by the Crown when he had been executed for plotting William's assassination. Anne became Queen, which would be significant for the marriage of one of Ralph's two surviving sons and the furtherance of his ultimate ambition: a dukedom.

Montagu House from street

Montagu House porter

Copyright of the subject

Montagu House courtyard screen

Montagu House

Montagu House courtyard

Montagu House Hall

Plate 14.

THE HALL and STAIR CASE.
BRITISH MUSEUM.
London Pub. 1 April 1808, at R. Ackermann's Repository of Arts 101 Strand.

Montagu House staircase from landing

STAIRCASE OF THE OLD BRITISH MUSEUM, MONTAGUE HOUSE

Montagu House staircase with giraffes

Copyright of the subject

Montagu House staircase

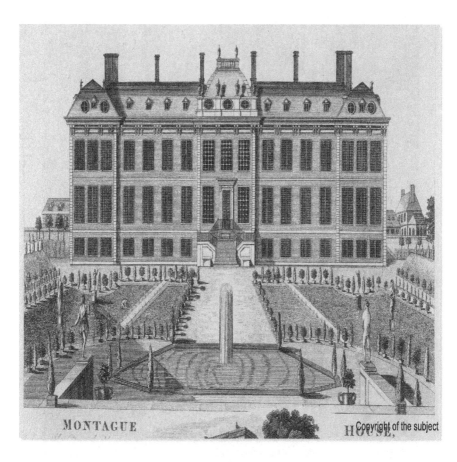

MONTAGUE HOUSE,

Montagu House garden

Gerrit Jensen Side Table and Pier Glass with RM monogram

Mortlake Tapestry, Elements Set - Fire Woven 1699

One of Monnoyer's many flower paintings for Montagu House

Mortlake Sumpter Cloth

I doe confesse To owe to
mr. cheron one hundred
& fftteene pounds which I promis
To pay him on the first of
november next augst The
26 1707 Montagu

Ap: 16 = 1712

3

Received of his Grace the Duke of Montagu as
Exect.r to the Late Duke his father by the hands
of mr mare Antonie one hundred & fifteen pounds
in full of this Note all acc.ts By me L. Cheron

David Sowerscad
Duc Mountague } 14 Augt 1711
This note or paper conteining was produced &
shewed to and Louis Cheron at the time of his
Examinaton

N° 42)

Promisory Note from Ralph Montagu to Louis Cheron

Marot panels for Montagu House boudoir

Chapter 8
Consolidation 1701 - 1703

Queen Anne's natural inclination, not least due to her religious outlook, favoured the Tories, who had long supported her in her disagreements with the Crown in the previous reign. But this was affected by her closeness to the Marlboroughs – John Churchill's career could only be furthered through the war that the Tories opposed. For some time therefore Godolphin as Treasurer and Harley as Speaker of the Commons were able to steer a middle way. There is no evidence that Ralph, now in his sixties, played any large political role although he doubtless discussed matters when he was with his Whig friends and colleagues. The frequency with which he had attended the Lords in the 1690s (such that on July 22 1697 he was one of only fifteen present in the House, and on September 28 1699 one of only eleven when Parliament was prorogued) fell away dramatically. Other than in May and June 1701 (when he was present on eighteen days), and December 1702 to February 1703 (twenty-five days) he was there on only a dozen or so days in eight years between Anne's accession and his death. We know that he was at Boughton shortly before the 1701 session from a letter he sent to Dr. Sloane on April 21: *Sir I am to acknowledge three of yours & to return you many thanks for the trouble you have given your self... Master is quite rid of his cold I hope. Though we have had, & shall have, the coldest weather was ever knowne, he neither takes any sort of milk in the morning nor syrop to sleepe at night. I am willing to let nature work. As for myself, I am much at the same rate, but quieter a little than your great men in town. I hope to be with you in ten or twelf days, & assure you of my being...* ("Master" is Ralph's son John).[310]

No longer did Ralph vote for Acts such as the one for repair of Bridlington's pier (April 12 1697) or sit on committees to consider bills like that for making Billingsgate a free market for the sale of fish (April 21 1699). Nonetheless just as Ralph was constantly asked for his help and support for all manner of people in a whole variety of ways, he in turn petitioned others. The papers of Robert Harley for example contain a letter from Ralph of March 8 1697 stating that *'as soon as I am well enough to stir abroad I will wait upon you and concur with you in everything you please to bring our Governors of the New River to reason'* [311] and five years later he asks Harley for assistance with the bill pending in the Commons *'called Hind's Bill about the building of Albermarle ground'* [312] (Harley was Speaker of the Commons and would later be made Lord

---

[310] BL Sloane Mss 4036 f.62
[311] HMC Portland vol. 3, p 581
[312] Ibid. vol. 4, p 38

Treasurer)[313]. Ralph did manage to get to the House when old political colleagues needed support, as Lords Somers and Orford did in June 1701 when they faced impeachment by the Commons. His vote helped ensure that they were acquitted.[314] There is an interesting record of what happened on the two days he attended the House of Lords in December 1702 given by Bishop Nicholson of Carlisle. On December 9 *'After a few private Bills, that against Occasional Conformity was read the 3rd time & (with its Amendments) sent back to the Commons. Immediately a debate began (much heated, the Earl of Sunderland's affirming that the Commons were just now considering how to tack this to a Money-Bill) which brought on a Division of the House, 51 against 47 & ended in the following Order:* That the annexing of any Clause or Clauses to a Bill of Aid or Supply, the matter of which is foreign to and different from the matter of the said Bill of Aid or Supply, is Unparliamentary and tends to the Destruction of the Constitution of the Government. *All Lords that please had leave given to subscribe this Order; which is to be added to the Roll of Standing Orders. In the Debate... The Lord Treasurer [Godolphin], Duke of Leeds, Earls of Nottingham, Rochester & Marlborough, argued that (tho' the thing was just in itself) it was now* unseasonable. *The Duke of Leeds was called upon by the Earl of Montague to explain himself; but the House thought there was no Occasion. However, some little Repartees 'twixt the Duke & Lord Halifax, in defence of his Chief".*

It seems that Ralph was known as Halifax's "chief" and a footnote by the editors of Nicolson's diary suggests that Ralph acted as his political mentor. On the following day: 'Thursday. *Upon complaint made to the House, by the Earl of Montague, that a quarrel had happened betwixt the Lords Osburn & Hallifax on occasion of Yesterday's Debate, and that Lord Hallifax was confined by the Queen, they were both sent for. The latter came presently in; and it was long debated – whether he might not be committed to Custody of (or attended by) the Black-Rod, for prevention of Evil, till the Lord Osburn could be likewise siezed. Whilst this was argueing, the Lord Osburn came in, and protested he knew of no Quarrel (but in Relation to a Suit at Law) that was between them. He confessed he had written a Letter last night, on this last mentioned Subject, to the Lord Hallifax but never intended it, as it appeared to be understood, for a Challenge. However, the Commands of the House were given that they should both declare (upon their word and Honour) that no future Quarrel*

---

[313] The New River Company had been established to bring fresh water into London. Albemarle Ground was the site of Albemarle House, where Ralph's wife had once lived. Hind began organising its development for building houses. Two of the main speculators were Henry Jermyn, Lord Dover and Sir Thomas Bond, after whom principal streets were named.

[314] PA (HLRO) mss mins 17 & 23 June 1701

should be between 'em on occasion of any thing that was past'. [315] Lord Osborne was Danby's son, and in the Commons. It is interesting evidence of the continued bad blood between Danby and the Montagus. In the Lords on the 10th Danby (now duke of Leeds) told Halifax publicly *'that his family was raised by rebellion, but his own suffered by it.'* [316] (Three years later: *1705, 7th Dec Friday Halifax challenged to duel by Carmarthen, Leed's son, in Hyde Park'*).

Ralph had many other things to occupy his time besides politics of course. He was still Master of the Great Wardrobe, the post he had purchased in August 1671. The Wardrobe supplied the materials for royal weddings, funerals and coronations, Garter robes, heralds' tabards, presents for foreign ambassadors and princes, furniture for royal palaces, ambassadors' residences abroad, royal carriages, yachts and barges, and robes for all royal servants. In 1674 it was decided that Ralph should receive a salary of £2,000 pa rather than a percentage of expenditure, plus a payment for his own livery of £106. In fact he still continued to receive a percentage on some goods, worth at least a further £300 pa. As might be imagined from the range of items that the Wardrobe was expected to supply it had many staff, from the deputy on £200 pa to a housemaid on £20. In addition there were some sixty tradesmen posts, all in the gift of the Master. Although only a few received a salary there was clearly kudos to be had in being a supplier to the royal household (an anticipation of the later royal warrants, still issued, that allow suppliers to advertise the fact that they are "By Royal Appointment"). An investigation into the workings of the Wardrobe in 1728 found that there was considerable room for creative accounting. At no point in the system, between the lord chamberlain's warrant to supply goods and the Master's declaration of accounts, was there any outside check or control. The estimated cost of the supply sent to the Treasury was not checked for accuracy before being counter-signed. Indeed, more often they were not counter-signed at all and the Wardrobe didn't wait for them before ordering the supply – in 1728/9 only 10% of almost £10,000 spent had been authorised. Furthermore what was ordered was not through written contract. Often there was not even a verbal contract, just an instruction to purchase at the cheapest possible price. As a result it was usually charged between 33% and 50% more than the market rate. There wasn't even a check on the quality of work done in the palaces, or the quality and quantity of materials delivered. The bills were simply accepted as accurate, entered into the accounts, and accepted by the auditors (who didn't require copies of the bills).[317] Despite this

[315]. C. Jones & G. Holmes ed., *The London Diaries of William Nicolson, Bishop of Carlisle, 1702-1718* (Oxford 1985)
[316] HMC 12th Report, Appendix ix [Beaufort Mss], p.96: Lord Coventry to his wife
[317] J.M. Beattie *The English Court in the Reign of George I* (Cambridge 1967)

Ralph did need occasionally to intervene. In June 1702 he wrote to Sir Charles Hedges, Secretary of State: '*Sr The same accounts of the great Wardrobe that I formerly troubled you about are as yet unsigned. I beg the favour of you at the first oportunitye to lay them before her Maiestye for her signatur. Though it be only a matter of forme I cannot without that be don proceede either with the auditors or commissionaires of accounts who call upon me very earnestlye I am Sr your most obedient humble servant Montagu*'. [318]

Did supplies intended for the royal palaces sometimes end up at Boughton, Ditton and Montagu House? Perhaps grateful craftsmen gave Ralph a preferential price. (Lionel Cranfield, James I's Master of the Wardrobe, got special deals from Flemish tapestry weavers by placing his orders at the same time as royal ones). With his long experience of the finest in French taste, which was fashionable throughout Europe, Ralph was well placed to secure the services of French craftsmen for both his and royal properties. He seems to have had close involvement with those he employed, often through his physician, Pierre Silvestre. A Huguenot, Silvestre had become a physician to the King William after arriving in Amsterdam. Offered a post with the army in Flanders, he had preferred to enter Ralph's household and at Boughton he was appointed Inspector of Architecture and Gardens. Ralph is likely to have seen little of the daily work of the Wardrobe. His deputy may well have had a little more direction, but certainly had outside interests too. From 1680 the post was filled by Robin Nott, who was removed when Ralph was deprived of the Mastership by James II. Both were reinstated in 1689. In c1706 Thomas Dummer became deputy and held the post for the next forty-four years. He also seems to have become Yeoman Tailor, yielding about £90 a year (as had Nott). (He succeeded Elias de Ritt who kept accounts for Ralph's household besides being a merchant supplying damasks to Whitehall). Ralph spent time supervising the work on his houses, and the accounts show that he paid for further training for his craftsmen.

Thomas Dummer's brother Edmund also held a Wardrobe post for some time. The fact that both were lawyers is proof that Thomas's post as Yeoman Tailor was purely a sinecure, a way to reward someone who was useful to Ralph. The family came from South Stoneham, near Southampton. They were related through their great-grandfather to the naval Dummers of North Stoneham which produced a pair of identically named brothers at the same period with whom they are often confused. The second Edmund was a civil engineer, appointed as surveyor to the Navy Board in 1689. As such he oversaw the establishment of the dockyard at Plymouth and extensive works at Portsmouth and Dover, representing the largest civil engineering project in England in the

---

[318] BL Add Mss 28927 f.43

seventeenth century. At Portsmouth he designed the first docks to be built of stone with stepped sides, which added to their strength and made easier the task of securing ships occupying them. He arranged for improvements at the Sowley ironworks, near Beaulieu, which were leased from Ralph to Roger Gringoe. The works had been set up by the Henry, earl of Southampton, in the 1590s and continued to operate for more than two centuries. Being on the west Solent its situation allowed heavy-weight production to be carried by water to the dockyards and other markets. The blast furnace at Sowley had long worked in association with the forge at Titchfield (Gringoe leased both sites), but the latter was not in Ralph's hands (having been inherited by his sister-in-law) so he financed the building of a forge at a cost of some £2,000. The Navy's defeat off Beachy Head in 1690 had led to orders for the construction of twenty-seven ships, financed by a tax on beer and spirits. The royal dockyards couldn't cope with such a number so contracts were given to civilian builders to construct some of them to Navy Board design. Fourteen ships were built in Southampton and on the river Hamble, and in 1696 Richard Herring, who had been foreman for some of the contracts, obtained one on his own account. He needed a site and entered into negotiations with Ralph for the lease of one on the Beaulieu river. Ralph also supplied the oak, elm and beech needed for construction from his lands in the New Forest. A year later Richard died and his brother took over, but there were serious cash-flow problems. Ralph was owed for the timber and arrears of rent, and so took possession of the site and uncompleted vessel. Thomas Dummer acted as Ralph's solicitor and came to an agreement with the Navy Board reported by the latter on March 3 1698 whereby *'his Lo(rdshi)pp would not interrupt the dispatch of said Shipp nor the launching and receiving her for the King but hopes his Lo.pp having an assignment of Herring's bills We will order the said Bills to be alter'd into his Lo.pp name and paid him when they come in due course'.* [319] Unfortunately the *"Salisbury"* when eventually launched didn't cover herself with glory. Just a few years later, in 1703, she was captured by the French. She wasn't renamed, which was as well since she was later recaptured by Admiral Byng.

Edmund Dummer (the lawyer) became Ralph's steward at Beaulieu in 1700 and Gringoe's lease was taken up in June by Henry Corbett, who had contracted to supply iron to Portsmouth dockyard the month before. A decade earlier Corbett had a business smelting and making copper and iron plates at Temple Mills on the river Lea, east of London. Edmund Dummer (the surveyor) had persuaded him to come down to Portsmouth. He also took Palace Farm at Beaulieu where, on the site of the old abbey church, he put up blacksmith's, carpenter's and plumber's shops, and a foundry. Despite making a revolutionary two-sectioned gate designed by Dummer

---

[319] Nat.Maritime Museum, Sergison papers 39

for dry docks he too fell into financial difficulties and next year owed Ralph and Dummer over £4,000. (The delay in getting settlement from the government was compounded by the payment, when it came, being in the form of undated Navy bills with only a nominal interest rate. The only way to cash them was to sell to London brokers at a discount). Dummer took over the business and paid Corbett to manage it. It produced some 300 tons of iron a year for Portsmouth dockyard. [320] One of the Dummer family was recommended by Ralph to Mr Cardenall, Marlborough's secretary: '*I desire Mr Cornelius Dummer may be recommended from me to be surgeon to one of the new raised regiments. I know him to be a verye goode surgeon & has had greate experience in the Hospitalls abroade. I am Sr, your most humble servant, Montagu*' Montagu House March 21 1704. [321] Although income from agriculture was the central component of a peer's wealth many shared Ralph's willingness to exploit whatever mineral and industrial possibilities their lands offered. Ralph's brother-in-law Newcastle had iron works in Sherwood Forest for example, whilst the duke of Bedford's father had headed a consortium formed to drain the Fens for agriculture.

Ralph had been able to obtain tapestries from his own works at Mortlake. Founded in 1619 so that tapestry did not have to be imported, it was taken over by the crown in 1637. Sir Gilbert Pickering, Cromwell's Lord Chamberlain was later put in charge of them. He married Sir Sydney Montagu's daughter, cousin to Ralph's father. Another connection came in the form of Sir Sackville Crow who married into the Manners family, as did Ralph's aunt, thus becoming countess of Rutland. Crow wrote to her concerning a set of tapestries that she was having woven in May 1670 and mentions that she will have a better account of them from her niece Lady Betty Harvey, since the manufactory was now in her hands. Through her agent Harry Baker Betty had managed to sell three sets of tapestry to Charles II between 1669 and 1673, the only Mortlakes he is known to have purchased during his long reign. Ralph had three identical sets to these: The Acts of the Apostles, after the Raphael cartoons purchased by Charles I (and now in the Victoria & Albert Museum (V&A), shown together with a fine example of a Montagu owned Mortlake tapestry), the Triumph of Caesar, after the Mantegna paintings Charles had similarly purchased (now at Hampton Court), and the Naked Boys. In 1674 Ralph took possession of the houses and materials at Mortlake from the earl of Sunderland and Lord Brouncker [322] and was thus in nominal charge of the only two tapestry manufactories in England, since the Wardrobe also employed tapestry

---

[320] A. J. Holland *Buckler's Hard* (Emsworth 1993)
[321] BL Add. Mss. 61298 f.118 Marlborough Mss
[322] W.G. Thompson, *A History of Tapestry: from the earliest times to the present day* (London 1930) pp.300/1

makers to provide for the palaces. It would seem that those who could afford tapestry (a luxury good far more expensive than paintings by even the most esteemed artist because of the time and labour they took to produce) preferred to source them from abroad and so the Mortlake works were not successful. In April 1692 a joint-stock company was formed by royal charter, presumably in the hope of saving the works, and Ralph made the first Governor. Although the charter forbade foreign imports the move seems to have been a failure. In 1701 the Surveyor General reported that he had gone to Mortlake to give a true state of the works. He found the buildings were very old and ruinous, consisting of two brick buildings, one fronting the track leading from Barnes to Mortlake, and the other extending towards the Thames. There were two workhouses, one with twelve looms, the other with four, over which were garrets and an old chapel. The ground floors provided small apartments for labourers and a tenement for the master workman which had been erected before the manufactory was built by King Charles I. There were several cartoons, but many old and unfit for use. Two years later Lady Harvey's son Daniel (who became the second husband of Ralph's daughter Anne) successfully petitioned the Queen for closure.

The extensive Montagu archives provide indications of Ralph's expenditure at this time. In 1707 £5,790 was paid out by the steward of Montagu House in the half year from March to Michaelmas. Of this £2,881 was for the costs of running the house, £479 on servants' wages, £390 given to Ralph (one assumes as his pocket-money), £510 for Ralph's son and heir Lord Monthermer, and £1,127 'on account of Work, enterest and annuity'. The larger items among the running costs include:

£107	Richard Bull: coffee, tea etc
£66 7s	Margeritte Sepoline: wax candles
£191	John Keeble: coles
£30 1s	William Child: cheese & bacon
£195	Robert Thacker: butcher's bill
£44 10s	Mrs Anne Walker: butter & eggs
£46	John Emery ye Confectioner
£77 11s	John Wheeler ye Brewer
£19	Davenant Sherborne, Oyleman
£66 13s	Ben Boultby, Sopemaker

£661 was spent on wine (including Moselle and Cannary), £145 17s 2d on fruit, £51 3s 8d on seven weeks' bills for the kitchen, £96 12s 8d for the Queen's tax for the previous year and £145 9s for disbursements at Ditton. Among the more unusual items are the £24 paid for a gold watch by

Thomas Tompion, £19 10d for a horse, £11 3s for books, £3 6s 6d for two guinea hens and the enormous sum of £337 2s 5d to Mrs Jane Guinicourt on account for tailoring.

The strangest entry is the £1 7s paid for asses' milk for Lord Hinchingbrook. Elizabeth, countess of Sandwich (daughter of the famous earl of Rochester) and a relation of Ralph's, was taken in by him when she parted with her husband, and Hinchingbrook was her son. She was as intelligent and high-spirited as her father had been, and far too much for her husband who was described by Jonathan Swift 'As much a puppy as ever I saw; very ugly and a fop'.[323] Nonetheless when she fell seriously ill in Paris in the summer of 1699 her husband had hurried to her sick-bed, and Matthew Prior wrote to Lord Jersey that he had had to hurry away again in fear of being arrested for unpaid debts. Jersey, in replying that he hoped she had recovered, said 'At Paris I did not think I was so much her humble servant as I find I really am, but one never knows a happiness till one misses it'.[324] She occupied apartments in the north-west pavilion at Boughton that Ralph's wife would probably have had if she had been sane. In 1705/6 Ralph ordered a tapestry bed for her, to Marot's design, and a silver toilet service from George Lewis. The 1707/8 accounts record two tables and a blanket being sent to her.[325] Whilst asses' milk was famously bathed in by Cleopatra and the Empress Poppaea to improve the whiteness of their skin it was more usually given to infants in place of breast milk. However the boy was 15 years old in 1707 - perhaps he was sickly, since it was also thought to be beneficial for invalids, especially consumptives.

Amongst the monies paid out on 'Work, Interest or Annuitys' was £20 to Monsieur Chevalier for perriwigs, £40 for plate, £40 to the apothecary, £70 for a mill to be made at Boughton, £35 to Mr David Hawkins for taking on Will Henson as an apprentice and £250 to glaziers, paviours, bricklayers, joiners and house painters. (The Executors' accounts show that Will Henson wasn't the only craftsman Ralph helped: in 1708 Thomas Drew (son of the stonemason at Boughton) was apprenticed to Thomas Hues, a bricklayer, and given some tools. He was taught drawing by Cornelius Gole (cabinetmaker) and geometry by the famous mathematician Abraham de Moivre). The final entries are for disbursements without receipts: £12 for a wheelbarrow for the stables; £1 5s for four umbrellas, £1 6s for a pound of Bokee tea and 1s 6d for dice, all sent to Boughton and 2s 6d for a chair to carry Natt Govsey to the nurse when sick. Natt apparently continued to be ill: the March – September

[323] The works of Jonathan Swift Dean of St Patrick's Dublin : containing additional letters, tracts and poems not hitherto published (London 1883) vol.xii, p.229
[324] Hist.Mss.Bath vol.3, pp.351,354
[325] Whilst the Countess's husband was merely a Tory, she was a keen Jacobite and corresponded with James III. She died in Paris (where she had lived for 27 years) at the age of 84 and was buried at St. Germain, as James II had been.

1708 accounts show a payment of £3 to Margeritt Litchfield for nursing him, and there are other entries in the accounts for nursing other servants. At Christmas they each received 6d for a '*minch pye*' whilst New Year gifts totalling £9 were given to tradesmen's servants.

The 1706 accounts show expenditure of £300 to Josiah Linnett, coachmaker, £13 9s to George Southwell for making of chocolate and vanillas, 6s 9d to a man for mustard, £1 3s for britches, shoes and stockings for the kitchen boy and 4s 6d for a bottle of liquor for a broken winded horse. Mrs Theodosia Barker seems to have been in charge of the seventeen maids, and was given £66 6s for their thirteen weeks' wages, whilst John Kerk was in charge of fourteen liverymen and had £61 15s for the same. The Montagu's livery colours were green lined with red, and yellow buttons.[326]

Unfortunately the accounts give little indication of what Ralph read – books may well have been purchased by him directly. The 1706 accounts have entries for sending a *book of Gardining* to Mr Lamotte at Boughton, for a book of Miscelanys by the late Lord Halifax, two books about the Armys in Spagne, and a history of England in folio volumes. The accounts also show payments to charities: £32 pa to the hospital in Chepstow (in his will of 1614 Sir Walter Montagu of Pencoyde, Monmouthshire left 120 acres at Hanging Houghton, Northamptonshire to financially support this almshouse and garden for ten poor people), £12 to Lady Sidney's hospital, and £2 to the churchwardens for Dr. Hayley's Easter offering. (William Hayley, who had been chaplain to Sir William Trumbull on his embassies to Paris and Istanbul, clearly found it more congenial to minister to his London parishioners at St. Giles in the Fields, Ralph's parish church, than to attend to his duties as Dean of Chichester). How did Ralph, even with the income he had from his estates, his marriages, and the Mastership, manage to have built (or rebuilt) three houses and completely furnish one of them, whilst maintaining an extravagant lifestyle? Montagu House alone was costing him some £7,000 pa. shortly before he died. The bundles of creditors' bills still extant give part of the answer – his son wrote that he left debts of some £50,000. Perhaps when Ralph had told the tax collector in 1689 that he owed £20,000 he was telling the truth. One of the great benefits of being a member of the nobility was that one couldn't be arrested for debt. However the possession of a peerage implied a commitment to a suitable (often ruinous) standard of living, a commitment that Ralph certainly believed in. The earl of Bedford had initially turned down the offer of a dukedom in 1689 because his sons would then be lords and he didn't have a large enough income to support the honour.[327] An

---

[326] Bedford County Archive X800/1-5
[327] Morrice Entring book vol. v, p.84

estimate of the income from the Montagu estates made the year after his death was £14,650 gross but only £6,465 net.

The presence of the countess of Sandwich at Montagu House may, in some way, have compensated Ralph for the loss of a close female friend of long standing - the duchess of Mazarin. In 1692 the Duchess had moved to Kensington Square and later went to a smaller house in Paradise Row, Chelsea with Pompey her negro and Polly her parrot. (Was this the same parrot who was apparently called Pretty?). It is probable that by the time of her second move she had lost Maurice her buffoon, Chop her dog and Pussy her cat, since she was deep in debt, not least due to her love of cards and fine food. When she died in 1699 at the age of 53 she owed Ralph £300 and St. Evremond 400 guineas. (The latter nonetheless described her in old age "as handsome as ever"). The Calender of State Papers records that: *'The Duchess of Mazarin died yesterday after a long lingering distemper, which ended in a lethargy without any manner of concern for what was past or what was to come, and has left the earls of Feversham and Montagu her executors. It was believed she had nothing to leave besides her monkies, parrots and Mustapha, a Mohamaton boy, but now it is reported she has bequeathed to somebody the title she had to 100 million crowns somewhere in France'*. The accounts show that Ralph also paid out £100 to ensure her body was sent safely back to France for burial, avoiding the threats of her creditors to seize it for ransom. (It is said that her unstable husband, rather than bury her, carried her coffin round with him on his travels and only later allowed it to be interred near her uncle the Cardinal). A letter from Ralph to the earl of Albermarle dated 28 June 1699 survives: *'Your Lordship, I am sure is so good natured as to pardon my giving you this trouble upon so sad & melancholye occasion as the Death of the Dutchesse of Mazarin; my Lord Feversham who by the marriage of his niece to her sonne the Duke de la Maillorye is allied to her & my self, whoe for soe manye yeares have had the honour of her acquaintance, thought we could doe noe lesse than take care of her familye & concerns till we receive his Maiestyes orders & directions who has so generoslye supported & protected her since his coming to the crown, & of which great favours & goodenesse to her she had so greate a sense & gratitude that about three weekes before her death she desired me to return her most humble thanks to him, assuring him she should dye wishing all the prosperity & happynesse might attende his glorious reigne, that if anye of her relations should pretend to importune him concerning a debt due to them of a debt of two hundred thousand crowns from the crown of England sent by the Cardinall Mazarin her unkle. She did owne & acknowledge that summe to have bin fullye repaide & satisfiyed by what she had received since her being in England from his maiestyes predecessors King Charles the second, the late King James & himself. The* house she hired in which his *Maiestyes greate bountye has given her for a terme of yeares & what may be due from my Lord Bradfords office may I hope pay her debts. If I may receive your advice what to doe in this matter I will persue it the best I can'.*[328] Her portrait (now at Boughton) was still hanging in Ralph's bedroom at Montagu House when he died.

Two letters written to Dr. Silvestre by St. Evremond [329] in around 1700 are full of longing for the pleasures of being entertained at Boughton:

Be satisfied, Sir, with your merit of Inspector, and don't encroach upon mine. I leave you your Architecture and Painting, but pray don't disturb me upon the Geography of Good Eating. However I must confess, that your Heath-Cocks, your Oysters, your Salmon, your Fruits, and the rest of that delicious abundance which you mention to me, give you some right to insult me, and leave me no relief, but in attributing all your advantages to the direction and magnificence of my Lord. Let but a thing please my Lord Montagu, and don't trouble you head any further: whatever expense is to be made; whatever care, whatever industry is to be employed to have it, you will be sure not to go without it. These are the words of the late Duchess Mazarin, which are as good as Oracles, and which were never more just than on this occasion. I never desired any thing so earnestly as to go to Boughton, to see my Lord, the good Company and Learning that is there in full lustre, when Monsieur le Vassor is there. I do not look upon my self as any thing, because I don't understand Greek' and

'If my new infirmities, or rather my old ones which are very much grown upon me, had no hindered me from going to Boughton, I should have been as happy as a man almost a hundred years of age can be. I lose a thousand pleasure which are all to my taste. That of seeing the fine House, the fine Water-works, the fine Ducks, would have pleased me extreamly, altho' I be but an indifferent Inspector. But you will easily guess the greatest of all, and that is being with my Lord Montagu, to enjoy his conversation twice a day, before and after the best cheer in the world. No person ever merited to be more magnificently receiv'd, and more handsomely entertain'd than my Lady Sandwich; no man was ever more proper to receive and entertain her well, than my Lord Montagu. I hope the Cascade, the Octogon, the Water-Sheafs, and the Water-Spouts, shall have made my Lady Sandwich forget France. And as my Lord is very happy in inspiring his taste and designs as to Buildings and Gardens, I

---

[328] BL Add Mss 63630 f.160

[329] Charles de St. Evremond (1610 – 1703) was a French essayist and critic who fled France for England in 1661. In other letters he praised the doctor's skill and ability to cure by his piercing look, *"le docteur aux regards salutaires"*. Pierre des Maizeaux, who edited St. Evremond's works for Sylvestre, recalled in later editions the doctor's delightful manner and conversation, his cheerfulness, good taste in music and painting, his deep knowledge of anatomy, medicine and chemistry. He died in Frith Street in 1718.

don't question but she will soon undertake some new work at Hinchinbrooke, which will not be behind those of Boughton, in any respect. It is impossible for any one to be more sensible than I am of the honour of her remembrance. There was nothing wanting to perfect any grief, for not having seen Boughton and the Master of the place, but my not having seen Hinchinbrooke, and its Mistress, who is the greatest ornament of all the places where she is.

If the poor Duchesse Mazarin had yet been alive, she would have had Peaches, of which she would not have fail'd to give me a share; she would have had Truffles, which I should have eat with her; not to mention the Carps of Newhall. I must make up the loss of so many advantages, by the Sundays and Wednesdays of Montagu House.[330]

There was an intellectual debate going on at this time about what should be placed on an English table, not least through defining what was particular about the English body and hence what food would keep it in good health. John Evelyn's "Acetaria, or a Discourse of Sallets" (1669) considered a diet which was mainly vegetarian to be best since gardening was a more suitable occupation for an Englishman than the pomp and grandeur of secular business. He condemned the French cuisine of made dishes and exotic sauces which the rich relished as expensive luxuries, eating not to live but to gratify their sensual appetites with Apician art. But Martin Lister's 1705 translation of a book on cookery supposedly by the first century Roman gourmet Apicius recommended this richer diet as most suited to an imperial race like the English. (It contains such delicacies as Isicia Omentata or beefburger, and Patina de pisciculis or fish soufflé). He particularly recommended the health benefits of the exotic spices and seasonings which had disappeared when the barbarians overthrew the empire. Garum, the fermented-fish sauce which was a staple of the Roman diet, Lister considered particularly beneficial to digestion. William King responded in 1708 with the mock-epic "Art of Cookery". King was a high-church Tory with an aversion to modernity, believing that the natural philosophy promoted by the (mainly Whig) Royal Society was throwing old certainties into doubt. He said that Lister's condiments were French rather than Roman, and pointed out that Lister had gone to France a decade before: '*Muse, sing the Man that did to Paris go, That he might taste their Soups, and Mushrooms know. How could Homer praise their Dancing Dogs, Their stinking Cheese, and Fricasy of Frogs!*' The Roman diet was not a suitable model for Englishmen, still less the French, but roast-beef was the proper food of the upper classes, and bread and cheese, or bacon and cabbage, for the middling sort. St. Evremond's letter suggests that Ralph was serving French fare to his guests. One wonders how much of Ralph's conversation was in French – whereas the English were famed for

---

[330] J. Hayward ed., *Letters of St. Evremond* (London, 1930)

plain speaking, the lexicon of wit was French. Badinage, persiflage and repartee had already crossed the Channel.

It is interesting to see from the letter that Ralph apparently held open house in London on Sundays and Wednesdays. St. Evremond's appreciation must have been heightened by Ralph's pension to him of £100 pa. A letter from him to Ralph written in the autumn of 1700 survives: *'No person can be more sensible than I am of the honour if being remembered by you. There is not one word in your letter that does not please me, except where you tell me that you eat truffles every day. I could not forbear crying, when I thought of eating them with the Duchess of Mazarin. I represented her to myself, with all her charms. I thought I was at Boughton: the Nile and the crocodiles appeared to me. I cannot continue this discourse without sorrow and therefore I must give it over. My Lady Sandwich has been at Windsor these nine or ten days. I sent her your letter. If she returns to London, as tis probable she will, I shall not fail my Lord to tell her of the music and truffles that wait for her. I do not doubt but that Dr Silvestre has caused these pieces of Corelli which he brought with him to be played over... I wish the Doctor would be so kind as to translate for me some chapter of the Author (Mr Asgill) who has taught us the way not to die. I have no hopes but in him. All the Doctors, Apothecaries and Surgeons are angry to distraction with him for disposing of death to their prejudice. I wish my Lord I could profit anything by his instructions, and live the Milleanos of the Spaniards, then I might continue so long to be your most humble and obedient servant'.*[331][332] A further letter from him to Silvestre gives a rare insight into the depth of Ralph's reading and conversation. *'Tis about ten years ago that my Lord Montagu explained to the Duchess of Mazarin and me, the meaning of the Depontani. I thought I had read all the good authors that speak of the customs of the Romans, but I had missed Festus, who teaches me what my Lord told us, but does not explain it so well. Depontani were old men good for nothing... who were thrown from the top of the bridge de ponte into the river. This discourse alarmed me'.*[333]

Another man of letters who was grateful to Ralph was William Congreve who, in March 1700, dedicated his new play "The Way of the World" to him:

My Lord

Whether the World will arraign me of Vanity, or not, that I have presum'd to Dedicate this Comedy to Your Lordship, I am yet in Doubt:

---

[331] *St. Evremond's works with the author's life* by Mr des Maizeaux 1714 vol. 2, p.421
[332] John Asgill published a work in June 1700 which suggested that, since death was the punishment of Adam's sin and Christ had redeemed that sin through his own death, those that believed in 'translation' would not die but go directly to heaven.
[333] Ibid p.447

Tho' it may be it is some degree of vanity even to doubt of it. One who has at any time had the Honor of your Lordship's Conversation, cannot be suppos'd to think very meanly of that which he wou'd prefer to Your Perusal: Yet it were to incur the Imputation of too much Sufficiency, to pretend to such a Merit as might abide the Test of Your Lordship's Censure.

Whatever value may be wanting to this Play while yet it is mine, will be sufficiently made up to it, when it is once become Your Lordship's; and it is my Security, that I cannot have overrated it more by my Dedication, than Your Lordship will dignify it by Your Patronage....

If I am not mistaken, Poetry is almost the only Art, which has not yet laid Claim to your Lordship's Patronage. Architecture, and Painting, to the Great Honour of our Country, have flourish'd under Your Influence and Protection. In the mean time, Poetry, the eldest Sister of All Arts, and Parent of most, seems to have resign'd her Birth-right, by having neglected to pay her Duty to Your Lordship; and by permitting others of a later Extraction, to prepossess that Place in Your Esteem, to which none can pretend a better Title. Poetry, in its Nature, is sacred to the Good and Great; the Relation between them is reciprocal, and they are ever propitious to it. It is the Privilege of Poetry to address to them, and it is their Prerogative alone to give it Protection.[334]

Theatre benefitted again in 1703: Ralph subscribed the large sum of one hundred guineas to the new Queen's Theatre in the Haymarket which Vanbrugh designed and operated in conjunction with Congreve and Thomas Betterton. (This wasn't a success – it was suggested that, as an architect, Vanbrugh was more concerned for the look of the place than the acoustics). From 1705 Vanbrugh was involved in the building of Blenheim for the Marlboroughs, which he had designed. (The papers preserved by the Duchess concerning her long dispute with the architect mention that Ralph was consulted).[335]

Even in the last few months of Ralph's life his patronage was being called on. On January 28 1709 the poet Matthew Prior was after a lucrative *'vacancy in the Commission of trade to which I have good reason to hope I may succeed: my Lord Duke of Montagu having spoken to my Lord Treasurer on that subject, and received his answer that his Lordship has a real inclination to befriend me...The Duke of Montagu, who is the chief of*

---

[334] J.C. Hodges ed., *William Congreve Letters & Documents* (London 1964)

[335] '*The Duke of Marlborough, your Grace, my late Lord Godolphin, the Duke of Shrewsbury, the late Duke of Montague, Sir Christopher Wren & several others were thoroughly consulted in this matter; & several meetings there were upon it, at Kensington, Montagu House &c when the Modells were inspected*' Vanbrugh to the Duchess of Marlborough ("Vanbrugh, Architect & Dramatist" by Lawrence Whistler, London 1938)

my friends here in this affair, bid me write the state of this thing to your Grace.' [336]

Whilst Ralph's main concerns seem to have been to climb the social ladder and to preserve his posterity, his most lasting legacy was arguably achieved through his patronage. That patronage was most influential through the work carried out in building and embellishing his houses. Unfortunately the work he commissioned at Ditton and Montagu House has gone, but one can see at Boughton how he had the north front extended with two pavilions in the French style joined by a series of state apartments. A fine stable block was also built and a false ceiling inserted below the roof of the great hall so that it could be frescoed and thereby modernised. Ralph would probably have liked to refront at least the west front of the house as well, and so present an added degree of uniformity to a building that had been enlarged at various times. But, strange though it might now seem to a visitor, Boughton was the poor sister of the three houses in that it was least used. Detrimental comparisons might be made with the country seats of Chatsworth or Burghley, but these were built by magnates who were politically out of favour and so did not have town houses. Montagu House was Ralph's prime concern – a magnificent house in which to entertain the great and the good, and which would add lustre to his name. A contemporary description of Montagu House mentions the slate roof and an *'Acroterion of four figures in the front, being the Four cardinal virtues. From the house the gardens are northward, where there is a fountain, a noble Terras, a Gladiator and several other statues...there are a great variety of noble Paintings, the Staircase and cupola room particularly curious, being Architecture done in perspective etc'.* [337] It is notable that Ralph chose to have statues of the Christian (rather than Classical) virtues of Prudence, Justice, Temperance and Fortitude on the plinth at the apex of the pediment over the grand front entrance into Montagu House. Ditton came next in importance because it was so much nearer than Boughton to London, accessible by road and river – ideal for the 'country house weekend'. Even with all the farming equipment and stock, the value of Boughton's contents on Ralph's death was less than two-thirds that of Montagu House. Ralph would probably be surprised by the richness of Boughton today and recognise furnishings brought from the other houses, added to by his successors.

Despite his position as Master of the Wardrobe, and the knowledge that many of the craftsmen he employed privately also worked supplied the Wardrobe, it is hard to provide absolute proof that Ralph's patronage influenced taste. Clearly visitors to his houses would have absorbed what

---

[336] BL Add. Mss. 61155 f. 188
[337] E. Hatton London views 1708

they saw but there is a rare case which shows something directly happening as a result. Madame de Rit, a member of Ralph's household, mentions in a letter to her husband that King William was coming for dinner and to see Montagu House. The visit led to a royal commission for the painter Jacques Rousseau to produce overdoors for Hampton Court. The French architect of the rebuilt House is uncertain: Colen Campbell in the first volume of Vitruvius Britannicus refers to a Mr Pouget. This may have been Francois Puget (1651 – 1707), son of the better known Pierre. The Pugets were based in Marseilles and Ralph may have met him when he was in Montpellier in the 1680s. In the centre of the main block of the house two halls stood back to back. The principal rooms were on the first floor, a grander conception than in most country houses where the saloon was on the ground floor. On either side of the north hall were apartments looking out on the gardens, and leading to the pavilions at either end. Round the walls of the 'painted stone hall' were five flower pieces and the ceiling, 'held up' by Ionic pilasters, was painted with allegorical figures. Two arches, with iron grilles, led to an expansive painted staircase, with a wrought-iron balustrade (an unusual feature in England at this date). Beyond the vestibule at the top of the stairs was the saloon. This occupied the centre of the house and so would have provided visitors with their first sight of the fine gardens. It seems from an account by Celia Fiennes to have been entirely painted: *'when the doores are shutt its so well suited in the walls you cannot tell where to find the door if a stranger, and it's a large roome every way. I saw a lady stand at one corner & turn herself to the wall and whisper'd, the voice came very clear and plaine to the Company that stood at the crosse corner of the room soe that it could not be carry'd by the side wall, it must be the arch overhead which was a great height'.*[338]

The team of painters worked under the direction of Rousseau and included Charles de la Fosse (until he was recalled to decorate the dome of Les Invalides), Jacques Parmentier (who specialised in painting sculpture in trompe d'eoil) and Jean-Baptiste Monnoyer (a flower painter). On May 9 1690 Madame de Rit wrote to her husband that she had drunk his health that day with de la Fosse and Rousseau, who had finished the salon and would soon start on the staircase. Monnoyer supplied more than fifty paintings, some of which survive at Boughton in the frames supplied by the Pelletiers (£924 was still owing to them at Ralph's death). The Pelletiers also supplied gilt-wood furniture. Money was also owed to Gedeon and Jean du Chesne, and Henri Nadauld for carving and

---

[338] C. Morris ed. *Journey of Celia Fiennes* (London 1947)

cornices.[339] An inventory of Montagu House's furnishings in 1707 survives, albeit incomplete. It shows, for example, that the corner room below the stairs at the west end of the house was hung with five white damask curtains trimmed with green and contained seats upholstered in green flowered velvet edged with gold lace, and "two little white India Cabinets" (japanned cabinets now at Boughton). The room next door contained marquetry furniture: the two sets (also at Boughton) were made by Cornelius Gole, son of a cabinet maker to Louis XIV.[340] The family were Protestants of Dutch origin, and Cornelius's daughter married Daniel Marot. Marot had entered William III's service and played a key role in the creation of the gardens and interiors at Het Loo. Following him to England, he then designed the semi-circular parterre for the garden at Hampton Court, and the Queen's apartments in the Water Gallery. "William's greatest single achievement as a patron was his employment". Marot "almost single-handedly brought the baroque style of the court of Versailles to Holland and England."[341] It is ironic that the accession of William hastened the end of the Dutch style that had become a phenomenon of the years following the Restoration. His enthusiasm for the style created under the aegis of his French enemy, "enthusiastically proselytised by the Duke of Montagu, replaced the plain dark interiors of Ham with the light, gilded and highly decorated interiors" of Montagu House. Marot is another candidate as architect of the latter, for which he may have provided five extant panels depicting scenes from the Loves of the Gods for a closet in the house: the designs by him of two of them are in the V&A. The flowers and garlands of fruit on the panels are ascribed to Monnoyer, mythological scenes to Lafosse, the putti, sphinxes and griffins to Parmentier and the architectural elements to Rousseau. The gilding may have been done by the Pelletiers, thus uniting in one work six of the great names patronised by Ralph. It is a "fascinating example of the full-blown Louis XIV style introduced to England in the early years of William III.[342] It also stands as a reminder of the House's lost beauty. Marot's name has also been put forward as the designer for Petworth, the house built by Ralph's step-daughter.

The use, almost exclusively, of French émigrés for the work at Montagu House can be ascribed to Ralph's exposure to, and love of,

---

[339] In 1705, after Ralph's elevation to a dukedom, Gedeon du Chesne records that he went to Boughton to cut the new duke's coat of arms over the stables, being twenty feet by twelve feet, and replaced the earl's coronet over his arms in the Great Hall with a duke's.
[340] Boughton also houses a bureau by Gole senior that can be identified with a piece in the earliest inventory of Versailles. Family tradition states that it was a gift from Louis to Ralph.
[341] Christopher Brown in "Art & Patronage in the Caroline Courts: Essays in honour of Sir Oliver Miller" ed. D Howarth (Cambridge 1993)
[342] Ibid

French style and to fashion. He has been described as "A missionary on behalf of European culture and civilisation, and deliberate framer of English taste."[343] Huguenot craftsmen were undoubtedly highly skilled, but there is apparently an intriguing reference by L E Dussieux in "Les Artistes Francaises a L'Entranger" (Paris 1876), citing a manuscript source in the Bibliotheque Nationale, which suggests that Louis XIV agreed to support the rebuilding of Montagu House financially on condition that only French craftsmen were employed. However, given Louis's attitude towards Huguenots, this would be surprising if true and French taste was not in need of subsidy to keep it in vogue. Boyer, in his obituary of Ralph, states that it was at Versailles *'his Grace formed the Ideas in his own Mind, both of Buildings and Gardens'*. Ralph's patronage may also have in it an element of support for those who he saw persecuted for their religion when he was in France. He seems to have paid to keep a pew in a Huguenot church (there are payments relating to the lock on the pew in both 1697 and 1700) which was probably the one in Hog Lane near the house.

Peter Rieusset provided the parquet de Versailles at Montagu House and Boughton, billiard tables at Boughton and Ditton in 1697 (the table for the former is still there, complete with cues of brazil wood and balls of ivory, and the bill for his trip to the house to set it up), and a large desk 8' long, 4'6" wide and 2'4" high, with a green cloth top, for Ralph's office at the Wardrobe. Also at Boughton is the State Bed, with crimson damask coverings and curtains, fringed with gold, that Francis Lapiere, upholsterer to the Royal Household took *'all to pieces and new making it up again to go to Boughton'* in 1705. In 1694 Lapiere had made Ralph a trustee of a £500 marriage portion for his daughter. She eventually married the tailor Joseph Boucher, whose name occurs in Ralph's accounts, supplying clothing to his family. Some of Ralph's silver was supplied by David Williaume, an eminent Huguenot goldsmith, who had a prestigious address in Pall Mall. In 1701 he provided Ralph with a pair of silver cisterns and wine fountains. A Huguenot silversmith is also likely to have made the octagonal silver basket chased with panels of fruit, foliage and drapery now at the Clark Art Institute of Williamstown, Massachusetts. It is engraved with Ralph's coat of arms and earl's coronet. Unfortunately little more of the silver he commissioned survives – though a tall, gilt chased vase now at Temple Newsam House, which comes from a garniture of vases and jars used to decorate mantelpieces, was probably his. At Ralph's death his plate amounted to more than a thousand items, valued at over £4,400 – about a quarter of the total value of his household goods. Gold teapots and cups were worth an additional £150. Inventories show that Montagu House had a set of silver-mounted table, stands and mirror, and

---

[343] J. Hook "The Baroque Age in England" (London 1976)

that the andirons, shovels and tongs for the grates in the state rooms were also silver-mounted, as was an eight-branch chandelier and multi-branched girandoles. This was the taste of the 1680s and 1690s. More personal purchases included a washing set with spitting pot and urinal which he may have used in the bathing room at Montagu House, which was furnished with tub, stools, four tables & eighteen prints. Ralph may also have kept some of the plate with which he was supplied for his embassies. Ambassadors were supplied by the Jewel House with plate for their household and chapel. This was to be returned at the end of the embassy, and the ambassador indented so to do. There is a record of the weight of the plate issued to Ralph as being 6,959 ounces and he implied in his petition to the King in 1683 that he had had to sell it to meet his own costs and to help the English soldiers from regiments disbanded by Louis.[344]

It is interesting that, according to the inventory taken after his death, the most important paintings were at Ditton, including works by Poussin, Snyders and Tintoretto. Perhaps it was felt that the finest works would be overwhelmed by the size of the rooms and the painted ceilings at Montagu House which did, however, have 35 small black and white paintings by van Dyck. These form about half of the total produced in preparation for engraving and printing as an *Iconography* of contemporary princes, generals, statesmen and artists. The London Gazette reported them missing after the fire of 1686 and offered a £10 reward to anyone who provided information on their whereabouts to Mr Edward Scawen at the two green posts over against Montagu House. The reward clearly worked, since they were in the house at the time of Ralph's death and are now at Boughton, which at that time was chiefly hung with tapestries rather than pictures.

Boughton has over one hundred tapestries, but it is clear from the inventories that at least a third of those owned by Ralph have disappeared. It also possesses eighteen carpets which *"both in number and quality...far outweigh in beauty, rarity, variety and art historical significance anything to be found in a similar environment in England."*[345] It is only a coincidence that John Vanderbank's £448 bill paid by Ralph's executors for cleaning and mending tapestries included doing the same work for eighteen carpets: the 1709 inventory of Montagu House mentions a chest containing twenty-six small and large carpets, together with velvet saddle furnishings ornamented with rich gold lace (total value £123 8s). The Armoury at Boughton holds a pair of sporting guns by Thuraine of Paris, makers to Louis XIV, with Ralph's crest. Unfortunately the gold hilted sword set with diamonds worth £200 which was listed on the inventory of

---

[344] HMC Rep XIII v.423
[345] I. Bennet & M. Franses in *Boughton House: The English Versailles* ed. T. Murdoch (London 1992)

his possessions has disappeared, as has the miniature of Louis set with diamonds that Ralph was given at the end of his first embassy.

Aside from the building, painting and furnishing of three houses, Ralph also wanted each to be set off by fine gardens. In 1685, the year he returned from exile in France, he appointed a Dutchman called van der Meulen as gardener. His name crops up subsequently in the accounts, and he apparently outlived Ralph - a Leonard van den Mulin was buried in Warkton in April 1717. Hints as to the scale of the undertaking come from various inventories, account entries and, occasionally, letters such as the one sent by Ralph (who was probably at Boughton) to Mr. Antonie at Montagu House, by the "London bag". *'I would have sent me down a Dutch lanthorn of horn upon a great stick, to light before a coach when it is dark, and four other little lanthorns of horn, to go in the passages and cellars when its is windy. You will find them ready done in going to St. Giles on the right hand...Speak to Mr Acres to send into Holland for ten thousand more plants of alders for this season. Tell George Keene I would have him go to Mr. Bland's, a bird man, on Tower Hill, to enquire what birds and monkeys he has come over of all kind'*. (The creditors' accounts record that Michael Bland was owed £2 5s for three India geese, £9 13s 6s for nine parakeets, and *'for 4 parrotts bought be his Grace's order which was returned & his Grace promised to allow me ten shillings a bird for my loss & trouble'*).

The letter is dated Sunday September 7 and so is likely to be from 1701 when the accounts have many entries for trees and seeds. One of the larger payments is £33 13s 8d for cockleshells for the garden (a way of adding lime to the soil). 1703/4 has entries for £13 13s for seeds, £30 12s 3d for trees and £71 18s 6d for great pots, all for Boughton, as well as £2 10s to van der Meulen for wages on account. The creditors' accounts include entries for providing 500 each of narcissi, tulips and crocuses, and 400 ranculus, and 53 baskets for hollies and 53 for yews taken from Montagu House to Ditton. Of the three houses Boughton, with its large estate, presented the greatest opportunity for landscaping. In 1694 Ralph's neighbour Christopher Hatton wrote from Burley that *'Here is great talk of vast gardens at Boughton; but I heard my Lord Montagu is very much concerned that ye water with which he hoped to make so fine fountains hath failed his expectations.'* Louis XIV had experienced similar problems in storing enough water in fairly flat countryside sufficient to create enough pressure for the fountains at Versailles. Unlike Louis, Ralph was not able to call upon the army to dig reservoirs: the creation of lakes and fountains was the garden equivalent of building a house – labour intensive and expensive. A Grand Etang was created on the higher ground to the north-west of the house to store water. Below the west front of the house were three parterres, the Parterre of Statues, the Parterre of Basins and the

Water Parterre with a large fountain in the centre that managed to reach a height of fifty feet, surrounded by smaller jets. The water then passed through a canal about 1500 yards in length where it fell seven feet in five cascades, at the top of which were vases, statues and more small fountains. Once the gardens were established they had to be maintained. The 1709 accounts have an entry for £57 10s paid to Mr Thomas Akres for keeping the garden (which one isn't specified) from March 9 to July 26. In January he had been paid £100 for trees and plants. The parkland beyond the gardens was stocked with deer (in 1706 £6 was paid in total for fifteen brace of fawns to the keepers of Lords Rockingham, Sunderland and Manchester). Given all this expenditure it is not surprising that the accounts also have entries for interest paid on loans – in 1708/9 on loans of more than £18,000.

One of Ralph's chief concerns would have been to pass on his patrimony and ensure the great name of Montagu endured. His will contains a clause that anyone inheriting his estate (such as the Harvey descendants of his daughter) must take the Montagu name within three months or be disinherited. Ralph may have felt that, having had three sons and a daughter by his first wife, the chances of his line continuing were good. This was one reason why, when he married for a second time, he could marry for money rather than to beget more children. Young Ralph had died in 1687 and Winwood, now Lord Monthermer, was prepared for his enhanced place in the world by being sent on the Grand Tour with Dr. Silvestre, and other young gentlemen. They left London on September 28 1699 for Paris, apparently via the Low Countries: a letter survives from St. Evremond to Silvestre written on behalf of the indisposed duchess of Mazarin. *"You have obliged her extremely by sending her news of yourself and of your little caravan. She was touched with your hard lot at Antwerp, in having nothing to drink but burgundy...My Lord Montagu had the sentiments of a true father, who sends his son to travel...I was very glad to hear that my Lord Monthermer accustomed himself to fatigue...If you return, bring monkeys and parrots, if you go to Rome, bring pardons and beads".*[346] After a month in Paris they spent four weeks travelling to Rome for the winter. They left that city for Genoa on March 28, arriving exactly a month later. From here Silvestre sent a report and a collection of 'natural curiosities' (earth, gum, Vesuvius salt etc) back to the Royal Society (of which he was a member). It describes *"the virtuosi I have seen in Italy and the state of learning there, chiefly as to natural philosophy and physick"*. His chief interest and skill was anatomy and his greatest excitement was expressed in seeing in Genoa a wax carving of a human body, in natural colour, made by a lecturer and compatriot, Desnoms, so perfect as to be indistinguishable from a newly embalmed corpse, which he urged as a

---

[346] des Maizeaux ibid p.379

marvellous aid to anatomical studies. (Silvestre's eclectic interests are illustrated by St. Evremond's comment that one souvenir of the doctor's trip was Corelli's violin sonatas).[347] On May 16 they sailed for Barcelona from whence to tour Spain: Guadalajara, Madrid, Badajoz, Merida, Trujillo, Toledo, Pamplona. There is a letter from Paul Methuen, the ambassador in Lisbon, to Ralph of early March 1701 stating that Winwood had arrived there in perfect health and was lodging with him. *'At his arrival I found him resolved to spend but little time in Portugal, and go from hence to France through Spain, in obedience to your Lordship's commands; but I thought it was my duty to represent to his Lordship how imprudent a thing it might be for him to engage himself in Spain or France in so critical a juncture as the present one, and the dangerous consequences of it, if a war should be declared between us and France...He intends to continue here till he...sees whether the present differences concerning the succession of the Spanish Monarchy will be amicably composed or no. P.S. I am honoured with your Lordship's of the 12th January under my Lord Manchester's cover. Your Lordship may be assured that I shall make it my business to serve my Lord Monthermer, but as for counsel or advice, it will be more fitting to take it from him than to give it, he being in the opinion of all men here the most accomplished man of his age that has been seen. I shall wait upon him to kiss the Queen Dowager's hands tomorrow, and have delivered to Mr. Marc Anthony your Lordship's two letters. I find my Lord Monthermer had no design to come hither, and that his taking this journey was only out of complaisance to monsieur Falaiseau, whose advice your Lordship has ordered him to follow in all things'.* Queen Catherine and Ralph had both been born in the winter of 1638. Did she remember Ned Montagu squeezing her hand almost forty years before, as his nephew kissed it in Lisbon? Having crossed the Pyrenees into France to visit Toulouse, Beziers, Montpellier, Avignon and Grenoble, they returned to Italy for Turin, Florence, Sienna and Naples. Back across the Alps for Geneva, Lausanne, Basle, Baden, Fribourg, Lausanne, Worms, Meiningen and finally to Hannover where, in May 1702, Winwood died.

Hanover ye 14th of May

I wood not writ to yr Lorsp ... with the ill news of the los of yor son. I take the liberty of this to ashur you ther was al the care as could be taken of him but tis thouht he had his ilnes before he came to hanover. I went often to see him; in a way I told him I hopt he wold not dy because he was not good and tho I did not think it for he was a very sweet youn[g man]. He told me he was not so bad as I thought... His servants sed the same,

---

347 *"Colladon & Mayerne"* Jnl Royal College Physicians London vol. 20 no 3 1986

which may be a grat comfort to yr Lorsp. Their never any had better servants then –tended him day & night with grat fidelety... Mr Antoney his gentlman one of the best of men. I had the same misfortune my Lord to loos my dear son at a distance from me so that I know the affliction which makes me compashonat.

Yr Lorsp he was quit recoverd but his time being come hee relaps again. My Lord let this be yr satisfaction as ther was al the care imaginable took of him for I took a great love to him as he to me for he told me al his - & as he was much trobled as somon had told you he was given to drink which he was far from it & sed he lovd you so he wood rather dy than disobleg you. He cauld much upon God so that I do not quston but that he is haper then this world could a made him. I hope you wil content yr self for I have bine fain that had the gratist los that ever hooman had. The good Electrice has given me grat comfort hear for many years after al my losis.

My Lord I am
  Your Lordsheps most humble sarvant   *Belamont*

In the absence of standard English spelling at the time, Lord Bellamont's is excusable. He was the son of Richard Coote, first earl who had died in New York on March 5 1701 and was not only of a similar age as Winwood at 21 but also like him was named after a grandparent. Winwood was somewhat more fortunate in this than Nanfan Coote. The precise date of his death is unclear – the news had reached London by the date this letter was written. (*1702 Tues May 5th The lord Mount Hermer, son to the earl of Montagu, is dead at Hanover*).[348] [349] Bellamont's reference to Winwood's concern that he had gained an unjust reputation for being a drunkard is interesting: the few references to him allege that he died drinking the Electress Sophia's health, or that he expired in Flanders of alcoholic

---

[348] Luttrell, vol.5

[349] Richard Coote had thrown in his lot with William of Orange the year before the Revolution, and was well rewarded with lands and an earldom two years later. He was Governor of New York, New Hampshire and Massachusetts and as such made acquaintance with the celebrated pirate Captain Kidd. In 1695 he put forward a scheme to Shrewsbury, Somers, Orford and Romney (and with the king as a secret partner) that Kidd should capture his fellow pirates who were harming English trade and process the takings outside the Admiralty courts for the benefit of him and his partners. Unfortunately Kidd's word was not his bond, and he sailed off to the Indian Ocean to join other captains to commit further acts of piracy, mostly on the ships of the East India Company. Naturally the Tories found this a golden opportunity to attack the Whigs who were out of power. An arrest warrant for Kidd was issued in November 1698 and Bellamont met and imprisoned him at Boston before sending him to England. Bellamont died shortly before Kidd was hung. The booty that was handed over by Kidd was sold and the proceeds used to buy the land for the new Greenwich Hospital. Nanfan died of palsy aged 27.

poisoning. After the many entries in the books of account for wigs, and payments to tutors teaching him to sing, dance and draw comes one for £21 10s to Thomas Cook on October 30 1702 for bringing Winwood's corpse from The Hague.

Just as Ralph had had to reconsider his posterity when his son Ralph had died and refocus on Winwood, he needed to adjust again: all now rested on twelve year old John. Ralph's illness at the end of September 1702, which was serious enough to be recorded by Luttrell, must have given him further impetus to do as much as he could to settle his family's future, especially given that he was now sixty-four years old in an era when one might expect to reach the age of sixty if one survived one's youth. In October he was complaining to Lord Godolphin of '*giddiness in his head, but I think he looks as he used to do*'.[350] This may well have been the reason that, though there is no evidence of a marriage planned for Winwood, just a year after his death plans were so far advanced for John that Luttrell noted on Tuesday, July 6 1703: '*A treaty of marriage is on foot between the lord Mount Hermon, only son to the earl of Montagu, and the lady Mary Churchill, daughter to the duke of Marlborough*'.[351]

[350] H. Snyder ed., *Marlborough – Godolphin correspondence* (Oxford 1975), p.136. Letter to the Countess of Marlborough, Wednesday October 21, 1702.
[351] Luttrell, p.315

Chapter 9
Apotheosis 1703 - 1709

Whilst Ralph seems to have further withdrawn from active political life after Queen Anne's accession, his old colleagues and rivals enjoyed the profits and pleasures of office. The 1st duke of Devonshire (formerly Lord Cavendish, and occupant of Montagu House when it burnt down) was Lord Steward from 1702 until his death in 1707, and Ralph's brother-in-law Newcastle held the post of Lord Privy Seal 1705-1711. The latter's own estates, added to those he had gained through his wife being the chief beneficiary of her father's will, made him the richest peer in England. He effectively controlled the elections to some ten Commons seats. If Ralph's second wife, rather than her sister, had been her father's favourite he might have been similarly placed – the reason why he and his brother-in-law the earl of Thanet continued for so long in their suit to have that will overturned. The longest spell in high office was enjoyed by the duke of Somerset, as Master of the Horse from 1702-1712 and in the Cabinet for all but the last eighteen months of that time. Somerset had an annual income of more than £20,000 pa (mostly from his marriage with Ralph's step-daughter Betty Percy). He and his wife had supported Anne when she felt slighted by William III, (they had offered her Syon House when she left Court) and she in turn rewarded them when she came to the throne. Somerset was nicknamed "the Sovereign" because of his pride in his position and Seymour lineage; his belief in his ability far outweighed his capability. The Duchess, as one of the Queen's ladies of the bedchamber, and a favourite (not least through her graciousness and civility – very different to her overbearing husband) was in a position to exercise influence but seems to have been very restrained in doing so. (In this she was unlike Sarah, duchess of Marlborough, another lady of the bedchamber and favourite of the Queen). There is no evidence (such as letters soliciting her influence for royal favour) that Ralph enjoyed a close relationship with her after his first wife's death.

Queen Anne's poor health and lack of intellect limited her ability to tackle the political and administrative burdens of the Crown. As a result she relied far more than her predecessor had ever done on her 'servants', although her Stuart blood would always respond to any attack on the royal prerogative. Permanent loss of her support would be the death of a political career and she learnt to be the arbiter trying to keep politicians in balance. Godolphin and Marlborough supervised the construction of Anne's first ministry in 1702, and continued to manage it until 1710, employing both Tories (like themselves) and Whigs. The duke and duchess of Marlborough were at the zenith of their influence in the early years of the reign. Having lost their only son at the age of seventeen in February 1703, their four daughters were their heirs. The eldest, Henrietta, had married the son and heir of Godolphin; Anne married Sunderland's widowed son and heir, (his first wife was another of the 2nd duke of Newcastle's daughters, and so Ralph's sister-in-law, and his mother was Dorothy Sidney, whose letters have been much used in this work); Elizabeth married the earl of Bridgwater. John Churchill had been appointed Captain General of the army, made a Knight of the Garter and raised to a dukedom. He was also made Master of the Ordnance, a lucrative post that he had coveted in William's reign. His wife Sarah was a woman of strong character (and trenchant opinions) who was thus able to influence her great friend, the placid Queen. The Marlboroughs were well acquainted with Ralph who had supported John a decade earlier when, with Lords Devonshire and Bradford on the Privy Council, he had refused to sign the warrant committing him to the Tower on a charge of treason in May 1693. Sarah was a great correspondent, especially with her husband (often away on campaign), so there is an unusual amount of information about their youngest daughter's marriage. Ralph's son and heir John was a potential husband.

The first concern was whether John wasn't too young, at thirteen, to marry the sixteen year old Mary. Like her mother and sisters, Mary had a forceful character. (That this trait came through the female line is indicated by the fact that it also showed itself in Sarah's mother and in Mary's older daughter). The Duke wrote to his wife from the army camp at Bonn on May 16 1703: '*You desire to know what I would have you answer to the Earl of Montagu. You know my mind in that matter, but whatever you do in it I shall like it; but I am very confident whenever you shall see the young man and Miss Mary together, you will think she is too much of a woman for him. However, you cannot do better than advise with the Lord Treasurer what is best to be done, for the proposal is very good if the young man were some years older*'. The advantages in the match that Sarah may have seen were not just in seeing her daughter married well to the son and heir of a wealthy aristocrat but also in having access to Ralph's influence as a Whig grandee. Whilst John Churchill, like Godolphin (and the Queen) were Tories, Sarah was more of a Whig and they realised that the prosecution of the war against France, and thus the Duke's destiny as a great commander, rested with that party. Nonetheless it is clear from the correspondence that other matches were being contemplated. On June 14 he wrote again: '*What you say concerning Lord Bradford's grandchild I hope will be noe temptation to you, for I love you and Miss Mary soe well that I hope you will not part with her easily, especially since her age is such as may very well alowe her not being disposed on for some few yeares.*" Duchess Sarah showed this letter to the Queen, who then wrote "*I fancy the other proposal dos not go on. I wish whenever you do dispose of this charming person, you may have the best match that is to be had'*. The Queen's belief in the failure of the match with John Montagu is confirmed by further letters the Duke found time to write on campaign: *'I find something within me against the match; for should Miss Mary not esteem the young man, it is neither title nor estate can make her happy…I am very glad that you are soe well parted with the Earl of Montagu, for a great many things happens in a year's time, which will make this match more or less reasonable'*. (June 25 1703) Thus it turned out – a year later the match was on once more. Sarah probably didn't need much help from Lord Treasurer Godolphin in the negotiations that took place over the marriage settlement. As she later wrote: *'the Duke of Marlborough left the care of all the settlements upon his children to me, I made them as advantageous to them as the circumstances of the families they were married into would allow of. The Dutchess of Montagu's settlement for herself was £800 a year pin-money, £3000 a year joynture, Ditton very well furnished, & all rent charge, free of all manner of taxes, and there was this provision made in the Settlement. That if she should happen to dye without sons, by which means the Estate might go by a second marriage from daughters, it is settled that, supposing she left only one daughter, it is to have £30,000 & if two daughters £20,000 each'*.[352] Sarah's insistence on the right settlement, and the youth of those intended for marriage, would have meant that she saw no need for haste, unlike Ralph. In 1704 he wrote to her:

Madame

I can make no other answer to the last letter your Grace did me the honour to send me but that you must be obeyed. I only ask the liberty to humbly represent how uneasye it must be to a man of my age & infirmity to see the settling of my son deferred. I am sure I have don, & alwaise will doe, what is in my power to showe with how much truth & respect I am, Madame, your Grace's most obedient humble servant

Montagu

PS I should beg my respects to Ladye Marye but that I heare she is not with your Grace [353]

There survives a series of letters from the Duchess to Ralph dating from this period showing a regular correspondence was maintained. In late July she wrote from Windsor that, since she has to take her turn as a Lady of the Queen's Bedchamber, she cannot fix the date of her visit to Althorp, but hoped *'before the summer is gone to have the honour to see you'*. She also looked forward to seeing Ralph's son in Northamptonshire *'where Lord Sunderland has made me promise to let Miss Mary go next week, and she is to stay with her sister till I come for her'*. One of the matters under

---

[352] BL Add.Mss 61451
[353] BL Add.Mss 61450, f.193

discussion seems to have been at what point they would truly be married. '*What my Lord Montague desires, that they may live together att sixteen, it is in my opinion impossible to refuse itt. I could wish with all my heart that they were older, but since that can't bee, when he is sixteen they must live together*'. (Letter from the duke of Marlborough to the Duchess, from the camp at Burcheim, 13 July 1704. Exactly one month later the Duke would be victorious at the Battle of Blenheim).

The uncertainty of the match didn't prevent Ralph from writing to the Duke asking for the occasional favour: '*My Lord, I am desired by the bearer mr Fawnt who has the honour to serve under your Grace to recommend him to your favour & protection. If you please to give him leave he will tell you what his pretensions are. His family has formerly had a relation to mine & any favour that you shall think fit to show him shall be owned as one to him, who is with greatest truth & respect*'. (October 2 1704). When the direct approach failed Ralph wrote to "Mr Cardinal" (Adam de Cardonnel), the Duke's secretary, enclosing Mr Fawnt's petition to be made a lieutenant.[354] The next month the Duchess wrote that she had received a letter from Mr Guydott, the lawyer, telling her that Ralph was finishing the marriage settlement '*which will be so near the time of Lord Marlborough's coming, that I hope you will think it reasonable to defer it till the term after, a month or two being of no consequence in such a great affair*'. Ralph would have known (as did all with whom she came into contact) that the Duchess called the shots, no matter what he thought was 'reasonable.' But she sweetened the request by adding '*I must not seal this letter without thanking you for a great many favours I have received from your Lordship since I had the honour to see you, and particularly for the little cakes. I thought it a deal of goodness that you should take notice, and remember what I liked*'. More characteristic was '*as to Mr Guydott, I am sensible he wants quickening in all business, though he is very old, and a good friend of mine. I saw him last night, and he told me your lawyer had been with him twice…If you please to order your lawyer to get the Attorney General to appoint a meeting, something may be done, for I have given him in writing all the conditions of the marriage that is necessary for him at present. I hope to have your company at dinner before Lord Marlborough goes*'.

An indication of the frequency of correspondence is given by a letter that Duchess Sarah wrote to Ralph on Saturday November 18 1704 from Windsor: '*Since your Lordship gives me this opportunity I will thank you for the favour of two letters at once…you are extremely obliging to think so much of a poor country person who is really so dull as to like this sort of life…but I will not be so obstinate as not to come to London in a very short time…I am very sorry to hear Lord Monthermont had had any*

---

[354] BL Add.Mss 61287, f.89

accident to make him keep up, especially in his feet, which otherwise I believe he would make a good deal of use of.'

The marriage finally took place on Saturday, March 17 1705, almost two years after Luttrell first mentioned it. *'This evening the lady Mary Churchill, daughter to the duke of Marlborough, is to be married to the lord mount Hermon, son to the earl of Montagu. Its said his lordship is to make the campagne with his grace the duke, who goes hence for Holland on Fryday.'* The ceremony seems to have occurred at St. James's, either at the Marlborough's apartments or in the Queen's chapel there. The decorative green and gold silk banners used, with the Montagus' griffin crest or their arms together with the Churchills', still survive. Unfortunately their wedding carriage, a 'five panelled bodyed Charriot' painted by James Thornhill, has not. (His outstanding bill for the work is in Ralph's executors' papers. He was just starting out on his career – it would be ten years before he decorated the dome of St. Paul's cathedral, and the Dining Hall at Greenwich Hospital). Through this marriage, and the Marlborough's influence with the Queen, Ralph finally achieved his crowning glory the following day: *'Sunday evening was a great council; tis said a warrant is signed to create the earl of Montagu a duke'*. The Executors' accounts show that shortly afterwards Gideon du Chesne was sent to Boughton to replace the earl's coronet over the large stucco coat of arms in the western lunette of the Great Hall with a ducal one. Unsurprisingly, not everyone considered this elevation to be deserved (it is notable that Godolphin and Sunderland, fathers-in-law to other Marlborough daughters, and arguably more important politically than Ralph, remained earls).

> The Queen, like Heaven, shines equally on all,
> Her favours without distinction fall.
> Great Read and slender Hannes, both knighted, show
> That none their honours shall to merit owe.
> That popish doctrine is exploded quite,
> Or Ralph had been no Duke, and Read no Knight;
> That none may virtue of their learning plead,
> This has no *grace*, and that can hardly *read*.

This poem by a Mr Gwinnett refers to Sir Edward Hannes, one of the Queen's doctors (who 'having been sometime mad, dyed July 1710') and Sir William Read, an oculist (a mountebank and barber of Ashdown, Essex, who could neither read nor write).[355]

---

[355] G E Cockayne, *Complete Peerage*

A day before the wedding the duchess of Marlborough replied to a letter from Ralph: '*Finding your Lordship so uneasy as you were t'other day at the proposal of exchanging your own life for your son's in the Great Wardrobe, and the apprehension I had, myself, that there was a possibility (in one case) that it might happen to your prejudice, I have done all I could to procure it, as I hope you will like, the Queen having at last consented that you son should have the reversion of the Master of the Great Wardrobe for life, with the same appointments as your Lordship now has*'. A week later this became public: '*Thurs 22ⁿᵈ March   The queen has been pleased to grant the reversion of the place of master of the wardrobe, worth 3000l per annum, to the marquess of Mounthermon, after the decease of his father. And her majestie has given his marchionesse a great quantity of gold plate upon her marriage*'. '*Thurs April 5ᵗʰ Queen ordered that marchioness to enjoy wardrobe if she survives her husband*'.[356] Ralph now wrote his will to make the settlement on John and Mary as agreed with Sarah Churchill. Luttrell records on Thursday March 29 that '*The honour and great part of the estate of the duke of Montagu, in case his son dies without issue male, are settled upon the lord Halifax*'.[357]

1705 saw the death of Ralph's son-in-law Alexander Popham who he had mentored. His daughter and heiress Elizabeth was married to the fourteen year old Lord Hinchingbrooke on April 12 1707 (the same boy who enjoyed asses' milk whilst living with his mother at Montagu House). It is clear from four pithy letters in the archives that the boy's father Lord Sandwich did not approve. Two were written on the 29ᵗʰ: '*Son I cannot but think myself very ill used in your marrying without my consent or rather against it, if you were of riper years I am afraid I could not forbear resenting it as a father ought to do, but I look upon what you have done to be very much the act of others and hope for the future you will behave yourself so towards me, as you may receive my pardon, from your loving father*'. To Ralph: '*Your Grace has done me the honour to acquaint me with a thing of great weight and moment, the circumstances whereof I am wholly ignorant*'. Clearly Ralph, Lady Hinchingbrooke and Ralph's daughter had settled the matter between them. It seems that Hinchingbrook then asked his father for a larger income. '*Son if you had shewed the Lady Sandwich the letter you sent lately to me, sure she could never have*

---

[356] Luttrell, pp.531-3

[357] Halifax was Ralph's nearest Montagu heir apart from the 4ᵗʰ earl of Manchester. As the fourth surviving son of the 1ˢᵗ earl he only inherited £50 p.a. and whilst he gained £1,500 p.a. when he married the widow of the 3ʳᵈ earl in 1688 he lost it when she died ten years later. He was unable to employ the financial abilities he had shown during William's reign because of Godolphin's eight year tenure of the Treasurership and Anne's dislike of his strong Whiggism. If the inheritance from Ralph came to pass Halifax's financial difficulties would have been at an end.

advised you to complain of an allowance of £400 pa which was thought sufficient for me when I travelled. As to your wifes fortune or way of living that ought not to be looked upon as any care of mine since I had not part in making the match. However I have at present so straightened myself to pay the Lady Sandwich and her debts that had you done what had been more honourable to me, I could not have made you a better allowance'. The earl of Sandwich was a strong Tory, unlike his cousins of Montagu and Manchester. In late June the new Lady Hinchingbrook apparently called upon her father-in-law, one assumes to soften his attitude to her marriage, but *'I am sorry I had no notice of my Lady Hinchingbrooks coming that I might have had time to make preparations to receive her. I hope your Grace and she will excuse what was amiss. As to my son Hinchingbrooks travelling, he may either go to travel or not as he thinks fit.'* Somehow money was found, probably by Ralph, since he went on a continental tour the next year.[358]

Less than a month after her wedding in 1707 Elizabeth's widowed mother Anne Popham married her cousin Daniel Harvey, the son of Ralph's sister, on May 8. Lady Betty Harvey had had two sons. The eldest had inherited Combe Park, Surrey, when his father had died in Istanbul in 1672. The local influence it brought him was only sufficient for him to get elected as MP for Bletchingley for one year, 1679, so it was undoubtedly through Ralph's help that he was an MP for Clitheroe from 1705-1713, and 1715-22. His brother Daniel was the second MP for that constituency in 1705, for the rotten borough of Dunwich in February 1709, and for Weymouth 1713- 1714. Daniel had risen from being the colonel in a regiment of horse to lieutenant general by the time he married. Having served in Portugal the year before he was then promoted to major-general – perhaps he too was benefitting from his closer family relationship to Marlborough. Although a Whig like Ralph, he was one of a small group of army officers who were in Marlborough's inner circle.[359]

From this period three letters survive from the Electress Sophia to Ralph. Since Sophia might well become Queen (although more than thirty-four years older than Anne she was in far better health) anyone hoping to enjoy royal favour in the future felt it important to make shows of loyalty. (Hence Ralph's son Winwood including Hanover on his European tour). The first letter, dating from April 16 1705, thanks Ralph for the proofs of his affection in his commiserations on the death of her daughter, Sophia Charlotte, Princess in Prussia, of pneumonia in January at the age of thirty-

---

[358] Just to keep everything in the family, and confuse historians, the widowed Elizabeth, Lady Hinchinbroke would marry Francis Seymour of Sherborne in 1728. His elder brother became 8th duke of Somerset, a title shorn of the Percy inheritance. Their mother was a Popham.
[359] G.S. Holmes *British Politics in the Age of Anne* (London 1967)

six. It also congratulates him on the recent marriage of his son John, to whom the Electress wishes happiness. (This letter was written only three days after Ralph's name had been noted as one of the peers who supported the Hanoverian succession).[360] The second, of October 25, responded to commiserations on the death of her brother-in-law (the duke of Brunswick) and suggests that she was equally unhappy about the marriage of her grandson (the future George II). The last, from June 1706, came after the earl of Halifax had given her a letter from Ralph during his visit. Ralph was apparently also asked to intercede with the duchess of Marlborough on her behalf: *'I have a letter from the princesse Sophia. She knows I have the honour of having sometimes accesse to your Grace, wherein she desires me to recommend Mr Wind* [?] *a servant of hers, to your Grace's favour & good offices & to her Maisety to whome she has writ herself in his behalf.'* (August 26 1707) [361] The winter of 1705 had seen the Tories attack the Queen for allowing her ministers to move away from a balanced ministry to one with a greater number of Whigs (who were willing to back the war). They did this by suggesting that there was a danger that her half-brother might be brought to the throne as James III if she died suddenly and by moving in the Lords that the Queen should be asked to invite Sophia to England. Like Elizabeth I, last of the Tudors, Anne hated discussion of her death and abhorred the idea of having a nominated heir as a rival in her own kingdom. The attempt failed miserably, and this alarmed Sophia. The Whigs hurried to reassure her and her son of their support.

Two months after the marriage Duchess Sarah wrote to Ralph from her home at St. Alban's that she was *'glad I did not hear of Lord Monthermer's illness till I had the satisfaction of knowing from your Grace that it is over; but I shall be in some pain till you are so good as to let me know you are well after the operation on your eye.'* She then mentions that Ralph had interested himself in Sunderland's mission to the Emperor and asks him to help Lord Essex *'being my neighbour, and having very little to do, he has done me the favour to come twice to St. Alban's. I think he has as good a heart as one can wish in any person, and I believe that helps to make his circumstances uneasy, which would be something mended by being Governor of the Tower. I should think that a man that is a soldier had a better title to an employment of that nature than my Lord Abingdon, who will never make a campaign but for Jacobite Elections. I have had many letters to condole upon that subject, but I have a great deal of philosophy upon such occasions, though I have been a little vexed at some things I hear has been reported of me, which I hope you don't believe, for the spirit of lying runs more with the Torrys'* (May 21

[360] Stowe Mss 224 f.330
[361] BL.Add.Mss 61450, f197

1705).[362] In the autumn Ralph had an opportunity to enjoy the precedence his new dukedom gave him. '*Tuesday Oct 23rd. This being the first day of the term, the new lord keeper was attended from the Middle Temple hall to Westminster by the dukes of Somerset, Newcastle and Montague, the lord treasurer, the earls of Kent, Essex, Orford, Stamford, lords Mohun, Colepeper, Cornwallis, Somers, Halifax and several other peers, together with the judges, serjeants at law etc.*'[363] On the previous Saturday a select number from this group (Ralph, Somerset, Ormond, Godolphin and Lord Chief Justice Holt) visited Lord Keeper Cowper.[364] Ralph had to wait until the opening of the new session of parliament in the following month for his introduction to the House of Lords as a duke. On November 15 the dukes of Bolton and Ormond stood on either side of him as he bowed to the Lord Chancellor. He now outranked his cousins the earl of Manchester, who officiated as Earl Marshal, and the earl of Sandwich. The Queen may have witnessed it – she had come to the House incognito (which meant everyone knew that she was there even if "officially" she wasn't) to hear a debate on the state of the nation, in which the Tories criticised the military stalemate, neglect of the Church of England, and the danger of a Jacobite restoration if the Queen died suddenly. The latter was to lay the path for a motion (mentioned above) and she was grateful to the Whigs for their support in defeating it. The suggestion that the Church was not supported by Anne was hurtfully untrue and the military stalemate was, as usual, down to the Dutch who supplied most of Marlborough's troops, rather than to the Duke.

Ralph had now surpassed his long held desire to be an earl but his ambition seems not to have been dimmed. He hoped that his son's marriage would allow access to the Queen, fount of all honours, through her favourite the duchess of Marlborough, but he knew how fickle fate could be and so seized the moment to ask for the ultimate royal favour. In a letter which is believed to date from February 1706 Sarah writes to him that '*There is many solicitors for the Garter, some that pretend promises, and others that think they merit favour from the Queen, who I find is unwilling to disoblige a great many, as her Majesty must do when she disposes of only one Garter; and therefore she has taken a resolution to keep this till she has more in her power. Knowing the Queen's mind on this occasion, before I received your Grace's commands, I have not acquainted her Majesty with what you have desired, being in some doubt whether you would have me speak in a thing that seems so remote*'. (Sarah's influence,

---

[362] Essex was the son of the 1st earl who had committed suicide in the Tower where he had been imprisoned after the discovery of the Rye House Plot, and was cousin to Ralph's first wife. He was a Whig. Sarah prevailed and he replaced Abingdon.
[363] Luttrell vol.5 p.604
[364] Diary of Lord Chancellor Cowper, Roxburgh Club 1833

never as powerful as her enemies claimed, had in any case started to wane by this time). Soon after this John, Lord Monthermer went to join his father-in-law and the army. He was sixteen years old and may have been homesick, since Marlborough wrote to his wife from The Hague at the end of April that the boy *'had pressed Lord Halifax and myself that he might return to England, saying he could have no happiness while he stayed abroad. I own to you that I do not disapprove of what he said, but my answer was that I desired he would consult Lord Halifax and take care not to anger his father. How it will end I do not know, but I am told tonight Doctor Silvester is for his staying'* (John was apparently to go on with Halifax to Hanover). On May 31 Marlborough wrote again. *'It is now four days ago since I sent for a pass for Lord Monthermer to come to the army, but the Marshal de Villeroy is either very much out of humour, or in so great a hurry, that he has not sent them. I am the uneasier at this because I think the young man is very desirous of returning for England, as would your humble servant if he was master of himself...I do hope that Lady Sunderland being with child will do her no hurt. For her sister Monthermer there can be no fear, for she is very strong'*. Perhaps young John had wanted to get home in time for the birth of his first child. There survives a letter from John's tutor to Ralph, of the same date from Nijmegen, saying that they had waited in vain for passports, but that he isn't surprised since Marlborough would have been extremely busy following up the great victory over the French at Ramillies a week earlier. He then mentions John's unhappiness and that they expected to be leaving for Bergen-op-Zoom (a Dutch port). John had written to his father-in-law and Dr. Silvestre to Marlborough's secretary Cardonel.

On July 27 1706 Ralph's uncle William (who had been a chief baron of the Exchequer) died. Sadness at losing a relative must have been relieved by the knowledge that when William's daughter Lady Drake died his estate would come to Ralph. A happier event took place on December 31 - a great procession to (the still unfinished) St. Paul's cathedral for a service to celebrate Ramillies. 1706 was one of the highest points in the long War of the Spanish Succession for the allies. The Duke had driven the French out of the Spanish Netherlands after the battle and the duchess of Mazarin's nephew Eugene of Savoy had ousted them from northern Italy in the autumn. (*'Weather good & Shew unspeakably fine'* recorded Bishop Nicolson of Carlisle in his diary). Ralph may well have enjoyed the City's banquet at the Vintner's Hall that followed even more. For all their civilities, the Marlboroughs apparently did not hold a high opinion of Ralph. The Duke wrote to his wife from The Hague in November 1706 regarding his daughter that *'tho I do from my heart believe that 125 [Ralph] is capable of everything that is ill, yet it is not for her's nor her husband's interest to see it."* The next summer *'8 [Ralph] is certainly very ill natured, but the devil is good when pleased"* (Meldert 9/20 June 1707) and in the autumn *"I am not at all surprised at any unreasonable or unjust thing done by 8"* (Helchin 1/12 September 1707) Perhaps if Ralph had known this he might have stop pestering the couple for favours. He certainly wrote to the Duke at the start of 1707, still angling for a Garter, for the Duke's reply to him survives: '*The Queen having reason to think the Kings of Sweden and Denmark may after the peace be desirous of having the Blew ribbon, makes you expedient impracticable'* (February 12 1707).

In the summer Ralph tried win the Duchess's support once more: '*The Duke of Devonshire being deade, I take the libertye to offer your Grace in case the Queen shall be pleased to give his sonne the place of Lord Steward, that then you woud shoe so much favour to my Lord Monthermer as to ask of the Queen the place of Captaine of the Yeoman of the Guards for him. It would introduce him extreamly well into the world, & enable him at present to make up my Lady Monthermers pin money, at present eight hundred pounds a year. I beg you pardon madame for this trouble'.*[365] The response was that '*there is so few employments, and so many to be gratified for the Queen's service, that I cant think of asking the Captain of the Yeoman of the Guards for my son-in-law who has (in reversion) one of the best things the Queen has to give, and his for life'*. Ralph wasn't convinced, so she wrote again. '*I am sorry your Grace does not think my answer reasonable concerning what is desired for Lord Monthermer, and though what your Grace writes is true, that the title and office was granted upon the account of the marriage, yet the Queen must look on it as a favour from her, and where there is so many expecting and desiring favours of that kind, her Majesty's circumstances will not allow her to give two great offices in her family* (household) *to one person'*. Ralph had experienced years of diplomatic negotiation and so wasn't going to give up easily. He responded from Boughton on August 30: '*I must beg your Grace's pardon if I trouble you againe upon the subject of the favour I begged you for my Lord Monthermer, but you have drawn it upon your self by furnishing arguments for doing what you seem to think not proper for you to do. The queen's mind is much altered in not allowing of two great offices in one famelye. My Lord Treasurer his son & daughter in law have three. My Lord Devonshire & his sonne have two. My Lord Sunderland & my ladye have two. The Duke & Duchesse of Ormond the same alsoe the Duke & Duchess of Somerset. The Duke of Bolton is warden of the new forest but admiral in those seas & governor of the Isle of Weight, all places of great honour & profit. These examples will I hope in some measure make my – with your Grace & shoe you Madame that I am not soe unreasonable in my pretensions for my sonne as you may*

---

[365] BL Add.Mss 61450, f195

perhaps judg me to be & for whoever they are that pretend to gratifications from her Maiestye I may without vanity say, that though my ill health dos not permitt me to be as diligent to make my court as I ought to doe, I have & doe for all occasions serve her Maiestye as effectually as any other can doe & will alwaise in what I can promote her service & interest & should my lord Monthermer have bin soe luckye as by your favour had this employment I alwaise designed that he should upon my death offered the queen that he would resigne that of captaine of the yeoman of the Guard. But [I]... resigne my selfe to God & then all be well & your Grace have noe more trouble from him whoe is with the greatest respect, Madame, Your Grace's most obedient humble servant'. [366] Yet a week later the rumour was that Ralph might attain his ultimate desire, even if he couldn't obtain the office for his son: *'Its said the duke of Montagu will have the garter of the late Duke of Devon and the earl of Manchester, ambassador at Venice, made captain of the yeomen of the guard, worth 1,000l per ann, in place of the present duke of Devon'.*[367] The rumour turned out to be false in both respects – Viscount Townshend was given the captaincy and Ralph would never have the garter. Luttrell also recorded that on Sunday August 17 Ralph had *'entertained at dinner the marquesse d'Alegre, one of the French prisoners, who being ask't what he thought of Toulon, answered, considering the account the last Paris Gazet gave of that siege, he was in fear for that place'.* (A further Luttrell reference to Ralph comes from September 18: *'This morning one Mr Chamberlain, a steward of the duke of Montagu's, stabb'd himself, and afterward cutt his throat, and his life is in great danger'*).

Ralph was also willing to lobby when he (or his family) seems to have had nothing to gain directly from doing so: *'Poore Madamoiselle Spanhems fate is very sad to fall from the agreeable hopes & expectations she has to return home with her ould father & mother. Methinks it would – with the queen's goodness & generosity to comfort her in this her misfortune to make her a present of a thousand guineas, & she rather because the court of prussia has been soe magnificent to all the English that have ever come there'* (Spanhem was the Prussian ambassador). Being a member of the aristocracy meant being part of a web of mutual obligations – the very fact of being asked to obtain a favour was an indicator of influence. The way in which the web was spun is shown by a letter from Ralph to Thomas Hopkins, an under-secretary of state, of June 5 1708. Having recommended one Colthurst for the office of Chief Justice of New York, he mentions that Lord Chancellor Cowper had *'promised me*

---

[366] BL Add.Mss 61450, f199
[367] Luttrell, Sept 9 1707

his friendship in the matter' and that Colthurst had been an active supporter of Sunderland's electioneering efforts in Northamptonshire.[368]

There is little record of Ralph aside from his correspondence with the Marlboroughs. The Duke's final surviving letter to his wife mentioning Ralph was sent from Brussels on January 30 1709: *'I think that I did acquaint you that towards the end of the campaign I had a letter from the Duke of Montagu to desire that he might buy the Earl of Albermarle's troop for his son. I made him a civil answer that the troop was not to be sold. I have since received the two enclosed letters. I would not have it known to anybody but the Lord Treasurer, but I own it to you I do not like the earnest desire the young man has to come into the army, for in his circumstances it must proceed from being very young or uneasiness at home'.* He was trying to embellish the Montagu name to the end - just over five weeks later he was dead.

Ralph must have been ill many times during his long life, even though there is only record of a few occasions such as the smallpox of his youth and his illnesses in March 1697 and at the end of September 1702. The household accounts for his later years occasionally give hints of ailments: an entry for October 1699 shows payment to a Mr Buissiere for bleeding Ralph twice and cupping him once, and a tip to the Duchess of Norfolk's footman *'who brought the king's drops to my lord'*. More than £25 had been spent the summer before on chocolate, which was considered to have medicinal properties, and shortly before Ralph died George Lewis supplied a 'fine polished Chocolat pot' and a four-ounce mill to grind the hard chocolate block. In 1705 Ralph was having severe problems with his eyes and so Mr Gerdard, a French oculist, was brought to England to couch them. One wonders whether the large bill of £61.18s.5 for sweetmeats for the year 1707 indicates a sweet tooth in old age rather than just a standard part of entertaining.

Ralph made another will on August 21 1707. Whilst his father and ancestors had been buried at Weekley, Ralph's first wife had been interred at Warkton, another church on the Boughton estate. He wanted his burial there to be 'very private' with only two coaches and to cost 'as little as conviently'. After directing that all his servants should have a suit of mourning clothes and half a year's wages, and that one of them, George Keen, should have a pension of £50 p.a., he left his estate in nine counties on trust until John reached the age of twenty-one. The trustees were to be Marc Antonie and John Warner of Weekley. Since John's son was then still alive it went to him after the death of his father. If the male line failed

---

[368] History of Parliament Trust, London, unpublished article on Ralph Montagu, duke of Montagu, for House of Lords 1660-1832 section by Robin Eagles.

the estate went to his sisters. After them Lords Halifax and Somers with the Dummer brothers of the Temple were to hold it in trust for Ralph's grand-daughter Lady Hinchingbrooke. After her family Ralph's nephew Edward Harvey and his issue would inherit, then Lord Halifax himself, then the earl of Manchester. If anyone succeeded who did not already bear the name of Montagu they were to adopt that name within three months and, where necessary, promote a private Act of Parliament to do so, otherwise they would be disinherited. Similarly Lady Hinchingbrooke was bound, if she inherited, to seek the consent of the trustees if she remarried. The will was signed by Hans Sloane, Dr Silvestre, Andrew Marchant and John Sergeant.[369]

Ralph died on March 9 1709 aged seventy. According to Boyer, he had been '*stricken with a distemper*' at the start of the month, and expired in Montagu House '*between the hours of 5 and 6*'.

The books of account for Ralph, duke of Montagu were closed off: £64 9s was paid to the doctors and surgeons who had not been able to save him, £330 to the servants for going into mourning, and £47 7s to Mr ffox '*on ye funeral account*'.

'*The duke of Montagu's death is much talked of and has produced a union between two sisters, the Duchess of Newcastle, and Lady Thanet; for yesterday they were seen in a coach together, and most say that the Queen has ordered the late Duchess of Albermarle shall live with Lady Thanet, but the Duchess of Newcastle and Lord Sunderland, whose first wife was these ladies' sister, to have equal concern with the keeping of her grace and equal advantage of her estate, which is £8,000 a year. None now questions her being alive. Some say the Queen will not meddle in this affair, but that the law decides that next relations must have the advantage and keeping of the lunatic, which she certainly is*'. (Lady Marow to her son-in-law, Sir Arthur Kaye, March 10 1709).[370] Another correspondent, after passing on the rumour that Ralph died £40,000 in debt and with a mortgage of £20,000 on Montagu House, reports that '*the Duchess has been seen by her sisters and is like to be begged for by her relations*'.[371]Ann Hadley wrote to her cousin Abigail Harley six days later that '*Here is no lamentations for ye Duke of Montague, but he by departing has given the inquisitive world ye long desired satisfaction of knowing his Mad Dutchess to be alive; they say she will be given to the Duke of Newcastle, when a commission of Lunacy is taken out, and whats more will come in for her thirds of her or her pretend husband Estate. For my part I'm apt to think he could have forseen or rather believed at what a*

---

[369] TNA Prob 10/7370
[370] Ormond Ms p.147 vol.II HMC Dartmouth
[371] Verney Ms mic M636/54 Margaret Adams to Viscount Fermanagh March 26 1709

distance this present world and he would soon have been, he for the wealth and honner sake of his family would discreetly have knockd her Ladyship on the head in good time' (Welbeck Mss). Had Ralph known that the Duchess would survive him by twenty-five years, dying in 1734 in her eightieth year and then buried in Westminster Abbey with her first husband, rather than with him, perhaps he would have done so. It is interesting to note the comment of 'pretend husband' – the judges had apparently had difficulty in ascertaining who had married them. On March 31 the Lunacy Commission found that 'the Duchess dowager of Montagu is a lunatic and not in her right understanding and does not enjoy lucid intervals'. In the Montagu archive there is a receipt affirming that she was 'delivered' to John Robb of the parish of St. Giles in the Fields. It is signed by him, Edward Dummer and Marc Antonie and bears the seals of Newcastle and Sunderland.[372] It is unclear whether she ever received the third of Ralph's estate during her life, as she was entitled to. She left some £120,000 to her nieces and so doesn't seem to have been in need of the funds.

Abel Boyer's "The History of the reign of Queen Anne" gives an obituary of Ralph which concludes that he *'lived with greater Splendor and Magnificence in his Family, than any Man of Quality perhaps in Great Britain'.* After compliments as to his relationships with his family, servants and friends, the truth of which is difficult to assess at this distance in time, it states that he was a *'Great Admirer and Encourager of Learning and the Liberal Arts. He daily entertained at his table several ingenious men; and had a particular esteem for Mr. de St. Evremond and some other French Gentlemen of Merit and Parts'.* The same day that he died a granddaughter was born.

---

[372] NRCO Montagu papers vol. 189

Epitaph

Metzger's seven page summary of Ralph Montagu's life in not complimentary. He points out that he was qualified through birth, education and wealth to achieve great things, '*yet did not see beyond his own gratification*'. He was a pure opportunist in his public, as well as his private, life and a planner but not a man of vision. In the Danby affair his '*traitorous actions*' had '*far reaching negative effects upon the government he served*' and his actions in the Exclusion crisis and Glorious Revolution '*reveal him as a man willing to parade his shameless conduct of betrayal under the guise of patriotism*'. His patronage of the arts was a cynical display of his belief that '*he could aspire to the nobility through culture and eventually be assimilated into the Court*'. Metzger acknowledges that Ralph loved good conversation and intellectual companionship but then states that he cultivated influential people in order to achieve the rewards he felt were his right. The author does suggest that nationalism was foreign to the late seventeenth century, and acknowledges that Ralph's life reflects the attitudes of the times in which he lived, but little else is offered to soften a critical view.

I offer a different perspective. Ralph, like his older brother and his sister, chose to go out in the world rather than stay at home and manage the family estate. The most exciting, and potentially career enhancing, place to be was at the newly restored Court of Charles II. Brother Ned was disgraced, in part no doubt due to other courtiers' jealousy of his closeness to the Queen, but also because his behaviour wasn't such as to win allies. He redeemed himself through his death, which made Ralph heir to his father's title and estate. The evidence of the copious correspondence from Ralph's years as ambassador suggests that he was diligent, and tried to do his best both for Arlington/Danby and for his monarch. The intrigue, bribery and intelligence work that was all part of the role is something he seems to have relished. He may well have shared Charles's belief that it was in England's best interest to ally with France and undermine the Dutch so that English trade could increase at their expense. Could they have predicted that ultimately Louis's ever greater ambitions in Europe would have to be thwarted by a long and expensive war? Even if Ralph privately believed Charles to be wrong in his policies it was his task to obtain the best possible price from Louis for English support. He knew that Parliament was being deceived but that was a concern for his masters in England - ambassadors in the seventeenth-century did not resign their posts on matters of principle.

Nineteenth-century historians in particular are critical of Ralph's 'treasonable activities' in trying to chisel more money from Louis at the same time that Charles was asking Parliament for cash to support a war against France. They can be incandescent at his revelation of these activities, and the consequent fall of Danby and end of the Long Parliament. Charles II, the Merry Monarch, was given a far less critical press. Ralph had been painted into a corner by Barbara Villiers and may well have considered that his career was already ruined, even though her accusations were quite possibly untrue. It seemed that the monarch and minister he had served, and who had offered little reward, would (at the least) abandon him. Ralph had a choice of fighting back or retiring to Northamptonshire. He was forty years old and his character was not that of a quitter, so he unveiled the duplicity of Danby and Charles to the Commons. This was at great personal risk, as his attempted flight shows, and he must have known that his actions would further blacken the royal family's view of him. Further opprobrium was garnered because Ralph subsequently accepted French money both on his own account, and to encourage others in opposition to Charles in Parliament. Yet many others did the same, not least Russell and Sidney who would become Whig 'martyrs'. Ralph may have known that, since the Court held the strongest cards, he was likely to be permanently on the losing side by siding with the opposition in Parliament. That was where Fate had placed him and, until he was smiled on again, he would exert himself in making life as difficult as he could for the King who had withdrawn his favour.

One cannot tell whether his support for William at the time of the Glorious Revolution was on principle or in the hope of the return of that favour. It is likely that it was both – human motives are often mixed. Like the majority of Englishmen he wanted James gone and, if what Barbara Villiers had reported of his views was true, he may well have hoped for a more limited monarchy. Evidence shows that he was active in his political support for William and exerted influence that led to the settlement reached. It must surely have been for those acts rather than his previous political deeds that he was rewarded with the long coveted earldom. Ralph was fifty years old at the Revolution and may still have hoped for office but the many rumours of his success never came true - he had to content himself with acting as a Whig grandee and host, influencing but not directing.

However much one tries, it is impossible to understand the mindset of someone born centuries ago. Reading the letters of Ralph and his contemporaries encourages a feeling that they were people not so dissimilar to ourselves, but of course the world they lived in was totally different. The weather was often a topic of conversation, as now, yet we are able to mitigate many of its effects, not least through artificial light and heat. People were concerned for their health, and that of their friends and neighbours, but they did not have access to anything than the most rudimentary medicines and a visit from a doctor was just as likely to make one's health worse. The agony of neuralgia suffered for years by Ralph's first wife is a reminder of that, as is the death of his children. Even those born into a wealthy family who survived the health perils of youth could be struck down with illness and die at any time.

Taking the judgements of Ralph's contemporaries of his character at face value is as fraught with difficulty as examining the views of later historians. All will have coloured those judgements with their own attitudes. Set against the political and moral behaviour of other men of his class of the later seventeenth century, Ralph's is better than some (Henry Saville, Buckingham and Charles II himself spring to mind) and no worse than many. Politicians are rarely lauded as shining lights of probity. His attempts to climb the slippery pole, and through doing so put his family in the very highest rank of society (which he considered it entitled to by descent and service), were what his peers would have expected of him. His second marriage may have exposed him to some ridicule, but his mad wife had had other suitors. That they had not succeeded in wedding her seems to have been because they didn't have Ralph's guile and imagination. Sarah Churchill apart (who rarely had a good word to say for anybody), Ralph seemed to be popular with women (often more discerning of the qualities of the opposite sex). He also held his own in the company of intellectuals and artists, although some of their praise may been oiled by gratitude for his patronage and the peaches and oysters served at dinner. He certainly seems to have been considered as an excellent host, good company and, as evidenced by all he did for the duchess of Mazarin, a faithful friend.

Readers of this biography will come to their own view of the man. His legacy to this age, apart from the fascinating archive, lies in the wonderful things he commissioned from many of the most skilled artisans of his day. The magnificence of Montagu House has gone, but some of its furnishings can still be seen and admired at his house at Boughton, as can the State Rooms with paintwork untouched and the State Bed still resplendent with its original red silk hangings and ostrich plumes. If Ralph surveyed his achievements as he lay dying, he would doubtless have been content that, after a long and eventful life, he was passing on an enlarged estate, three fine houses and, above all, a dukedom to his son. Since he had married that son to the daughter of the greatest man in England, and she had given him a grandson, he had done all that might have been expected of a Montagu. Ralph may well have decided to have this appropriately commemorated – one of the last works he commissioned at Boughton, three years before he died, was to have a coved ceiling inserted below the early Tudor timber roof of the Great Hall. The subject he chose to have Cheron paint on the vault was the Apotheosis of Hercules, the hero who had laboured hard and overcame incredible obstacles to win his place in the heavens.

**Ralph's arms, impaled with those of his first wife, surmounted by a ducal
coronet, in the Great Hall at Boughton House**

BIBLIOGRAPHY

Primary and Archival Sources
Bodleian Library, Oxford: Carte Ms. Series
Belvoir Mss, II
HMC Bath
HMC Finch
HMC Lindsey Mss
HMC Essex Papers
HMC Montagu of Beaulieu
HMC Ormonde letters
HMC Rutland
HMC Letters of Sir Robert Southwell to 1st Duke of Ormonde
HMC 12th Report, Appendix ix Beaufort Mss
HMC 13th Report v
HMC 15th Report, *The Mss of the Duke of Somerset, the Marquis of Ailesbury, and the Revd. Sir T H G Puleston, Bart.* (London, 1898)
Hatton correspondence
Locke, John. Case notes preserved at Royal College of Physicians Mss 405
National Archives, Kew
Devonshire Mss., Chatsworth, Halifax Collection, Group B/10
British Library, London
Additional Ms Series: 3280, 5751a, 23894, 25119, 28044, 28927, 3957, 32095, 34526, 38849, 61155, 61298, 63630, 70074, 70114, 70119, 72483, 72588
Egerton Mss 1533
Egmont Mss
Portledge Papers
Welbeck Mss
Sloane Mss
Verney manuscripts kept as Ms mic.636
CA 117, 119
TNA SP78/126, 129, 132
PRO 30/32/38, 31/3/153
PRO Prb.II.379
Calenders of State Papers (Domestic, Venetian, Treasury Books)
National Maritime Museum, Sergison papers
Bedford and Luton Archives and Record Service, Bedford: County Archive X800/1-5
Beinecke Rare Book and Manuscript Library, Yale University, New Haven: Osborn fb. 191 "Diary of Ralph Montagu"
Lords Journals
Wiltshire County Record Office: Ailesbury Mss 1300/856

Printed Primary Sources

Ailesbury, Thomas, Earl of, *Memoirs* (Roxburghe Club, 1890)

Airy, O. (ed.), Burnet's *History of my own time*

Bebington, T. ed., *Lettres du Comte d'Arlington au Chevalier Temple (aux Comtes de Sandwich, & de Sunderland; & aux Chevaliers Fanshaw, Godolphin, & Southwel)* (Utrecht, 1701)

Beddard, R., *A Kingdom without a King: the journal of the provisional government in the revolution of 1688* (Oxford, 1988)

Bertie, Charles *Diary* (Lindsey Mss)

Boyer, A., *The History of the reign of Queen Anne, year the 8th 1710*

Blencowe, R.W. (ed.), *Henry Sidney: Diary of the Times of Charles II* (London, 1843)

Burnet, Gilbert *History of my own time* ed. O. Airy (1897-1900)

Christie, W.D. (ed.), *Letters addressed from London to Sir Joseph Williamson while Plenipotentiary at the Congress of Cologne in the years 1673 and 1674* (Camden Society, 1874)

Curran, M.B., 'The despatches of William Perwich' *Camden Soc. 3rd Ser. V* (London, 1903)

Dalrymple, J., *Memoirs of Great Britain and Ireland. From the dissolution of the last Parliament of Charles II till the capture of the French and Spanish Fleets in Vigo* 3 vols. (London, 1790)

Ellis, G.J.W.A., *The Ellis Correspondence* (London, 1829)

Evelyn, John diary 6 vols (Oxford, 1955)

Esher, Sir Ralph *Adventures of a gentleman of the Court* (1832)

de Fonblanque, E.B., *Annals of the House of Percy, from the Conquest to the opening of the nineteenth century* (London, 1887)

Grey, Antichel *Debates of the House of Commons 1667-1694* (10 vols. 1769)

Hamilton, A., *Memoirs of the Life of the Count of Grammont* (London, 1965)

Hatton, E., *New View of London* (1708)

Hayton, D. W.,*The Parliamentary Diary of Sir Richard Cocks, 1698-1702* (Oxford, 1966)

Hayward, J. (ed.), *Letters of St. Evremond* (London, 1930)

Hodges, J. (ed.), *William Congreve, Letters & Documents* (London, 1964)

Jones, C. & Holmes, G. (ed.), *London diaries of Wm. Nicholson, Bishop of Carlisle* (Oxford, 1985)

Kerr, R.J. & Duncan, I.C. (eds.), *Portledge Papers : being extracts from the letters of Richard Lapthorne to Richard Coffin* (London, 1928)

Locke's Travels to France 1675-1679 as related in his journals (Cambridge 1953)

Luttrell, N., *A brief historical relation of state affairs from September 1678 to April 1714* (6 vols., Oxford, 1857)

Marlborough, *Letters & Despatches of John Churchill, First Duke of Marlborough, 1702-12*. Ed. Sir George Murray (5 vols. 1838)

Marlborough, *Letters: Private Correspondence of Sarah, Duchess of Marlborough*. Ed. Lord John Russel (2 vols. 1838)

Marlborough – Godolphin Correspondence: Ed. Henry L Synder (3 vols. Oxford, 1975) St.Evremond's *works with the author's life* by Mr des Maizeaux 1714

Singer, S.W. (ed.), *The Correspondence of H. H., Earl of Clarendon, and of his brother, Laurence Hyde, Earl of Rochester; with the Diary of Lord Clarendon from 1687 to 1690* (London 1828)

Macky, *Memoirs of the secret services* Roxburghe Club 1895

Marlow, N., *The diary of Thomas Isham of Lamport (1658-81), kept by him in Latin from 1671 to 1673 at his father's command* (Farnborough, 1971)

Morrice, R., *The Entring Book of Roger Morrice 1677-1691* (Woodbridge, 2007)

Osborne, T., *Copies and Extracts of some Letters written to and from the Earl of Danby, (now Duke of Leeds,) in the years 1676, 1677, and 1678, with particular remarks upon some of them* (London, 1710)

Parker, J.H. (ed.), *The Autobiography of Symon Patrick, Bishop of Ely* (Oxford, 1829)

Simons, J. (ed.), *Robert Persons, Certamen Ecclesiae Anglicanae* (Assen, 1965)

Robinson, H.W. & Adams, W. ed., The diary of Robert Hooke F.R.S., 1672-1680 : transcribed from the original in the possession of the Corporation *of the City of London* (London 1935)

Russell, Lady Rachel *Letters of....* (London, 1773) vol.1 of 1853 ed

Snyder, H. ed., *Marlborough – Godolphin correspondence* (Oxford 1975)

Swift, J. *The works of Jonathan Swift Dean of St Patrick's Dublin : containing additional letters, tracts and poems not hitherto published* (London, 1883) vol.xii

Stowe, J.A., survey of the cities of London and Westminster…by J. Strype (London 1842)

The Court in Mourning. Being the Life and Worthy Actions of Ralph, Duke of Montagu (London,1709)

Uffenbach, London in 1710. From the travels of Z C von Uffenbach (London 1934)

Swift, J. *The works of Jonathan Swift Dean of St Patrick's Dublin : containing additional letters, tracts and poems not hitherto published* (London 1883)

Westergaard, W. (ed.), *The First Triple Alliance: The Letters of Christopher Lindenov, Danish Envoy to London 1668-72* (Yale, 1947)

Printed Secondary Sources

Aylmer, G., 'The Crown's Servants', *Govt. & Civil Service under Charles II* (Oxford, 2002)

Barbour, V., *Henry Bennet, Earl of Arlington* (Washington, 1914)

Baxter, S. B., *William III* (London, 1966)

Beattie, J.M., *The English Court in the Reign of George I* (Cambridge, 1967)

Becket, J. V., *The Aristocracy in England1660-1914* (Oxford, 1986)

Bevan, S., *The Duchess Hortense* (London, 1987)

Bonfield, L., *Marriage Settlements 1601-1740* (Cambridge, 1983)

Browning A., *Thomas Osborne, Earl of Danby & Duke of Leeds 1632-1712* (Glasgow, 1951)

Budd, E.F. (ed.), *The Dramatic Works of William Burnaby* (London, 1931)

Cannon, J., *An Aristocratic Century* (Cambridge, 1984)

Caygill, M. & Date, C., *Building the British Museum* (Cambridge, 1999)

Chapman, H.W., *Great Villiers* (London, 1949)

Cockayne, G.E., *The Complete Peerage of England, Scotland & Ireland* (London, 1910 – 59)

Colvin, H., *A biographical dictionary of British Architects 1600-1840* (London, 1978)

Cooper, M.A.R., *A more beautiful city: Robert Hooke and the rebuilding of London* (Stroud, 2003)

Cope, E.S., *1ˢᵗ baron Montagu of Boughton, Life of a public man* (Philadelphia, 1981)

Corp, E., 'The Last Years of James II' *History Today* (September 2001)

Doebner, R. (ed.), *Memoirs of Mary Queen of England* (Leipzig, 1886)

Falk, B., *The Way of the Montagues: A Gallery of Family Portraits* (London, 1947)

Feiling, K., *British Foreign Policy 1660 – 72* (London, 1930)

Fox Bourne, H.R., *The Life of John Locke* (London, 1876)

Glassey, L.K.J., *Politics & the appointment of Justices of the Peace, 1675-1720* (Oxford, 1979)

Goldie, M.A., 'Locke & Anglican Royalism' *Political Studies 3, 1983*

Habakkuk, H.J., 'English land Ownership 1680-1740' *Economic Hist. Review 1939-40;Marriage, Debt & the estates system* (Oxford, 1994)

Haley, K. H.D. *The 1ˢᵗ Earl of Shaftesbury* (Oxford, 1968)

Hamilton, E., *The illustrious lady: a biography of Barbara Villiers, Countess of Castlemaine and Duchess of Cleveland* (London, 1980)

Hansard, T.C., *The Parliamentary History of England from the Earliest period to the year 1803*

Harris, F.R., *Life of Edw. Montagu, 1ˢᵗ earl of Sandwich* (London, 1912)

Hartmann, C.H., *Charles II & Madame* (London, 1934)

Hayton, D.W., Cruickshanks, E.C. and Handley, S.N. (eds.), *The House of Commons, 1690-1715*

Henning, B.D. (ed.), *The House of Commons, 1660-1690*

Holland, A. J., *Bucklers Hard, a rural shipbuilding centre* (Emsworth, 1993)

Holmes, G., *British Politics in the Age of Anne* (London, 1967)

Hook, J., *The Baroque Age in England* (London, 1976)

Hoppit, J., *A Land of Liberty? England 1689-1727* (Oxford, 2000)

Horwitz, H., *Parliament, Policy & Politics under William III* (Manchester 1977)

Howarth, D. (ed.), *Art & Patronage in the Caroline Courts: Essays in honour of Sir Oliver Miller* (Cambridge, 1993)

Jacobsen, H., *Luxury and Power: the material world of the Stuart Diplomat, 1660-1714*(Oxford, 2012)

Jameson, Mrs. A., *Beauties of the Court of Charles II* (1838)

Jones, J.R., *County & Court: England 1658 – 1714* (London, 1978)

Jones, J.R., *The First Whigs* (London, 1961)

Jusserand, J.J., *A French Ambassador at the Court of Charles II* (London, 1892)

Kenyon, J.P., *The Nobility in the Revolution of 1688* (Hull, 1963)

Kenyon, J.P., *Robert Spencer, Earl of Sunderland, 1641-1702* (Westport, 1975)

Langford, P., *Public life & the propertied Englishman 1689-1788* (Oxford, 1991)

Lee, M.D., *The Cabal* (Illinois, 1965)

Popham, F.W., *A West country family, the Pophams from 1150* (Sevenoaks, 1976)

Long, J. & B., *Plot Against Pepys* (London, 2007)

Maccubin, R. & Hamilton Phillips, M. (eds.), *The age of Wm III & Mary II: power, politics & patronage 1688 – 1702* (Williamsburg, 1989)

Metzger, E.C., *Ralph, First Duke of Montagu, 1638-1709* (New York, 1987)

Miller, J., *James II: a study in kingship* (1989)

Milen, D. J., 'Results of the Rye House Plot' *Transactions of the Royal Historical Society* 5 (1951)

Morris, C. (ed.), *Journey of Celia Fiennes* (London, 1947)

Murdoch, T. (ed.), *Boughton House: The English Versailles* (London, 1992)

Ollard, R., *Edward Montagu, 1ˢᵗ Earl of Sandwich, "Cromwell's Earl"* (London, 1994)

Reese, M.M., *The Royal Office of Master of the Horse* (1976)

Rubini, D. A., *Court & Country 1688 – 1702* (London, 1967)

Sachse, W.L., *Lord Somers: a political portrait* (Manchester, 1975)

St John Brooks, E., *Sir Hans Sloane* (London, 1954)

Schwoerer, L.G., *Lady Rachel Russell: "one of the best of women"* (London, 1988)

Scott-Giles, C.W., *Sidney Sussex College* (Cambridge, 1975)

Somerville, D.H., *The King of Hearts: Charles Talbot, Duke of Shrewsbury* (London, 1962)

Speck, W.A., *Tory & Whig: the struggle in the constituencies 1701-15* (London, 1970)

Speck, W.A., *Reluctant Revolutionaries: Englishmen & the revolution of 1688* (Oxford, 1988)

Stone, L., *An open elite?: England,1540-1880* (Oxford, 1984)

Stone, L., *The Crisis of the Aristocracy 1558-1641* (London, 1965)

Swift, J., *The works of Jonathan Swift Dean of St Patrick's Dublin: containing additional letters, tracts and poems not hitherto published* (London, 1883)

Thompson, W.G., *A History of Tapestry: from the earliest times to the present day* (London, 1930)

Thornton, A. P., *West India policy under the Restoration* (Oxford, 1956)

Vigne, R 'Mayerne & his successors', *Journal Royal College of Physicians London*, vol. 20, no. 3

Ward, A.W. & Waller A.R. (eds.), *The Cambridge history of English literature* (Cambridge, 1953)

Ward, E.F., *Christopher Monck, Duke of Albemarle* (London, 1915)

Wilson, D., *All the King's Women: Love, Sex and Politics in the Life of Charles II* (London, 2003)

Index

Lightning Source UK Ltd.
Milton Keynes UK
UKOW06f1322200715

255492UK00001B/2/P